Exploring Leadership

Susan R. Komives
Nance Lucas
Timothy R. McMahon

JB JOSSEY-BASS

Exploring Leadership

For College Students Who Want to Make a Difference

Second Edition

John Wiley & Sons, Inc.

Published by Jossey-Bass
A Wiley Imprint
989 Market Street, San Francisco, CA 94103-1741   www.josseybass.com

Jossey-Bass books and products are available through most bookstores. To contact Jossey-Bass directly call our Customer Care Department within the U.S. at 800-956-7739, outside the U.S. at 317-572-3986, or fax 317-572-4002.

Jossey-Bass also publishes its books in a variety of electronic formats. Some content that appears in print may not be available in electronic books.

Library of Congress Cataloging-in-Publication Data
Komives, Susan R., 1946-
  Exploring leadership : for college students who want to make a difference /
Susan R. Komives, Nance J. Lucas, and Timothy R. McMahon. — 2nd ed.
      p. cm.
  Includes bibliographical references and index.
  ISBN-13: 978-0-7879-8213-3
  ISBN-10: 0-7879-8213-X
  1. Student activities—United States. 2. Leadership—Study and teaching (Higher)—United States. 3. Interpersonal relations—United States. I. Lucas, Nance, 1960- II. McMahon, Timothy R., 1951- III. Title.
  LB3605.K64 2007
  378.1'98—dc22   2006029663

Printed in the United States of America
SECOND EDITION
PB Printing 10 9 8 7 6

The Jossey-Bass
Higher and Adult Education Series

Contents

Part IV: Making a Difference with Leadership

Part V: Leadership Development and Renewal

Preface

What comes to mind when you hear the word *leadership*? Do you think of international or national figures like Condoleezza Rice, Tony Blair, Hillary Clinton, Wilma Mankiller, Martin Luther King Jr., Barack Obama, Mohandas Gandhi, Nelson Mandela, Elaine Chao, or Rudy Giuliani? Our brains somehow immediately translate the word *leadership* to mean *leader*. You probably just did the same thing. You probably imagined a company president, a prime minister, your professor, your supervisor at work, or the person standing at a podium with a gavel. However, the premise of this book is that leadership is *a relational and ethical process of people together attempting to accomplish positive change*. In other words, leadership is about relationships. And you can be part of the leadership process, whether as a formal leader or as an active, committed group member.

Purpose of this Book

Chances are that you are reading this book because you want to learn more about leadership. You may be taking a leadership course, attending a workshop, learning to be a resident assistant, or just reading for your own development. Somehow, you want to be more effective in accomplishing change, making a difference, or working with others. Perhaps you have just accepted a new leadership role or selected a career in which you will be called on to assume leadership responsibilities. Maybe you have had many leadership experiences, or maybe you have never thought of yourself as a leader at all. Indeed, you may have thought of leadership as emphasizing leaders—not followers or group members.

A popular sentiment wisely reminds us that all of us are smarter than one of us. The wisdom, common purpose, inclusivity, sense of community, and personal empowerment embedded in that statement are profound. Leadership is not something possessed by only a select few people in high positions. We are all involved in the leadership process, and we are all capable of being effective leaders. Through collaboration with others, you can make a difference from any place within a group or organization, whether as the titled leader or as an active member.

Scope of the Book and Treatment of Topics

Our rapidly changing world needs each of us to do what we can to make a difference in our own communities. Each of us is a member of many communities—our family, neighborhood, religious group, workplace, classroom, or sports team. In this book, we will ask you to examine yourself and your communities: where you live, where you work, whom you care for, what interests you, and how you want to develop. Together, we will explore how you see yourself in relation to others and how you prefer to interact with others in group settings. Our aim in this book is to help you use your own college context and your experience as a college student as the frame within which to understand leadership. The students who helped us with this book said, "Most students skip the preface!" We are glad you did not do that. You will understand the book better for having read this section.

The three of us have, for many years, taught leadership courses, advised students in formal leadership roles, mentored student leaders and group members, supervised student workers, sought to bring students into campus governance, served as leaders ourselves, and read and researched leadership. When we developed the first edition of this book, we were keenly aware that when we have taught a leadership course, we shared a frustration that the scholarship and literature in leadership studies did not connect with most students. Business majors often find themselves in the literature because so much of it comes from their major. Psychology and sociology majors usually relate to it because the leadership field is interdisciplinary and draws heavily from their fields. But many students have trouble relating to the leadership literature, much of which is written for corporate chief executive officers (CEOs). Some students find the leader-focused approaches to be self-centered, and some say, "I'm not a leader. I just want to make a difference."

Leadership can be viewed from various frames: political science addresses power and influence, business management sees leadership as effectiveness in outcomes or emphasizes supervisor-subordinate relationships, anthropology views cultural influences and such factors as symbols and norms, history looks to the influence of key figures during significant times or when leading major social movements, and psychology or sociology looks at individuals and groups as they interact. One book cannot do justice to all these diverse perspectives, but we challenge you to explore how your field or fields of study approach leadership.

The primary perspectives or frames we use in this book are a combination of psychological and educational approaches; we emphasize learning about yourself and understanding yourself in the context of others. Being aware of your personal values, beliefs, and commitments builds a strong foundation for your position as a member in the world's many communities. Self-awareness is central to being able to understand others and interact effectively in groups, organizations, and communities.

We believe that you can learn to understand yourself and others, that organizations are most effective when they are learning environments, and that our rapidly changing world will require people leading together toward meaningful change. The belief that leadership is grounded in learning together must be modeled in our educational environments. Yet the world does not always work this way. You constantly will be challenged to understand how things are, see how they could be, and be a part of change if necessary.

Throughout the book, you will find quotes from students from across the country. We think you will find their attitudes and experiences interesting.

Summary of the Contents

Because personal awareness and personal development are central to learning leadership, the focus of this book is as much on you and your relationships with others as it is on understanding leadership theory, styles, practices, and applications.

We organized the book around five major themes: leadership for a changing world (Part One), with an emphasis on the Relational Leadership Model; relationships as the foundation of leadership (Part Two); the context of leadership in groups, organizations, and communities (Part Three); understanding change and how to make a difference using leadership (Part Four); and leadership identity and personal renewal (Part Five). This second edition includes a number of revisions and updates to the original chapters, along with new chapters on understanding change, strategies for change, and developing a leadership identity.

In Chapter One, we introduce the concepts in this book with specific attention to the variety among groups of students with different experiences who learn leadership for different purposes and practice it in various settings. In Chapter Two, we show how the study and understanding of leadership has evolved through recent times and how rapidly changing times lead to new leadership approaches. In Chapter Three, we present the Relational Leadership Model (RLM). This model emphasizes the nature of relationships that are the building blocks in working with others to make a difference and accomplish change. The new graphic in this chapter is a more clear interpretation of the RLM than the graphic in the first edition.

In Part Two (Chapters Four, Five, and Six), we ask you to explore yourself, others, yourself in relation to others, and the nature of leading with integrity. Understanding self includes understanding your values, character, and the preferences you have in interacting, deciding, and learning. Self-awareness is an essential foundation for understanding leadership and helps you respond to the differences and commonalties you have with others. We also promote the concept of leading from your strengths and talents. Please note that although we have a dedicated chapter on leading with integrity, the treatment of values, ethics, and character is a theme throughout this book.

Part Three (Chapters Seven, Eight, Nine, and Ten) examines the various settings in which leadership is needed; for example, in groups and teams. It also examines aspects of complex organizations and how these may raise distinct issues for the practice of relational leadership. It explores the core elements of communities and emphasizes collaborative processes, and it presents the need for organizational renewal in all the contexts of leadership.

Part Four (Chapters Eleven and Twelve) is new for this edition. It presents material on the nature of change, the change process, and being change agents. It explores such strategies as service learning, coalition building, and activism. This part also contains another widely used model of leadership development, the Social Change Model of Leadership Development.

Part Five (Chapters Thirteen and Fourteen) brings the focus back to you as the reader. This section presents the importance of individual self-efficacy for leadership and research on how a leadership identity develops, along with the need for you to stay renewed and balanced. These two chapters close the circle and bring you back to where you started, with the most foundational aspects of self-awareness and the importance of staying renewed in the leadership process.

Leadership Can Be Learned

This book (and perhaps the course you are taking as well) is designed to expose you to key concepts of leadership and to provide activities that will encourage you to learn leadership. You will need to practice these new skills and help your classmates and peers practice them as well. If you want to learn to play the piano, you might imagine playing with gusto, but you know it will take practice to do that. If you want to learn to play tennis, you can imagine hitting a cross-court backhand, but you know you have to hit many of them to perfect that stroke. Likewise, if you imagine a group coming to agreement after much conflict and going forward with shared vision and a sense of respectful community, then you have to learn a lot about yourself and practice the skills of listening and collaborating. You would not drop piano lessons when the first scale you learn gets boring or sell your tennis racket when you develop a sore muscle. Likewise, you do not give up on practicing leadership because you find it hard or challenging. Practicing together will help each person learn leadership.

If you are using this book as a textbook for a class, you will find it is designed to help your class become a learning community. After an introduction to leadership, the book focuses on you. Learning activities are designed to help you reflect on yourself and show you how to listen to and learn from others. This will not always be easy or painless. But the classroom provides an opportunity to practice the difficult skills of building learning communities in which to experience collaborative leadership. Many students tell us they dislike group projects, but unless you learn the skills required for working effectively with others and building common purpose with others, including handling frustration when things do not go well, you have not practiced collaborative leadership. Most great things were not accomplished by an individual acting alone. Even when one person is singled out for credit, there were usually many others who contributed or collaborated to make that accomplishment possible.

As you read and discuss this book, we encourage you to think about yourself. Do not distance yourself from the pages, but connect with the concepts and ask yourself, In what ways could this help me be more effective? Not everything will relate to you all the time, but think about your life right now and the many roles and responsibilities you anticipate acquiring as you go forward. We invite you to begin your leadership journey as you explore yourself in various contexts. Each step of the way will enhance your sense of self-awareness and help you realize that you are leading when you are actively working with others toward a shared purpose. You do make a difference.

We are still on our own leadership journey and know this is a lifelong activity. As we change and as times change, we will always need to be sensitive to the relational process of leadership. We hope you will enhance your own abilities to be effective in this leadership journey.

Acknowledgments

In the process of writing both editions of this book, we tried hard to practice what we were preaching. Our collaborative effort constantly affirmed for us the benefits of working together in a caring and supportive manner. We treasure each other. We became travelers in cyberspace and made great use of e-mail. We learned from each other, constantly wishing we had more time together, and in the process became our own learning community. We also learned from the many people who assisted us.

Since the first edition of the book we have been gratified to see the growth in campus efforts on student leadership development and in the plethora of leadership education resources. We are proud to have contributed to the movement to challenge college students to take an active role in their communities.

We recognize the tremendous support we have received from others and feel truly blessed to have such an array of loving and giving families, friends, and colleagues. For the first edition of *Exploring Leadership* we continue to offer special appreciation to Marcy Levy Shankman, Elizabeth McGovern, Mike Sarich, Reena Meltzer, Carrie Goldstein, Mary Campbell, and Alice Faron. The second edition stands on their shoulders. The second edition was greatly shaped by Julie Owen, Maryland doctoral student and a remarkable leadership educator, who worked with every step of this revision and worked on major revisions to the instructor manual. Special thanks to members of Julie's graduate leadership educator's class and other Maryland colleagues who edited chapters and provided activities for the instructor manual (Jennifer Armstrong, Kristan Cilente, Krystal Clark, Keith Edwards, Jeff Grim, Paige Haber, Anthony Kraft, Karol Martinez, Jim Neumeister, Darren Pierre, Jessica Porras, Terry Zacker, and Seth Zolin). We also thank Jen Edwards and Paige Haber, both Maryland master's students. Jen managed many logistics such as copyright permission releases and tracking the exhibits. Paige diligently coordinated the work of undergraduate research assistants Anthony M. Kraft and Jeffrey L. Chow in the solicitation and organization of hundreds of remarkable student quotes from across the country that illuminate each chapter of the book.

Susan offers special thanks to her husband, Ralph, for his unfailing support and phenomenal Macintosh skills. She is particularly grateful to her leadership identity research team (Julie Owen, Susan Longerbeam, Felicia Mainella, and Laura Osteen—then Maryland doctoral students) for their amazing leadership identity development project presented in this book (see Chapter Thirteen) and for her current nineteen-person research team with Co-Principal Investigator John Dugan, coordinator of Maryland Co-Curricular Leadership Programs, and project manager, Tom Segar, both Maryland doctoral students engaging in their 54-campus study of leadership.

Nance is grateful for family members and mentors who taught her about leadership through their example, and especially to Joel Rudy, an early professional mentor, and to the late Don Clifton for his influence on understanding and practicing leadership using talents and strengths. A thank-you to best friends Dee Mazza (aunt as well as friend), Checka Leinwall, and Mel Ampthor for their unyielding moral support, love, and confidence. Special appreciation goes to New Century College faculty and staff at George Mason University for their encouragement of her involvement in this book-writing venture. And to Tony Chambers, Karen Silien, Helen and Alexander Astin, and John Burkhardt—thanks for their collaborations in the leadership education field that have had a lasting impact on her. A hearty thank-you goes out to her many students for influencing her philosophy of leadership.

Tim thanks his parents, Jim and Irene, and brother Tom for all of their support; Curt Kochner for sharing ideas, laughter, and experiences in the last, best place; and longtime friend and college roommate Rick Howser for all the great times at Wrigley. Thanks also to Kathy Allen, Gary Althen, Steve Axley, George Bettas, Pam Boersig, Bruce Clemetsen, Barbara Maxwell, Richard Preuhs, Denny Roberts, Karen Roth, and Dave Strang for helping shape his thoughts about leadership. Finally, thank you to his Oregon friends and colleagues in the Office of Student Life, CoDaC, and ALS for their ongoing support—most especially Laurie Jones Neighbors.

We are all grateful to Jossey-Bass's David Brightman for his unfailing continued guidance, patience, and motivation. Special thanks to Craig Slack, director of the National Clearinghouse for Leadership Programs, for his ongoing support of this work.

The Authors

Susan R. Komives is associate professor and director of the college student personnel graduate program at the University of Maryland, College Park. She is former president of the American College Personnel Association (ACPA) and former vice president for student development at Stephens College and the University of Tampa. She is author or coauthor of eleven books or monographs and over forty articles or book chapters, and she has delivered more than four hundred keynote speeches. She is cofounder and publications editor of the National Clearinghouse for Leadership Programs and a senior scholar with the James MacGregor Burns Academy of Leadership. She was a member of the ensemble that developed *The Social Change Model of Leadership Development* and was principal investigator (PI) of a team whose research resulted in a grounded theory of Leadership Identity Development. She is co-PI of the Multi-Institutional Study of Leadership, a 54-campus study of college student leadership outcomes and campus practices that contribute to those outcomes. She was the 2004 recipient of the National Association of Student Personnel Administrators (NASPA) Robert H. Shaffer Award for Academic Excellence as a Graduate Faculty Member and in 2006 received both the NASPA Contribution of Scholarship and Literature Award and the ACPA Contribution to Knowledge Award. Komives received her bachelor of science degree (1968) in mathematics and chemistry from Florida State University, as well as her master of science degree (1969) in higher education administration. Her doctorate in educational administration and supervision (1973) is from the University of Tennessee.

Nance Lucas is the associate dean and associate professor of New Century College at George Mason University and former special assistant to the provost and director of the James MacGregor Burns Academy of Leadership at the University of Maryland. Prior to becoming director of the Academy of Leadership, Nance was the cofounder and first director of the National Clearinghouse for Leadership Programs. Her research and scholarship interests focus on ethics and leadership. She served as the co-editor of the *Journal of Leadership and Organizational Studies* for special issues and a member of the Journal's editorial board. She has published chapters and articles on topics of leadership and ethics and was a contributing author of *Leadership Reconsidered* and *The Social Change Model of Leadership Development*. With her goal of improving the quality of leadership in organizations and communities, Nance is a keynote speaker, leadership development facilitator, and leadership coach to numerous organizations. She served as the creator and convener of the 1997 Global Leadership Week Program (a worldwide leadership program initiative that spanned five continents), cofounder of the National Leadership Symposium, and a past chair of the National InterAssociation Leadership Project. Nance was a faculty member at the National LeaderShape Institute and a faculty member and assistant conference coordinator at the 1995 Salzburg Leadership Seminar in Salzburg, Austria. She served on the Kellogg Forum on Higher Education National Dialogue Series Planning Team, the Kellogg Foundation Leadership Studies Project Ethics Focus Group, the Kellogg Foundation College Age Youth Leadership Program Review Team, and the International Leadership Association Board. Lucas received a doctorate in college student personnel with a concentration in leadership studies and ethics at the University of Maryland, and a master's degree in college student personnel administration and a bachelor of arts degree in industrial psychology from the Pennsylvania State University.

Timothy R. McMahon is a faculty consultant in the Teaching Effectiveness program at the University of Oregon. In this position, he helps faculty and graduate teaching fellows teach better. Prior to coming to Oregon he worked at Western Illinois University as a faculty member in the Department of Counselor Education and College Student Personnel. Tim also has professional experience in student affairs at Western Illinois University, the University of Iowa, Washington State University, Lakeland College, and the University of Wisconsin–River Falls. McMahon has made numerous national presentations on topics related to leadership education and has taught undergraduate leadership and diversity courses. McMahon's current professional interests include leadership, chaos and systems theory, diversity, and issues related to teaching and learning. He received a bachelor of science degree (1973) in astronomy and a master of education degree (1975) in higher education administration from the University of Illinois. He received his doctorate (1992) in college student services administration from Oregon State University.

Exploring Leadership

Part I

Leadership for a Changing World

More than ever, today's times demand that diverse people work flexibly and respectfully together. The chapters in this section establish a foundation for understanding how leadership has been perceived over time and how today's rapidly changing, networked world calls for new approaches to leadership. This section ends with the exploration of a model of relational leadership and its elements of being purposeful, inclusive, ethical, and empowering. These four elements are embedded within an overall process orientation, which is the fifth component of the Relational Leadership Model.

The leadership process is not about things—it is about people. As you read this section, challenge yourself to think how it relates to you and to those you have worked with in groups or communities. Try to see what new awareness or skill you might need to be more effective in working with others.

The writings of the Chinese philosopher Lao Tzu are wise guides to self and others. In the book *Tao of Leadership*, Heider (1985) adapts Lao Tzu's proverbs. Lao Tzu advises us:

> The superficial leader cannot see how things happen, even though the evidence is everywhere. This leader is swept up by drama, sensation, and excitement. All this

confusion is blinding. But the leader who returns again and again to awareness-of-process has a deep sense of how things happen. (p. 69)

The model presented in this section promotes a relational process to leadership.

1

An Introduction to Leadership

You will most likely find yourself—your interests and your attitudes—reflected on every page of this book, regardless of your age, gender, race, ethnicity, or academic major. You can find ideas that apply to your interests whether you are majoring in engineering or English or are planning a career in journalism, education, or law. Any number of other majors pertain to leadership as well.

Your habits are also reflected here. You might like details or you might only focus on the big picture. You might think best by speaking aloud or by turning thoughts over in your head before saying anything. However you work and think best, your perspective is distinctly yours and is represented in these pages.

Your unique experiences have shaped your view of yourself as a leader or member of a group. Think of the various leadership roles you have held or observed. Think about the various ways you have led formally, led informally, or been an active participant in various groups. Think about the leadership exhibited by the people you have admired in the national or international news, in your home community, on campus, at work, or in the career field you are choosing. Think ahead to the places and relationships in which you could become more active—your classes, class projects, student employment position, residence hall, honor societies, student government, Greek organizations, athletic teams, PTA meetings, your family, friendship groups, your off-campus work, community service settings, your church or temple—the possibilities are endless.

You draw on your personal characteristics, experiences, and the settings in which you might be involved for different leadership purposes. Some readers may want to further personal development; others may want to enhance a career skill, still others to accomplish social change. Whatever your purpose, your journey through the leadership process will make a difference in all aspects of your life.

Chapter Overview

In this chapter, we introduce key concepts and models that will be developed throughout the book, and we provide an overview of what we mean by leader, follower, and leadership. We show that new views on leadership are needed—views that call for ethical collaborations—and we describe ways to understand these new views. We assert our belief that leadership develops best when organizations and the individuals in them are open to learning together.

Foundational Principles

We encourage you to critique and analyze the perspectives and frames we present in this book. You will probably agree and connect with some ideas and disagree with others. But try to figure out *why* you agree or disagree. Exercising critical thinking is a key to furthering your understanding about leadership. We encourage you to learn about leadership using different perspectives. To do that, you will need to identify the principles that are important to you and relate those beliefs to these perspectives. The foundational principles in this book are as follows:

1. Leadership is a concern of all of us. As individuals and groups, we have a responsibility to contribute effectively as members of organizations, local communities, nations, and in the world community. Members of communities (work, learning, living, and ide-

ological communities) are citizens of those various groups and have a responsibility to develop shared leadership and participatory governance.

2. Leadership is viewed and valued differently by various disciplines and cultures. A multidisciplinary approach to leadership develops a shared understanding of differences and commonalities in leadership principles and practices across professions and cultures.

3. Conventional views of leadership have changed. Leadership is not static; it must be practiced flexibly. The rapid pace of change leads people to continually seek new ways of relating to shared problems.

4. Leadership can be exhibited in many ways. These ways of leading can be analyzed and adapted to varying situations. Different settings might call for different types of leadership. Pluralistic, empowering leadership values the inclusion of diverse people and diverse ideas, working toward common purposes.

5. Leadership qualities and skills can be learned and developed. Today's leaders are made, not born. Leadership effectiveness begins with self-awareness and self-understanding and grows to an understanding of others.

6. Leadership committed to ethical action is needed to encourage change and social responsibility. Leadership happens through relationships among people engaged in change. As a relational process, leadership requires the highest possible standards of credibility, authenticity, integrity, and ethical conduct. Ethical leaders model positive behaviors that influence the actions of others.

Leadership development is greatly enhanced when you understand how important relationships are in leadership; that is, when you see the basic relational foundation of the leadership process. Three basic principles are involved: knowing, being, and doing:

- *Knowing*. You must know—yourself, how change occurs, and how and why others may view things differently than you do.

- *Being.* You must be—ethical, principled, open, caring, and inclusive.

- *Doing.* You must act—in socially responsible ways, consistently and congruently, as a participant in a community, and on your commitments and passions.

It is unrealistic to think that certain proven behaviors are required if you are to be an effective leader or collaborator in this time of rapid change. Leadership cannot be reduced to a number of easy steps. It is realistic, however, to develop a way of thinking—a personal philosophy of leadership—and identify core values that can help you work with others toward change. In today's complex times, we need a set of principles to guide our actions.

"Leadership is an electric current of believing. The energy created from people believing in each other fuels a constant positive reaction to work together and achieve."—Lisa M. Stevens attended the Jepson School of Leadership Studies at the University of Richmond and was active in the Women's College Government Association and at the campus radio station.

Rapidly Changing Times

Peter Vaill (1989, 1991, 1996, 1998) describes these times as similar to swirling rapids—permanent white water. We can easily feel overwhelmed; we gasp for air as we navigate our fast-paced days with our many responsibilities. Your clock radio may awaken you to the news of suicide bombers and the latest horrific crimes in your community. You go to class to learn something you hope you can apply to real life, but you often find the material irrelevant. Just as you settle in to write a paper for class, one of your children falls and breaks her leg, changing your plans for days to come. You get to your job in the student activities office and find that the work you left unfinished yesterday is needed in fifteen minutes, instead of in two days as you had thought. You just saw publicity for a program being sponsored on campus that confronts the very foundational beliefs that one of your organizations holds; you are incensed and have to figure out what to do. And the problems continue.

We no longer have simple problems with right and wrong answers but are increasingly faced with complex dilemmas and paradoxes. For example, we may want to be civil yet affirm freedom of speech, or we may want to find community and common purpose but also value individuality and individual differences.

Vaill (1989) observes that traditional approaches like simply working harder may no longer be the most effective strategy to deal with rapid, complex change. The paradigm of hard work solving all problems is now too simplistic. Instead of working harder, we need to work smarter. Vaill challenges us to work

- Collectively smarter
- Reflectively smarter
- Spiritually smarter (p. 29)

Working collectively smarter means knowing, as the old saying goes, that all of us are smarter than one of us. Working collectively smarter recognizes our interdependence. It means believing that coalitions can accomplish more than single groups; it means knowing that collaborative practices build more community and commitment than isolated, individual actions do. It recognizes the transcendent importance of relationships in the leadership dynamic. Allen and Cherrey (2000), in their book *Systemic Leadership*, observe that "relationships are the connective tissue of organizations, relationships built on integrity are the glue that holds organizations together" (p. 31).

Working reflectively smarter means taking the time to make meaning out of what is happening in order to gain perspective and understanding. Reflection keeps priorities in order; it helps new paradigms become clear and enables us to identify patterns as they emerge. Reflection helps us keep a sense of common purpose and becomes the beacon that guides us through the rapids.

Working spiritually smarter means being aware of the values, beliefs, and principles that become our rudder in white water and build our character. Instead of bouncing around with the swirl of the rapids, knowing our values and beliefs provides a rudder to guide ethical actions. Working spiritually smarter does not necessarily refer to an involvement in religion, but it does signal a personal purpose and centering that transcends unexamined action. "Spirituality is a way of being in the world" (Brussat & Brussat, 1996, p. 29). Working spiritually smarter means seeking wholeness. Some envision that we are in a "spiritual renaissance" and are recognizing the value of "a renewed search for contemplative values in the flurry of our active lives" (Palmer, 1990, p. 6).

Developing a personal approach to leadership that joins one person with others in an effort to accomplish a shared goal is difficult. It requires being intentional and thoughtful. Working to become smarter means examining our own assumptions and realizing that others might see things differently. Gaining new insight means learning to identify and understand paradigms.

Understanding Paradigms

In every aspect of our lives, change is more rapid, confusing, and unpredictable than ever before. You buy and learn one word processing program only to find a new version released three months later. Daily newspapers bring awareness of complex local issues, and the nightly news flashes images of conflict at home and abroad. The conventional ways of thinking about and organizing our shared experiences do not seem helpful anymore. Instead of individual determinism, competition, and predictable structures, we seem to need quickly responding, nimble systems; collaboration; and a new awareness of shared values that honor our diversity.

These different perspectives might be called different world-views, frames, or paradigms. Paradigms are patterns and ways of looking at things in order to make sense of them. Some paradigms are clear and help us function well. For example, you have fairly clear paradigms about playing baseball, going to class the first day, going to the airport, or attending the first meeting of an organization you wish to join. Consider going to that first class. You may sit in a preferred spot, expect to greet the person sitting beside you, get a syllabus, learn what text to buy, and perhaps even get out a bit early. That paradigm might be shattered if you arrived to find no chairs, or a professor who said, "I have not yet organized this class. What do you want to learn?" It is hard then to figure out what will happen; the rules no longer work; your established paradigms do not help fill in the gaps. Indeed, you might judge this class to be more exciting or more terrifying because it is unpredictable. We are surprised when some paradigms change, but we can adjust to the new paradigm. Imagine your customer-service paradigm. Until recently, when you called the customer service number for your telecommunications provider at the company's headquarters in Pittsburgh, Pennsylvania, you expected to be conversing with a person located at that site. With this same scenario today, you could be calling a Pittsburgh number but reach a customer service representative who answers the phone at an office in India.

There are widely divergent paradigms for what it means to be a good leader. For some, a good-leader paradigm signals a verbal, self-confident person clearly in charge and directing followers with confidence. Some would see a good leader as someone who delegates and involves others in the group's decisions and actions. Still others think beyond "good leader" to consider "good leadership." Some imagine a good leadership paradigm as a group of colleagues sharing in leadership, with each contributing to the group outcome and no one dominating others. Deliberately thinking about leadership paradigms may help identify what was previously unclear or even unseen and what now might be very obvious.

"I used to view the leader of a group as the director of a play, telling people what to do and teaching them how to do it. Over the past five years however, I realized the director approach may get things done, but it does not motivate people, help them understand the importance of what they are doing, or ensure that the group will function in the absence of the leader. I have learned that the best leaders empower the individuals they lead, enabling them to contribute to the group and succeed on their own."—Daniel Gregory, majoring in Communication Arts and Sciences at the Pennsylvania State University, is the Marshall and Chaplain of Theta Chi Fraternity.

As times change, standard approaches to a topic may no longer be effective. An awareness of needing new ways to approach problems may signal a paradigm shift. There was a time in our country's history when the predominant paradigm held that women were not capable of understanding issues sufficiently to vote; at other times, the prevailing paradigm has held that education should be a privilege of only the elite, or that corporations could do anything to enhance their profits, or that smokers could light up anywhere they pleased. A paradigm shift means a shift in the previously held patterns or views. A paradigm shift in paying your bills means that instead of writing checks, you pay your bills through direct electronic banking deductions from your account. Instead of rushing to the bank in their limited open hours to get money from your account, you can use an ATM twenty-four hours a day, seven days a week, in thousands of locations. When your grandfather says, "We had no TV when I was a boy, and all our social life revolved around the church," he is observing a paradigm shift in how we spend leisure time, brought on by technology and transportation.

There have been numerous shifts in how people acquire information over time. Think of the changes from the early, sagelike scholars imparting wisdom to small groups of students sitting at their feet, to the volume-filled libraries we could borrow from, to the electronic retrieval systems that allow us to acquire information on the Web. Instead of going to the library to borrow a book, many of us now download articles from a web site. How reasonable is it in these changing times to use an old paradigm of measuring the quality of universities by the number of volumes in their libraries when any student can access thousands of volumes through interlibrary loan?

A paradigm shift, however, does not necessarily mean completely abandoning one view for another. The new paradigm or view often emerges "alongside the old. It is appearing inside and around the old paradigm . . . building on it, amplifying it and extending it . . . not replacing it" (Nicoll, 1984, p. 5). We encourage you to examine the conventional paradigm of command and control as a method of leadership and seek to identify other paradigms that may be emerging, through your own experiences as well as from reading this book.

If old patterns or paradigms no longer work well, those who see things differently and hold new paradigms begin to employ new approaches and paradigm shifts emerge. As we all begin to seek new ways to make sense out of the frequent confusion in our shared times, together we can find new solutions to our problems and more effective ways of relating through leadership. We are fully engaged now in the emergent paradigm that values collaborative processes among authentic people in organizations. Yes, there are bad or toxic leaders in some groups (Kellerman, 2004; Lipman-Blumen, 2005), but group expectations have largely shifted to expect ethical processes among people of integrity.

Examining the Paradigms

Leadership has long been presented as an elusive, complex phenomenon. Thousands of books and articles have been written about leaders and leadership, seeking to identify traits, characteristics, situations, and behaviors that signal leadership effectiveness (Bass, 1990). We will present an overview of several of these approaches in the next chapter so you can see how these paradigms have emerged and how leadership has been socially constructed over time. This impressive number of publications provides insight, but leadership is perhaps best described as using your personal philosophy of how to work effectively with others toward meaningful change.

Research in leadership studies is largely centered on the individual leader rather than the process of leadership. Most approaches examine what a leader does with followers to accomplish some purpose. Only in the last decade has the literature focused extensively on followers or group members themselves. The conventional way of looking at people in groups (whether work groups or friendship groups) is first to identify a leader (or leaders) and then describe their followers. However, "understanding the relational nature of leadership and followership opens up richer forms of involvement and rewards in groups, organizations, and society at large" (Hollander, 1993, p. 43).

Most leadership literature focuses on how managers function in organizational settings and assumes that the manager is also a leader. Therefore, much attention has been focused on the leader's behaviors to get followers to do what the leader wants. This kind of leader usually holds a positional role like chairperson, president, or supervisor. This emphasis on positional leaders frequently promotes a passive approach to followers, often ignoring the role or effect followers have in the organization including the way followers affect the positional leader. This approach clearly does not adequately describe the leadership relationship among people in groups. Concepts of transforming leadership value how these followers could become leaders themselves (Burns, 1978).

We must reconstruct our view of leadership to see that "leadership is not something a leader possesses so much as a process involving followership" (Hollander, 1993, p. 29). Further, followership is really leadership in action among people in the group. In this book, we view leadership as *a relational and ethical process of people together attempting to accomplish positive change*.

Some leadership approaches, such as participative leadership, acknowledge that followers must be meaningfully involved in everything from setting goals to decision making. Followers must be active participants. Often, these approaches do not go far enough to genuinely engage followers while sharing power with them. This difference signals a paradigm shift from controlling follower behavior to empowering followers to be central to an organization's outcomes. Indeed, followers quickly see through and reject those leaders who ask for advice and input but rarely change their opinions. Followers usually embrace positional leaders who introduce issues to the group for discussion and decision.

"I believe that everyone needs to be a follower many times in life. Followers are essentially the drive behind most groups. It is the power of all that accomplishes much, but one person can change the direction of that power. Often followers have the clearest sight of all involved."—Laura A. Bennett was founder of Residents Against Substance Abuse at the University of Kansas and a member of the Friends of the Johnson County Libraries.

The Search for a New Conceptualization of Followers

Since childhood, we have heard the lesson "Follow the leader." We have been taught that someone is in charge, so we let that person take the lead and we follow. If we are the leader, we expect others to cooperate and follow our lead. The leadership literature includes a range of perspectives on followers, largely based on the role of the leader. On one extreme, if the leader is viewed as hierarchically apart from the group, then followers matter less and are to be more compliant with the leader's views. On the other extreme, when the leader is embedded in the group, it is a shared leadership process and followers are perceived as colleagues.

Followership

Most hierarchical organizations are designed with manager or leader roles and follower or staff roles. To honor and recognize the important role of the follower, the term *followership* started being used in conjunction with the term *leadership* (Kelley, 1992). Followership skills are those skills and processes practiced by members of groups. However, not all followers are alike. One taxonomy, presented in Figure 1.1, presents approaches to being a follower by considering both their commitment to performing in the group and their interest in group relationships. Imagine Maria, who is passive and unengaged in her group. She will do what is asked of her but is a passive participant; she is a subordinate. James does not engage much with other members of the group, but he is diligent about getting his tasks done and meeting his obligations; he is a contributor. Tonya uses her interpersonal skills and really knows how to network with others, but she does not always get her work done or show commitment to the group's task; she is a politician. Carl both embraces the task and wants to do good work as well as join others in a successful team effort; he is a partner.

USAF Lieutenant Colonels Sharon Latour and Vicki Rast (2004) summarize their review of followership research and define effective followers as "individuals with high organizational commitment who are able to function well in a change-oriented team environment. Additionally, they are independent, critical thinkers with highly developed integrity and competency" (p. 6). They posit that dynamic followership is a prerequisite for effective leadership. Chaleff (1995) went a step further and encouraged followers to be

Performance Initiative

	Low	High
High	Politician	Partner
Low	Subordinate	Contributor

Relationship Initiative (vertical axis label)

Figure 1.1. Follower Types.

Source: Adapted from Porter, Rosenbach, & Pittman (2005), p. 149. Used with permission.

courageous. Followers have special responsibilities to speak truth to leaders and to take risks when the leadership practices being used are not effective for the organization.

Just as there are skills or capacities to develop in leadership, many assert there are skills and capacities to develop to be an effective follower. Clearly there is a reciprocal relationship between the leader and the follower. Some authors advise followers how to be effective with their positional leaders. Lussier and Achua (2004) suggest that as a follower you should

- Offer support to the leader
- Take initiative
- Play counseling and coaching roles to the leader, when appropriate
- Raise issues and/or concerns when necessary
- Seek and encourage honest feedback from the leader
- Clarify your role and expectations
- Show appreciation

- Keep the leader informed
- Resist inappropriate influence of the leader (p. 237)

Latour and Rast (2004) promote several categories of important follower competencies (see Exhibit 1.1). These authors clarify that followership skills help develop leadership skills and are essential perspectives for teamwork.

Because most of the followership models are presented in the context of a hierarchical authority figure interacting in some way to influence followers, these models do not transfer well to non-hierarchical groups or community contexts in which public leadership seeks to address shared issues (Luke, 1998). Using public leadership as the context, Luke illustrates how the leader-follower dynamic differs in the public sector:

> In an interconnected world, this model is simply inac-
> curate. One individual may be the leader who galvanizes
> and stimulates initial action. Then other leaders and
> autonomous stakeholders will refine the initial burst of
> vision, agree on directions for action, and pursue specific
> initiatives aimed at solving the program. Public leader-
> ship does not engage followers; rather, it involves col-
> laborations, audiences, and other self-organizing groups
> . . . effective leaders are forced to become "leader-fol-
> lowers" simultaneously. Public leadership shifts, changes,
> and is shared at different times by different people in dif-
> ferent organizations. (pp. 32–33)

We need to reconceptualize how we view followers and the nature of relationships in groups. It seems woefully inadequate to call group members by the term *followers*, implying they are follow-ing someone or something, unable to think for themselves, or remaining indifferent to the group's goals, when actually they are creating and shaping the context themselves.

Exhibit 1.1. Follower Competencies.

Competency	Description
Displays loyalty	Shows deep commitment to the organization, adheres to the boss's vision and priorities, disagrees agreeably, aligns personal and organizational goals
Functions well in change-oriented environments	Serves as a change agent, demonstrates agility, moves fluidly between leading and following
Functions well on teams	Collaborates, shares credit, acts responsibly toward others
Thinks independently and critically	Dissents courageously, takes the initiative, practices self-management
Considers integrity of paramount importance	Remains trustworthy, tells the truth, maintains the highest performance standards, admits mistakes

Source: Latour & Rast (2004), p. 111. Used with permission.

What New Term for Followers?

Leadership scholars have been searching for a new term to more adequately describe followers. Followers have been called members, employees, associates, or subordinates. Kouzes and Posner (1993) suggest calling them the *constituents*. "A constituent is someone who has an active part in the process of running an organization and who authorizes another to act on his or her behalf. A constituent confers authority on the leader, not the other way around" (p. xix). Although the concept is usually found in describing how their constituents from their voting districts authorize political leaders, it is useful in other situations as well.

Imagine the senior class council discussing changes the provost's office is planning in the commencement ceremony; the president of the senior class will likely be empowered by her constituents and expected to carry the wishes of the council to the provost for consideration. The president would be speaking on behalf of others, not just carrying a personal opinion forward.

Crum (1987) likes the term *co-creator*, elevating the empowered, collaborative, transformational role of group members. "When we choose co-creation, we end separation, the root cause of conflict . . . They know through responsible participation that they can empower each other and ultimately their institutions and society, thereby creating a life that is meaningful and satisfying for everyone" (p. 175). Positional leaders who see group members as co-creators will take important decisions to the group and ask, "What do we want to do about this?"

Rost (1991) believes that the traditional meaning of the word *follower* is too embedded in all of our minds to adequately shift to a new meaning. He implores us to see that we have moved from an industrial worldview to a postindustrial era. In the industrial view, people in the organization are merely resources—like steel or other raw materials—whereas in the postindustrial view, people are essential because they bring information and wisdom and the capacity to adapt. Rost now encourages the use of the term *collaborator* for the role of people in this new way of working together. He clarifies, "I now use the word followers when I write about leadership in the industrial paradigm. I use the word collaborators when I write about leadership in the postindustrial paradigm . . . no amount of reconstruction is going to salvage the word [follower]" (Rost, 1993, p. 109).

In this book, we use the term *participant* to refer to people involved in groups in this new paradigm. Participants are involved in the leadership process, actively sharing leadership with other group members. Participants include the informal or formal positional leader in a group as well as all active group members who seek to be involved in group change. Participants are active, engaged, and intentional.

A Word About Leaders

The word *leader* is used in this book in two primary ways. One use of the term refers to a person in a leadership position who has been elected, selected, or hired to assume responsibility for a group working toward change; this leader has defined responsibilities for decision making and action. Such a *positional leader* usually has a title of some kind, such as supervisor, general, team captain, chairperson, or vice president. Clearly, being in such a position does not mean that the person knows how to lead, is a good leader, or is looked to as a leader by others. We all have known committee chairs, supervisors, or organization officers who did not seem to know what they were doing, let alone know how to lead anyone or anything toward change. When we use *leader* to mean a positional leader, we will say so.

The other meaning of *leader*—and the one that we generally use—is entirely different. It refers to any person who actively engages with others to accomplish change. Whether as the positional leader or participant-collaborator-group member, a person can be a leader by taking initiative and making a difference in moving the group forward toward positive change. You can be that kind of leader.

Purposes of Leadership

Leadership should attempt to accomplish something or change something. Leadership is purposeful and intentional. On a more profound level, leadership should be practiced in such a way as to be socially responsible. This kind of social responsibility is involved both in the outcomes or content of the group's purpose as well as in the group's process.

We are concerned about leadership that advances the welfare and quality of life for all. The outcomes of this ethical leadership approach on a broad scale—on your campus or in your community—would contribute to the public good. On a small scale, like in a club, this leadership would seek to incorporate the common good. The concept of common good does not mean the majority view but does mean shared purposes and common vision. This commitment to the public good or common good is a valuing of the role of social responsibility.

Social responsibility is a personal commitment to the well-being of people, our shared world, and the public good. It is "a way of being in the world that is deeply connected to others and the environment" (Berman & La Farge, 1993, p. 7). Being socially responsible also means you are willing to confront unfair and unjust treatment of others wherever it may appear—in classes, at work, or in your organizations. It means functioning within your organizations in ways that value relationships and act ethically with honor and integrity toward your responsibilities and each other.

Somehow, too many people have developed into observers instead of activists in their daily lives. They act as if they are spectators instead of citizens and active participants. Instead of complaining or doing nothing, we need to become engaged in the processes of improving our shared experience, whether at work, in clubs, in class, on a residence hall floor, on an intramural team, or in any of our other communities. Civic engagement is a heightened sense of responsibility for all those communities.

"After being an active member for a year I saw the potential for improving the club. I thought that my vision was in unison with the clubs, and that I stood out as one of the more vocal candidates to play a leadership role. Also, I was passionate about what the club was out to achieve."—Aaron Burke was vice president of En Circulo (Hispanic Club) and active in the Fiesta Del Pueblo volunteer group at North Carolina State University.

Civic Engagement and Civic Responsibility

Civic engagement is not as narrow as what ninth graders learn about in government class. Civic responsibility is the sense of personal responsibility individuals should feel to uphold their obligations as part of any community. Certainly, civic responsibility may mean voting in campus, local, state, or national elections. Yet civic responsibility means far more. It means noticing that key campus parking lot lights are broken and stopping by an office to report them instead of merely thinking, "I sure hope someone doesn't get assaulted in the dark." Civic engagement means attending your academic department's brown-bag lunch seminar to support your friends who planned the event and to be part of this learning community. Civic responsibility means saying, "If I am a member of this community, I have a responsibility to work with others to keep it functioning and make it better."

Making a Difference

Following the decade of the 1970s—in which some political leaders seemed less than honest, some religious leaders shattered their vows, and sports figures admitted to drug abuse and other offensive and illegal behaviors—it was no wonder that college students identified very few personal heroes. By the early 1990s, however, over 75% of 18- to 22-year-old students said they could name people they admired—people who made a difference (Levine, 1993). These admired people were local heroes: parents, the neighbor who started a local recycling movement, a minister, or the people who drove hundreds of miles to stuff sandbags to reinforce the levees in the Midwest floods or to rebuild houses after a hurricane in southern Florida. These were not major world leaders or rich corporate executives. These real heroes were average people who, together with others, made a difference in their communities, sometimes overcoming seemingly insurmountable odds to do so. The nightly CBS news began identifying a weekly hero—average Americans who made extraordinary contributions. The community service movement in the 1990s solidified the practice of people helping others in their local communities. On May 29, 1995, the cover of *Newsweek* magazine featured two youths active in service to their neighborhood with the caption, "Everyday Heroes: Yes, You Can Make a Difference." In a 1998 study of over seven hundred diverse youth (aged 18 through 30), summarized in Exhibit 1.2, respondents' confidence in the average person in local communities to solve complex societal problems was clear.

Steven Covey (1991), author of the popular *Principle-Centered Leadership*, encourages people to say, "I am not a product of my culture, my conditioning, and the conditions of my life; rather, I am a product of my value system, attitudes, and behaviors—and those things I control" (p. 257). This responsibility operates from a philosophy of being proactive instead of reactive. Instead of complaining about what "they" are not doing, this commitment to civic awareness acknowledges what "we" must do together. Clearly, oppressive structures such as racism and sexism can keep people from realizing their potential, but all of us can be more active agents in our own lives than we perhaps are.

Leadership Viewed from Different Frames

Leadership cannot be touched, smelled, or tasted, but it can be understood by how it is seen, heard, thought, and felt. Leadership is, therefore, a socially constructed phenomenon. To understand social construction, think of the fact of most people being one of two sexes—a woman or a man; however, the concepts of feminine or masculine are socially constructed. Many phenomena are given meaning by how they are constructed. Seeing, hearing, thinking, and feeling are all perceptual processes. People interpret their perceptions and draw meaning from them.

Many disciplines provide their own framework for viewing social constructions like leadership. Leadership is explored in many majors—including anthropology, history, sociology, psychology, political science, education, and business—as well as through literature or the arts. Leadership comes in various forms and relates to different disciplines and majors in different ways. When we think of leadership, we often think of political science—the study of

Exhibit 1.2. Young Americans' Model for Leadership.

Which Would You Prefer?

71% The best model for leadership is to build from the bottom up, that is, for many people to share responsibility for making decisions and moving forward.

25% The best model for leadership is to build from the top down, that is, for strong leaders to assume responsibility for making decisions and moving forward.

78% No one group is mostly responsible for solving social problems, and communities and individuals are responsible for solving their problems collectively.

17% Big institutions, such as government and business, are best suited to take responsibility for the well-being of citizens and for solving social problems.

65% We should look for leadership from ordinary people in the community, regardless of their position or level of authority.

31% We should look for leadership from people who have achieved an important position and earned the authority and respect that comes with that position.

79% Average people have the resources and practical know-how to solve most of their problems in their community.

18% Our problems are very complex, and we need experts to solve them.

Source: Hart & Associates (1998), p. 6.

systems of governance at local, state, and national levels in countries around the world. But leadership is also evident in other fields of study.

Consider how leadership might be constructed in your major. What paradigm might professionals in your field assume as a shared view? Anthropologists might study indigenous groups and try to discover how their leaders are selected and the qualities that the members of their culture believe are most important. Sociologists might study grassroots movements of people who embrace certain causes and how leadership develops in such groups. Psychologists might study the characteristics of leaders and followers and try to further the understanding of why they act in certain ways. Speech and speech communications majors often study how the messages leaders convey influence or inspire others to act. Organizational communicators are often concerned with how communication works in large, complex organizations and how various interpersonal communications can help or hinder such leadership processes. Education majors study leaders and leadership at all levels—from leadership in the classroom to being a district superintendent to running a college or university. Business majors study leadership in many different forms, including leading work teams, entrepreneurship, and providing a vision for large businesses. Fine arts majors often learn the challenges of leadership firsthand through being a first chair in an orchestra or directing a school play, and science majors experience leadership in research teams and various application projects. And the list goes on.

Each field of study may emphasize different elements of leadership, yet each field has an interest in how people can work more effectively together toward some outcome. "Leadership is like beauty: it's hard to define, but you know it when you see it" (Bennis, 1989, p. 1). Every academic major can benefit from a better understanding of the nature of leadership. Think about your own major. How can knowing more about leadership make you more successful in your future career or other endeavors?

Leadership Requires Openness to Learning

The story is told of philosopher-author Gertrude Stein lying on her deathbed. Her longtime partner, Alice B. Toklas, leaned over in despair at the impending passing of her companion and asked, "Gertrude, what is the answer?" Gertrude thoughtfully looked up at Alice and replied, "What is the question?" Leaders and participants ask questions, inviting others into the dialogue, and are open to diverse ideas. The question mark becomes a tool of leadership because participants need to ask questions, listen, and learn. In his classic *Rules for Radicals*, Saul Alinsky (1971) writes, "The question mark is an inverted plow, breaking up the hard soil of old belief and preparing for the new growth" (p. 11). Asking questions invites the group to examine its purpose and practices instead of thoughtlessly continuing old practices.

> Conventional leaders, who may think they have all the answers and that their passive followers should merely obey, are the dinosaurs of rapidly changing times. These times call for leaders who know how to let go of the past in the face of uncertainty because they have done it before and have succeeded. It is a paradox. Effective leaders will be the ones whose experience has shown them that they cannot rely on their experience. . . . they will use the expertise they have gained through experience to tap the experience and creative energies of others. (Potter & Fiedler, 1993, p. 68)

Leadership today shows that there is great wisdom and energy in the group. All members of the group have a great deal to learn from each other. Certainly, learning occurs inside the classroom, but it is very real in the world of experience. Involvement on and off campus provides the laboratory for enriching this learning.

Watkins and Marsick (1993) present a useful model that applies to learning (see Figure 1.2). The model also applies to the learning that occurs in the teams and groups. This model presents three components to learning: focus, or knowing about the learning opportunities; capability, including the resources and skills to learn; and will, or the motivation to engage in learning. You begin your exploration of yourself in the leadership equation when you examine your own goals, roles, and capabilities. Stop for a minute and think about something you are trying to accomplish. What is your focus? What do you need to accomplish this goal? What is your motivation or will to persist? On an even more complex level, we believe that the most effective organizations and communities are learning environments in which learning is ongoing, constant, pervasive, and valued.

Rapidly changing times and exploding information indicate we must all be lifelong learners. Vaill (1991) comments that we must all be comfortable being beginners again all the time. "It is not an exaggeration to suggest that everyone's state of beginnerhood is only going to deepen and intensify so that ten years from now each of us will be even more profoundly and thoroughly settled in the state of being a perpetual beginner" (p. 81). This means admitting when we do not know something, yet having the confidence that together among a diverse group working together on a shared problem we can figure it out. Remember, all of us are smarter than one of us.

Personal Responsibility for Learning

The conventional view of leadership assumes that leaders do the planning and motivating and that they carry a major share of responsibility for accomplishing anything with their group. We do not believe this is true. All of us are responsible for ourselves and for helping others. The whole group of participants, including positional leaders, needs to make sure the environment is open to learning, making mistakes, and sharing knowledge. Any behaviors or circumstances that block learning in organizations are likely to block empowerment and inclusion as well.

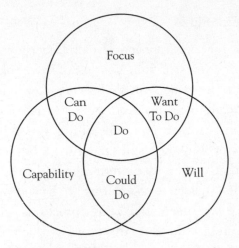

Figure 1.2. The Learning Model.
Source: Watkins & Marsick (1993), p. 37. Reprinted with permission.

Self-development, with the goal of students becoming more effective leaders and participants, is a primary goal of most colleges and universities. Leadership skills are life skills that can be applied to personal relationships as well as to work and organizational responsibilities. By redirecting your own life in the context of family, values, and dreams, you can become a productive colleague with others. As we said in the Preface, we believe in this approach to leadership because all of us can learn about ourselves, about others, and about change. Through learning, we stay vital and renewed.

"Through participation in classroom activities and student organizations, I have learned that the differences between a leader and a follower is his/her ability to take initiative to make things happen and to accept personal responsibility for his/her choices."—Gideon Craymer is a criminal justice and Spanish major at Grand Valley State University. He serves as secretary of Alpha Phi Sigma Criminal Justice Honors Society.

Experiential Learning

Understanding how you learn and develop leadership will be important to exploring yourself in the context of this book. David Kolb (1981) built on the work of such scholars as Lewin and Dewey to explore how learning occurs. Kolb suggests that we come to new information in one of two ways: by doing something (concrete experience) or by thinking about something (abstract conceptualization). We then process that information either by reflecting on that information (reflective observation) or by applying that information (active experimentation). This process is best understood as a cycle. Figure 1.3 illustrates this process. Much of how leadership is learned is in the real, concrete experiences of being in groups that are trying to accomplish something. Imagine you have just had an experience. To learn from that experience, you would want to reflect on it and make meaning from it. Next, you would form some hypotheses about it, and in thinking about it you would wonder if this is true for others—if it would work in other situations—and you look for connections to other information you possess. Then you would want to apply this new theory or learning in a real situation. And the cycle continues. This may be best understood as "What?" "So What?" and "Now What?" Kolb reminds us that what happens to us does not become experience without reflection. Without it, events are just things that happened. Many things happen from which we learn nothing because we do not reflect on those experiences to seek their deeper meaning.

Relational Leadership

This book will explore the evolution of leadership thinking and some of the many theories that help make meaning out of the varied and complex approaches to leadership. Yet studying leadership does not magically make you a better leader or participant. As learners about leadership in the context of today's challenges and opportunities, we propose that you focus on core, basic principles of

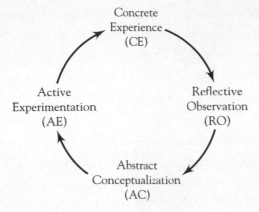

Figure 1.3. Kolb's Experiential Learning Model.
Source: Adapted from Kolb (1981), p. 235. Used with permission.

leadership that can guide your effectiveness. To reiterate: we define leadership as *a relational and ethical process of people together attempting to accomplish positive change*.

There is not one right way to lead. Leadership should not be studied as a recipe or a checklist. It is more important to develop a philosophy of leadership to guide your actions. This philosophy would value being ethical and inclusive. It would acknowledge the diverse talents of group members and trust the process to bring good thinking to the socially responsible changes group members agree they want to work toward.

"Leadership is a role open to anyone. Leadership is living by a personal set of rules in which you motivate others to do the right thing, be engaged in the world, and to listen to others and their concerns. Leadership is focused on the other person."—Chandra Johnson was an officer in Alpha Xi Delta and Dance Marathon as well as serving as a member of Order of Omega of the University of Iowa.

Relationships are the key to leadership effectiveness. Because leadership is inherently relational, it is perhaps redundant to use the term *relational leadership*. There is, however, strength in the affirmation of repetition. As leaders and participants in all our communities, we should be and expect others to be

- Purposeful

- Inclusive

- Empowering

- Ethical

- Process-oriented

These aspects of relational leadership then become foundational to working smarter. How we relate and work together in all of our communities (families, classes, organizations, work sites, and neighborhoods) matters. You need to examine your role as a member of these communities, whether they are made up of five people in your family or fifty people on your residence hall floor.

The Real World

Does this approach to leadership seem ideal and unrealistic or real and possible? Why don't we see these leadership practices widely embraced and used by all around us? This confusion between a preferred and an actual state is called cognitive dissonance (Festinger, 1962). When the president of your university speaks eloquently at the opening convocation about the campus being an ethical, learning environment open to change, yet your experience is that campus administrators resist trying anything new and even seem fearful of change, you likely feel dissonance. When the president of a student organization says, "We want to have all your feedback on this plan before we decide" and then proceeds to represent the plan so defensively that all comments are quickly silenced and you would not dare raise a question, there is dissonance.

Conversely, think of the times you have been treated with serious purpose, included, and aware that your contributions matter—perhaps in your study group, your favorite class, your office, or your committee planning a project like a clothing drive for a homeless shelter. These are the places where you matter because you find congruence in the principles you value and in the values the group practices.

Even when things are not what they ought to be, each of us can practice a personal philosophy of being the kind of person, leader, or participant we value. This brings a sense of personal congruence and authenticity. Educators have been challenged to see that "it is not nearly enough to teach students how the world is. We must also encourage them to think about how it ought to be. Without some hope for a better world, it is all too easy to think only of oneself and all too easy to leave the responsibilities of citizenship to others" (Harriger & Ford, 1989, p. 27). Clearly, community is not someone else's responsibility. It is a commitment from each participant. Likewise, leadership is not someone else's responsibility. It is a shared responsibility among participants. In short, as a participant, leadership is your responsibility.

Chapter Summary

In this chapter, we have asked you to explore aspects of your unique characteristics and experiences that you bring to leadership. Rapidly changing, complex times indicate a need to work together in different ways than those promoted by conventional or industrial approaches to leadership. This chapter introduced the value that leadership must be for socially responsible purposes. An overview of leadership with an emphasis on followers as active participants in the leadership process was presented in this chapter. This relational approach to leadership is committed to positive change, inclusive, empowering, ethical, and process-oriented. Relational leadership is best practiced in learning organizations.

What's Next?

The next chapter presents an overview of how leadership has been understood over time. It discusses how the complexity of today's times demands a more relational way of solving shared problems.

Chapter Activities

1. Which of the six foundational principles used to develop this book do you most closely agree with and why? Which is most difficult to endorse and why? Which is the most difficult to practice and why? Which is the easiest to practice and why?

2. Create words that could substitute for the term *follower* that would have an empowering connotation to others. How do you, or would you, react to being called a follower?

3. In response to the question "What is the purpose of leadership?" reflect and answer that question for yourself. What is your leadership purpose?

4. What community are you associated with or do you know about that is the most involving, ethical, empowering, and inclusive? How do people in this group empower others, make decisions, elicit feedback, and share power and authority? How does this community introduce and implement change?

5. How can knowing more about leadership make you more successful in your future career or other endeavors?

6. Using the Learning Model, stop for a minute and think about something you are trying to accomplish. What is your focus? How are you able to accomplish this goal? What is your motivation or will to persist?

7. What experiences have you had that you reflected on and from which you drew a leadership lesson? Using Kolb's model, describe that process.

Additional Readings

Allen, K. E., & Cherrey, C. (2000). *Systemic leadership: Enriching the meaning of our work*. Lanham, MD: University Press of America.

Kelley, R. E. (1992). *The power of followership: How to create leaders people want to follow and followers who lead themselves*. New York: Currency/Doubleday.

Lussier, R. N., & Achua, C. F. (2004). *Leadership: Theory, application, skill development* (2nd ed.). Eagan, MN: Thomson-West.

2

The Changing Nature of Leadership

Leadership often is perceived as a prized, coveted phenomenon in our society. It is mentioned daily in newspapers, classrooms, student organization meetings, news broadcasts, and dinner conversations. The leaders who are revered by some people are admonished by others. As prominent leadership scholar James MacGregor Burns (1978) remarked more than twenty years ago, "Leadership is one of the most observed and least understood phenomena on earth" (p. 2). That is still true today.

For decades, hundreds of leadership scholars have attempted to define the term, postulate theories, conduct research, and write about the topic; others believe that all you need is common sense to understand and practice leadership. As noted in Chapter One, the social construction of leadership makes it difficult to arrive at a single definition of the term *leadership* because "leadership means different things to different people" (Yukl, 1994, p. 2).

The meaning of leadership varies from one country to another. Leadership in a collectivistic society like Japan's looks different from leadership in an individualistic country such as Germany because of cultural norms, cultural values, and the use of power (Hofstede, 1980). Scholars have remarked that "there are almost as many definitions of leadership as there are people who have attempted to describe the concept" (Stogdill, 1974, p. 259). Still others believe that "leadership is not a mysterious activity" (Gardner, 1990, p. xv) and that the tasks of leadership can be identified. What is your understanding of leadership?

Aside from the struggles and difficulties of studying leadership, society is crying out for capable and willing leaders to step up and make a difference in our communities and in our world. John W. Gardner (1993), former presidential cabinet member and founder and former chair of Common Cause, entitled his essay (first published in 1965) "The Antileadership Vaccine." Thus, he made the point that people are less willing to take on the challenges of leadership because of the growing distrust society has shown toward leaders. Leading, whether through a formal position or without a formal title, can be a rewarding and self-fulfilling experience. It can also be a frustrating, exhausting, and difficult process.

Despite the sharp criticisms of leadership studies, many advancements have been made in the field to increase our knowledge of and appreciation for the complexities of leadership (Heilbrunn, 1994). We know more about leadership today than our forebears did at the turn of the twentieth century. Through research and analysis, many myths of leadership have been dispelled. Colleges and universities are developing academic majors, centers, and schools devoted to the study and practice of leadership. Our understanding of leadership is sharpened by recent research on the interactions between leaders and followers, the concept of change, self-leading teams, individual expressions of leadership, and shared leadership. Distinctions have been made between studying specific leaders—such as Malcolm X, former New York City mayor Rudy Giuliani, or Tennessee basketball coach Pat Summit—and studying leaders in general.

An extremely important consideration in our understanding of leadership is the context in which it is practiced. Leadership for what purpose? is a central question in our effort to dissect and understand leadership processes. The kind of leadership necessary to move social movements forward is very different from the type of leadership required in a military setting, especially on the battlefield.

Chapter Overview

In this chapter, we explore how the definitions and theories of leadership have changed over the years; we introduce some myths and truths about leadership, along with various metaphors of leadership. We also present some new perspectives about leadership that are now emerging out of recent scientific advances.

Myths About Leadership

The myths about leadership date back to the turn of the twentieth century, when leadership was first formally studied by psychologists and sociologists. In ancient Greece, only men with potbellies were thought to be great leaders. In Celtic lands, birds were thought to confer leadership powers. Some believe that only people with a charismatic personality make powerful leaders. The myths of leadership include

- Leaders are born, not made.

- Leadership is hierarchical, and you need to hold a formal position (have status and power) to be considered a leader.

- You have to have charisma to be an effective leader.

- There is one standard way of leading.

- It is impossible to be a manager and a leader at the same time.

- You only need to have common sense to be an effective leader.

Truths About Leadership

The truths about leadership that we propose are based on our collective research, years of study and teaching, and on our own experiences as leaders. We propose the following:

1. Leaders are made, not born. Many people have the capacity to lead an organization, community, family, profession, and, most important, themselves. Some individuals will not describe themselves as leaders based on traditional notions of formal leadership when, in fact, they do make a difference in their organization through their commitment, values, and action toward change. Leaders are not born with innate characteristics or skills predisposing them to be leaders (Gardner, 1990). A person's environment can influence the development of leadership skills and interests (Hughes, Ginnett, & Curphy, 1993; Komives, Owen, Longerbeam, Mainella, & Osteen, 2005).

2. In today's fluid organizations, leadership occurs at all levels. Progressive organizations are striving to flatten their hierarchies to empower people throughout the organization to participate in the leadership process. Manz and Sims's (1989) self-managing teams concept is an example of people at the "worker-level" being responsible for high-level decision making and behavioral control over an organization's process and outcomes. People find meaning in their organizational life and work through shared experiences and a feeling of being empowered to make a contribution or difference.

3. Having a charismatic personality is not a prerequisite for leadership. A charismatic leader is one who has "profound and unusual effects on followers" (Yukl, 1994, p. 318). Charismatic leaders are often described as visionaries who have a strong desire for power; leaders have been called impression managers who have a keen ability to motivate others and set an example for others to follow (Yukl). However, many effective and accomplished leaders are not described as charismatic. For every positive example of a charismatic leader, we can find a negative charismatic. For example, Martin

Luther King Jr. is described positively as a charismatic leader who organized a nation to fight for civil rights for all its citizens, whereas Adolph Hitler is viewed negatively as an example of a charismatic leader who influenced a nation to senselessly and unmercifully kill millions of people because of their race, religion, sexual orientation, or disability.

4. There is not one identifiable right way to lead an organization or group. On an individual level, a person's leadership approach or style might be influenced by his or her sex, cultural identity, or personal value system. On an organizational level, the context of the setting might determine the type of leadership required to be effective. Leading a volunteer civilian organization calls for a very different leadership approach than does leading a for-profit organization.

5. Some leaders and scholars believe it is important to make a distinction between the processes of management and leadership (Bennis & Nanus, 1985; Gardner, 1990). Gardner goes to great lengths to describe the differences between the functions of managers and leaders. He defines a manager as "the individual so labeled [who] holds a directive post in an organization, presiding over the processes by which the organization functions, allocating resources prudently, and making the best possible use of people" (p. 3). In Gardner's view, the manager is closely bound to an organization or institution, whereas a leader may not have an organization at all. Florence Nightingale is an example of such a leader. Yet others find the exercise of determining the differences between leadership and management to have little utility and use the terms interchangeably (Yukl, 1994).

Another proposition is that managers are preoccupied with doing things *the right way*, whereas leaders are focused on doing *the right thing* (Zaleznik, 1977). There are distinctions between management and leadership, and there is also overlap in the functions associated with both processes (Gardner, 1990). It behooves leaders who also perform managerial tasks, such as allocating resources and organizing systems, to be effective managers and to perform those functions well. It is possible, and in some cases desirable, for a person to be an effective leader while being an effective manager. The functions of both leadership and management, if they can be distinguished, are necessary in organizations.

6. Leadership is a discipline that is teachable (Gardner, 1990; Parks, 2005). Any participant with a desire to lead or to assume leadership responsibilities can be taught certain skills and processes. Leadership is not just common sense. Catherine the Great, John F. Kennedy, Sitting Bull, and Harriet Tubman did not rise to greatness serendipitously. They had a mission or purpose and they all experienced life events that shaped their values and sharpened their skills. Learning about leadership and developing as a leader is a lifelong process involving preparation, experience, trial and error, self-examination, and a willingness to learn from mistakes and successes. Your own leadership development might start early in elementary school as the lead in your sixth-grade play, or it may begin later in your career when you become an elected official or community activist at the age of fifty. We will explore how a leadership identity may develop in Chapter Thirteen.

Definitions of Leadership

The study of leadership has produced hundreds of definitions of the term, spanning several decades and dating back to the early 1900s (Rost, 1991). Although the term *leader* can be traced in the English language to about 1300, the word *leadership* emerged in the 1800s and was used in the context of political influence (Greenwood, 1993; Stogdill, 1974). Fewer than a dozen formal definitions of leadership existed from 1900 to 1929. In the 1980s, we witnessed a keen interest in the task of defining leadership, with 110 definitions of leadership created by scholars from a wide range of academic fields (Rost, 1991). According to Rost, at least 221 definitions of the term can be found in books and other scholarly publications—and at least 366 publications on leadership do *not* include a formal definition of the term.

An early definition offered by Mumford (1906–1907) defined leadership as "the preeminence of one or a few individuals in a group in the process of control of societal phenomena" (as cited in Bass, 1981, p. 7). Mumford's definition portrays the leader as controller of events and infers control over people. Early definitions such as Mumford's typically describe leadership as one person controlling others or inducing them to follow his or her command.

Contemporary definitions describe leadership as a relational process, based on mutual goals, toward some action or change. Another common aspect of most current definitions is that there is a level of interaction between leaders and followers who are working together to accomplish a goal or some type of action, and the interaction often is based on some type of influence. For example, Gardner (1990) defines leadership as "the process of persuasion or example by which an individual (or leadership team) induces a group to pursue objectives held by the leader or shared by the leader and his or her followers" (p. 1). Rost (1993) defines leadership as "an influence relationship among leaders and their collaborators who intend real changes that reflect their mutual purposes" (p. 99). Larraine Matusak, a leadership scholar and author of *Finding Your Voice: Learning to Lead . . . Anywhere You Want to Make a Difference* (1996), states that the leadership process entails "initiating and guiding and working with a group to accomplish change" (p. 5). And again we want to emphasize that leadership, as defined in the Relational Leadership Model (to be discussed in the next chapter), is *a relational and ethical process of people together attempting to accomplish positive change*.

What does all of this mean, and why does it matter? Our understanding of how leadership works in contemporary organizations is influenced by an integrated framework of leadership definitions and theories that have emerged over time. Various academic fields— such as anthropology, psychology, history, sociology, the arts, and philosophy—add to the rich interdisciplinary nature of how leadership is studied and practiced. We know more about leadership now than we knew at the turn of the nineteenth century, when only one scholarly definition of leadership could be found. Today, we know there is not one correct definition of leadership. This causes us to return to the question What is the purpose of leadership? in deciding which definition best fits a given context or situation.

Metaphorical Definitions of Leadership

Leadership also has been defined in interesting ways with the use of metaphors; that is, as "figure[s] of speech in which a word or phrase literally denoting one kind of object or idea is used in place of another to suggest a likeness or analogy between them: figurative language." (*Webster's Ninth New Collegiate Dictionary*, 1986, p. 532). Cohen and March (1974) and Weick (1979) provide comprehensive examples of how leadership and organizations can be described and understood through metaphors. Cohen and March (1974) use eight metaphors to describe how one might perceive university governance and the functions of presidential leadership: the competitive market metaphor, administrative metaphor, collective bargaining metaphor, democratic metaphor, consensus metaphor, anarchy metaphor, independent judiciary metaphor, and plebiscitary autocracy metaphor. Metaphorical examples provide us with a clearer or more visual understanding of a concept, process, or phenomenon.

A common contemporary metaphor likens leadership to an orchestra or symphony. Think for a moment of the role and tasks of a symphony conductor and the musicians. The conductor is responsible for bringing out the artistic talents and gifts of each symphony member, while the musicians work together to blend and harmonize the music.

Peter Vaill (1991) uses the metaphor of managing as a performing art to describe artistry associated with management and leadership. Vaill encourages leaders to look at "action as a performing art" (p. 117), which allows examination of both the parts and the whole, as well as the interrelationships between the two. Form matters in art. Vaill illustrates how form or the quality process (p. 118) is inherent in management and leadership, using the example of whether the ends justify the means in weighing the importance of process and outcome.

Max De Pree (1989) also illustrates leadership as an art and parallels the leadership process, not as a science or a set list of tasks, but rather as a "belief, a condition of the heart" (p. 148). De Pree's use of the art metaphor describes leadership as something intangible, a set of values, convictions, intimacy with one's work and passion. He goes on to say, "the visible signs of artful leadership are expressed, ultimately, in its practice" (p. 148). De Pree (1992) also uses the metaphor of a jazz musician to illustrate the leadership process:

> Jazz-band leaders must choose the music, find the right musicians, and perform—in public. But the effect of the performance depends on so many things—the environment, the volunteers playing in the band, the need for everybody to perform as individuals and as a group, the absolute dependence of the leader on the members of the band, the need of the leader for the followers to play well. What a summary of an organization! (De Pree, 1992, pp. 8–9)

De Pree's leadership jazz metaphor is powerful in illustrating inclusiveness, valuing individuality, showing the importance of the public good, and empowering people to realize their gifts and talents. The leadership jazz metaphor describes the emerging new model of leadership in today's organizations and communities.

Rost (1993) uses the metaphor of leadership as an episodic affair. "Any time people do leadership, they are involved in a process that is bounded by time, subject matter, specific leaders and collaborators engaged in the process, place, and context. . . . it is an episode in people's lives" (p. 103). Leadership then is time-specific, place-specific, and context-specific; individuals experience leadership in episodic moments. For example, leadership does not occur routinely in people's lives during every moment they are working or volunteering in the community. People "do leadership episodically—ten minutes here, a half hour there, fifteen minutes now, and two hours later" (p. 103).

We even have a metaphor—the "Fosbury Flop"—to describe the paradigm shift in leadership (McFarland, Senn, & Childress, 1993):

> In high jumping years ago, from high school track meets to the Olympics, the men and women who won always used the traditional scissors kick. Then Dick Fosbury showed up and invented a whole new way to jump over the bar, which came to be called the "Fosbury Flop." Very soon, if you couldn't convert your old belief in the scissors kick to a new belief in this more effective "Fosbury Flop," then you could no longer compete in the event. (p. 184)

And so it is with leadership in an ever changing world in which we live. Our technology is changing, our demographics are changing, the concept of a neighborhood has changed, our religions are changing, how we learn is changing, and our governments are being reinvented. Maybe the first test of leading a dynamic and contemporary organization should be whether or not we can do the Fosbury Leadership Flop.

Generations of Leadership Theories

Next, we will explore the evolution of leadership theories and provide you with a glimpse of several major theories. This will give you a conceptual understanding of leadership theory. There is a wealth of information on leadership theories—so much that this chapter could be the basis of a book on leadership theory. At the chapter's end, you will find a list of sources that will give you a more in-depth description and analysis of leadership theories.

It cannot be overstated that leadership is a complex and elusive phenomenon. It can be bewildering to wade through the swampy waters of incomplete leadership theories and often inconclusive research. The multidisciplinary nature of leadership adds to its contextual richness and reinforces the metaphor of leadership as an art form.

A metaphor can also be used to describe the state of leadership theory and research: leadership as an atom (Van Fleet & Yukl, 1989, p. 65). In earlier studies of the atom, it was proposed that the atom was "thought to be the simplest, single indivisible particle of matter" (Van Fleet & Yukl, p. 65). Just like the earlier scientific assumptions about the atom, leadership nearly a century ago was viewed as a simple, predictable, and uncomplicated construct. When leadership was placed under the microscope of social and behavioral scientists, it was discovered, as was the case with the atom, that leadership has many properties and many forms (Van Fleet & Yukl). "Where we once thought of leadership as a relatively simple construct, we now recognize that it is among the more complex social phenomena" (Van Fleet & Yukl, p. 66). Despite its criticisms and noted shortcomings, the field of leadership studies has been characterized as having a "robust (and respectable) intellectual history" (Heilbrunn, 1994, p. 66).

There are many ways to categorize the generations of leadership theories that have evolved over time. For the purposes of this chapter, leadership theory will be summarized using the following classification schema:

- Great man approaches

- Trait approaches

- Behavioral approaches

- Situational contingency approaches

- Influence theories

- Reciprocal leadership approaches

- Chaos theories

We will describe key leadership theories that have influenced scholars' and practitioners' understanding of leadership. These generations of leadership theories are presented in Exhibit 2.1.

Great Man Approaches

Great man theories preceded trait approaches. Darwinistic thinking dominated the first theories in the nineteenth century, under the assumption that leadership is based on hereditary properties (Bass, 1981). The great man folklore is based on brothers of reigning kings who were ascribed to have abilities of power and influence. It was believed that the intermarriage of the fittest would produce an aristocratic class superior to the lower class (Bass). Great women such as Joan of Arc and Catherine the Great were ignored as examples of leaders who were born with innate or natural gifts.

Trait Approaches

In the early 1900s, great man theories gave way to trait theories of leadership. Trait approaches marked the emergence of the second generation of leadership theories. If leadership depended not on who the leader was, then perhaps leadership could be understood by characteristics of those seen as leaders. It was assumed that leaders had particular traits or characteristics, such as intelligence, height, and self-confidence, that differentiated them from nonleaders and thus made them successful (Bass, 1981; Bass, 1990; Yukl, 1994).

Trait studies produced varying lists of personal traits that would guarantee leadership success to an individual who possessed these extraordinary qualities. The research questions based on trait theory were, What traits distinguish leaders from other people? and What is the extent of those differences? (Bass, 1990, p. 38). Ralph Stogdill provided evidence that disputed trait theories, with the premise that "persons who are leaders in one situation may not necessarily be leaders in other situations" (Greenwood, 1993, p. 7). In summary, research failed to produce a list of traits to ensure which characteristics leaders must possess to be effective; this paved the way for the behavioral approach of leadership research (Rost, 1993). What a leader *does* became more interesting than what a leader *is*.

Behavioral Approaches

The "one best way" approach to leading is a phrase commonly used to describe behavioral leadership theories that promote the notion that there is one best way to lead (Greenwood, 1993; Phillips, 1995; Van Fleet & Yukl, 1989). If leadership could not be explained by leader traits and characteristics, then attention turned to the things leaders do—their behaviors, skills, and styles. The behavioral approach includes the analysis of "what managers actually do on the job" (Yukl, 1994, p. 12), which is related to the content of managerial activities, roles, functions, and responsibilities. Effective and ineffective leaders also were compared in behavior studies to find out how the behaviors of effective leaders differed from those of ineffective leaders (Yukl). Historically, the field of psychology largely influenced studies on the behavioral approach to further knowledge of leadership in the 1950s and 1960s (Hughes, Ginnett, & Curphy, 1993).

The Ohio State studies and the University of Michigan studies are known as the seminal research projects on behavioral leadership theories (Yukl, 1994). Results from the Ohio State studies produced two dimensions of managerial behavior toward subordinates: consideration and initiating structure. Consideration was described as "the degree to which a leader acts in a friendly and supportive manner, shows concern for subordinates, and looks out for their welfare" (Yukl, p. 54) and initiating structure as "the degree to which

Exhibit 2.1. Summary of Leadership Approaches.

Approach	Time Period	Major Assumptions	Major Criticisms
Great Man	Mid-1800s to early 1900s	• Leadership development is based on Darwinistic principles • Leaders are born, not made • Leaders have natural abilities of power and influence	• Scientific research has not proved that leadership is based on hereditary factors • Leadership was believed to exist only in a few individuals
Trait	1904 to 1947	• A leader has superior or endowed qualities • Certain individuals possess a natural ability to lead • Leaders have traits that differentiate them from followers	• The situation is not considered in this approach • Many traits are too obscure or abstract to measure and observe • Studies have not adequately linked traits with leadership effectiveness • Most trait studies omit leadership behaviors and followers' motivation as mediating variables
Behavioral	1950s to early 1980s	• There is one best way to lead • Leaders who express high concern for both people and production or consideration and structure will be effective	• Situational variables and group processes are ignored; studies failed to identify the situations in which specific types of leadership behaviors are relevant
Situational Contingency	1950s to 1960s	• Leaders act differently, depending on the situation • The situation determines who will emerge as a leader • Different leadership behaviors are required for different situations	• Most contingency theories are ambiguous, making it difficult to formulate specific, testable propositions • Theories lack accurate measures

Approach	Time Period	Major Assumptions	Major Criticisms
Influence	Mid-1920s to 1977	• Leadership is an influence or social exchange process	• More research is needed on the effect charisma has on the leader-follower interaction
Reciprocal	1978 to present	• Leadership is a relational process • Leadership is a shared process • Emphasis is on followership	• Research is lacking • Further clarification is needed on similarities and differences between charismatic and transforming leadership • Processes of collaboration, change, and empowerment are difficult to achieve and measure
Chaos or Systems	1990 to present	• Attempts to describe leadership within a context of a complex, rapidly changing world • Leadership is a relational process • Control is not possible, so leadership is described as an influence relationship • The importance of systems is emphasized	• Research is lacking • Some concepts are difficult to define and understand • Holistic approach makes it difficult to achieve and measure

a leader defines and structures his or her own role and the roles of subordinates toward attainment of the group's formal goals" (p. 54). It is possible for an individual to be high on consideration and low on initiating structure, because the two dimensions are independent of one another. An individual also could be high on both consideration and initiating structure. Blake and Mouton proposed a two-factor approach: concern for people and concern for production. They developed the Managerial Grid Model in 1964 (as cited in Greenwood, 1993; Yukl). Research using their model concluded that effective managers show high concern for people and production.

The Michigan studies on leadership behavior included the "identification of relationships among leader behavior, group processes, and measures of group performance" (Yukl, 1994, p. 59). Three types of behaviors were identified that provided a distinction between effective and ineffective managers: task-oriented behaviors, relationship-oriented behaviors, and participative leadership. These studies suggested that leaders focus on high performance standards. Like the Ohio State studies, the Michigan studies showed that effective leader behaviors vary with the situation. To date, there is little research on leader behaviors that shows which specific behaviors are appropriate for specific situations (Yukl). The main criticisms of the behavioral approach are that it offers simple explanations to complex questions (Yukl) and that certain leadership behaviors have not resulted in specific outcomes (Northouse, 2004). The majority of research on leader behaviors has ignored situational variables and group processes. The results have been inconclusive and inconsistent, which opened the door for situational contingency approaches.

Situational Contingency Approaches

Situational contingency approaches propose that leaders should vary their approach or their behaviors based on the context or situation. The situation determines who will emerge as the leader—

the leader being "the product of the situation" (Bass, 1990, p. 38). The major research question is, "How [do] the effects of leadership vary from situation to situation?" (Yukl, 1994, p. 285). Contingency theories incorporate situational moderator variables to explain leadership effectiveness (Yukl). Situational theories emphasize that leadership behavior cannot be explained in a vacuum; elements of the situation must be included (Bass).

The Least Preferred Co-Worker (LPC) model and the Path-Goal theory are two major situational contingency theories. The LPC model was developed by Fiedler in the mid-1960s and "describes how the situation moderates the relationship between leader traits and effectiveness" (Yukl, 1994). This contingency theory of leadership focuses on the importance of the situation in explaining leader effectiveness. The Path-Goal theory originated in 1957 by Georgopoulos and others but is well known for its later applications by Robert House in the early 1970s (as cited in Van Fleet & Yukl, 1989). Van Fleet and Yukl note:

> If a group member perceives high productivity to be an easy "path" to attain personal goals, then he or she will tend to be a high producer. On the other hand, if personal goals are obtainable in other ways, then the group member will not likely be a high producer. The task of the group leader is, then, to increase the personal rewards to subordinates for performance in order to make the paths to their goals clearer and easier. (p. 71)

Personal characteristics of group members and the work environment are the two contingency variables associated with Path-Goal theory. Skills, needs, and motives define personal characteristics of group members, whereas task structure, formal authority, system of organization, and the work group as a whole define the work environment (Van Fleet & Yukl, 1989). The effect of leader behavior is contingent on elements of the situation, which are task and subordinate characteristics (Yukl, 1994). These variables influence others' "preferences for a particular pattern of leadership behavior, thereby influencing the impact of the leader on subordinate satisfaction" (Yukl, p. 286). Concerns about this theory of leadership include a lack of supporting research and an unclear association between the commitment and competence of subordinates and their level of development (Northouse, 2004).

"Leadership is a process in response to a situational need for change facilitated by a vision and tangible action motivating others to the achievement of that vision."—Michelle Swartz is the captain of the University Mock Team Trial and a member of the Varsity Field Hockey Team at the University of Richmond.

Influence Theories

In 1924 and 1947, Max Weber used the term *charisma* in a managerial context "to describe a form of influence based not on traditional power or formal authority but rather on follower perceptions that the leader is endowed with exceptional qualities" (Yukl, 1994, p. 317). Interest in charismatic leadership initially grew out of political, social, and religious movements in situations in which a leader would emerge out of a crisis or exhibit extraordinary vision to solve a problem (Bass, 1990; Yukl). It was not formalized until 1977, when Robert House proposed a formal theory of charismatic leadership that could be explained by a set of testable variables (Yukl).

Charisma is often attributed to leaders by their followers and is based on the perceptions of followers and the attributions of the leader, the context of the situation, and the needs of individuals and the group. There are several theories of charismatic leadership, including House's theory of charismatic leadership, the attribution theory of charisma, a self-concept theory of charismatic leadership, and psychoanalytic and social contagion explanations of charisma (Yukl, 1994). These theories vary based on the variables associated with the influence processes and how charismatic leadership behavior is defined.

House's theory of charismatic leadership is used for its noted comprehensiveness and proposed set of testable propositions. House's theory "identifies how charismatic leaders behave, how they differ from other people, and the conditions in which they are most likely to flourish" (Yukl, 1994, p. 318).

Conditions that facilitate charismatic leadership include times of crisis and times when followers are willing to challenge the status quo (Hughes, Ginnett, & Curphy, 1993). Charismatic leadership has received mixed reviews as a standard of practice in leadership situations. Too much deference to an individual leader by followers can create a dangerous scenario in which the leader misuses the power or delivers a vision with an empty dream (Yukl, 1994). Just as there are positive charismatics, society has been blemished by negative charismatics who were powerful and influential enough to lead others to their deaths or lead organizations to their destruction.

Reciprocal Leadership Theories

Since the late 1970s, a grouping of leadership theories has emerged that focuses on the relational and reciprocal nature of the leader-follower interaction. These theories emphasize the mutual goals and motivations of both followers and leaders, and elevate the importance and role of followers in the leadership process. In other words, these theories posit, leadership is not just something that a leader does to followers; rather, leadership is a process that meaningfully engages leaders and participants, values the contributions of participants, shares power and authority between leaders and participants, and establishes leadership as an inclusive activity among interdependent people. Participants are empowered to provide leadership and make significant contributions to achieving the vision of the organization. In some cases, the participants are transformed into leaders. The leadership process encompasses the essential role of all people, including participants. We call theories describing this process *reciprocal leadership theories*.

Several theories could be included in the reciprocal leadership theory category. In this chapter we focus on what we consider to be the major theories, because they most closely relate to the Relational Leadership Model, which will be presented in the next chapter. The major theories are transforming leadership, servant leadership, and followership. We will present another model of leadership, the Social Change Model, in Chapter Twelve.

Transforming Leadership Theory

A major reciprocal leadership theory—transforming leadership—was formulated by James MacGregor Burns in 1978. Burns (1978) defines transforming leadership as "a process where leaders and followers raise one another to higher levels of morality and motivation" (p. 20). Transforming leadership can result "in a relationship of mutual stimulation and elevation that converts followers into leaders and may convert leaders into moral agents" (p. 4). Leaders appeal to followers' "higher ideals and moral values such as liberty, justice, equality, peace, and humanitarianism, not to lesser emotions such as fear, greed, jealousy, or hatred" (Yukl, 1994, p. 351).

Transforming leadership is based on the assumption that leadership is "inseparable from followers' needs and goals" (Burns, 1978, p. 19) and that the "essence of the leader-follower relation is the interaction of persons with different levels of motivations and of power potential, including skill, in pursuit of a common or at least joint purpose" (p. 19). Power is used to realize common goals and purposes and not for purposes of exploitation or manipulation. A unique aspect of transforming leadership theory is its moral component.

The end goal of transforming leadership is that both leaders and followers raise each other to higher ethical aspirations and conduct. Burns believed that transforming leadership could be practiced at all levels of an organization and by both leaders and followers.

Examples of frequently mentioned transformational leaders include Gandhi, John F. Kennedy, Mother Teresa, Martin Luther King Jr., Abraham Lincoln, and Franklin D. Roosevelt (Bass, 1990; Burns, 1978). It is transforming leaders whom most people identify when they think about positive examples of leaders or role models (Bass).

Transforming leadership was contrasted with transactional leadership by Burns (1978) to demonstrate that the leader-follower interaction has two dimensions: transforming leadership and transactional leadership. Burns defines transactional leadership as the process whereby "one person takes the initiative in making contact with others for the purpose of an exchange of valued things" (p. 19). It is possible for a leader to engage in both transforming and transactional leadership. Transactional leadership appeals to the self-interests of followers, whereas transforming leadership appeals to higher ideals and moral values of both leaders and followers (Burns; Yukl, 1994).

For example, Gandhi, as a transforming leader, "elevated the hopes and demands of millions of Indians whose life and personality were enhanced in the process" (Burns, 1978, p. 20). Transactional leadership is exercised when a political candidate asks for votes in exchange for a promise to build more schools. Exhibit 2.2 lists the fundamental values associated with transforming and transactional leadership (Burns; Yukl, 1994). Critics of this theory focus on the its overall lack of clarity and specificity (Northouse, 2004).

Exhibit 2.2. Transforming and Transactional Leadership.

Transforming Leadership	*Transactional Leadership*
(Based on higher or end values)	(Based on exchange or modal values)
Order	Honesty
Equality	Fairness
Liberty	Responsibility
Freedom	Due process
Justice	Courage

Servant-Leadership Theory

Servant-leadership theory begins by viewing the leader first as a servant—a person who first wants to serve others. The servant, through focusing on the primary needs of others and the organization, then transforms himself or herself into a leader (Greenleaf, 1977). A servant-leader is someone who joins a club, a community, or a social movement with the sole goal of serving others to make a difference. The individual does not engage in these activities in order to lead the group or enhance a résumé. Mother Teresa was commonly characterized as a servant-leader (Rogers, 1996). There are many examples of servant-leaders in local communities—people who dedicate themselves to building the community so it becomes a better place for others. These servant-leaders can be residents, local business people, community activists, and politicians.

Servant-leaders view institutions "in which CEOs, staffs, directors, and trustees all play significant roles in holding their institutions in trust for the greater good of society" (Spears, 1995, pp. 6–7), which is the reciprocal nature of this leadership process. Peter Block (1993) refers to this concept as stewardship. In the servant-leadership process, both leaders and participants are stewards of the organization who dedicate themselves to taking care of the needs of others and the organization's needs and to uplifting the mission and values of the enterprise.

"A good leader must also [be] willing to serve first and foremost and have the ability and capability to lead or direct others in a way that is beneficial to their lives. Being able to lead by example and actually having the experience and knowledge of what the task entails is needed. A good leader is kind and knows how to speak to his/her followers in a non-demeaning way."—Sophia McIntosh is the Community Assistant Coordinator, President of Junior Missionary, and the Gospel Choir Director at SUNY Stony Brook.

The biggest difference between a servant-leader and a person who wants to lead an organization is the servant-leader's motive of putting the needs of others before his or her own needs. A person who joins the student government association because she wants to provide better academic services and advising based on the desires of the student community is an example of a servant-leader. Someone who gets involved with student government because she wants to run for office and maybe someday even be president is simply an example of someone with leadership aspirations. The end goal of servant-leadership is for those who are served to grow, to become more knowledgeable and empowered, to gain interdependence or independence, and to become servant-leaders themselves.

Followership Theory

Followers in many ways have been viewed in the leadership literature as sheep in need of a leader to tell them what to do, how to do it, and when to do it. Important thinking about followership has been provided by Robert E. Kelley, a professor in the Graduate School of Industrial Administration at Carnegie Mellon University. Kelley redefines followership and leadership. He does not subscribe to the industrial model of leaders, in which leaders are superior to followers (Kelley, 1992), but defines the roles of leaders and followers as having equally important but different activities. Followership is a role people assume in the leadership process.

Kelley (1988, p. 144) outlines five followership patterns along the dimensions of independent, critical thinking and dependent, uncritical thinking: alienated followers, sheep, yes people, survivors, and effective followers. Effective followers share these qualities:

- They manage themselves well.

- They are committed to the organization and to a purpose, principle, or person outside themselves.

- They build their competence and focus their efforts for maximum impact.

- They are courageous, honest, and credible.

The reciprocal nature of leadership and followership is that followers see themselves as "coadventurers" (Kelley, 1988) with leaders. Organizational successes result from both effective followership and effective leadership. Effective followers need to be empowered, honored for their contributions, and valued for the satisfaction and pride that they take in their roles of helping the organization achieve its goals and vision.

Two examples of followership in action come from opposite ends of the organizational continuum. New members of an organization can have an incredible impact by demonstrating their commitment through the aspects of followership just mentioned. This is also true of past officers of an organization. If they are able to stay connected to the organization, their positive impact can be extremely helpful to the current leaders.

"In order to be a good leader you have to be a great follower, and once you have become a good leader you must continue to be a great follower by helping others achieve."—Bernard Ford is the National Communications Coordinator-Residence Hall Presidents' Council, Keeper of Exchequer-Georgia Southern University Chapter of Kappa Alpha Psi Fraternity, Inc., and a senator in the Student Government Association at Georgia Southern University.

Emerging Leadership Paradigms

Rost (1991) describes the leadership theories in the twentieth century using the Industrial Paradigm Model. Leadership theory in the twentieth century mirrored the industrial era in that the theories were "structural-functionalist, management-oriented, personalistic in focusing only on the leader, goal-achievement dominated, self-interested and individualistic in outlook, male-oriented, utilitarian and materialistic in ethical perspective, and rationalistic, techno-cratic, linear, quantitative, and scientific in language and method-ology" (p. 27).

In summary, the theories that emerged from the early 1900s to the early 1970s are grounded in the industrial paradigm. For this reason, Rost (1993) calls for a "total transformation of our concept of leadership" (p. 98). The reciprocal leadership theories have allowed us to experience a paradigm shift from the industrial para-digm to the postindustrial paradigm of leadership. We believe that a more integrated understanding of contemporary leadership the-ory is necessary—one that relies on new ways of thinking about leadership. In the following sections, we will examine various aspects of this new, postindustrial paradigm.

Leadership Maps for a Rapidly Changing World

As Luthans and Slocum (2004) note in their introduction to a spe-cial issue of *Organizational Dynamics,* "Faced with an unprecedented economic, technological, socio-political, and moral/ethical tumul-tuous sea of change, there is a need for new theories, new applica-tions and just plain new thinking about leadership" (p. 227).

Much of what is taught in school has prepared people to live and lead in a neat, controllable world. But recent discoveries have indi-cated that the world is a lot messier than it once was believed to be. This may be an orderly world but the order is often obscured. It is a world in which control is not possible, especially if other people are involved—a world filled with chaos but one in which chaos is viewed as something to be embraced rather than feared. To suc-cessfully navigate in this world, new maps are needed—maps describing the leadership that is needed in an era of rapid change. As Stacey (1992) notes, "An old map is useless when the terrain is new" (p. 4), and the world is certainly a different place than it was fifty, forty, thirty, or even twenty years ago. Exhibit 2.3 highlights some of the differences between the conventional and emergent perspectives of how the world operates.

Another way of conceptualizing this new world is to ask two questions. First ask, How is my life (or organization) like a machine? The words you might use to describe your life (or organization) using a machine metaphor apply to the rational, orderly side of life. For example, just as with machines, certain operating procedures must be followed to make organizations work in a bureaucracy. When using organizational or institutional funds or reserving meeting rooms, certain procedures must be followed. These procedures are predictable and do not vary from month to month. Not following these procedures will cause problems for the organization. You need tools to function.

Now ask, How is my life (or organization) like a weather system? The nonrational, unpredictable, uncontrollable side of life will be included in the words you will use. For example, like the weather, organizational crises are usually unexpected. They can occur without warning, and their emergence cannot be predicted precisely. Yet the organization must be prepared to deal with these storms.

Both of these qualities are in operation at all times in the universe. To embrace only one perspective is to deny the other part of life. A former student government leader described the differences between these two perspectives in this manner: "The (rational/controllable) world is how I wish things were. The other (unpredictable/uncontrollable) world is how I know things are." Allen and Cherrey (2000, p. 20) summarize these "competing expectations and realities" in Exhibit 2.4.

The World of Chaos and Systems

Chaos, as we are using the term, has been defined as "order without predictability" (Cartwright, 1991, p. 44). As Stacey (1992) notes, "Chaotic behavior has two important characteristics. . . . it is inherently unpredictable, while at another level it displays a 'hidden'

Exhibit 2.3. Moving from the Conventional to the Emergent.

Conventional Perspectives	Emergent Perspectives
Stability	Change/Risk
Discussion	Dialogue
Structure	Order
Balance	Disequilibrium/Confusion
Certainty	Uncertainty
Controlled	Chaotic
Permanent	Temporary
March in Step	Dance in Rhythm
Talk	Listen
Local or Global	Local and Global
Known	Unknown/Unseen
Facts	Force Fields of Information
Share Information	Create Knowledge
Hierarchy	Web
Safe	Dangerous
Problems are "out there" (theirs)	Problems are "in here" (ours)
Proven Pasts/Products	Creative Solutions/Futures
Money and Bottom Line	Values and Vision
Policies and Procedures	Opportunities and Purposes
Restructuring	Recommitting
Divisions of the University	Communities of Learning
Teaching	Learning
Covering the Subject	Uncovering the Subject
Hearing	Thinking
Explaining	Exploring
Protecting	Connecting
Providers	Partners
Individual	Integrity/Collaboration
Contract	Trust
Skill Development	Personal Development
Programs	Outcomes
Learning in the Classroom	Learning Everywhere
Receiving	Reflecting
Driving by Dollars	Sailing with Soul
Set Limits	Set Expectations
Critical Analysis	Critical Thinking

Source: Adapted from Kochner in McMahon, T., Kochner, C., Clemetsen, B., & Bolger, A. (1995). Reprinted with permission.

Exhibit 2.4. Competing Expectations and Realities.

The way things ought to be	The way things actually are
Perfection is expected the first time.	Informed experimentation is necessary.
Goals are predictable with complete certainty.	Additional and new goals will always appear.
Control is expected.	Absolute control is rare and cannot be maintained over the long term.
Efficiency is the standard of competence.	Redundance and detours fuel creativity and innovation.
Predictability is assumed.	Probabilities are the norm.

Source: Allen & Cherrey (2000), p. 20. Used with permission.

pattern" (p. 62). This view of a world as turbulent, ever-changing, risky, and always challenging is echoed and expanded in some recent work describing the quantum or chaotic world. When you hear the word *chaos,* what do you imagine? Do words like *unorganized, untidy, wild, scary, anarchy, messy,* and *unproductive* come to mind? If you can let go of your need to have the world be completely rational and orderly, you may recognize this list of adjectives as a set of descriptors for how the world really operates. This notion of the world as yin and yang, rational and nonrational, orderly and messy is at the heart of how this real world is described. Using chaos and related concepts to describe leadership and life has been the focus of a number of different authors (Allen, 1990; Briggs & Peat, 1999; Eoyang, 1997; Holland, 1998; Lewin & Regine, 2001; Pascale, Millemann, & Goija, 2000; and Wheatley, 1999).

The chaotic world is a quantum world—a world of wholes, not parts. It is a connected world in which relationships are everything. It is a world filled with "strange attractors of meaning" (Wheatley, 1999, p. 115) and force fields that help shape the behaviors of individuals and organizations. It is a world in which multiple realities exist and it is difficult to identify exactly what caused something to occur. It is a world in which living things invariably organize themselves based largely on the feedback they gather from the environment around them. Finally, it is a world that cannot be controlled (Wheatley, 1999). This chaotic world has much to offer as we think about the changing nature of leadership. This section will explore the key elements to framing the world as more chaotic or more like a weather system than a machine.

Sensitivity to Initial Conditions

There are some basic concepts that are used to operate successfully in the world of chaos. Sensitivity to initial conditions (also called "the importance of initial conditions") implies that how something begins greatly determines where it ends up. Two objects may be initially positioned very close together, yet after their movements are amplified over and over again by feedback loops, they may be far apart after a relatively short period of time. This points to the great importance of the first committee or group meetings, first meetings with advisers, or the first days of class or on the job. As a shampoo commercial succinctly put it, "You'll never have another chance to make a first impression."

Relationships, Connections, and Anding

Relationships and connections are so important that Margaret Wheatley (1992) wrote, "None of us exists independent of our relationships with others" (p. 34). Another way to realize the importance of connections is to consider the concept of "andness." Andness occurs when you make a connection with something or someone—you are literally "anding" with it or them. Unless you "and" with something or someone, no exchange occurs, nothing is produced, no new energy is created. Think about it this way. We all know that $1 + 1 = 2$. But think about this in human terms. Think about your very best friend or coworker. When you two get together, you accomplish amazing things, much more than any two people you know. In this case, a synergy exists and $1 + 1 = 5$ or 10 or even 100. Now consider working on a project with someone with whom you cannot "and" or connect. In this case, the two of you are like two skewed lines in space, never to intersect: 1 + 1 = 0 (Meadows, 1982). If you can successfully "and" with the concepts of chaos theory, you will see countless examples of it in action every day. It is also important to note a need to shift our thinking. As Allen and Cherrey note (2000), "Systemic leadership is 'both-and,' not 'either-or'" (p. 21). Something might not be right or wrong, it might be right *and* wrong. Love and Estanek (2004) discuss this concept of dualism in detail and state, "One cannot understand one without the other" (p. 17).

Multiple Partial Solutions

If you are trying to solve a problem, the tendency can be to look for a single answer to it. But because people have such different perspectives, a better idea is to look for multiple partial solutions (Kelly, 1994). You will be more likely to come up with some possible answers and can begin solving the problem. To use a baseball example, it is a lot easier to hit several singles than a home run. An obvious question is, Do multiple partial solutions solve problems completely or only partially? The underlying assumption behind this question is that all problems have complete solutions. Most problems facing communities, groups, and organizations are difficult and have no simple answer. If there is an answer that seems obvious, it will have been tried some time in the past and may or may not have succeeded. Because of the complex nature of these problems, partial solutions may be all you can expect to develop. But you will be surprised at how much several partial solutions can accomplish.

Self-Organizing Systems

The chaotic world is filled with self-organizing systems; that is, collections of living things whose behaviors are constantly being shaped by the surrounding environment and by the actions of those around them. This may sound nebulous, but think about how a peer group shapes the behaviors of its participants or the profound impact that a culture has on its society. Try not to underestimate the influence that participants in an organization have on each other, even if they are not designated leaders of the group. Groups of people will organize themselves (Wheatley & Kellner-Rogers, 1996). As a participant, you need to work hard to see that the principles that shape this organizing are the ones that support the organization's mission.

"In times of uncertainty it is the leader's job to create clear goals and objectives. It is impossible to lead a group toward something that is ambiguous. Unfortunately even after the parameters have been defined, there are forces out of our control that can cause uncertainty. In this case, I force myself to regroup and establish smaller more short-term goals that will act as a concrete method of working toward achieving our long-term goal even if it is clouded by certain ambiguous aspects at that moment. It is important to always have an objective and clear direction for reaching such goals. If something should impede upon the original plan I must remember to be flexible and take a minute to redefine these goals."—Megan Huckins is a member of the Endicott College Leadership Advisory Board and head of the Endicott Chapter of the Philadelphia Project, and she volunteers with the Mexico Community Service Project. She majors in visual communications at Ellicott College.

We believe that leadership must be purposeful, inclusive, empowering, ethical, and process-oriented. Helping the group create and continually incorporate such a compelling vision into its organizational life is a challenge for any leader. Most newly elected officers want to begin doing things immediately. The very idea of taking some time to thoughtfully reflect on why the organization exists and to determine what values and ideals it needs to reflect can seem like a complete waste of time. Yet we guarantee that time spent reflecting will be time well spent.

Authentic Leadership

One exciting new development in leadership is a review of many reciprocal leadership models and postindustrial research, leading some scholars to see an underlying theme in all these approaches, which they have called *authentic leadership*. Authentic leadership has received a great deal of attention in recent years (Avolio & Gardner, 2005; Avolio, Gardner, Walumbwa, Luthans, & May, 2004; Gardner, Avolio, Luthans, May, & Walumbwa, 2005; Gardner, Avolio, & Walumbwa, 2005; Gardner & Schermerhorn, 2004; May, Hodges, Chan, & Avolio, 2003; Luthans & Avolio, 2003; Shamir & Eilam, 2005) and has been the subject of a special edition of *The Leadership Quarterly* (Vol. 16, Issue 3, 2005). As May, Hodges, Chan, and Avolio (2003) note, "Starting from a very basic point of view, authentic people are at the center of authentic leadership, and authentic leadership is at the base of all positive, socially constructive forms of leadership" (p. 249).

Luthans and Avolio (2003) describe authentic leadership as the confluence of positive psychology, transformational leadership, and moral, ethical leadership, and the authentic leader as someone who is "confident, hopeful, optimistic, resilient, transparent, moral/ethical, future-oriented, and gives priority to developing associates to be leaders" (p. 243). In a similar vein, Avolio et al. (2004) describe authentic leaders as "persons who have achieved high levels of authenticity in that they know who they are, what they believe and value, and they act upon those values and beliefs while transparently interacting with others" (p. 802).

The concept of authentic leadership adds much to our understanding of leadership. Avolio et al. (2004) describe authentic lead-

ership as a "root construct"—"at the very base or core of what constitutes profoundly positive leadership in whatever form it exists"
(p. 818). As such, it recognizes the need to understand the powerful impact of hope, trust, and positive emotions and the need to
understand the attitudes and behaviors of followers (Avolio et al.).
Followers are especially important to authentic leadership. Shamir
and Eilam (2005) note that "authentic leadership includes authentic followership as well, namely followers who follow the leaders for
authentic reasons and have an authentic relationship with the
leader" (pp. 400–401). Gardner, Avolio, Luthans, et al. (2005)
describe the relationship between authentic leader and follower as
"characterized by: a) transparency, openness, and trust, b) guidance
toward worthy objectives, and c) an emphasis on follower development" (p. 345).

Avolio et al. (2004) note that "authentic leadership theory
stresses the idea of leading by example (i.e., role modeling) through
setting high moral standards, honesty, and integrity" (p. 807). May,
Hodges, Chan, and Avolio (2003) offer the following "tasks" of
authentic leadership: build followers' self-efficacy; create hope; raise
optimism; and strengthen resilience (pp. 274–278). Shamir and
Eilam (2005) describe authentic leaders in the following way:

1. Authentic leaders do not fake their leadership.
2. Relatedly, authentic leaders do not take on a leadership role or engage in leadership activities for
   status, honor, or other personal rewards.
3. Authentic leaders are originals, not copies.
4. Authentic leaders are leaders whose actions are
   based on their values and convictions. (pp.
   396–397)

It is important to remember that authentic leaders

can be directive or participative, and could even
be authoritarian. The behavioral style per se is not what

necessarily differentiates the authentic from the inauthentic leader. Authentic leaders act in accordance with deep personal values and convictions, to build credibility and win the respect and trust of followers by encouraging diverse viewpoints and building networks of collaborative relationships with followers, and thereby lead in a manner that followers recognize as authentic. (Avolio et al., 2004, p. 806)

"Over the years, I have learned that the leader isn't always right. I wasn't necessarily taught this but I found it to be a misconception. While the leader is there to guide others in the right direction, they don't always have all the answers. I learned this in high school by questioning my leader, but also experienced it as a TA."—Kathryn Graham is a Learning Edge Academic Program mentor, Mammalian Anatomy Teaching Assistant, and a member of the Daily Collegian Sports Staff. She helped plan the IFC/Panhellenic Dance Marathon at Penn State University.

Although related in some ways, it is important to note how authentic leadership differs from similar conceptualizations of leadership, particularly transformational leadership. Shamir and Eilam (2005) state that "transformational leaders can be authentic or inauthentic and non-transformational leaders can be authentic" (p. 398). Relatedly, Avolio et al. (2004) offer that "authentic leadership theory does not necessarily delve into the essence of transforming leadership articulated by Burns, which was to transform followers into leaders" (p. 807). Although there are certainly similarities with other descriptions of leadership, authentic leadership, with its emphasis on core or root construct and positive emotions, offers a unique view of leadership.

Chapter Summary

The studies on leadership theory are often described with what we call the "but" phenomenon: there are numerous theories on leadership, "but" we still know very little about if and how leaders make a difference and their effectiveness on the organization; leadership has been studied as a scientific discipline for several decades, "but" we still have made little progress; there are numerous research studies on leadership, "but" the results are often inconclusive and ambiguous.

Scholars, practitioners, and students of leadership just within this decade are making progress in reformulating their ideas and research questions to fit the changing nature of our organizations and our world. Yukl (1994) calls for researchers and scholars to greatly improve the quality of leadership research and theory. Perhaps researchers need to experience a Fosbury Flop in their formulation of leadership theory and research design.

Leaders and leadership researchers need to work collaboratively to forge new knowledge and discoveries about leadership processes in contemporary organizations. Scholars and researchers cannot work in isolation from individuals who practice leadership "out in the field" at all levels of an organization or in a community. As we continue to search for answers and knowledge about leadership, we see the glass as half full rather than half empty.

In this chapter, we also explored a new world—the world of chaos and systems—and noted how it is different from the linear, rational world that has been traditionally used as a model for how the world works. Leadership in this new world requires embracing rapid change and constant learning. These are exciting, challenging, turbulent times in which to be alive. They call for new and different ways of conceptualizing and leading in organizations and the world.

Finally, we introduced the emergence of authentic leadership. With its focus on leadership as a core aspect of our very being; hope, trust, and positive emotions; and concern for understanding the attitudes and behaviors of followers, authentic leadership offers a new way for us to look at leadership.

What's Next?

The next chapter presents a leadership model that emphasizes the role of relationships. This Relational Leadership Model highlights the importance of being inclusive, empowering, purposeful, ethical, and process-oriented.

Chapter Activities

1. Describe your personal best leadership experience—an experience in which you were most effective. What theory or metaphor best describes your leadership approach and why?

2. What motivates you to take on leadership responsibilities or roles and why? Why do you lead?

3. For each of the leadership theory categories (trait, behavioral, and so on), provide examples of specific leaders and participants whose leadership can be described based upon that approach. Give examples of people who practice these theories.

4. Using Rost's postindustrial leadership definition and paradigm, describe what an organization, office, or community in which you belong would look like if this type of leadership were practiced. What would be the same? What would be different?

5. If the glass is half full of our understanding of leadership theory and concepts, what do you think we need to learn to further our knowledge of how leadership works in contemporary organizations?

6. Think about your life. What provides the order in your chaotic world? Is it values? Relationships? Family? Your faith? Now think about your organization. What provides the order or structure within this group? Does it need to be changed? If so, how can you do this?

7. Think about the last time you did something in your organization that others would describe as being "outside the lines." What was it? Why did others think it was "way out"? Was it successful? Why or why not?

8. Consider how Luthans and Avolio (2003) describe authentic leaders. Describe your own sense of hope and optimism. Similarly, consider the sense of hope and optimism within an organization with which you are familiar. How can you nurture the sense of hope and optimism in followers? How might a leader enhance the sense of hope and optimism within this organization?

Additional Readings

Avolio, B. J., & Gardner, W. L. (2005). Authentic leadership development: Getting to the root of positive forms of leadership. *Leadership Quarterly, 16,* 315–338.

Kelly, K. (1994). *Out of control: The new biology of machines, social systems, and the economic world.* Reading, MA: Addison-Wesley.

Luthans, F., & Avolio, B. (2003). Authentic leadership development. In K. S. Cameron, J. E. Dutton, & R. E. Quinn (Eds.), *Positive organizational scholarship: Foundations for a new discipline* (pp. 241–258). San Francisco: Berrett-Koehler.

Northouse, P. G. (2004). *Leadership: Theory and practice* (3rd ed.). Thousand Oaks, CA: Sage.

Senge, P. M. (1990). *The fifth discipline: The art and practice of the learning organization.* New York: Currency/Doubleday.

Wheatley, M. J. (1998). *Leadership and the new science: Learning about organization from an orderly universe* (2nd ed.). San Francisco: Berrett-Koehler.

3

The Relational Leadership Model

In the previous chapter, we reviewed how theorists' view of leadership has changed, from the belief that leaders are simply born to the idea that the best way to learn about leadership is to study the behaviors or practices of people who are viewed as leaders. Theorizing has evolved even further into an understanding of leadership as a complex process. Indeed, leadership is a transforming process that raises all participants to levels at which they can become effective leaders.

Leadership may best be understood as philosophy. At its core, understanding philosophy means understanding values. "Affect, motives, attitudes, beliefs, values, ethics, morals, will, commitment, preferences, norms, expectations, responsibilities—such are the concerns of leadership philosophy proper. Their study is paramount because the very nature of leadership is that of practical philosophy, philosophy-in-action" (Hodgkinson, 1983, p. 202). When we examine historical leaders, we often are analyzing the values and ethics that characterized their leadership. It is critical that we each develop our own personal philosophy—one we hope will include the elements of the model presented in this chapter.

Chapter Overview

This chapter presents a relational model of leadership to consider in building your own personal philosophy. Each of the elements of the model is presented in detail to give you more information about each component.

Relational Leadership

Leadership has to do with relationships, the role of which cannot be overstated. Leadership is inherently a relational, communal process. "Leadership is always dependent on the context, but the context is established by the relationships we value" (Wheatley, 1992, p. 144). Although a person could exert leadership of ideas through persuasive writings or making speeches, most leadership happens in an interactive context between individuals and among group members. We emphasize once again: we view leadership as *a relational and ethical process of people together attempting to accomplish positive change*.

Chapter Two presented an overview of how leadership theories and models have changed over time. These changing frameworks are reflected in the descriptive terms that have been affixed to the word *leadership*. Examples of these leadership theories and concepts include situational, transforming, servant-leadership, authentic leadership, and principle-centered leadership. We have used the term *relational leadership* as a reminder that relationships are the focal point of the leadership process.

Relational leadership involves a focus on five primary components. This approach to leadership is purposeful and builds commitment toward positive purposes that are inclusive of people and diverse points of view, empowers those involved, is ethical, and recognizes that all four of these elements are accomplished by being process-oriented.

The model provides a frame of reference or an approach to leadership in contemporary organizations. With these foundational philosophies and commitments, an individual can make a meaningful contribution in any organization. This model is not a leadership theory in itself, and it does not address the change outcomes

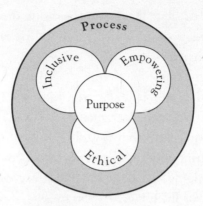

Figure 3.1. Relational Leadership Model.

for which leadership is intended. The Relational Leadership Model does not seek to describe the way leadership is currently practiced in all groups or organizations, but is an aspirational model that we propose in developing and supporting a healthy, ethical, effective group. It is a framework connecting five key elements that can serve as a responsive approach to leadership. Figure 3.1 offers a visual image of the elements of the model.

The components of relational leadership are complex concepts. Think about your own level of comfort or knowledge about each component as you read the related dimensions of each element. The model reflects how the organization's or community's purpose influences the components of being inclusive, empowering, and ethical. For example, the purpose of the Habitat for Humanity Club on campus is to engage its members to assist in providing houses for those who cannot afford them on their own. The purpose includes others, empowers them to use their leadership and talents to make a difference, and is ethical in that it benefits others and improves the quality of life in a community. How that purpose is achieved (the process) is just as important as the outcome. How the goals are accomplished and how others are involved in the process matters in the leadership process. The purpose is vision-driven and not position-driven. Leaders and members promote the organization's purpose through a shared vision and not for self-gain such as achieving a higher leadership position or fame.

Exhibit 3.1 identifies some important knowledge, attitudes, and skills that are embedded in each element. These reflect the knowledge, attitudes, and skills that would be helpful in understanding relational leadership. Brief applications of the core elements to the knowing-being-doing model conclude each section. For example, in order to practice inclusiveness, you must

- Know yourself and others; engage yourself in learning new information as you develop the competencies required in your role (knowledge)

- Be open to difference and value other perspectives (attitudes)

- Practice listening skills, coalition building, interpersonal skills, and effective civil discourse (skills)

Knowing-Being-Doing

Individuals involved in the leadership process (leaders, members, co-creators, and so on) need to know themselves well before they can effectively work with others to influence change or achieve common purpose. It is not enough to simply drive an agenda or accomplish small or big wins. The leadership process calls for those engaged in it to be knowledgeable (knowing), to be aware of self and others (being), and to act (doing). The knowing-being-doing model represents a holistic approach to the leadership development of yourself and others. These three components are interrelated— the knowledge you possess can influence your ways of thinking, which can influence your actions. And it is also true that your beliefs and way of existing in this world (being) can influence your actions, which can influence your behaviors. This pattern of influence is circular and not on a straight path.

Other ways to view this holistic approach is by using the framework of knowledge, skills, and attitudes or head, heart, and practice. Palmer (1998) uses the phrase "head, heart, and practice" to describe the paradoxes in teaching and what happens when we keep the head (knowing and intellect) separated from the heart (being) and even further separated from practice (doing). Palmer argues that we need a synthesis of all three components in the teaching process. The same applies in the leadership process.

The Army coined the phrase "know, be, do." People will collaborate with those who are credible (both leaders and members)—those who are knowing. Leaders need to demonstrate competence and maintain a certain amount of knowledge. Hesselbein and Shinseki (2004) offer four levels of skills essential to leadership: interpersonal skills, conceptual skills (ability to think creatively), technical skills (expertise required for position), and tactical skills (negotiation, human relations, and other skills necessary to achieve objectives) (p. 12). Knowing is an ongoing process that allows leaders to continue to develop, learn, and grow.

In the Army, the "be" means knowing what values and attributes define you as a leader (Hesselbein & Shinseki, 2004). "Your character helps you know what is right; more than that, it links that knowledge to action. Character gives you the courage to do what is right regardless of the circumstances or consequences" (p. 11). The Army's acronym of leadership is LDRSHIP: Loyalty, Duty, Respect, Selfless service, Honor, Integrity, Personal courage (p. 11). That is the essence of the "be" of leadership. The Lao Tzu quotations throughout this book are another example of being. This Eastern reflection of having a sense of self and being centered in self-awareness is important to relating well with others.

The "doing" of knowing and being means acting. Character and knowledge are not enough in facilitating change in the leadership process. Doing attempts to produce results, accomplishes the vision, creates change, and influences others to act. Sometimes leaders will fail to act because of indecision or due to a fixation on perfection. "Competent, confident leaders tolerate honest mistakes that are not

Exhibit 3.1. Relational Leadership Model Compared to Knowing-Being-Doing.

Leadership Component	Knowing (*Knowledge and Understanding*)	Being (*Attitudes*)	Doing (*Skills*)
Purposeful	How change occurs	Hopeful	Identifying goals
	Core elements of change	Committed	Envisioning
		"Can do" attitude	Meaning-making
	Role of mission or vision	Likes improvement	Creative thinking
		Commitment to social responsibility	Involving others in vision-building process
	Shared values		
	Common purpose		
Inclusive	Self and others	Open to difference	Talent development
	Citizenship	Values equity	
	Frames and multiple realities	Web-like thinking	Listening skills
		Believes everyone can make a difference	Building coalitions
			Framing and reframing
			Civil discourse
Empowering	Power	Believes each has something to offer	Gate-keeping skills
	How policies or procedures block or promote empowerment	Self-esteem	Sharing information
		Concern for others' growth	Individual and team learning
	Personal mastery	Values others' contributions	Encouraging or affirming others
	Control is not possible	Willing to share power	Capacity building
			Promoting self-leadership
			Practicing renewal

the result of negligence. A leader who sets a standard of 'zero defects, no mistakes' is also saying, 'Don't take any chances'" (Hesselbein & Shinseki, 2004, p. 15).

Learning is an outcome of the knowing-being-doing developmental model or feedback system. Be attuned to how new learning

Leadership Component	Knowing (Knowledge and Understanding)	Being (Attitudes)	Doing (Skills)
Ethical	How values develop How systems influence justice and care Self and others' values Ethical decision-making models	Commitment to socially responsible behavior Confronting behavior Values integrity Trustworthy Authentic Establishes sense of personal character Responsible Expects high standards Puts benefit to others over self-gain	Being congruent Being trusting Being reliable Having courage Using moral imagination
Process-Oriented	Community Group process Relational aspect of leadership Process is as important as outcomes	Values process as well as outcomes Quality effort Develops systems perspective	Collaboration Reflection Meaning making Challenge Civil confrontation Learning Giving and receiving feedback

is changing your attitudes and behaviors or is changing you in general. It is important to reflect upon how and what you are learning as you go through those cycles. "Leaders promote learning in at least three ways: through their own learning on a personal level, by helping others in their units [organizations] learn, and by shaping and contributing to an organizational culture that promotes learning" (Hesselbein & Shinseki, 2004, p. 133).

As you continue reading this and the following chapters, consider how this model is adding to your knowledge. How can you take this information and incorporate it into your beliefs surrounding leadership? What actions can you take with this new knowledge? Consciously examining your thoughts, feelings, and actions allows you to continue to learn and grow both as a leader and as a human being.

Relational Leadership Is Purposeful

Being purposeful means having a commitment to a goal or activity. It is also the ability to collaborate and to find common ground with others to facilitate positive change. Creating positive change can mean working hard toward resolving differences among participants, finding a common direction, and building a shared vision to improve the organization or enhance others in some way. Even if a participant does not have a vision, that person knows enough to ask others, "Remind me what we are working toward. What do we all hope will happen?" Trusting the process, several in the group will chime in with their ideas, and someone will have the talent to express those words in terms of the vision and purpose that will bring nods of agreement from nearly every person present. It is important that all group members be able to articulate that purpose and use it as a driving force. That is an essential element in relational leadership.

The conventional paradigm of leadership often asserts that the positional leader must have a clear vision. Research, however, has shown two primary types of vision activity: personalized vision and socialized vision (Howell, 1988). Personalized vision refers to a person, usually the person with legitimate authority, announcing a dream or plan and imposing it on others. Participants seem to have little choice and must adopt this vision, which results in varying degrees of personal ownership or commitment. Jack Welch, the former CEO of General Electric (GE), is an excellent example of an authoritative leader with a personalized vision. Although Jack Welch was a strong leader with a public presence, he did not single-handedly raise the profile of GE. Even though Jack Welsh had the legitimate power to do so, it did not automatically ensure commitment from his employees. He started his tenure as CEO as a commanding leader and then, over time, developed a more humanistic leadership approach that inspired GE's employees with a values-based vision (O'Toole, 2003).

Socialized vision is building a vision from among group members, recognizing that people support what they help create. Sharing vision does not mean that each person must create and possess a vision, but that each person must be involved in the process of building a vision with others. "Effective leaders don't just impose their vision on others, they recruit others to a shared vision. Especially in our digital age, when power tends to coalesce around ideas, not position, leadership is a partnership, not a sinecure" (Bennis & Thomas, 2002, p. 137). Think about your personality preferences. Do you think creatively and see possibilities in everything, or are you shaking your head right now, thinking "No way!" Do you have ideas about your future and a vision of how things might be? Such a vision is a picture of "a realistic, credible, attractive future" for yourself or your organization (Nanus, 1992, p. 8).

After hearing a presentation on empowering leadership and the importance of shared vision, one of our colleagues approached the presenter. She said, "I just am not creative or cannot articulate a vision. I am practical and realistic. I feel capable but am more of a maintainer than a builder. I can keep things going more than I am able to think them up in the first place." The first piece of advice that organization consultant Burt Nanus (1992) shares with those trying to avoid failures in organizational vision is, "Don't do it alone" (p. 167).

Being purposeful with a group vision that includes a positive change effort helps you set priorities and make decisions congruent with that dream. "Vision animates, inspirits, and transforms purpose into action" (Bennis & Goldsmith, 1994, p. 101). This action component to vision is described well by the engraving in an eighteenth-century church in Sussex, England:

> A vision without a task is but a dream,
> a task without a vision is drudgery,
> a vision and a task
> is the hope of the world.
> (*From* Transcultural Leadership, *p. 106, by G. F. Simons, C. Vázquez, & P. R. Harris. Copyright © 1993, with permission from Elsevier.*)

"To be motivating, a vision must be a source of self-esteem and common purpose. . . . The core of the vision is the organization's mission statement, which describes the general purpose of the organization" (Yukl, 1989, p. 336). One approach that is used by executives to develop shared visions is an exercise involving magazine articles. Organizational members are asked to identify their favorite magazine or a magazine closely related to the organization's purpose and write a feature story that will describe the organization in the future (four or five years from the present time) using headlines (Yukl). This powerful activity allows everyone to dream together and to begin the visioning process using creativity, imagination, and passion.

Your individual, purposeful commitment to the shared vision of a group project means you will do your part, share resources, and support your teammates because you expect the same of them. Vision guides action. "It's not what a vision is, it's what a vision does" (Kazuo Inamori, as cited in Senge, 1990, p. 207). A vision of a homecoming weekend reaching the broadest possible group of alumni will guide all the committee's choices about how to diversify that event.

"Success can be measured in many ways such as reaching your goal, involving new groups or individuals with new perspectives, and creating awareness or change. In the organizations I have been involved with, success has come by including those who are highly motivated and want to make a difference and have a clear understanding of the goal to be achieved. When this happens, it becomes easier to accomplish tasks because everyone is working towards the same goal. It is beneficial to utilize special groups or individuals who have expertise on your project to gain new insight, help motivate others, and provide additional resources and support."—Brynn DeLong is a member of the Blue Chip Leadership Program and majors in political science at the University of Arizona.

A vision inspires energy and purpose. Retired General Norman Schwarzkopf observed, "I have found that in order to be a leader, you are almost serving a cause" (Wren, 1994, p. 4).Purposeful participants have emotionally identified with a purpose and a dream. "There is no more powerful engine driving an organization toward excellence and long-range success than an attractive, worthwhile, and achievable vision of the future, widely shared" (Nanus, 1992, p. 3).

Working for Positive Change

One common purpose that pulls people together is working toward change. Change processes can have various motives associated with them. The Relational Leadership Model supports positive change— that is, change that improves the human condition and that does not intentionally harm others. The antithesis of this is facilitating change that is destructive, like the attacks on the World Trade Center in New York City. When facilitating a positive change process, the means justify the ends.

Rost (1991) proposes that leadership happens when the group *intends* to accomplish change, not just when they *do* accomplish change. Having the intention of improving a situation, accomplishing a task, or implementing a common purpose is part of the change process. Change may not happen for many reasons, but the core fact that the group intended to make a difference is central. John Parr (1994), president of the National Civic League, writes, "Positive change can occur when people with different perspectives are organized into groups in which everyone is regarded as a peer. There must be a high level of involvement, a clear purpose, adequate resources, and the power to decide and implement" (p. xiii).

Some situations are profoundly hard to change. It is hard to move away from the status quo—the way things are. Change theory proposes that change often begins when something unfreezes a situation. The cycle is often presented as unfreezing → changing → refreezing. This "unfreezing" may be caused by a trigger event, such as a carjacking in a remote campus parking lot, a campus riot following a sporting event, or a disappointingly small attendance at a group's expensive activity. People pay attention to the problem with a focus they did not have prior to the incident. Unfreezing may also occur when external policies change—when a new law is enacted, for example. Unfreezing makes it possible to address an issue or policy that has not commanded the attention of those who need to address it. The change process is then engaged and the issue is addressed.

Even after a change is implemented, it would be an error in these times even to consider any issue "refrozen." Instead, it is best to consider the outcome to be "slush," so that the solution is seen not as final but as permeable and open to be readdressed easily. It may be best to consider solutions as automatically open for review, regularly evaluated, and flexible. The classic change model (Lewin, 1958), describing the change process as moving from the present state through a transition state to a desired state, still works, but we encourage a caution that the desired state should now be viewed as less rigid.

Change can be thought of as moving some situation away from the status quo to a different place. To understand why that movement is hard, examine the driving forces pushing for change and the resisting forces striving to keep change from happening to preserve the status quo. Clearly, not all change is appropriate or supportable. When it is, the driving forces working toward change should be enhanced and the restraining forces minimized. This "force-field analysis" is a useful method for identifying aspects of the situation that could enhance change (Lippitt, 1969, p. 157).

Kotter and Cohen (2002) refer to the concept of "removing barriers in the mind" as another reason why people are resistant to change or to changing. "After years of stability, incremental change, or failed attempts at change, people can internalize a deep belief that they are not capable of achieving a leap. They may not say out loud 'I can't do it,' but at some level they feel it, even when it is not true" (p. 112). It is important to understand that the mind can both disempower and empower individuals toward change.

We are constantly faced with the dynamic tension of how things are and how we think they ought to be. This "is-ought" dichotomy asks us to face reality but work toward true transformative change, real change—to move toward the more hopeful vision. This "creative tension" brings energy to the change effort (Senge, 1990, p. 150). Connecting personal hopes and commitments to a group vision is a creative process. This process can be time-consuming. As we describe more fully in Chapter Seven, when a group is newly formed, the process of building a group vision can be energetic and hopeful if the group quickly comes to agreement and commitment, or it can be anxious and cautious if the group shows little agreement. When joining an ongoing group in which a vision has already been established, new participants have to determine whether they can connect to that vision or feel they can help shape the continued evolution of the group's vision over time.

Relational Leadership Is Inclusive

Being inclusive means understanding, valuing, and actively engaging diversity in views, approaches, styles, and aspects of individuality, such as sex or culture, that add multiple perspectives to a group's activity. As a foundation for valuing inclusion, you will have a chance to explore your own attitudes and attributes in Chapter Four and examine those of others in Chapter Five. Exhibit 3.1 highlights aspects of being inclusive to illustrate how you might explore this component. It means understanding how different groups or individuals might approach issues from different perspectives or frames, maintaining the attitudes that respect differences, and valuing equity and involvement. It means thinking of networks and webs of connection instead of seeing issues and problems as isolated and discrete. Being inclusive embraces having the skills to develop the talent of members so they can be readily involved. Listening with empathy and communicating with civility are communication skills that facilitate the inclusion of others. Inclusiveness breeds new leadership and creates a positive cycle that sustains the quality of an organization over time.

You saw in the last chapter that although many things seem unpredictable and even unconnected, there is unity in nature; seemingly unrelated parts influence each other as well as the whole. By applying these concepts to the leadership world, we learn to understand that the group or organization represents unity or wholeness built from and influenced greatly by the smallest subunits of that system. "As we move away from viewing the organization as a complex of parts and deal with it as a unity, then problems met in leadership can make more sense and solutions become obvious" (Fairholm, 1994, p. 59).

Individuals are important because they concurrently represent and influence the whole. The purpose, vision, and values of the whole come to life as each individual member describes and applies them. The goal is not to overcome the variations and differences among participants—indeed, those variations bring creativity and energy—but to build shared purpose. "Leading others to lead themselves is the key to tapping the intelligence, the spirit, the creativity, the commitment, and most of all, the tremendous, unique potential of each individual" (Manz & Sims, 1989, p. 225).

"When, as a leader, you are able to empower others and create a sense of community among members, everyone will be compelled to contribute their unique talents. The group will then meet its potential to fulfill its purpose."—Gina Pagel is a volunteer for the American Cancer Society Relay for Life and the president of the Student Wisconsin Education Association Chapter at Edgewood College.

Being inclusive means developing the strengths and talent of group members so they can contribute to the group's goals.

> Leaders enhance the learning of others, helping them to develop their own initiative, strengthening them in the use of their own judgment, and enabling them to grow and to become better contributors to the organization. These leaders, by virtue of their learning, then become leaders and mentors to others. (McGill & Slocum, 1993, p. 11)

It is not sufficient just to be a participative leader involving group members in the work of the organization. Organizations have to go further and recognize that in many cases the organizational culture has to change to effectively involve people who have different backgrounds and different views and who may not embrace the dominant cultural norms. In addition to its practice, the language of inclusivity is exceptionally important. How we talk about people in the organization, how we refer to them (colleagues versus subordinates or participants versus followers), and how the organization is structured are indicators of inclusive environments (Hesselbein, 2002). Think about the message being sent by using the word *we* instead of the word *I*. You might engage in a conversation with someone and hear an excessive use of the word *I* from that person. What impression did that individual make on you? Did you feel engaged in the conversation? Hesselbein describes the model of inclusion best by stating, from her own experiences,

> Building the inclusive, cohesive, vibrant institution does
> indeed require the biggest basket in town—for it has to
> have room for all of us. Not just the favored few, those
> who look alike and think alike, but all who are part of
> the community of the future. When equal access pre-
> vails, the synergy of inclusion propels us far beyond the
> old gated enclaves of the past into the richness of oppor-
> tunities that lie beyond the walls. (p. 20)

Groups would benefit by examining practices that might block
inclusivity. A group might be so accustomed to voting on every
decision that it has alienated members who find this process uncomfortable. Those members might like to use a consensus model of
decision making to ensure that the views of all are included in each
significant decision. For example, the extreme use of Robert's Rules
of Order has the potential to cut off discussion when issues are unresolved and the direction is unclear. Another illustration is when a
student union program committee traditionally provides music or
movies of interest to only one segment of the campus. They would
need to examine that practice and involve others with different
interests in order to diversify programming. Organizational practices, such as always meeting at 9 P.M., might exclude the involvement of people such as adult learners and those who cannot be on
campus at that time because of family or work obligations, or
because commuting is a problem. When the group realizes, for
example, that no commuter students, or students of color, or men
are involved in their activities, that should be a signal that something is wrong. Other ways of communicating and consulting with
people should be found, as should other ways of including diverse
interests in group decision making.

Involving Those External to the Group

Being inclusive also means identifying the shareholders and stakeholders external to the group who have some responsibility (a share)
or interest (a stake) in the change that is being planned. It would

be exclusive, not inclusive, for a group to assume that they should or could accomplish a major change alone. For example, an organization like the Latino Student Union might seek to change a campus practice about how scholarship programs are advertised to new Latino students. Being inclusive means the Latino Student Union should also consider which other campus groups or offices might be stakeholders in resolving this issue because they have a shared interest or could be affected by the consequences of any action (Bryson & Crosby, 1992). The Latino Student Union might then reach out to form coalitions or some involvement with such groups as the Council of Black Fraternity and Sorority Chapters, the Black Student Union, the Multicultural Affairs Committee of the Student Government Association, and other related student organizations like the Honors Program. In addition, the Latino Student Union should identify the shareholders in resolving the issue— the Financial Aid Office, the Dean of Students Office, and the Office of Minority Affairs. These offices would each want to get the word out to students about their programs and need not be thought of as negative or antagonistic to the changes. They might in fact appreciate help in resolving problems they too experience in the current process.

Stakeholders may not all hold the same view of a problem, and they may not all seek the same solutions. Bryson and Crosby (1992) clarify how a stakeholder's position on an issue (ranging from high support to high opposition) is influenced by the importance with which they view the issue (ranging from least important to most important). This makes stakeholders' responses more understandable (see Figure 3.2). As they work toward being more inclusive, relational leaders will want to assess possible stakeholder reactions in determining their approaches.

Even if stakeholders disagree on an issue, they should be involved. Involvement helps stakeholders gain new views on issues and may build support among various stakeholders toward an intended change. They also bring in an outside viewpoint, which contributes to the overall knowledge of the group. Stakeholders

Perspective or stand on the issues

		High Opposition	High Support
	High Importance	Antagonistic	Supportive
	Low Importance	Problematic	Low Priority

(left vertical axis label: Degree of importance to the stakeholder)

Figure 3.2. Responses of Stakeholders to Shared Issues and Goals.
Source: Adapted from Bryson & Crosby (1992), p. 268. Used with permission.

might see dimensions of an issue that the group is blind to. Building support and forming coalitions are related skills for relational leaders.

Relational Leadership Is Empowering

"Thriving on change demands the empowerment of every person in the organization—no ifs, ands, or buts" (Peters, 1989, p. xiv). Empowerment has two dimensions: (1) the sense of self that claims ownership, claims a place in the process, and expects to be involved, and (2) a set of environmental conditions (in the group or organization) that promote the full involvement of participants by reducing the barriers that block the development of individual talent and involvement. Empowerment is claimed ("I have a legitimate right to be here and say what I feel and think") as well as shared with others ("You should be involved in this; you have a right to be here too; tell us what you think and feel"). Being empowering means mitigating aspects of the environmental climate that can block meaningful involvement for others. Empowering environments are learning climates in which people expect successes yet know they can learn from failures or mistakes. It is important to establish organizational environments that empower others to do and to be their best.

The root word in the concept of empowerment is *power*. Understanding power dynamics is essential in moving toward a philosophical commitment to empowerment. Where possible, positional leaders must be willing to share their power or authority, and participants must be willing to assume more responsibility for group outcomes. Power has traditionally been viewed on a zero-sum basis. Conventional approaches assumed that if one person in an organization is very powerful, then someone else has less power. In truth, different types of power exist concurrently among people in any kind of relationship. Power dynamics range from power "over" (autocratic approaches) to power "with" (collaborative approaches) or power "alongside" (collegial approaches). Some approaches to leadership would go further and describe power "from," referring to the authority and power afforded to a leader from a group of participants. Effective positional leaders know that their power and ability to be effective comes from the members of their group—their participants (Kouzes & Posner, 1987).

Sources of Power

How a person uses power and reacts to the power of others must be examined in relational leadership. In their classic work, French and Raven (1959) identify five primary sources of power that individuals bring to their relationships with others. These bases of social power are expert power, referent power, legitimate power, coercive power, and reward power.

Expert power is the power of information or knowledge. Expertise may come through professional development and formal education (such as that received by engineers or dentists), from possessing specific information (such as remembering the results of a recent survey or knowing the rules in the student handbook), or from extended experience (such as being the mother of three children or being a seasoned baseball player). We trust experts and give them power over us based on their assumed higher level of knowledge or experience.

Referent power refers to the nature and strength of a relationship between two or more people. Think of the wise senior who is so highly regarded that her words carry great weight in the group discussion.

Legitimate power is due to the formal role a person holds, usually because he or she has the responsibility and authority to exert some degree of power. For instance, the president of a student organization has power to make certain decisions due to the nature of his or her role. However, those in authority generally know that their legitimate power is fragile.

Coercive power influences individuals or groups through imposing or threatening punitive sanctions or removing rewards or benefits. Coercion accomplishes behavior change but usually at great cost to the relationships among those involved. Because leadership is an influence relationship, it is essential that this influence be "noncoercive" (Rost, 1993, p. 105).

Conversely, reward power influences behavior through the ability to deliver positive outcomes and desired resources. Rewards may be extrinsic, like raises, plaques, or special privileges. They may also be intrinsic—intangibles like praise or support.

You may intentionally use some source of power. For example, you might prepare very well before a meeting so you will be an expert on some topic. Conversely, others may attribute some source of power to you without your knowing what is happening, as, for example, when someone fears your disapproval because you have referent power. To empower ourselves and others, it is essential to understand power.

Understanding Power

In many cases, we give power away. We do it when we do not trust our own opinion if it contradicts that of an expert. We assume the expert knows more. Yet when the doctor too readily concludes that you just need bed rest and you know it's something more serious, you should insist that your doctor explore other alternatives. When the person with legitimate power announces a plan or an approach, we give power away if we do not say, "We would like to talk about that first because we might have some additional ideas that would be helpful." We may also have power attributed to us that is undeserved. When the group assumes that because you are an English major you would be best at writing the group's report, they may be in error.

Power is not finite and indeed can be shared and amplified. Some think that power should be framed differently and seen with a similar frame as love: the more you give away, the more you get. If the leadership paradigm of your colleagues is very conventional, they may see the sharing of power as indecisiveness or an avoidance of responsibility. Others may abuse the power shared with them, but those in legitimate authority roles who share their power usually find that they build stronger groups.

For the society to get its work done, leaders and the systems over which they preside must be granted some measure of power. It is a common experience for leaders today to have far less power than they need to accomplish the tasks that we hand them. They must have the power to get results (Gardner, 2003, p. 201).

Gardner goes on to say that those who hold power must be held accountable. Leaders are in a greater position of power when they hold themselves accountable first before waiting for others to implement a system of checks and balances.

Hoarding power in leadership risks negative responses from others, such as sabotage, withdrawal, resistance, anger, and other behaviors that would contradict the positive goals and objectives of the group. "The key gift that leaders can offer is power" (Bolman & Deal, 2003a, p. 341). When people can use and hear their voices in the life of an organization or community, they will feel a sense of justice and a belief that they matter.

Self-Empowerment

Empowerment is claiming the power you should have from any position in the organization. Self-empowerment then is the recognition that you have a legitimate right to be heard and the self-confidence to be part of a solution or the change process. "The E-word by itself, is a non sequitur unless it's used with self-discovery . . . it provides a means of empowering yourself as you explore your natural, educational, and professional attributes in sizing up your leadership prospects" (Haas & Tamarkin, 1992, p. 35). Murrell (1985, pp. 36–37) presents six methods through which you might become empowered:

1. Educating (discovering/sharing information and knowledge)
2. Leading (inspiring, rewarding, directing)
3. Structuring (creating structural factors such as arranging your day, bringing people to the table, changing policies or processes so that the change lives beyond the people who created it)
4. Providing (making sure others have resources to get their job done)
5. Mentoring (having close personal relationships)
6. Actualizing (taking it on—being empowered—claiming it)

Valuing the empowerment of all members creates a larger group of participants or citizens who generally take more ownership of group tasks and processes and who feel committed to the outcomes of the change.

Mattering and Marginality

Empowerment places you at the center of what is happening rather than at the edges, where you might feel inconsequential. This may be understood best by examining the concepts of mattering and marginality. Schlossberg (1989b) has extended and applied the work of sociologist Morris Rosenberg on mattering to her own work in studying adults in transition. "Mattering is a motive: the feeling that others depend on us, are interested in us, are concerned with our fate . . . [which] exercises a powerful influence on our actions" (Rosenberg & McCullough, as cited in Schlossberg, 1989b, p. 8). In new situations, in new roles, or with new people, we may feel marginal, as if we do not matter unless the group welcomes us and seeks our meaningful involvement. In contrast, mattering is the feeling that we are significant to others and to the process. Think of the anxiety and perhaps marginalization of potential new members coming to their first meeting of the Campus Environmental Coalition—or any group. They could be scarcely noticed, become isolated, and perhaps be ignored, or they could be welcomed, involved, and engaged, and know that they matter. Think about the positive feelings imparted to a first-year student when an upper-class veteran of an organization requests his or her opinion on an issue.

Empowering Environments

Groups, organizations, or environments can promote mattering or can keep people on the periphery—in the margins. We need environments that promote the development of the human spirit on a local scale, thus creating a "fundamental shift of mind, in which individuals come to see themselves as capable of creating the world they truly want rather than merely reacting to circumstances beyond their control" (Kiefer & Senge, 1984, p. 68).

Empowerment is likely to happen in organizational environments where people recognize that things can always be better than they are now. These organizations expect to learn and seek new solutions. Empowering organizations seek to eliminate fear or humiliation and operate on trust and inclusivity. If you do not feel empowered in a particular group, you might assess the dynamics in the organization to see if they are encouraging or controlling. There may be an in-group and an out-group, and those in the out-group are excluded from access to information and opportunities to shape decisions (Kohn, 1992). If the organizational dynamics are basically supportive, however, perhaps you need to enhance your self-empowerment by building competencies, networks, or attributes to let you make a meaningful contribution.

Empowerment and delegation are not the same thing. A leader cannot give tasks to participants to do, no matter how important those assignments may be, and simply assume that participants will subsequently feel empowered. Indeed, if the leader retains a great deal of power or control when delegating, participants may feel manipulated, unprepared, resentful, or victimized. Conversely, if a positional leader has clearly acted congruently in sharing authority and responsibility with the group and has its trust, then sharing tasks can be empowering and can enhance community. Empowerment is achieved by enabling the involvement of group members and conveying faith in them.

"I was recently elected President of the Executive Board at Endicott College, after residing as Vice President of my class for a year. The role of the executive board is to organize and run the Student Government Association (SGA). As the new Executive President, I plan to make some changes in the organization of the SGA. I am planning on making more class officers be involved in the activities and events run by the SGA. I aspire to make everyone feel as though they have a significant role in every issue that comes across SGA's path. I believe when people feel that they are important they realize their potential. They also realize that when contributing to a greater whole, much personal satisfaction is gained. Once an individual is given the chance to take action and lead, they become more involved and dedicated on their own thereafter because they realize what they are accomplishing makes such a difference to the community."—Elyse Goldstein is vice president of the class of 2007 at Endicott College and a student curator of the David Broudo Gallery.

Relational Leadership Is Ethical

A seven-year-old goes into the grocery store with his father. Upon arriving home, the father discovers that little Johnny has a pocketful of candy that was not a part of the purchase. Horrified at Johnny's stealing, the father demands that Johnny return the candy to the store, confess to the store manager, apologize for his behavior, and promise never to steal from any store again. For some of us, an incident like this was our first real lesson in what is good and what is bad, what is virtuous and what is immoral. Early in our lives, in lessons such as this one, we were taught to value honesty over dishonesty, kindness over cruelty, and doing the right thing over breaking the law.

Ethical and Moral Leadership

The Relational Leadership Model emphasizes ethical and moral leadership, meaning leadership that is driven by values and standards and leadership that is good—moral—in nature. The language we use to examine ethical, moral leadership is of utmost importance. Some have a tendency to use the terms *ethics* and *morals* interchangeably (Henderson, 1992; Walton, 1988). Others differentiate between them, yet draw a strong relationship between ethics and morals (Shea, 1988). Shaw and Barry (1989) define ethics as "the social rules that govern and limit our conduct, especially the ultimate rules concerning right and wrong" (pp. 2–3).

The derivation of ethics is from *ethos*, from the Greek words for "character" and "sentiment of the community" (Toffler, 1986, p. 10). Other definitions of ethics include "the principles of conduct governing an individual or a profession" and "standards of behavior" (Shea, 1988, p. 17). Being ethical means "conforming to the standards of a given profession or group. Any group can set its own ethical standards and then live by them or not" (Toffler, 1986, p. 10). Ethical standards, whether they are established by an individual or an organization, help guide a person's decisions and actions. For the purposes of this model, ethics will be defined as "rules or standards that govern behaviors" (Toffler, 1986, p. 10).

Stephen Covey, author of the best-selling book *The 7 Habits of Highly Effective People* (1989), uses the metaphor of "leadership by compass" to illustrate principle-centered leadership (p. 19). Principles, like values, ethics, standards, and morals, "provide 'true north' direction to our lives when navigating the 'streams' of our environments" (p. 19).

Professions often establish codes of ethics or standards that serve as normative expectations for people in a particular profession. Lawyers must adhere to the American Bar Association's code of ethics for attorneys, and the American Medical Association promotes a code of ethics for physicians. Every McDonald's restaurant prominently displays a code of standards that pledges excellence in its food and service. Upon closer examination, these organizations are promoting standards by which they expect professionals and employees to live.

Moral means "relating to principles of right and wrong" (Toffler, 1986, p. 10) or "arising from one's conscience or a sense of good and evil; pertaining to the discernment of good and evil; instructive of what is good or evil (bad)" (Shea, 1988, p. 17). Morals are commonly thought to be influenced by religion or personal beliefs. Moral leadership is concerned with "good" leadership; that is, leadership with good means and good ends.

Our philosophy of leadership is values-driven. Again, our definition underscores this: *leadership is a relational and ethical process of people together attempting to accomplish positive change*. Using this philosophy, leaders and followers act out of a sense of shared values—the desire to cause real change and a commitment to mutual purposes. The actions of leaders and participants emanate from a set of values, which we hope are congruent and shared. Values are "freely chosen personal beliefs" (Lewis, 1990, p. 9) or the "guiding principles in our lives with respect to the personal and social ends we desire" (Kouzes & Posner, 1993, p. 60). Simply stated, values are our personal beliefs.

Although there is much disagreement in the leadership literature over definitions and theory, and about whether leadership is values-neutral or values-driven, it is safe to say that most people expect leaders to do the right thing. In a 1988 Gallup poll of 1,200 workers and managers, 89% of the respondents "believed it was important for leaders to be upright, honest, and ethical in their dealings" (Hughes, Ginnett, & Curphy, 1993, p. 170). Unfortunately, only 41% of those surveyed believed that their supervisor exhibited these qualities (Hughes et al.). A 2003 Gallup Poll on Governance found that only 53% of those surveyed had "a great deal" or "a fair amount" of trust in the government of their state (Jones, 2003, p. 1). Trust in state governments has declined since the events of September 11, 2001. Securing and keeping the trust of your constituencies is central to leadership. When 1,500 executives from 20 countries were asked what the requirements were for an ideal chief corporate officer, personal ethics was ranked at the top of the list (Kidder, 1993). A Gallup Youth Survey conducted in 2003 revealed that 67% of youth between the ages of 13 and 17 reported "a great deal" to "a fair amount" of cheating in their schools, with half of them indicating that they also cheated (Kidder, 2005, p. 267).

As leaders and citizens, our challenge today is to close the gap between our expectations of ethical leadership and the reality of frequent breaches of ethical conduct by our leaders. We need bold, courageous leadership—leadership that is by word and deed ethical and moral. It is encouraging that a growing number of people express their abhorrence of the breaches of ethical conduct by national and local leaders and that a vast majority of the populace believe that ethics play a critical role in leadership.

John Gardner (1990) thoughtfully makes the connection between shared values and a moral commitment to do the right thing. He reflects:

> In any functioning society everything—leadership and
> everything else—takes place within a set of shared beliefs
> concerning the standards of acceptable behavior that
> must govern individual members. One of the tasks of
> leadership—at all levels—is to revitalize those shared
> beliefs and values, and to draw on them as sources of
> motivation for the exertions required of the group. Lead-
> ers can help to keep the values fresh. They can combat
> the hypocrisy that proclaims values at the same time that
> it violates them. They can help us understand our his-
> tory and our present dilemmas. They have a role in cre-
> ating the state of mind that is the society. Leaders must
> conceive and articulate goals in ways that lift people out
> of their petty preoccupations and unite them toward
> higher ends. (p. 191)

Gardner implies that leadership "toward higher ends" is ethical in nature and includes positive, constructive ends rather than results or outcomes that are destructive, harmful, or immoral.

To underscore the importance of the relationship between lead-ership and ethics, we join with those scholars who propose that ethics is the central core of leadership. Without a commitment to doing the right thing or a sound code of ethical standards, leader-ship cannot emerge. Although some argue that the phrase "ethical leadership" is redundant because leadership cannot be experienced without an element of ethics, we feel that leadership that lacks eth-ical behavior and actions is anything but leadership. Consider the example of Adolf Hitler. Indeed, right now you may be thinking that Hitler was a leader but you are averse to what he was leading, and some leadership theorists would agree with you. We share the views of other scholars, however, that Hitler's actions were not aligned with our notions of leadership. They were acts of dictator-ship (Burns, 1978).

Burns (1978) elevates the importance of values and ethics in the leadership process through his theory of transforming leadership. He notes that "the ultimate test of moral leadership is its capacity to transcend the claims of multiplicity of everyday wants and needs and expectations, to respond to the higher levels of moral development, and to relate leadership behavior—its roles, choices, style, commitments—to a set of reasoned, relatively explicit, conscious values" (p. 46). Aligned with Burns's bold thinking to cast leadership in a moral foundation is the recent shift in societal views, from leadership as values-neutral to leadership as values-driven (Beck & Murphy, 1994; Bok, 1982, 1990; Gandossy & Effron, 2004; Kouzes & Posner, 2002; Northouse, 2004; Piper, Gentile, & Parks, 1993). Moral or ethical leadership is driven by knowing what is virtuous and what is good.

Leading by Example

As an exercise, a leader and a participant must ponder soul-searching questions such as, What do I stand for? How far am I willing to go to advance the common good or to do the right thing? Based on their research on leaders, Kouzes and Posner (1987) propose five practices of exemplary leadership. One of these practices is "Modeling the Way" or practicing what one preaches. Leaders "show others by their own example that they live by the values that they profess" (p. 187). What one stands for "provides a prism through which all behavior is ultimately viewed" (p. 192).

Leading by example is a powerful way to influence the values and ethics of an organization. This means aligning your own values with the worthy values of the organization. Exemplary leadership includes a congruency between values and actions. The aphorism attributed to Ralph Waldo Emerson—"What you do speaks so loudly that I cannot hear what you say"—implies an even greater emphasis on the importance of values being congruent with actions. Nobel Peace Prize recipient Jimmy Carter is the first contemporary president said to have pursued higher goals after the presidency. Indeed, his work in diplomacy and in community service such as Habitat for Humanity attests to the congruence between his values and his actions. It is one thing to profess values and quite another to act on them.

Terry (1993) provides a cautionary note that action without authenticity erodes what can be considered ethical or moral leadership. Terry defines authenticity as "genuineness and a refusal to engage in self deception" (p. 128). Being true to oneself as a leader is a prerequisite for ethical and moral leadership.

The task of leading by example is not an easy one. Most, if not all, leaders begin with the goal of wanting to do the right thing. Some leaders get derailed by peer pressure or the temptation to trade leading for the common good with leading for personal gain or the uncommon good. What sustains ethical and moral leadership is a stubborn commitment to high standards, which include honesty and trustworthiness, authenticity, organizational values, and doing the right thing. It takes courage and chutzpah to stand among your peers and advocate a decision that is right yet unpopular. Imagine the tremendous courage of a fraternity chapter member or ROTC junior officer who says, "No, I do not think we should make our pledges drink until they pass out and then drop them off naked in the woods. It is not only dangerous but it is not how I want to bring them into our brotherhood. I won't be a part of it, and I hope you will not either. I will help plan activities that are fun and more worthwhile, but we cannot do this." Or the courage of a student who steps in and stops his peers from flipping over a car during a campus riot.

"To handle ethical dilemmas, the single most important quality to remember is to be honest with yourself and others. Tell the parties involved honestly and openly how you feel about the particular issue. Help them understand delicately your position, but stand strong in the dilemma. One other important aspect is listening and not jumping to conclusions."—Andrea Jean Grate, from Alfred University, was a director of student orientation.

Although it appears that we are stating the obvious by stressing the importance of leading by example and with integrity, there are, regrettably, numerous accounts of local and national leaders who have been caught embezzling, putting humans at risk for the sake of profit, and hiding the truth. Richard M. Nixon began his presidency with good intentions and then succumbed to political corruption. Leading with integrity is not a neat and tidy process, yet it probably is the driving force that allows leaders to continue in their capacities. We will return to the topic of ethical leadership in Chapter Six with a closer examination of ethical decision making, ethical theories, and creating and sustaining ethical environments in groups and organizations.

Relational Leadership Is About Process

Process refers to how the group goes about being a group, remaining a group, and accomplishing a group's purposes. It refers to the recruitment and involvement of members, how the group makes decisions, and how the group handles the tasks related to its mission and vision. Every group has a process, and every process can be described. Processes must be intentional and not incidental. The process component of the Relational Leadership Model means that individuals interact with others and that leaders and other participants work together to accomplish change. The process creates energy, synergy, and momentum.

When asked how her view of the universe as orderly in its chaotic state has influenced her work with organizations, Wheatley (1992) observed, "The time I formerly spent on detailed planning and analysis I now use to look at the structures that might facilitate relationships. I have come to expect that something useful occurs if I link up people, units, or tasks, even though I cannot determine precise outcomes" (p. 43–44). When groups design and implement ethical, inclusive, empowering processes that further a shared purpose, they can trust the processes to take them through difficult times, resolve ambiguous tasks, and be assured that together they will be better than they might be individually.

Too often, processes devalue the people involved by being highly controlled, valuing winning at all costs, excluding or shutting out those who have an interest in change, or expecting everyone to think and act alike. Attending to the process means being thoughtful and conscious of how the group is going about its business, so participants might say, "Wait a minute. If we do it this way, we'll be ignoring the needs of an important group of students and that is not our intent." Wheatley (2003) believes that we live in a process world. She states that "we would do better to attend more carefully to the process by which we create our plans and intentions. We need to see these plans, standards, organization charts not as objects that we complete, but as processes that enable a group to keep clarifying its intent and strengthening its connections to new people and new information" (p. 516).

Several key processes are essential to relational leadership. These processes include collaboration, reflection, feedback, civil confrontation, community building, and a level of profound understanding called *meaning making*. We will discuss several of these here and in subsequent chapters. Being process-oriented means that participants and the group as a whole are conscious of their process. They are reflective, challenging, collaborative, and caring. Being process-oriented means being aware of the dynamics among people in groups. Many groups jump right into the task or goal and lose a focus on the process. When participants focus on the process of group life or community life, they are forced to ask, Why do we do things this way? How could we be more effective? Participants ensure that the groups keeps working and learning together.

Cooperation and Collaboration

Competition seems embedded in many of our American structures. The adversarial legal system, sports teams, the game of poker, and the competitive free market economy all illustrate the way competition permeates our shared life. It is hard to imagine a different paradigm. Even while avoiding trying to beat others and not needing to always be number one, many people feel a strong need to compete with themselves. Perhaps they need to better that last exam grade or beat their last video game score.

In the early 1980s, researchers at the University of Minnesota reviewed 122 studies conducted over a fifty-year period on the role of competitive, cooperative, or individual goal orientations in achievement. Researchers concluded that "cooperation is superior to competition in promoting achievement and productivity" (Johnson, Maruyama, Johnson, Nelson, & Skon, 1981, p. 56). They further distinguished the strong benefits of cooperation (not competition) in the internal functioning of the group from the incentives when competing with other external groups (Johnson et al.). Working cooperatively with other participants is a desirable process.

Studies consistently show that members of various kinds of groups prefer positional leaders and colleagues who establish cooperative or collaborative relationships with them instead of competitive relationships (Kanter, 1989; Spence, 1983; Tjosvold & Tjosvold, 1991). Even a group member who enjoys competition in athletics is not likely to enjoy working in a setting such as a sports team, committee, study group, or job site in which others are competitive and try to beat each other or use competitive practices like withholding information or degrading others' contributions. Indeed, "the simplest way to understand why competition generally does not promote excellence is to realize that trying to do well and trying to beat others are two different things" (Kohn, 1992, p. 55). A person's best work is done under conditions of support and cooperation, not under fear, anxiety, or coercion.

The concepts of cooperation and collaboration are different.

> Collaboration is more than simply sharing knowledge
> and information (communication) and more than a rela-
> tionship that helps each party achieve its own goals
> (cooperation and coordination). The purpose of collab-
> oration is to create a shared vision and joint strategies to
> address concerns that go beyond the purview of any par-
> ticular party. (Chrislip & Larson, 1994, p. 5)

Wood and Gray (1991) assert that "collaboration occurs when
a group of autonomous stakeholders of a problem engage in an interactive process, using shared rules, norms, and structures, to act or
decide on issues related to that domain" (p. 146). For example,
Microsoft and Intel collaborated on developing wireless applications for PDAs and smart phones. These companies had a shared
vision that was achieved by working together rather than in competition with each other. Former presidents George H. W. Bush and
Bill Clinton, who were once in fierce political competition with one
another, worked collaboratively on natural disaster relief projects
in the face of the Southeast Asian tsunami in 2004 and Hurricane
Katrina in 2005.

Both cooperation and collaboration are helpful processes: cooperation helps the other person or group achieve their own goals,
whereas collaboration joins with another person or group in setting
and accomplishing mutual, shared goals. The "collaborative
premise" is a belief that "if you bring the appropriate people together
in constructive ways with good information, they will create
authentic visions and strategies for addressing the shared concerns
of the organization or community" (Chrislip & Larson, p. 14). It
would be cooperation for the Habitat for Humanity group to send
their membership recruitment flyer out with the Food Cooperative
flyer to save postage or for them to attend another group's event. It
would be collaboration for those two groups and several others with
a common environmental purpose to design a new flyer to attract

new members to these shared causes or to work collaboratively together to plan a larger event.

"Part of being a leader is being a participant as well because by being a leader, you need to lead by example. Taking part in whatever you are leading will show that you are proud and enthusiastic to be involved with your particular group. Other members will also respect the fact that you are not only a leader, but that you are humble enough to participate like everyone else."—Betsy Dedels is a member of Phi Beta Kappa and team captain of intramural volleyball. She majors in sociology at the University of Kentucky.

For the group to be effective, all members must be prepared to do their part.

Chapter Two described how music provides a good metaphor for this kind of teamwork. Musicians must be individually skilled and committed, yet know that they are part of a collective—a team. Further, imagine a performance of jazz music with improvisational dance. Both dancers and musicians find wonderful rhythms and sounds, simultaneously interpreted, shaping each other's work. The collaboration, respect, and commitment to their common purposes as dancers and musicians are obvious. Yet those artists did not just walk into a studio and create movement. The dancers knew their bodies and the musicians knew their instruments. They knew how and why and when to react. Their self-awareness of their own strengths, limits, talents, and abilities created the collaboration in their joint effort. In a parallel manner, think of a terrific class project in which individuals volunteer their knowledge and skills ("I can do the PowerPoint presentation" or "I can call those businesses for donations"), and the division of labor starts to shape a strong project. Knowing yourself well and seeking to know the members of the group creates a group atmosphere conducive to collaboration.

Meaning Making

Leadership requires a process of truly understanding (that is, making meaning) throughout the shared experience of the group. Meaning has both cognitive (ideas and thoughts) and emotional (feelings) components, which "allows a person to know (in the sense of understand) some world version (a representation of the way things are and the way they ought to be) and that places the person in relation to this world view" (Drath & Palus, 1994, p. 4). Part of this meaning making involves the recognition that in our rapidly changing world, we are continually challenged to see that data become information, information becomes translated into knowledge, knowledge influences understanding, understanding translates into wisdom, and wisdom becomes meaningful thought and action. Imagine this flow as

DATA → INFORMATION → KNOWLEDGE → UNDERSTANDING → WISDOM → THOUGHT AND ACTION

Meaning making is "the process of arranging our understanding of experience so that we can know what has happened and what is happening, and so that we can predict what will happen; it is constructing knowledge of ourselves and the world" (Drath & Palus, 1994, p. 2). Drath and Palus make it clear that two understandings of the word *meaning* guide our thinking about meaning and leadership. One use is when symbols, like words, stand for something. This process of naming and interpreting helps clarify meaning and is essential for the perspectives needed in reframing and seeing multiple realities. For example, one person might call a particular action lawlessness, and another might call it civil disobedience. What one person might call destructive partying, another might see as group bonding and celebration. Coming to agreement on the interpretations of symbolic words and events helps a group to make meaning. Senge (1990) refers to these as "mental models."

The second use of the word *meaning* involves "people's values and relationships and commitments" (Drath & Palus, 1994, p. 7). People want to matter and to lead lives of meaning. When something is of value, one can make a commitment, find personal purpose, and risk personal involvement—it matters, it has meaning. In contrast, if something is meaningless or of no value, then it does not engage emotion and build commitment. However, we should be careful not to judge too quickly. Sometimes, important matters may seem to have no value. For example, a group of students expressing concern about getting to their cars in remote parking lots after late-night classes deserves a careful hearing. Those listening may be student government officers who live in nearby residence halls or campus administrators who have parking spaces near their buildings. The relational empathy skill of trying to see things from the perspective of another will validate that meaning. (Refer to Chapter Five for more on relational empathy.)

Understanding how we make meaning helps a group frame and reframe the issues and problems they are seeking to resolve. The framing process involves naming the problem and identifying the nature of interventions or solutions that might be helpful. If a problem is framed as, "The administration won't provide money for additional safety lighting," it leads to a set of discussions and strategies focused on changing the administration. Reframing means finding a new interpretation of the problem that might create a new view that helps a group be more productive (Bryson & Crosby, 1992). Reframing this same problem might bring a new awareness of coalitions, shareholders, and stakeholders if it were readdressed as, "How can we unite the talent of our campus to address the problem of a dramatic rise in crimes against women?"

Reflection and Contemplation

Vaill (1989) proposes that the rapid pace of change and the need to make meaning from ambiguous material requires individuals and groups to practice reflection. Reflection is the process of pausing, stepping back from the action, and asking, What is happening? Why is this happening? What does this mean? What does this mean for me? What can I learn from this? Lao Tzu (Heider, 1985) encourages time for reflection:

> Endless drama in a group clouds consciousness. Too much noise overwhelms the senses. Continual input obscures genuine insight. Do not substitute sensationalism for learning. Allow regular time for silent reflection. Turn inward and digest what has happened. Let the senses rest and grow still. Teach people to let go of their superficial mental chatter and obsessions. Teach people to pay attention to the whole body's reaction to a situation. When group members have time to reflect, they can see more clearly what is essential in themselves and others. (p. 23)

Smith, MacGregor, Matthews, and Gabelnick (2004) believe that "reflective thinking should be metacognitive" (p. 125). Metacognition is "thinking about one's thinking—now considered essential for effective learning and problem solving" (p. 126). Reflection can be accomplished when a group intentionally discusses its process. If groups discuss their process at all, they usually reflect only on their failures. They try to find out what went wrong and how to avoid those errors again. To be true learning organizations, groups also need to reflect on their successes and bring to every participant's awareness a common understanding of answers to such questions as, Why did this go so well? What did we do together that made this happen? How can we make sure to work this well together again? Horwood (1989) observes that "Reflection is hard mental work. The word itself means 'bending back.' . . . The mental work of reflection includes deliberation . . . rumination . . . pondering . . . and musing" (p. 5). Reflection is a key process in becoming a learning community.

In a study of successful leaders, Bennis (1989) observed that these effective leaders encouraged "reflective backtalk" (p. 194).

They knew the importance of truth telling and encouraged their colleagues to reflect honestly what they think they saw or heard. "Reflection is vital—at every level, in every organization . . . all [leaders] should practice the new three Rs: retreat, renewal, and return" (p. 186). One form of group reflection is when the group processes (discusses) a shared experience. As a difficult meeting winds down, any participant (or perhaps the group's adviser) might say, "Let's take time now at the end of this meeting to process what we liked about how we handled the big decision tonight and what we think we should do differently next time." Reflection is also useful for keeping a group on track. A group might intentionally review its goals and mission in the middle of the year and discuss how their activities are supporting that mission or whether they should be redirected. Reflection is an essential component of a process to keep individuals and the whole group focused and intentional.

Contemplation is a form of reflection that allows us to think deeply about the events around us, our feelings, and our emotions. Chickering, Dalton, and Stamm (2006) describe contemplation as "the cerebral metabolic process for meaning making. The food that we chew and swallow, that then enters our stomach, only nourishes us, only becomes part of our bloodstream, muscles, nerves, and body chemistry when it is metabolized" (p. 143). The experiences of life operate in a similar way. In the absence of reflection and contemplation, the knowledge that we acquire and the experiences that we go through can "end up like the residue from food we don't metabolize" (p. 143). Reflective practices allow us to think about what is occurring around us and to us and then to make meaning from those experiences.

What Would This Look Like?

You will acquire many leadership skills over time. It is easy to confuse some management tools—like running meetings or planning agendas—with real leadership. Using the principles of relational leadership, you can reframe typical skills like agenda planning so that they are more effective. The goals of the agenda for your group meeting will not be just to get through the topics to be presented or decided in the quickest time but will involve the most people, empower voices that might have been excluded before, make sure no one is railroaded and that fair decisions are made, involve others in building an agenda, and use collaborative practices.

Remember the times you have been to a meeting whose leader made all the announcements. A small group of two or three in-group members seemed to run the whole show, and you never said a word. We have all had that experience. You felt marginalized and might have wondered why you even bothered to attend. Think of a meeting in which people disagreed hotly and then someone quickly moved to vote on an issue. A vote was taken with the resulting majority winning and a dissatisfied minority losing or feeling railroaded.

Imagine the differences in a meeting whose positional leader or convener says, "It is our custom to make sure everyone is involved and heard before we try to resolve issues. The executive committee has asked three of you to present the key issues on the first agenda item; we will then break into small groups for fifteen minutes to see what questions and issues emerge before we proceed and see what we want to do at that point. In your discussion, try to identify the principles that will be important for us to consider in the decision we eventually make." Even if you do not agree with this approach, you would feel more comfortable suggesting a different model because the tone of the meeting is one of involvement and participation.

Chapter Summary

Conditions in our rapidly changing world require that each of us become effective members of our groups and communities in order to work with others toward needed change and for common purpose. The way we relate to each other matters and is symbolic of our social responsibility. Taking the time needed to build a sense of community in a group acknowledges that relationships are central to effective leadership. Relational leadership is purposeful, inclusive, empowering, ethical, and about process. Attention to those practices builds a strong organization with committed participants who know they matter.

What's Next?

After understanding the various ways leadership has been viewed and the current need for new models of leadership that value relational approaches, it is essential to understand people as participants in those relationships. Perhaps the most important person to understand is you. The next chapter, which begins Part Two, encourages you to explore aspects about yourself that are important in leadership; following that is a chapter exploring aspects of others and how they may be different from yours. The final chapter in Part Two addresses the importance of integrity in the leadership process and in establishing relationships with others.

Chapter Activities

1. Think of a leader whom you would consider to be a role model, someone who practices what he or she preaches and lives by high standards. Think of local, national, or historical exemplars. What is it about the role model you identified that qualifies that person as an exemplary leader? What values does he or she profess, and what practices does he or she consistently live by?

2. Describe your leadership philosophy using all three components of the knowing-being-doing model.

3. Describe your leadership compass. What principles or ethics guide your personal life and your leadership?

4. Identify a situation in which you successfully used one or more of French and Raven's sources of power. What contributed to your effective use of each of those sources of power? Think of an example of a leader who abused one of these sources of power. What were the consequences of that person's leadership?

5. As you review the five elements of this Relational Leadership Model, which are most comfortable for you and why? Which involve knowledge, skills, or attitudes that you have not yet learned or developed?

6. In their simplicity, models often omit concepts that could have been included. What concepts would you add to any of the five elements of this model, or what new elements do you think should be included?

Additional Readings

Bennis, W. G., & Thomas, R. J. (2002). *Geeks and geezers: How era, values, and defining moments shape leaders*. Boston: Harvard Business School Press.

Chrislip, D. D., & Larson, C. E. (1994). *Collaborative leadership: How citizens and civic leaders can make a difference*. San Francisco: Jossey-Bass.

Drath, W. H., & Palus, C. J. (1994). *Making common sense: Leadership as meaning-making in a community of practice*. Greensboro, NC: Center for Creative Leadership.

Gandossy, R., & Effron, M. (2004). *Leading the way: Three truths from the top companies for leaders*. Hoboken, NJ: Wiley.

Kouzes, J. M., & Posner, B. Z. (2002). *The leadership challenge* (3rd ed.). San Francisco: Jossey-Bass.

Part II

Exploring Your Potential for Leadership

The Relational Leadership Model (RLM) emphasizes the importance of relationships among participants in the process of purposeful change. Developing and maintaining healthy and honest relationships starts with a knowledge of self and an openness to appreciate and to respect others.

This part of the book contains three chapters to enrich your self-awareness. These chapters help you explore yourself in relation to others as foundational components of developing a personal leadership philosophy. The last chapter of this part explores the importance of the ethical dimension of the RLM and of being a person of character, living a life of integrity. The chapter asserts that in all settings, relational leadership must be grounded in ethical processes, create ethical climates, and produce moral actions and outcomes that reflect the interests of the common good. Creating an ethical climate in all contexts is an important dimension of the RLM.

Lao Tzu (Heider, 1985) noted,

> The wise leader's ability does not rest on techniques or gimmicks or set exercises. The method of awareness-of-process applies to all people and all situations.
>
> The leader's personal state of consciousness creates a climate of openness. Center and ground give the leader stability, flexibility, and endurance.
>
> Because the leader sees clearly, the leader can shed light on others. (p. 53)

In the Relational Leadership Model presented in the previous chapter, we encouraged you to be purposeful, inclusive, empowering, ethical, and process-oriented. Think again about what you need to know, or be, or do to participate effectively in relational leadership. You might return to Exhibit 3.1 to assess yourself and these concepts again.

Ask yourself some thoughtful questions to explore your self-awareness and awareness of others, leadership, and this model:

Purposeful: Do you have clear goals and an awareness of commitments that are important to you? Do you have to get your own way, or are you able to find common purpose with others? Do you know how change occurs?

Inclusive: How comfortable and effective are you with including others? Do you understand your own motivations when you agree or disagree with others? When you interact with people different from you, are there differences you find easy to accommodate or difficult to understand?

Empowering: Do you know how to build on your own strengths and on the strengths of others? Do you find it easy or difficult to share authority and responsibility?

Ethical: Do you find it easy to act with integrity and authenticity? Can you identify the values and principles that guide your actions? Are you trusting or distrustful of others?

Process-Oriented: Do you know what approaches you prefer for facilitating change and accomplishing goals? Do you prefer collaboration or competition? How effective are you at civil discussions, even when you strongly disagree with someone?

The most productive thing you can do to become more effective as a leader and as an active participant is to learn to see yourself clearly. This part of the book will help you explore what you value, how you are developing character, how you learn best, and how aspects of yourself (such as your gender, culture, and communication pattern) have been shaped. In learning to see these aspects of yourself, we hope you can explore these same things in others.

4

Understanding Yourself

Imagine the times you have been sitting in class or a meeting and had thoughts like these:

I have a solution to this problem, but I don't want to say it out loud in front of all of these people. What if it sounds stupid?

When my classmate came to me for advice, I was able to listen and help him feel better about himself and his situation.

Here I am again, rushing to finish my paper the night before it's due. Why do I always procrastinate when I have known this was due for months?

I wish my professor would stop revising the syllabus. I like to know everything I need to do in the semester early so I can plan when I want to work on assignments.

Why in the world do I always pick away at all the details of an idea and end up sounding so negative?

I am so proud that I didn't hesitate a minute to disagree when she made such a hurtful comment.

My sense of humor really helped the group get through the tense moment tonight and keep things in perspective.

Seeing your own strengths and weaknesses and those of others so clearly requires focused reflection. Being aware of how you prefer to think, to relate, to learn, and to find personal meaning is an important self-awareness skill. Being able to articulate what you believe and what you value helps you understand your own motivations and behaviors. Knowing your strengths and weaknesses helps you grow and relate to others with authenticity and credibility.

Because leadership happens in the context of interpersonal relationships, self-understanding is essential to authenticity in those relationships. Perhaps the most basic life trait that translates to leadership effectiveness is honest, authentic self-awareness that is open to growth, learning, and change.

Chapter Overview

This chapter challenges you to think of the things about yourself that shape your personal identity and fuel your motivations. It explores the role of self-awareness in leadership, including aspects of self-concept and self-esteem. It also explores how you form your values and the role of values in developing character. Your personality preferences for how you approach decisions and how you learn also are addressed. Along with studying leadership, you must understand yourself.

Development of Self for Leadership

The *Star Wars* movies were filled with deeper meaning behind their adventurous entertainment. In *The Return of the Jedi*, young Luke Skywalker seeks to learn the secrets of the famous Jedi Master, Yoda. Luke is initially incredulous that this small green creature is The Master and further disappointed not to be given or taught Yoda's secrets. Yoda instead takes Luke on a journey into himself, teaching him to focus and trust his own internal power to literally move mountains.

This inward journey provides the self-awareness of identifying abilities, strengths, and weaknesses. The journey develops a sense of trust in yourself to be congruent and to truly know the basis of your effectiveness.

"It is of great importance to recognize one's strengths and weaknesses because only then can one realize one's capability and limitations. Recognizing capacity allows leaders to commit themselves in such a way as to utilize their capability. Recognizing limitations allows for humility and the acknowledgment that leaders can not succeed at everything."—Kevin Panicker is a participant in the Banner Scholar Community Service Program at the University of Richmond and member of the South Asian Student Alliance.

The common observation of many acknowledged leaders is that no one can teach you about yourself except you (Bennis, 1989). Counselors, advisers, friends, or family can help with this process, but awareness ultimately requires you to study yourself. Bennis (1989) observes four lessons from which to develop self-knowledge:

- You are your own best teacher.
- Accept responsibility. Blame no one.
- You can learn anything you want to learn.
- True understanding comes from reflection on your experience. (p. 56)

"Leadership means self-discovery, getting a better yield out of your attributes" (Haas & Tamarkin, 1992, p. 6). In your life so far, you have probably learned to set goals, motivate yourself to meet them, and feel personally responsible if you do not. It is hard for some people to translate the life skills of self-control and internal motivation into guides of action as members of a group. If you often sit in a meeting and think, "It's not my responsibility; I will just let the leaders do it. After all, it's their job," then you need to develop more self-leadership skills.

Your decision to be a person who can make a difference (evidenced by reading this book) is a statement about self-leadership. You know you cannot credit or blame external factors such as teachers, supervisors, parents, or positional leaders for your motivation. Sadly, there may be acts of discrimination or oppression that have held you back, but you are now looking ahead and asking, What can I do to matter and to make a difference in the things that are important to me?

Strengths and Weaknesses

Each person brings a different mix of strengths and weaknesses to any situation. The irony is that some of your strengths, if overemphasized, become your weaknesses, and things you consider weaknesses may actually be seen as strengths by others. You may be a strong critical thinker who can readily find flaws in logic. That can be a terrific strength in helping your group prepare and present its position on a topic, or it can be seen as negative and blocking if someone is presenting an idea to you and you just naturally begin to be critical instead of trying to connect and listen. The converse can be true as well: to be humble and quiet may mean your opinion is never heard and your voice is left out of decision making. But it can also mean you are a keen listener who is very tuned in to others' thoughts. Leadership self-awareness grows when you can identify your personal strengths and weaknesses in working with others toward change.

Identifying Your Passions and Strengths

Clifton and Nelson (1992) suggest that you pay attention to the things you see others doing and to your inner mind saying, "Oh, I would love to try that." Sometimes it is hard to identify strengths. Listen for the times you say, "I feel I've accomplished something great when I do that." Clifton and Nelson recommend that you find your strengths by trying these strategies:

1. Listen to yourself when you have done something well, even if no one else noticed.

2. Identify the satisfaction you feel when you know something you did was terrific and gives you a feeling of well-being.

3. Know what things you find easy to learn quickly: organizing your lab report, talking to strangers, mastering a new computer technology, reading patiently to a small child.

4. Study your successes for clues of excellence, for glimpses of what can be excellent—for what things you do very well. Whether giving a speech or helping someone feel very special, by examining whatever your success has been, you will discover what you can do well.

5. Think about your patterns of excellence—when you are able to sing every word of a song you like, when you are able to grasp the deeper meaning in a complicated class lecture, when you practice a skill (whether cooking, playing basketball, or public speaking) and you feel it improve each time you do it. Clues to your strengths are all around you. Identifying and labeling them can affirm your confidence and self-esteem by acknowledging that you do bring reliable talents to situations and can contribute to the leadership of a cause.

Developing Your Talent

One of our greatest assets as human beings is talent (Buckingham & Clifton, 2001). Everyone has talent. Knowing yourself well includes knowing your talents—the things that you are naturally good at. Unfortunately, we often work from the deficit model—focusing on, and maybe even obsessing about, our weaknesses. Trying to fix our weaknesses takes away from our ability to lead and work from our talents and strengths. We do not have enough time in our life span to fix our weaknesses or to try to transform our weaknesses into strengths while also trying to work from our natural talents.

Effective leaders know what they do best and apply their strengths in all aspects of their lives. This does not mean that you should ignore your weaknesses. Instead, you should be aware of those things that you do not do well and find ways to manage them so that you can be more productive and more fulfilled. One strategy of managing your weaknesses is to surround yourself with others who have talents that are different from yours and are needed to successfully achieve results or accomplish change. If you manage your weaknesses rather than trying to fix them, you will have more time to focus on your strengths.

When you play to your strengths, you are working from the philosophy of talent. Buckingham and Clifton (2001) propose two assumptions that can guide you in your leadership:

1. Each person's talents are enduring and unique.
2. Each person's greatest room for growth is in the areas of his or her greatest strength. (p. 8)

Too often, we believe that our best strategy to grow and develop is to improve our weaknesses. The Gallup Organization conducted more than two million interviews over ten years asking high-performing individuals to describe what they did that made them excel (Buckingham & Clifton, 2001). They discovered thirty-four patterns or prevalent themes of human talent. Their research shows that these thirty-four themes of talent can explain a broad range of excellent performance. Buckingham and Clifton observe that "the real tragedy of life is not that each of us doesn't have enough strengths, it's that we fail to use the ones that we have" (p. 12). Strength is defined as "consistent near perfect performance in any activity" (p. 25). Buckingham and Clifton define talent as "your naturally recurring patterns of thought, feeling, or behavior" (p. 29).

Leading from a philosophy of talents and strengths is an outgrowth of an emerging new field called *positive psychology*. This new field of psychology has moved away from the clinical diagnostic approach of looking at what is wrong with an individual to paying attention to what is right within each person. Leading from this framework will energize you and others in a positive way, open up more new possibilities, and allow you and others to do what you are best at. Here is a simple yet powerful metaphor you can use to guide your daily actions and interactions: it's called "Don's Theory of the Dipper and the Bucket" (Rath & Clifton, 2004). Everyone has something like an invisible bucket that can get filled or emptied on a regular basis by an invisible dipper. When your bucket gets emptied, you feel negative and let down. When your bucket is full, you feel positive. The dipper is a powerful tool in leadership, allowing us to fill another's bucket by saying positive things and focusing on what that person is good at. You can also use the dipper to dip from someone's bucket, making that person feel diminished. Your own sense of esteem is enhanced when you use the dipper to fill someone's bucket. When you fill your own bucket and others', you are affirming your own and others' strengths and talents.

Think about what you do best, then think about how you felt when you received recognition for a job well done. You were probably motivated to continue doing what you did because you were good at it and you enjoyed doing it. When someone filled your bucket, it probably made you feel good about yourself. Organizational research has shown that when you have opportunities to do what you are best at doing and when you are recognized for that, you will experience more meaning and satisfaction in what you are doing and your productivity will increase as a result (Buckingham & Clifton, 2001). Leading from your talents and strengths will keep your bucket filled.

Managing Our Weaknesses

All of us can learn to manage our weaknesses. Some think that weaknesses "can be removed but they cannot be transformed into strengths. The goal, therefore, is to manage weaknesses so the strengths can be freed to develop and become so powerful they make the weaknesses irrelevant" (Clifton & Nelson, 1992, p. 73). A person can either manage weaknesses so that they do not repress other strengths or overcome them and turn them into strengths.

What do Tom Cruise, Orlando Bloom, Keanu Reeves, Whoopi Goldberg, Leonardo da Vinci, Pablo Picasso, Thomas Edison, Albert Einstein, and John Lennon have in common? Each of them has coped with dyslexia. They may struggle to be quick readers or accurate spellers, but all learned to manage those weaknesses and found ways to prevent them from blocking their strengths. Tom Cruise said, "I had to train myself to focus my attention. I became very visual and learned how to create mental images in order to comprehend what I read." (http://www.dys-add.com/backiss.html# famous).

Others cope with different weaknesses. Helen Keller could not see, hear, nor speak, but she learned to communicate remarkably well. Olympic athlete Jackie Joyner Kersey deals daily with asthma. Whatever their weaknesses, all these gifted people learned to manage weakness so that it did not hold back their strengths.

We encourage you to focus on your strengths and develop your talent. Some weaknesses, however, may be problematic because they cause you to function poorly. These need to be tackled directly. For example, you may not speak well in front of a group. You can, however, manage this weakness by learning ways to make a presentation more comfortable for you, like using overhead transparencies or handouts, or encouraging group interaction. The actor James Earl Jones had a debilitating childhood stutter, which he overcame so successfully that he became a remarkable orator. One of our students observed that she thought herself to be a terrible speaker, but she enjoyed class discussions and had fun arguing her points. She clearly had a talent that could help her manage a weakness. One of her classmates pointed out how related those skills are. What she perceived as a weakness was viewed differently by others. Assessing your strengths and weaknesses is critical to self-awareness (Conger & Benjamin, 1999; Lee & King, 2001).

Esteem and Confidence

John W. Gardner (1990) tells a story of sitting beside Martin Luther King Jr. at a seminar on education. The first presentation was a speech entitled, "First, Teach Them to Read." After observing this title, King whispered to Gardner, "First, teach them to believe in themselves" (p. 10).

How you think and feel about yourself is the energy that fuels your motivation. Self-concept is how we objectively describe ourselves; usually, it is based on our roles and attributes. You might say, "I am a mother of a two-year-old and like to go with the flow, keeping all my options open" or "I am an older-than-typical student with above-average intelligence and high motivation" or "I am a creative person with musical abilities." Self-esteem is the subjective element of how you feel about yourself. For example, you might say, "I am a creative person with musical abilities but am unskilled socially and uncomfortable around those in authority. I feel proud of my musical and creative skills and feel disappointed in myself for not being more socially skilled." Self-awareness would lead to having an accurate self-concept. Honoring your strengths and addressing your weaknesses are essential first steps toward higher self-esteem.

Self-esteem is enhanced if you can identify your strengths and weaknesses and know that you are growing and progressing in the areas you want to improve. High self-esteem is a result of valuing your self-concept. Low self-esteem may mean you expect something better or different than you feel. You may have a 3.3 grade point average as a biology major, have a group of supportive friends, and have just been elected vice president of your campus chapter of Amnesty International. You may feel proud and have high regard for those accomplishments. If, however, you are working for a 3.9 because you want to go to medical school, you may feel bad about your grades and have low self-esteem about your academic ability.

Self-confidence is the ability to know that you can rely on your strengths, competencies, and skills in the many contexts in which you find yourself. Some people consistently do well in whatever they do, but they are never sure they can do well and therefore have low self-confidence. Perhaps self-confident people have better memories and know that they have done well before and can do so again.

Accepting ourselves is perhaps one of the hardest life tasks. Realizing that you cannot change some things about yourself is a step toward higher self-esteem. For example, you will not become six foot two if you are now five foot six; you will not become another race, change your siblings, or get rid of your freckles. You can, however, learn new skills and add to your knowledge base.

If some aspects of yourself are negative influences on your self-esteem, you must differentiate between those you can actually do something about and those you just need to think about differently, which can lead to a higher level of self-acceptance. Perceiving things differently is called cognitive reframing—a different way of thinking. You may have felt bad when thinking of your personality as shy and quiet, but you might feel empowered to frame those same characteristics as thoughtful and reflective. Reflecting on her own youth, singer-actress Bette Midler said, "I didn't belong as a kid, and that always bothered me. If only I'd known that one day my differentness would be an asset, then my early life would have been much easier" (as cited in *The Quotable Woman*, 1991, p. 39).

Understanding Yourself

What makes you the way you are? How much of your perception, values, temperament, personality, and motives come from the way you were raised, the influence of your surroundings, and your contextual environment? How much of the way you are is inborn or genetic?

Debates have raged for years over whether to attribute human behavior to nurture (socialization) or nature (heredity). Becoming aware of the influence of either nurture or nature in your own development is essential to understanding yourself. For example, you may be tall and may have learned that some people find you imposing; they assume you will be outgoing and aggressive, even though you are quiet and shy. Or you may be small but have learned that people react eventually to the quality of what you have to say. Some might even say, "You seem bigger than your height." You may have learned to be relational or thoughtful or funny or anxious.

Regardless of how you came to be the way you are, you can intentionally choose to develop desired traits or skills. You cannot change your height or some other genetic attribute, but you can address many of the things you have learned by bringing them into your awareness. Although you cannot always change the way others view you, because they bring their own biases and attributions, you can at least be authentic as you try to be the person you would like to be.

Discussing your self-awareness is a form of the psychological study of individuality. If you feel uncomfortable with the concept of individuality, it could be because describing human perception or behavior in categories or types makes you feel boxed in or stereotyped. You may feel constrained or categorized. You may also feel uncomfortable because focusing on your own needs or on yourself is considered selfish or inappropriate in your family or culture. We hope that you will instead welcome the opportunity for personal insight by reviewing the ways scholars understand the ranges of human behavior. By knowing how others respond, you can assess how their response is like or unlike your own. For example, if you have had a death in your family or the loss of someone you love, you may find comfort in knowing that there are predictable stages in the grief process for many people (denial, anger, bargaining, depression, and acceptance) and that your personal reactions are very normal (Kübler-Ross, 1970). Because you are unique, however, you may find your grief reaction to be more pronounced or less severe than Kübler-Ross's model suggests, based on such factors as how close you were to the person who died, the comfort you receive from your family, or your religious practices. Whatever the phenomena being presented in various theories about human behavior, you can then connect with what is most like you or least like you to better understand yourself and to see how others might be similar or different from you.

Factors That Shape Your Identity

Several central, salient characteristics have probably made you the person you are and the person you will become as you age. Consider how your ethnic, racial, or cultural background has made a difference and shaped the way you are. How do you believe or behave differently because you are a man or a woman? How has your sexual orientation influenced your attitudes and behaviors? How does your age influence your interests and views? Do you have specific abilities or disabilities that shape your perceptions or skills? How has your birth-order position in your family influenced your development? What significant roles do you have that bring responsibilities that shape your decisions—being a son or daughter, a volunteer, a parent, an office manager, a Sunday School teacher, or an athlete? How has your sense of spirituality shaped your worldview? How important is religion in guiding your thinking? How has your family's socioeconomic status influenced your development and your views of leadership? Individuals may do things differently because they are male or female, old or young, Irish Catholic, Jewish, or Muslim. Mapping your personal context must include many elements that contribute to your sense of identity.

We believe the capacity for leadership is within each of you. As we noted in Chapter Two, many observers of leadership agree that leaders are made, not born, and that everyone has a "leader within" (Haas & Tamarkin, 1992). Meaningful interaction and effective leadership processes can result if individuals are aware of their own motivations and where others are coming from. The leader within you may be willing to assume positional leadership roles or may be more comfortable with active participant roles. Either way, within you is the capacity to make a difference.

Values, Beliefs, Ethics, and Character

As difficult as it may be to determine how characteristics like your gender, ethnicity, or religion influence the way you think and act, it is even more complicated and important to identify the values and beliefs that lead to your ethical behaviors and build your character.

Values and Beliefs

Among the hardest things to articulate are the values that guide actions. If your actions and thoughts are a mystery to you, you may not have adequately examined your own value system. Beliefs shape values, which influence thoughts and actions. If you can articulate your values, then you are likely aware of the principles and beliefs that serve as your guides.

Contrasts in value systems are rarely as clear as when *Star Trek*'s Mr. Spock dispassionately says to Bones, the surgeon on the U.S.S. *Enterprise*, "You are too emotional, doctor. That is not logical." Bones explodes and shouts back, "Mr. Spock, how can you be half human and not have one ounce of feeling in you?" Each of us has preferences in how we construct our own value systems. You may prefer to be logical and scientific, or you may be emotional; you may prefer to be concrete, or you may just come to know what is important by using your intuition. Knowing that you have preferences in how you construct your value system should help you understand yourself and others better. No one process is preferred over others; your process reflects how you have come to construct meaning from your experience.

The discussion of values should always raise the crucial question, Whose values and for what purpose? Some values, such as promise keeping and nonviolence, are so fundamental that they have been found to be norms in most civilized societies (Bok, 1990). Understanding values becomes a central component to understanding others and to achieving a common purpose. Imagine this scene:

> Shaking his head, Scott approaches his two friends, Khalil and Michael. "I just cannot believe it!" Scott laments. "I just heard that James vetoed the activity fee allocations to the student Hillel Association. I think he is biased and power hungry and I'm quitting student government. I just won't have anything to do with student government anymore, not with a president who does stuff like that!"
>
> "Hey, just wait a minute, Scott," Michael implores. "I've always known James to be fair and reasonable, and I trust him. Something else must be going on that we just don't understand. He must have a reason if he did this, and knowing him like we do, I bet it is a good reason. There's probably more behind his decision than we can see right now."
>
> "Yeah, I agree completely," Khalil adds. "I know him pretty well and he's OK. Let's go talk to him."

James's character and reputation for integrity among those who know him are solid and defensible. When a person is known for a solid value system grounded in integrity and authenticity, others may disagree with a decision but cannot find fault with the character of the decision maker. Concurrently, Scott did not know James well enough to form the opinion Michael and Khalil shared, but he did have the strength of his convictions that he would quit an organization over such actions. That is also a measure of someone's integrity and is also a possible reaction to an intolerable ethical dilemma or values conflict. Values were behind these students' reactions.

Character and Ethical Behavior

Integrity in relationships is central to the value systems needed among people working together toward change. Authenticity is rooted in action that is "both true and real in ourselves and in the world" (Terry, 1993, pp. 111–112). Whether framed as integrity, authenticity, or credibility, the very core of your character is central to sincerely linking with others in the spirit of community to work toward change. When asked what leadership qualities he looked for in leaders in the U.S. Army, Desert Storm's retired General Norman Schwarzkopf said, "Probably far more important to me than competence was character . . . integrity . . . ethics . . . and morality . . . I looked for people who . . . were willing to serve a cause and were what I would call selfless leaders rather than self-serving leaders" (Wren, 1994, p. 2).

"Trust has been crucial in my relationships with others. If I don't think I can trust someone, then I won't pursue a relationship with the person. I think trust has to be earned through consistency and honesty. In building relationships with others, I try to never lie and always be there for the person. Being faithful to a person breaks down barriers and builds trust. Being trustworthy also makes others feel like you are someone they can follow. Without trust, I don't think a meaningful relationship is possible."—Erin Fogleman is a volunteer leader of Young Life, president of Quest, and a tutor at the University Writing and Communication Center. She studies English at East Tennessee State University.

A person of character promotes ethical decision making and expects ethical behavior from others. The Josephson Institute of Ethics proposes six pillars of character that are "enduring and indispensable" to ethical leadership practices (Jones & Lucas, 1994, p. 4). These pillars are trustworthiness, respect, responsibility, fairness, caring, and citizenship.

Trustworthiness is far more than telling the truth. Being worthy of trust means being honest, demonstrating integrity, keeping promises, and being loyal. It means being known for standing up for your own convictions. *Respect* means that you treat others considerately, not that you admire or agree with all their views or behaviors. Being respectful is a commitment to treating others in ways that do not demean or take advantage of them. *Responsibility* means accepting accountability for your own actions and being conscious of the moral and ethical implications of deciding not to act. Being responsible means being accountable, pursuing excellence, and exercising self-restraint. *Fairness* is working toward an equitable outcome. Being fair means being open-minded and willing to listen, and confronting your own biases that might influence your decisions. *Caring* means your awareness of being concerned for each person's well-being and your attention to not being hurtful. Care requires empathy and kindness. *Citizenship* is the civic virtue of knowing that as a member of a community, you have responsibilities to do your part to contribute to the well-being of the group. Citizenship means you are willing to abide by laws and societal obligations.

After a concert on campus one Friday night, two students were counting the ticket sales receipts. The money in the cash drawer was $120 short for the number of tickets sold. Baffled at the difference, the students turned in the accounts the next day and presented the problem to the Student Activities Office. That afternoon, a third student came into the office carrying an envelope containing $120. The money had apparently come in during a ticket sales rush and had been set aside instead of being locked in the cash drawer.

The office accountant clerk asked her, "Why didn't you just keep the money? No one would have known."

The student's quick, indignant reply was, "But I would have known, and I don't do things like that!"

A Person of Character:

- Is trustworthy (is honest, has integrity, keeps promises, is loyal)

- Treats people with respect (is courteous, nonviolent, nonprejudiced, accepting)

- Is responsible (is accountable, pursues excellence, shows self-restraint)

- Is fair (just, equitable, open, reasonable, unbiased)

- Is caring (kind, compassionate, empathetic, unselfish)

- Is a good citizen (is law-abiding, does his or her share, performs community service, protects the environment)

That student's consciousness of her own value system and commitment to integrity was so embedded that she could not imagine behaving any differently. The trust and respect she earned in her relationships led to an assessment of her character that was above reproach. Another example in the news was when a student volunteer, who was helping with the cleanup after Hurricane Katrina, found $30,000 in cash in a vacated house and turned the money in to the authorities. "Leadership . . . requires a special kind of dedication, a special kind of belief. I think that you must have defined for yourself a set of moral and ethical values in which you chose to make your decisions in life as you move along. Then you must be true to yourself" (Schwarzkopf, as cited in Wren, 1994, p. 5). Vaill's analogy (1989) that our values become our rudders in times of permanent white water rings true (see Chapter One).

"Self assessments have helped me better understand myself because they allow me to evaluate my personality from an impartial perspective. Identifying habits and traits within my personality increases my understanding of how I interact with others. It also makes it easier to determine character flaws in things that I should improve in order to become a more effective communicator and leader."—Audrey K. Hicks attends Florida State University and majors in international affairs with a minor in Spanish. She was the senior class president, a member of the National Board of Directors of Omicron Delta Kappa Society, and an intern at the Florida House or Representatives.

Personal Style Preferences

Understanding how you express your values through your preferred interactions or decision making helps you understand yourself and serves as a bridge to exploring diversity within groups. You may see yourself as a caring person committed to being fair and just, yet you are puzzled as to why some people perceive you as judgmental or rigid. Understanding your personality preferences helps explain how you function in the world and how you are perceived by others.

Psychological Type

How humans adapt to the world around them is different for each one because of personality preferences. The study of personality consumes the content of many psychology courses, books, and specialized journals. You are so accustomed to the way you view things, get things done, interact, and make decisions that you perhaps cannot imagine doing them differently. It is essential to realize that you have the capacity to broaden your approaches, but the first step is to identify them.

Carl Jung (1923) identified four core functions of human adaptation that he called personality archetypes or temperament types.

These four functions include how we relate to the world, perceive the world, make judgments, and make decisions. Jung's typology includes four pairs of adaptive orientations that are diametrically opposed to each other. These combinations describe where we get our energy (extravert-introvert), how we gather information from the world around us (sensing-intuiting), how we prefer to process that information (feeling-thinking), and how we prefer to make decisions (judging-perceiving).

The first of these four core functions concerns our mode of relating to the world. There are differences between those who are oriented to the outer world (extraverts) and those who prefer their own inner world (introverts). Those who are extraverts (E) prefer the outer world of people and things. Extraverts do their best thinking out loud and in dialogue with others. Extraverts get energy from being around people; they are sociable. When given twenty minutes of free time before she has to leave her residence hall room, an extravert will go out into the floor lobby to see what is going on. People who are introverts (I) are more oriented to their inner world of feelings and ideas. Introverts prefer to think things through and reflect before forming or stating their opinions. They do their best work through internal reflection. Introverts gain energy by creating private space, even when in a crowd. Introverts may do very well in highly interactive settings but leave those settings drained of energy and need private time to renew. Given the same twenty-minute break, an introvert might write an entry in his journal or pull out the file on his upcoming meeting and review what will be covered. The use of these words is sometimes confusing because extravert does not mean outgoing, and introvert does not mean shy and withdrawn. The terms refer instead to a preferred orientation to the outer or inner world.

The second core function covers your preferences for perceiving the world around you—sensing or intuiting. Sensing people (S) rely on the five senses and prefer concrete facts and details. Sensing people are very practical and realistic, preferring the present or past to the abstractions of the future. Intuiting people (N) prefer the big picture and like to see things as a whole. They are innovative and use imagination to develop many possibilities. Intuitive people like to project into the future, living in anticipation of how things can be better, improved, and changed. Sensing people might say, "If it's not broken, don't fix it," whereas intuitives might say, "There has to be a better way" (McCaulley, 1990, p. 407). The differences in these two preferences are the source of great misunderstandings, and this "places the widest gulf between people" (Keirsey & Bates, 1984, p. 17). You may hear this gulf being expressed in a discussion when one person says, "Wait a minute. We need more information before we decide" or "What do the rules in the student handbook say?" The other person then might say, "We cannot know everything, and we are close enough to have an idea of what might work. Let's just give it a try and see what happens." Groups need both kinds of people—those grounded in reality and those who think of possibilities.

The third core function is the mode of judging—thinking or feeling. Those who prefer thinking (T) use logic and rationality—the head rules rather than the heart. Thinking approaches, through critical thinking, analysis, and reliance on the objective scientific method, are rewarded in school systems. Feeling-type people (F) prefer to make judgments that account for relationships and the importance of human values and beliefs, with an emphasis on personal friendships. Those who prefer feeling (Fs) may find those who prefer thinking (Ts) to be cold and too objective, whereas Ts may find Fs too emotional and unable to stand firm on a decision. This is the only scale that shows a gender pattern, with men making up 60% of the T preference group and women making up 60% of the F preference group. Misunderstandings that are on occasion attributed to gender differences may actually reflect personality differences.

The fourth core function involves how you prefer to make decisions—by judging or perceiving. Those with judging preferences (J) prefer order and emphasize resolving issues and making decisions to create order. People who use J preferences like tying up loose ends and seeking closure; they like clear beginnings, deadlines, and endings. Perceiving-type people (P) prefer to keep things open-ended by gathering as much information as possible and being flexible. People with P preferences handle ambiguity well, are known to go with the flow, and are comfortable leaving things open-ended or unresolved. Those with J preferences may seem close-minded or driven, and those with P preferences may seem unfocused and have a hard time getting anything done.

We each have developed preferences of how we most comfortably perceive and judge our worlds. These pairs (and the sixteen primary personality types that emerge) help us understand ourselves and others (Myers, 1980). Your four-letter composite profile is a combination, then, of E or I, S or N, T or F, and J or P. See Exhibit 4.1 for cue words that provide additional explanation of these preferences. Which set seems most like you?

We can and do use all eight of these processes but generally prefer a consistent pattern. If you are right-handed, you could write with your left hand if you had to, but you prefer your right hand. If you are an introvert, you can and do enjoy people and good conversation, but you must have time and space to think and reflect to do your best work. If you are an extravert, you certainly can listen and reflect, but you prefer the energy of interacting with others to build and refine your ideas because you like to "think out loud." Understanding the impact of our preferences and comfortably using our nonpreferred strategies is a skill to acquire. Indeed, the secondary subtitle of *Developing Leaders* (Fitzgerald & Kirby, 1997) is *Integrating Reality and Vision, Mind and Heart*.

Perhaps the best-known method of assessing Jungian personality types is the Myers-Briggs Type Indicator (MBTI). Your college counseling center will likely have this instrument. You might also like to complete the Keirsey Temperament Sorter, which is based on the same principles, from *Please Understand Me* (Keirsey & Bates, 1984). You may not need the instrument at all if you identified with

Exhibit 4.1. Type Indicator Cue Words.

Extravert (E)	versus	Introvert (I)
(75% of population)		(25% of population)
Sociability		Territoriality
Interaction		Concentration
External		Internal
Breadth		Depth
Extensive		Intensive
Multiplicity of relationships		Limited relationships
Expenditure of energies		Conservation of energies
Interest in external events		Interest in internal reaction

Sensing (S)	versus	Intuition (N)
(75% of population)		(25% of population)
Experience		Hunches
Past		Future
Realistic		Speculative
Perspiration		Inspiration
Actual		Possible
Down-to-earth		Head-in-clouds
Utility		Fantasy
Fact		Fiction
Practicality		Ingenuity
Sensible		Imaginative

the descriptions of each of the four core functions in the MBTI and could identify your preferences.

The MBTI is useful in understanding relationships in a leadership setting. Research using the MBTI indicates that 65 to 75% of the general population are extraverts (E) and that women are slightly higher than men in this preference. Introverts (I) predominate in fields of study such as science and among careers such as university teaching. Those who prefer sensing (S) are three times more prevalent in the population than intuitives (N). "Groups at

Thinking (T)	versus	Feeling (F)
(50% of population)		(50% of population)
Objective		Subjective
Principles		Values
Policy		Social values
Laws		Extenuating circumstances
Criterion		Intimacy
Firmness		Persuasion
Impersonal		Personal
Justice		Humane
Categories		Harmony
Standards		Good or bad
Critique		Appreciate
Analysis		Sympathy
Allocation		Devotion

(handwritten: →So I can be →)

Judging (J)	versus	Perceiving (P)
(50% of population)		(50% of population)
Settled		Pending
Decided		Gather more data
Fixed		Flexible
Plan ahead		Adapt as you go
Run one's life		Let life happen
Closure		Open options
Decision making		Treasure hunting
Planned		Open ended
Completed		Emergent
Decisive		Tentative
Wrap it up		Something will turn up
Urgency		There's plenty of time
Deadline!		What deadline?
Get show on the road		Let's wait and see . . .

Source: Keirsey & Bates (1984), pp. 25–26. Adapted with permission.

the intuitive end . . . are more likely to include educators, consultants, and student leaders" (McCaulley, 1990, p. 407). Approximately two-thirds of men prefer thinking (T), and two-thirds of women prefer feeling (F). However, among female graduate students, engineering students, and business executives, the majority prefer thinking approaches. Among men in the arts, counseling, and some health fields, those with feeling preferences predominate. The general population contains about 55% judging types (J), but studies of leaders show this to range upward to 91%, clearly indicating the preferences among positional leaders to reach closure and get decisions made (McCaulley, 1990). Leaders come from all groupings of preferences, but clearly certain patterns of preferences may exist in some careers or fields that draw on those preferences as strengths. McCaulley asserts, "From the type perspective, one would not ask the question, 'What type is the best leader?' Rather, one would ask, 'How does each type show leadership?'" (p. 412).

This theory of psychological type has been widely used in leadership assessments to understand self, others, and the dynamics of relationships and leadership processes, but it is not without flaws. There is some indication that type is not stable, that you can change your pattern over time. The action-oriented extravert may become a more contemplative and reflective introvert later in her life. Scores on the MBTI may be related to the context you have in mind when you complete the instrument. Assessments like the MBTI are occasionally used inappropriately. It would be inappropriate in hiring decisions to assume that someone can be no different from her four-letter score, when actually she may be well developed in using several preferences. However, the concept of personality preferences is helpful in understanding ourselves and as a framework for your own self-exploration.

Becoming aware of your personality preferences helps move you further toward self-awareness. As awareness grows, you begin to see the need to build other skills and to have a wider range of responses in decision making and in your relations with others. A useful application occurs when you realize that the conflict you have with another may be because of a clash in preferences, which can lead to more understanding ways of relating. You will then find it comfortable to say, "Sorry, I know it seems like I am jumping the gun, but I just do my best thinking out loud," or "I know I am asking lots of detailed questions, but it helps me understand the bigger picture" or "These were interesting ideas presented today; I am just not yet ready to decide. I need to think about this overnight. Can we decide at our meeting tomorrow?"

Approaches to Learning

One of the elements of leadership is its focus on accomplishing something or changing something. How individuals understand the need for change and how effectively individuals and groups can adapt to change is a learning process. Human beings go through a continual process of adaptation to changing conditions, whether those conditions are imposed or induced.

There are learning applications of the Jungian types presented as personality preferences in the previous section. Use of the MBTI would bring a complex understanding of the combinations of your four codes (E/I, S/N, T/F, and P/J). For purposes of illustration, some simple applications follow.

If you are extraverted (E), you are likely to enjoy group learning tasks and projects, learn readily from group discussion, and think aloud as you respond to questions and comments in the group. Extraverts value experience and often "leap into academic tasks with little planning . . . they prefer trial-and-error process because it allows them to think while they are active" (Jensen, 1987, p. 183). If you are an introvert (I), you listen keenly and find you carry on a great dialogue in your head. You might prefer to keep a journal, and you probably do well with written assignments when there is time to reflect. When something important comes up, you prefer to think about it first and not jump to a hasty conclusion.

If you are a sensing (S) learner, you like details and facts and might prefer inductive thinking. You value the history and background of an issue to establish the context to learn about it. If you are an intuitive learner (N), you like the big picture and do not retain the small details well. You may be quick to jump to conclusions with little information. You like possibility thinking, and you cast a wide net to gather a great deal of information from diverse sources. The sensing or intuition preference may relate to a preference for either deductive or inductive ways of thinking. Being deductive means you like to see the big picture and know what the final outcome is likely to be—or what the whole is—and then you are comfortable looking at the parts and pieces. You like to see the forest before you examine all the trees. If you are inductive, you like to build up to the big picture or conclusion by assembling all the parts and evolving your conclusion. You prefer to see each tree before you stand back and see the forest. A deductive learner might be frustrated with an inductive learner and say, "Where in the world are you going with this argument? Can you just get to your point?" Understanding the difference in approach, that same deductive learner might say, "It would help me to know where this is going so I can fit your examples into the bigger picture."

Think of the classes or organizations you know that are made up of one predominant type. Often a major will attract students who are more similar than different. If, however, you are mismatched in learning style, you may wonder why the group does not readily see the benefit of your suggestions or perhaps even rejects a process you propose. Groups that may be composed of one predominant type of learning preference will find strength in including other approaches to enrich the outcome.

Highly diverse groups of learners need to acknowledge that people learn differently and offer options and choices that will appeal to the diversity within a group. For example, student government organizers who are planning a retreat during which goals and plans for the year are to be set might:

- Send out materials ahead of time (appealing to the introverts and intuitors)

- Plan large-group presentations (appealing to the introverts and the thinkers)

- Plan small-group discussions (useful for the extraverts and feelers)

- Plan case study applications

Also, they might work through how a possible goal might be put into an action plan with a related budget (useful to the sensers and judgers). If only one approach were used, it would relate less well to the entire group. It is clearly helpful to know your own preferred learning style and understand how others may prefer to learn differently.

Preferences in how we take in information, relate to others, make decisions, and learn are all essential areas of awareness in relational leadership. These applications of Jung's principles may help you explore your own personality and attitudes in new ways.

Chapter Summary

This chapter discussed some important aspects of your self-awareness that become key to understanding yourself as a participant and as a leader. The chapter explored ways to examine your strengths and weaknesses, with a goal of developing your talent, and having a realistic self-concept with healthy self-esteem and self-confidence. We then reviewed basic values that are essential in a person of character. Building on the psychological and educational approaches to leadership, we presented some models to assess your personality preferences and your learning preferences.

What's Next?

Understanding yourself and building your capacity for self-leadership is a foundational asset for effectively relating to others. Chapter Five will encourage you to explore yourself in the context of others. The chapter will further present how interpersonal relations can be enhanced by understanding differences and commonalties with others. This understanding is helpful in communicating and building empowering relationships with other participants.

Chapter Activities

1. Think about your gender, ethnicity, sexual orientation, special abilities or disabilities, age, socioeconomic status, religion, birth order, and any other possible influences that come to mind. How have these factors influenced your personality and learning preferences?

2. Write your own personal mission statement. What is your purpose in life? What values are important to you? What do you want to be? What attributes and capabilities are important to you?

3. Review Bennis's lessons for developing self-knowledge and provide examples from your own life. When were you your own best teacher? When did you accept responsibility for something that did not go well? When did you learn something you really wanted to learn? When did you learn something through the process of reflection?

4. Identify two of your top talents. Write in your journal about how those talents help you in leadership situations. How do you apply these talents in your leadership?

5. To learn more about the talent philosophy, go to the Gallup Organization's web site about StrengthsQuest at www.strengthsquest.com and click on the student box to learn more about the StrengthsQuest web-based assessment and to view a demonstration of it. You can also read more about leading with your strengths at this site.

6. Contact your college counseling center to complete the

Myers-Briggs Type Indicator (MBTI). That will help you understand your personality preferences.

7. Many people use positive affirmations to enhance their self-esteem. Although these will not make up for a lack of skill or ability, they can help you develop your confidence. An example might be, "I am going to do a good job speaking in front of this group." Saying this phrase over and over to yourself, up to twenty times throughout the day, can help you believe in yourself. Develop two or three affirmations that you can use to strengthen your self-confidence.

8. Another technique is creative visualization. Again, this will not make up for a lack of skill or ability, but it can help you develop your confidence. Identify something you have to do in the next couple of days that is causing you to worry. Now visualize yourself accomplishing this activity successfully. Repeat this visualization whenever you begin to worry about the upcoming event. After the event is over, consider whether or not using visualization helped you.

9. Using the dipper and bucket metaphor, go to the Gallup Organization web site at: http://www.bucketbook.com/drops/electronic/ and send someone an electronic drop to fill his or her bucket.

Additional Readings

Conger, J. A., & Benjamin, B. (1999). *Building leaders: How successful companies develop the next generation.* San Francisco: Jossey-Bass.

Covey, S. (1989). *The 7 habits of highly effective people.* New York: Simon & Schuster.

Keirsey, D., & Bates, M. (1984). *Please understand me: Character and temperament types* (4th ed.). Del Mar, CA: Prometheus Nemesis Books.

Lee, R. J., & King, S. N. (2001). *Discovering the leader in you: A guide to realizing your personal leadership potential.* Center for Creative Leadership. San Francisco: Jossey-Bass.

Rath, T., & Clifton, D. O. (2004). *How full is your bucket? Positive strengths for work and life.* New York: Gallup Press.

5

Understanding Others

Consider this situation:

Place yourself in a typical meeting of an organization in which you are a member. Have you ever found yourself wondering . . .

Laurie wonders why the men in the organization seem to dominate the discussions.

Martina wonders why some of the group's members never say anything.

James wonders why some of his peers enjoy controversy so much. They seem to enjoy the disagreement and heated debate.

Patrick wonders what it's like to be one of the few students of color in the room.

Julianna wonders if the students in the organization who are gay feel safe.

Angela wonders if those students who are very religious are offended by any of the conversations going on during the meeting.

Martin wonders how they could get some international students interested in joining the organization.

What do you wonder about the motives and behavior of others when you're sitting in a typical organization meeting?

A central goal of understanding yourself is to develop a sense of awareness that can result in true community and common purpose with others. There are three central questions (Komives, 1994, p. 219) to ask yourself in any setting:

- How am I like no one else here?

- How am I like some others here?

- How am I like everyone here?

Each of us brings uniqueness and individuality to any situation. As we explored in Chapter Four, your skills, background, and preferences create a unique person—you. But you are not alone. To be truly inclusive and empowering, you must also understand others. The importance of this cannot be overstated. As the nation becomes more diverse and the world becomes smaller and more connected through technology, it becomes "flatter" (Friedman, 2005). Understanding others is a necessity for all leaders.

Chapter Overview

This chapter briefly explores some characteristics of gender, ethnicity, and culture that illustrate how differences need to be understood as you work toward leadership that is inclusive and empowering. The chapter also explores various leadership processes—including communication, conflict resolution, and decision making—that are influenced by diverse approaches. The chapter concludes with a discussion of communication skills, such as empathy and assertiveness, that are useful in working effectively with others in leadership.

Individuality and Commonality

In Chapter Four you explored your value system and your psychological preferences. Others might be similar to you or very different from you. Even if others look the same, they may have different values, preferences, or approaches to learning. Some of these differences in ourselves and others come from our gender, ethnicity, or culture; some come from our environments.

In the grand scheme of living human species, we are more alike than we are different. Research into the human genome has certainly confirmed this. Finding common human purpose is the focus on which to center our perceptions of difference. The poet Maya Angelou (1994) has remarkable insight into the commonalties of being human. In her poem "Human Family," she describes all of our uniqueness as people that set us apart, but concludes, "We are more alike, my friends, than we are unalike" (pp. 224–225).

In any group setting, you can look around and see others who look like you. You will see men or women, people with visible racial or ethnic characteristics, or people of different ages. Also, you might see people wearing symbolic attire like your own: a wedding ring, a sorority pin, a pink triangle, a Star of David, or tennis whites. You might also identify with others when they express ideas you agree with, share experiences you have had, or have goals you also hold, regardless of visible characteristics that might have initially made them seem unlike you. You may begin to find similarities of interests: being in the same major, living close together, thinking alike about current politics, working out daily, being parents, or being affiliated with the same religion. Finding some people like you creates a feeling of association called social identity and leads to the identification of subcommunities.

On a transcendent level, something binds you to everyone around you, no matter how different they may seem: you all want to learn the subject in a particular course; you all value the goals of the organization meeting you have attended, be it the residence hall association, the aikido club, or a Bible study class; or you all want to work toward a common purpose like changing the university's policy on weekend library hours. The challenge of leadership is coming to common purpose from the vast differences that individuals bring to a situation. Finding the purpose, vision, and common commitments that create a "we" from a group of individuals is the challenge of community.

"I believe that every individual can provide a new perspective on a situation. No matter what your experiences are, they are different from mine and therefore we see things differently. Using this perspective in addition to one's ideas allows for better communication, better solutions, and better leadership."—Cathy Ragan was formerly the student government president at Rowan University.

The English language may well be the only one that values the individual to such a degree that the word for the first person singular—I—is capitalized. This emphasis on the individual is grounded in a predominantly Western tradition. Those with non-Western roots may find it easier to envision *we* because those cultural traditions emphasize the collective, the family, or group. To truly establish a sense of *we*, the individual needs to let go of self enough to see the connections to others.

Buber (1958) encouraged an exploration of "I-Thou"; leadership educators have encouraged "I→you→we" (National Invitational Leadership Symposium, 1990). This might best be expressed symbolically by showing that the focus on the individual (I) needs to be de-emphasized (i) to truly listen and engage with another (you)

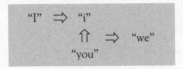

Figure 5.1. I, You, and We.

as equals, so that all can move forward to become a community (we) (see Figure 5.1).

One challenge, then, is to understand yourself well enough to know how you are seen by others and to modify your own behaviors and attitudes to encourage a spirit of openness and connection with others. The second challenge is to engage in the hard work of understanding others so that together you can form meaningful community and engage in coalitions for group change.

Groups are made up of great diversity. Even if members are all of one sex or one race or one major, there are great differences in personality, learning preferences, and experiences. The pluralism of a group refers to the plethora of differences that need to be understood in order to accomplish shared purposes. Pluralistic leadership results when heterogeneous groups of people work together to accomplish change. Pluralistic leadership is enhanced when a person understands, develops an appreciation for, and possesses the skills needed to communicate across these borders and come to common understandings.

Understanding Gender Diversity

It is salient to ask yourself, How does my gender influence my attitudes and behaviors? How does my experience as a man or woman shape my worldview and how might it shape the worldview of others? Characteristics of gender differences are too numerous to develop fully, but it is important to realize that we all deal with both sex roles and gender roles. The two terms are often used inter-changeably, but sex roles are those expectations resulting from biology, like pregnancy or muscle mass, whereas gender roles are socially constructed expectations that get labeled masculine or feminine.

Gender roles are often limiting and inaccurate when assigned to individual men and women. For example, although only women can bear children, women are not the only sex to be nurturing of children. Historically, men's involvement in the development of children has been limited because that role has been considered feminine and nurturing. Likewise, women may be athletic, but it has been hard for women to engage in sports that require high physical contact, like football and rugby, because those sports are considered masculine. Women who are not nurturing or men who are not athletic may suffer from gender role discrimination by acting or being different from conventional paradigms. Likewise, those who hold a conventional leadership expectation that leaders should be decisive, in charge, competitive, and self-reliant may be holding a traditional masculine paradigm that excludes many women, as well as many men who are very capable but who do not lead from that perspective.

From the beginnings of our lives, our gender role perceptions are shaped by the many messages we receive from the environment. Even those parents who make sure the storybooks their children read do not promote gender role or sex role stereotypes and who give dolls to their sons and trucks to their daughters soon realize that other socialization agents (like peers, toys, television, and conversations on the bus going to school every morning) reinforce traditional gender messages. Many boys learn to be tough, objective, unemotional, and competitive, and many girls learn to be polite, caring, emotional, and supportive.

To understand how men and women have come to be as they are, we can learn from children's development. The way we play in childhood establishes patterns of how we work and communicate as adults. Boys often play outside in rough-and-tumble games, and extraverted leaders shout commands in competitive settings. Winning or losing becomes very important. Most games are played using teams. Even inside games like video or computer games often have elaborate hierarchical systems with complex rules and procedures that involve dominating or annihilating enemies and are frequently preferred by boys. Girls, however, often play inside in calm settings with one another or with a small group of friends. Their play stresses intimacy and values social relationships. Many of their preferred games have no winners or losers but every person gets a turn. Such games are jumping rope, hopscotch, or playing house (Tannen, 1990).

The social learning that happens with play and many other experiences often leads females to seek and value intimacy and relationships, whereas males often seek and value independence.

Intimacy is key in a world of connection in which individuals negotiate complex networks of friendship, minimize differences, try to reach consensus, and value the appearance of superiority which would highlight differences. In a world of status, *independence* is key, because a primary means of establishing status is to tell others what to do, and taking orders is a marker of low status (Tannen, 1990, p. 26).

Think of how rare it is in entertainment to find people who play roles that are different from conventional gender roles. Can you think of a television show or movie in which a woman played a role traditionally viewed as being for a man? Or in which a man played a role traditionally reserved for a woman?

Childhood play experiences also contribute to the development of the thinking or feeling orientation described in the Jungian preference types in Chapter Four. Remember that there is great variation among men and among women, but these patterns do raise our awareness and understanding of differences.

Men and women tend to hold different attributions for their successes and failures. Many women tend to credit their successes to external factors like luck and being in the right place at the right time. They might say, "Oh, I don't deserve the credit. So many people helped." They credit their failures to internal factors like not being prepared or not having the right skills or not having enough time. Many men, in contrast, tend to credit successes to internal factors like being prepared and capable and attribute their failures to external factors like fate, others not doing their part, or bad luck.

However, "psychological and physiological data on sex-linked traits suggest that the degree of overlap between the sexes is as important, or more important, than the average differences between them" (Lipman-Blumen, 1984, p. 4). Both men and women are capable of making good decisions, leading effectively, being responsible group members, and communicating with clarity, but they may go about doing those things differently than the other sex would (Eagley, Karau, & Makhijani, 1995). The fact that we persist in observing differences speaks to the power relationships that continue to exist in which men's ways, views, and artifacts have had higher status. Because men have traditionally held many visible leadership positions, the conventional paradigm of leadership was often socially constructed as having these same male characteristics.

Expectations that limit people's range of roles and suppress their individuality will likely inhibit their effectiveness in their communities. Sex or gender, however, is only one identity perspective we bring to a situation. We all have other salient social identities that are based on attributes such as our culture, ethnicity, age, or sexual orientation.

Understanding Cultural Diversity

Culture encompasses everything about how a group of people thinks, feels, and behaves. It is their pattern of knowledge. It is a "body of common understandings" (Brown, 1963, p. 3). Culture is "the sum total of ways of living; including values, beliefs, esthetic standards, linguistic expression, patterns of thinking, behavioral norms, and styles of communication which a group of people has developed to assure its survival in a particular physical and human environment. Culture, and the people who are part of it, interact, so that culture is not static" (Hoopes & Pusch, 1979, p. 3). We may be so embedded in our culture that it is hard to see it clearly.

Culture is, therefore, a broad term that could be applied to an office or a campus, to aging, or to a group of people who share a common race or ethnicity. Many cultures coexist simultaneously in any group. Effective leaders need to develop an appreciation for multiculturalism to build inclusiveness, collaboration, and common purposes. A prerequisite to developing a greater sense of multiculturalism is the conscious awareness of culturally informed assumptions (Helms, 1992; Pedersen, 1988).

Culture has often been described in terms of race and ethnicity. We encourage you to be cautious about the construct of race. Race is a "somewhat suspect concept used to identify large groups of the human species who share a more or less distinctive combination of hereditary physical characteristics" (Hoopes & Pusch, 1979, p. 3). The California Newsreel entitled *Race—The Power of an Illusion* explores this concept in detail in this three-hour video series and presents evidence that the very concept of race has no biological foundation. According to their web site,

> The division of the world's peoples into distinct groups—
> "red," "black," "white," or "yellow" peoples—has became
> so deeply imbedded in our psyches, so widely accepted,
> many would promptly dismiss as crazy any suggestion of
> its falsity. Yet, that's exactly what this provocative three-
> hour series by California Newsreel claims. *Race—The
> Power of an Illusion* questions the very idea of race as biol-
> ogy, suggesting that a belief in race is no more sound
> than believing that the sun revolves around the earth.
> Yet race still matters. Just because race doesn't exist in
> biology doesn't mean it isn't very real, helping shape life

ht158EING LSHIP

chances and opportunities. (http://www.newsreel.org/
nav/title.asp?tc=CN0149)

As noted educator Derald Wing Sue (2003) states, "Many difficulties exist, however, in using race as a descriptor" (p. 34).

Yet, historically, race has been a very powerful aspect of life in
the United States and continues to impact every campus today. It
has been used to marginalize whole groups of people, and students
on campuses experience racism every day. The Relational Leadership Model, with its emphasis on inclusion and empowerment,
embraces the belief that the group, team, organization, community,
nation, and world will be made better when all participants are
heard, made visible, and valued for their contributions.

Historically, the dominant culture—the culture in the powerful
majority—has not had to examine its beliefs and practices because
it is not disadvantaged by them. The majority norms often became
the standards used to judge others who are not in the majority.
America's attention to racial and ethnic diversity has led to new
awareness of what it means to be White and of European origin in
the American culture. Peggy McIntosh (1989) coined the phrase
the "invisible knapsack" to describe the concept of "White privilege." This weightless knapsack is filled with provisions that help
you travel through life more easily. Even well-meaning people in
the majority culture often take for granted the benefits of White
privilege, which include shopping without being followed, being
able to buy or rent housing of their choice, and easily finding toys
and pictures that look like themselves (Talbot, 1996). In a general
sense, it is useful to think of the privileges afforded any of us by
virtue of personal characteristics that place us in a powerful "majority" (for example, being male, heterosexual, able-bodied, educated,
financially comfortable) and examine closely how unconsciously
affirming the privileges associated with those characteristics may
actually cause or influence the oppression of others, even though
oppression is unintended. Cris Cullinan (1999) describes privilege

in a slightly different way. She notes that people with privilege are presumed to be innocent, worthy, and competent. We must examine how the characteristics of these forms of privilege may be attached to our expectations of what it means to be a leader or to not be a leader, and we must learn to value, or at least recognize, that leadership may take on different characteristics.

Understanding International Diversity

Understanding how to work with persons from other countries is even more complex but can be an exciting and rewarding experience. At times, it can also be very challenging. One of the great opportunities afforded to college students is the chance to get to know and work with students from other nations and, if you have the opportunity, to study abroad. As Javidan and House (2001) noted in describing global leaders, "To be successful in dealing with people from other cultures, managers need knowledge about cultural differences and similarities among countries. They also need to understand the implications of the differences and the skills required to act and decide appropriately and in a culturally sensitive way" (p. 292). Kets de Vries and Florent-Treacy (2002) note that global leadership development means increasing one's adaptability, cultural empathy, acceptance of ambiguity, lack of xenophobia, cultural relativity, awareness of one's own roots and cultural biases, and "as if" quality (p. 307). They go on to note, "An outlook of cultural relativity, excellent relational skills, curiosity, and emotional intelligence distinguish successful global leaders" (p. 304).

Project GLOBE (Global Leadership and Organizational Behavior Effectiveness), an extensive international study of thousands of middle managers, defined culture as "a set of shared values and beliefs" in which the values are "people's aspirations about the way things should be done" and the beliefs are "people's perceptions of how things are done in their countries" (Javidan & House, 2001, p. 293). This study identified nine dimensions of culture that differed from country to country: assertiveness, future orientation, gender differentiation, uncertainty avoidance, power distance (power expected to be shared unequally within the culture), institutional emphasis on collectivism versus individualism, in-group collectivism (membership in small groups and families), performance orientation, and humane orientation (fairness, generosity, caring) (Javidan & House). Some countries seem to be higher than others in different dimensions. For example, people in the United States are thought to be more male-dominated than people in England but less than people in Germany. (See House, Hanges, Javidan, Dorfman, & Gupta, 2004, for the complete report.) As with any attempt to generalize large groups, information in reports such as this should be viewed and used with great caution. That being said, when working with others from different nations, realizing they may differ from you in the dimensions mentioned in this report can help you understand them better and work with them more effectively.

Knowledge about other countries becomes increasingly important as the world becomes more connected. It is also an area in which U.S. students could improve. Rebekah Nathan (2005) is the pen name of an anthropologist who went "undercover" and lived in a residence hall posing as a freshman. As she discovered, "The single biggest complaint international students lodged against U.S. students was, to put it bluntly, our ignorance. As informants described it, by 'ignorance' they meant the misinformation and lack of information that Americans have both about other countries and about themselves" (p. 84).

Your Cultural Heritage

We encourage you to read about your cultural heritage to see how you may have acquired the values and beliefs of your culture or ethnicity and in what ways you have diverged from them. Read also about a group that is different from your own. You might study the White or European American cultures, African American or Black culture, Asian American cultures, Latino or Hispanic or Chicano cultures, Native American traditions, and international students who come from other countries. Learn more about aging and adult development, deaf culture, religious diversity, and regional differences. In any case, it will be useful to be aware of the assumptions that a person coming into a group might have that would influence that person's behavior. It may be most useful to start with you.

"The benefits of working with people who are different from you are extreme. If you are an effective leader, you will be inclusive in many facets of the word. . . . As an individual in a leadership position, it is crucial to possess the ability to hear and be open-minded and inclusive of different people or different ideas. This ability to accept and work with one another strongly adds to the knowledge base of the group."—Annie Millstone is a dance teacher and majors in retailing and consumer sciences at the University of Arizona.

Building Multicultural Appreciation

Being an effective leader or participant in a diverse organization or being a leader who brings diversity to the organization requires that we know more about developing an openness and appreciation of various cultures and aspects of how others may differ. Paul Pedersen (1988) supports this idea by noting that individuals need to develop their awareness, knowledge, and skills to be able to work effectively in a multicultural environment. David Hoopes (1979) presents an Intercultural Learning Process Model (see Exhibit 5.1) that describes how we develop and learn to communicate clearly and understand people and cultures that seem different from our own. The first stage is ethnocentrism. In this stage, we believe that our own culture or way of doing things is best—even superior to others. People with ethnocentric views can be intolerant and even hostile to others from different cultures. Racism and sexism grow

Exhibit 5.1. Hoopes Intercultural Learning Process.

Ethnocentrism	A human survival response that tells us our own culture is best. Individuals at this stage may exhibit intolerance and outright hostility or aggression towards other cultures. Individuals who do not move beyond this stage tend to feel their culture is superior and impose it on others.
Transition stages	
Awareness	A first step out of Ethnocentrism. This stage involves the acknowledgment that other cultures exist and the awareness that they have a culture. The individual at this stage becomes aware that differences are culturally based and that they are part of a given people's way of thinking and acting.
Understanding	This stage involves the acquiring of knowledge and information about other cultures on a rational, cognitive level. The individual begins to piece together the "puzzle" of the other culture from pieces of information about values, customs, etc. Occurs in a detached and separate way.
Acceptance/Respect (tolerance)	Individuals at this stage accept the validity of other cultures without comparing or judging them against one's own culture. A change in attitude of "It's OK for them" occurs, a relativistic approach. A "live and let live" attitude results and the value of other cultures is for others, not me.

from this base. As we expand our experiences, we begin to move out of ethnocentrism and our awareness is raised. We begin to acknowledge that many different cultures exist. As awareness of culture grows, we move to some level of understanding derived by experiences, learning and acquiring information, and knowledge. Learning about other cultures is somewhat objective in this transition and is more thought about than felt.

These two transition stages of awareness and understanding lead to a willingness to accept and respect that others do have a legiti-

Transition stages	
Appreciating/Valuing	At this stage, one begins to understand that cultures have strengths and weaknesses; such an understanding leads to appreciation and valuing of specific aspects of other cultures. A change occurs from objectivity to subjectivity considering cultural aspects in terms of one's own identity and values.
Selective Adoption	The individual at this stage tries and adopts new attitudes and behaviors from other cultures which are believed to be useful and desirable to emulate. Aspects of another culture which have value and worth for the individual personally are integrated into her/his way of thinking, feeling, or acting.
Multiculturalism	An ideal state and an ongoing PROCESS where a person is able to feel comfortable in and communicate effectively with people from many cultures and in many situations. Identities, self-concepts, outlooks, and value formation transcends cultural considerations. Very open to new experiences.

Source: Leppo (1987), pp. 56–60. Copyright 1987 by the National Association of Campus Activities. Adapted with permission. (Original work from Hoopes, 1979, pp. 17–20. Copyright 1979 by Intercultural Press. Adapted with permission of Intercultural Press, Inc., Yarmouth, MA.)

mate cultural view. This tolerance has led not to an examination of one's own culture but to the recognition that it may be all right for others to hold the views and values they possess from their cultural view. Some would say that acceptance is still a negative attitude; it may lead to the civility of tolerance but does not yet place the same value on another's views as on one's own (Riddle, as cited in Leppo & Lustgraaf, 1987).

The transition from the tolerance step in the process toward multiculturalism moves forward with appreciating and valuing certain aspects of other cultures. This does not mean that every-thing about another culture or way of doing things is appreciated but that a recognition of the strengths, assets, and value of another cultural view has occurred. For example, we have learned to appre-ciate the international foods, music, and dance that are incorpo-rated into our daily American life. This stage means comparing others to our own cultural view and becoming more subjective about this assessment. This leads to the next transition in selectively adopting values or aspects of another culture that are worthy of admiration. Aspects of value in another culture (for example, the role of elders or the role of the environment) are integrated into a person's own life out of admiration and choice.

The goal of this process is multiculturalism, which is not a final state but an ongoing process of comfort in learning about and appre-ciating other cultures—a lifelong learning task. This openness to new experiences enriches a person's own life and makes it possible to share aspects of a person's own culture that may be of value to others.

Imagine this model (see Exhibit 5.1) helping the aging culture to be more open to youth culture or the Black Student Union and the Jewish Student Union coming to an appreciation of each other's perspectives. Think of the lessons many could learn from Native Americans. A benefit of multiculturalism is to grow beyond seeing the world only in our own terms to seeing the legitimate views of others. This appreciation does not mean we will agree or even find decision making easy, but it should mean that we will understand other views.

Attitudes Toward Differences

How we view others who are different from ourselves is complex. There is some evidence that this is a developmental or sequential process during which we move from complete unawareness as a child to some degree of acceptance or appreciation as a mature adult. Through the years, we begin to learn through positive and negative experiences. As a result of these experiences, some people learn to dislike and fear differences. In extreme cases, fears can lead to racism, homophobia, or sexism. Other experiences lead us to be appreciative and to embrace many differences.

"Diversity is an essential aspect of our society. To deny diversity is to short change yourself and society. Many talents are lost daily due to discrimination. As the Co-Chair of the Houston Transgender Unity Committee, we produce the world's largest single day event for the transgender community at our annual Houston Transgender Unity Banquet. At this banquet we have successfully involved such corporations as IBM and Motorola as sponsors."—Josephine Tittsworth is vice president, Student Outreach and Communication Student Government Association; president, Omicron Delta Kappa Atrium Circle; treasurer, Unity Club and Women's Studies Student Association; member of the Multicultural Advisory Board at the University of Houston—Clear Lake; and cochair of the Houston Transgender Unity Committee.

In the previous section, we illustrated the progression from ethnocentrism to multiculturalism. One model that applies to attitudes toward many differences is the Riddle Scale (cited in Leppo & Lustgraaf, 1987). As depicted in Exhibit 5.2, the first four stages of the scale (repulsion, pity, tolerance, and acceptance) are negative attitudes because they come from a belief that the person who is different is somehow of less value than oneself. The second group of four stages of the scale (support, admiration, appreciation, and nurturance) are positive levels of the scale because the other person is of value just as oneself is. Dorothy Riddle developed this model originally as a Scale for Homophobia to understand attitudes toward gay and lesbian people, but our students have found it helpful as a

Exhibit 5.2. The Riddle Scale: Attitudes Toward Differences.

Negative Levels of Attitudes	
Repulsion	Views people who are different as strange, sick, crazy, and aversive. Views anything that will change them to be more "normal" or part of the mainstream as justifiable.
Pity	Views people who are different as somehow born that way and feels that that is pitiful. Sees being different as definitely immature and less preferred, so to help those poor individuals one should reinforce normal behaviors.
Tolerance	Sees being different as just a phase of development that most people "grow out" of. Thus one should protect and tolerate those who are different as one does a child who is still learning.
Acceptance	Implies that one needs to make accommodations for another's differences; does not acknowledge that the other's identity may be of the same value as one's own.
Positive Levels of Attitudes	
Support	Works to safeguard the rights of those who are different. One may be uncomfortable oneself but one is aware of the climate and the irrational unfairness in our society.
Admiration	Acknowledges that being different in our society takes strength. One is willing to truly look at oneself and work on one's own personal biases.
Appreciation	Values the diversity of people and is willing to confront insensitive attitudes.
Nurturance	Assumes the differences in people are indispensable in society. Views differences with genuine affection and delight and is willing to be an advocate of those differences.

Source: Adapted from Leppo and Lustgraaf (1987). Copyright by John Leppo. Adapted with permission from Dorothy Riddle, "Scale for Homophobia," unpublished document.

conceptual model for understanding other differences, as well as attitudes toward people with physical disabilities or different religious practices.

Cultural Influences on Leadership Behavior

Awareness of how such aspects of diversity as sex, race, ethnicity, age, sexual identity, religion, ability, or socioeconomic status influence our own behavior and that of others in groups is a step toward being an effective relational leader. No group is totally homogeneous; we differ in personality preferences, attitudes, styles, value systems, beliefs, and opinions, based on our cultural influences. Relational leadership values effective leadership processes within heterogeneous groups. Many leadership practices could be described as participative because they value the empowerment of followers, but relational and pluralistic leadership seeks to change the very culture of the organization or group to see the diversity of the group as a true asset (Loden & Rosener, 1991).

It clearly would be inaccurate to describe people based on only one aspect of their identity. Behaviors grow from a complex interaction of many salient background factors; it is more useful to observe people's behaviors and seek to understand their attitudes than to presume differences among people that are based on stereotypes. It is useful to examine the range of human behaviors that are essential in leadership settings. Consider the cultural influences in such leadership processes as communications, conflict resolution, and decision making.

"Again and again, the issue of diversity arises at both the writing center where I work and in Residence Life. For both, it is a part of training that receives a lot of attention. Having, and appreciating diversity in a group is a great way to involve several unique points of view. An ignorance of the benefits of diversity can truly hinder any group. To be successful as a leader, or in a leadership role, one should *always* consider perspectives from a variety of people or groups."—Rebecca Mooney is a resident assistant at the University of Maryland. She is employed as a technician in the Department of Business Services Copy Center and is a member of the Golden Key Honor Society.

Communication

You may observe a range of behaviors in a group. Some people may be highly verbal, with strong oral traditions; others may be verbally reserved, preferring thoughtful writing. Some may be outgoing, expressive, and emotional, whereas the cultural assumptions of others lead them to be thoughtful, objective, and analytical. Depending on the mix of individuals, some will be open and revealing, whereas others will be closed and guarded. Some cultural assumptions lead people to be direct and factual; others have learned to be symbolic and metaphorical. Some have been taught to value direct, bold eye contact; others find respect in indirect body language. Some have learned to be timely and to value promptness; other cultures value casual approaches. Understanding the mix of preferred communication patterns in any group helps the group be more informed in its interaction. Instead of judging another to be wrong or disrespectful, it is useful to ask yourself, Within that person's context, how do I understand this action or practice? And how would they want to be treated?

One aspect of communication we have found to be useful is the idea of *speech communities*. "A speech community exists when people share norms about how to use talk and what purposes it serves" (Wood, 2004, p. 115; citing Labov, 1972). This can be important to keep in mind, because persons from different speech communities may misunderstand each other (Wood). Speech communities can be determined by gender, ethnicity, workplace, interests, or other groupings that share a common core of patterns about language and how it is used. "Recognizing and respecting different speech communities increases our ability to participate competently in a diverse culture" (p. 119). For example, students who are devoted players of a particular game like Halo have a language all their own that people who do not play this game probably would not know. Experienced members of a student government organization can develop their own language, using acronyms and inside jokes, that can be less than inclusive when used around newly elected representatives.

Finally, it is important to remember the key role that nonverbal communication plays. As Wood (2004) notes, "Like verbal communication, nonverbal patterns reflect the values, perspectives, norms, and heritage of specific cultures" (p. 134). We communicate with our physical appearance, personal space, facial expressions, gestures, touching, eye contact, the expression of emotions, and orientation toward time—all of which have cultural components (Andersen, 2003; Wood). This is one of those areas in which we can find ourselves saying, "I don't know what the big deal was; this wouldn't have bothered me." When we are trying to connect with others, it is imperative to remember that "different is just different; different is not wrong."

Conflict Resolution

You might observe individuals with a range of behaviors, from the confrontational to the very subtle. Some may encourage taking responsibility and being accountable; others will tend to blame; still others will seek harmony and face-saving. Some believe their way is right and are closed to other options, whereas others seek connections among options. Some resolve conflict by being deferential to authority, whereas others have learned to be confrontational to authority figures. Finally, some people will link resolution to values like harmony with nature. Conflict resolution is a critical aspect of relational leadership. Almost any change effort will involve some degree of conflict. Remaining focused on the purpose of the change while maintaining positive relationships is necessary. At the same time, it is also important to remain ethical and inclusive. This is certainly challenging, but even more necessary in times of conflict when the tendency can be to try to go it alone or to try to just make it all "go away."

Decision Making

The way in which decisions are made reflects either those who value the power of majority rule and prefer voting or those who seek inclusion of the minority opinion and value consensus. In some groups, if the will of the group does not emerge as apparent, an issue may be dropped completely and brought up at a later time. Some believe the hierarchy and authorities should decide, whereas others think the experts or those involved should decide.

Relational leadership requires communication skills that help each person seek to understand others, not just persuade them. All communicators should constantly ask themselves, How do my perspectives and preferences shade my view? In what ways could I be understood more correctly and understand with greater insight?

Leadership and Communication

Just about everything done in life is enhanced by being a more effective communicator. Communication skills involve far more than persuasive talking or skillful writing. As one student leader told us, "God gave me two ears and one mouth; I figure that's a message to listen more than I talk." The Chinese language, like many Asian languages, includes symbols that depict related concepts to create new meaning. The Chinese pictogram for listening is made up of the symbols for ears, eyes, and heart (see Figure 5.2).

For most of us, hearing is a natural and almost automatic process. Listening, however, is more difficult and is a "purposive activity" requiring one to be intentionally "mindful" (Gudykunst, 1991, p. 38). True listening is far from a passive activity.

Listening and communicating in a pluralistic context requires one to listen with empathy. Listening with empathy is an "intellec-

Listening is when you use . . .

Ears   Eyes

                                                              Heart

To give undivided attention.

Figure 5.2. Listening.
   Source: From Simons, Vázquez, & Harris (1993), p. 37. Copyright 1993 with permission, from Elsevier.

tual and emotional participation in another person's experience" (Bennett, 1979, p. 418). Empathy means you are using another person's standards and reference points to understand that person's experience. In contrast, sympathy is putting yourself in the other person's place but retaining your own perspective and still using your own standard of judgment. In other words, "sympathy is about feeling sorry for or sad about" the other person (Cormier & Hackney, 2005).

You are using empathy if you are able to see yourself understanding the experiences of others from their point of view, imagining how they feel, and connecting with the emotions others are experiencing when they communicate. This means trying to see others as they would want you to see them and becoming able to understand what others are feeling without being told directly (Gudykunst, 1991, p. 122).

Imagine a friend with low self-confidence who confides, "I made a comment in our meeting today and it was awful! People laughed at me." Showing sympathy and remembering times you have said things like that when you just needed a morale boost, you might say, "Oh, I am sure it wasn't that bad, and what you said was just humorous; probably no one even remembers." Responding with empathy, however, you might say, "I know how hard it is to speak up in that meeting. You don't talk much in that setting and it must have been very scary." The second response leads to more genuine dialogue than the first, which denied your friend's emotion and the apparent pain of the experience.

Renowned psychologist Carl Rogers would often require someone to restate what was said by a previous speaker, to build a listening skill and an awareness of empathy. You learn to listen for empathy if you try to find a point of agreement or genuine understanding with a previous speaker and build on it instead of immediately criticizing, rejecting, or denying the point. "Seek first to understand, then to be understood" (Covey, 1991, p. 123). This requires one to pause, think, restate for understanding, then build on that point. Criticism that comes too quickly leaves the first speaker thinking he or she was not heard.

Empathic communication is difficult. Think of the complexity of processes in typical conversation. The content of what we say and how we say it influence the receiver in forming meaning from what we shared. Communication involves both verbal and nonverbal components. Think of the complexity in this verbal process:

What I meant to say

What I actually said

What you heard me say

What you think I mean

What you mean to say

What you actually say

What I hear you say

What I think you mean

Each element in that process is influenced by our cultural and gender lenses. For example, who would you say talks more, men or women? Common stereotypical perception is that women talk more, yet in almost any coeducational class or setting, men likely will be the first to speak, and they will speak more often for longer periods (Hart & Dalke, 1983). What men and women include in their speech varies as well. Deborah Tannen (1990) notes a difference in public speaking and private speaking. Another way of stating that is that males prefer report-talking and females engage in rapport-talking (p. 77). Men's speech promotes their independence and is often used to share information or opinions, to tell jokes, or to relate stories. Women's speech, even in public settings like meetings or classes, seeks to find connections with others and build relationships. Often, women will add a tag line to the beginning or end of an opinion to provide bridges for others in the conversation. They do not want to stand out or apart. For example, a woman might say, "It's just my opinion, but . . ." or "I know there are many different views, but . . ." or "I think . . . Do you agree or disagree with that?"

Assertive Communication

Socialization has clearly played an important role in how we have learned to converse with each other. Some women feel silenced, or have silenced themselves, by assuming their opinions were of less value than others or by being socialized to avoid conflict. They have learned to be harmonizers or peacemakers. Some men feel it is more manly to be aggressive, assuming that their opinions are of more value and that others should acquiesce.

In every communication, each person has a right to be heard and a responsibility to listen. Each has a right to make a request or ask a question, and the recipient has the right to make his or her own decision without apology. Imagine an assertiveness continuum with three positions: a person might be unassertive, assertive, or aggressive (Alberti & Emmons, 1974). If you are unassertive, you passively give up your rights to others and let them take advantage of you. After an encounter, you may often wish you had said or done something different. Exhibit 5.3 illustrates this continuum.

Being assertive does not mean that you get your own way but that you did what you could to be understood. In a similar way, practicing relational leadership does not mean that the group will go along with what you think should happen in the group, but that you would have done your best to respect their involvement, listen for true understanding, and be a productive community member.

Relational Empathy

Working effectively together requires "relational empathy" (Broome, 1993, p. 97). Relational empathy goes beyond merely understanding another "in which the emphasis is upon the re-creation in the listener of the meaning originally created by the speaker" (p. 98) and seeks shared meaning. Relational empathy recognizes the importance of context.

It may mean creating a new "third culture" (p. 103) that synthesizes the positions from the two individual perspectives, culture, and context and builds a new culture, an environment of empathy and insight. "As sharing of contexts takes place, organizations of diverse people start weaving a new context" (Simons, Vázquez, & Harris, 1993, p. 39).

This third culture, or common context, develops its "own jargon, definitions, visions, and understandings" through which members from different contexts can come together (Simons et al. 1993, p. 39). In these organizations, the culture says

- People are good, honest, and trustworthy

- People are purposeful

- Each individual has a unique contribution to make

- Complex problems require local solutions

Exhibit 5.3. Illustrations of Unassertive, Assertive, and Aggressive Communication.

The Question: " Could you substitute for me at the event tonight? I have had something come up and cannot go after all."

Unassertive response: Even though you have several plans, you reply almost meekly. You deny your own rights and are intimidated into compliance. You may feel trapped or afraid to say no. You are fairly passive.	"OK, sure. I guess I can."
Assertive response: This response acknowledges that the other person had every right to ask, and you have a right to make your own decision. Being assertive means you can say no without feeling guilty or without apologizing.	"No, I have other plans and cannot do it." Depending on your style, you might say, "I am sorry I cannot substitute. You might ask me again sometime when I would have a little more time to change my plans, but thanks for thinking of me."
Aggressive Response: This response denies the other person had any right even to ask for your help and is rarely appropriate.	"How dare you ask me to do this? You always slack off on your responsibilities, and I won't stand for it."

- Me and you versus me or you (Kiefer & Senge, 1984, pp. 75–78)

These beliefs about the goodness of people guide how we approach others. "Self-fulfilling prophecy" demonstrates that people may indeed become as you see them (Argyris, as cited in Yukl, 1994, p. 176). If you think no one will get along in the group, conflict is bound to occur and be harmful. If you believe people will avoid responsibility, then you may shape your own behavior to be controlling and negative, and you may act discouraged. Those with whom you are engaged are likely to become as you anticipate. Conversely, if you think people will try to get along, want to face their sources of conflict, be helpful, and take responsibility, then you approach your behaviors in hopeful ways that make that prophecy come true.

Imagine going to your first group project meeting thinking that people will just slack off, that you will end up doing all the work, and that no one really cares. You then look for evidence of those assumptions, and at the smallest indication you think, Aha!—I knew it! Imagine instead going to your first project committee meeting thinking, We are all busy so we will have to be careful about what we take on, but people will want to do their part, and we can come up with something worthwhile. There are very real differences in environments, and groups may be negative in one setting and welcoming in another. The biggest difference in how a setting is perceived is the internal assumptions that guide expectations—how one will be in that setting and how being that way brings out responses in others. Building this new third culture meets the challenge inherent in the opening question: How am I like everyone else here?

Chapter Summary

The ability to understand others, be understood by others, and together create an effective organizational or group environment is the challenge of relational leadership. Truly understanding the influences of our cultural heritage, gender, and other aspects of our difference helps us work together toward change. We usually find we are more alike than we are different. Expecting commonalties, good will, and shared purposes can become a self-fulfilling prophecy. This awareness helps us create a new third culture in any group.

What's Next?

The next chapter provides an overview of leadership and ethics, underscoring the importance of leading with integrity. Strategies for creating and sustaining ethical organizations and models of ethical decision making will be reviewed.

Chapter Activities

1. How are your communication, conflict-resolution, and decision-making behaviors or tendencies influenced by your perceptions of the gender, race, ethnicity, family practices, or other characteristics of others in the group?

2. Referring to David Hoopes's Intercultural Learning Process Model, think about where you are currently in this model. What stage best describes you now? What experiences will help you expand your openness to others?

3. Ask a friend who is different from you to take you to an event or gathering at which the majority of others will be like your friend. What is easiest and hardest for you to understand about the practices in that group? Which of your own characteristics make it hardest for you to gain this understanding?

4. Refer to the Illustrations of Unassertive, Assertive, and Aggressive Communication chart (Exhibit 5.3). Think of a recent communication in which someone asked you to do something or asked for a favor. Based on this chart, what type of response did you give? Are you satisfied with that response? Why or why not? If not, how would you respond differently if you could do it over again?

Additional Readings

Andersen, P. A. (2003). In different dimensions: Nonverbal communication and culture. In L. A. Samovar & R. E. Porter (Eds.), *Intercultural communication: A reader* (10th ed.). Belmont, CA: Wadsworth.

Cullinan, C. (1999). Vision, privilege, and the limits of tolerance. *Electronic Magazine of Multicultural Education, 1*(2) (n.p.).

Friedman, T. L. (2005). *The world is flat: A brief history of the twenty-first century.* New York: Farrar, Straus, and Giroux.

Gudykunst, W. B. (1991). *Bridging differences: Effective intergroup communication.* Thousand Oaks, CA: Sage.

Helms, J. E. (1992). *A race is a nice thing to have.* Topeka, KS: Content Communications.

House, R. J., Hanges, P. J., Javidan, M., Dorfman, P. W., & Gupta, V. (Eds.). (2004). *Culture, leadership, and organizations: The GLOBE study of 62 societies*. Thousand Oaks, CA: Sage.

Johnson, A. G. (2006). *Privilege, power and difference* (2nd ed.). Boston: McGraw-Hill.

Nathan, R. (2005). *My freshman year: What a professor learned by becoming a student*. Ithaca, NY: Cornell University.

Sue, D. W. (2003). *Overcoming our racism: The journey to liberation*. San Francisco: Jossey-Bass.

Wood, J. T. (2004). *Interpersonal communication: Everyday encounters* (4th ed.). Belmont, CA: Wadsworth.

Video Resource

Adelman, L. (Executive Producer). (2003). *Race—The power of an illusion*. (Three-episode video). (Available from California Newsreel, Order Department, P.O. Box 2284, South Burlington, VT 05407).

6

Leading with Integrity
and Moral Purpose

I magine yourself in the following situations:

• You are a new participant in a residence hall programming committee. Your committee rents DVDs from one of the major distribution companies to show in the residence halls on a rotating basis during the semester. The committee's regular practice is to copy all of the DVDs that are used. When you ask about this practice, you are told, "Everyone does it." What do you do?

• You are in charge of the elections committee in your organization. Your by-laws note that all officers must have a minimum grade point average at the time they are elected. Candidates must sign a statement verifying that they have good enough grades to be eligible for office, but these statements are never checked or verified. Your best friend is running for office and has signed such a form. You know his GPA is lower than the required minimum. In the past, other candidates have signed such a form without having the necessary grades, and this by-law is considered a joke by the organization. What do you do?

• You are collecting money for a major campus philanthropy to support cancer research. The daughter of your physics professor is also participating in this project as a member of the philanthropy. You notice that she takes some cash to buy a case of beer at the end of a long day of soliciting donations. What do you do?

Too often, we find ourselves in ethical dilemmas like these, and our tendency is to either react quickly to resolve them or pretend we did not notice. However, avoidance leaves you troubled, and quick decisions preclude careful thought about all the aspects of the situation, which could raise questions of character and ethics if participants rush to decisions that are void of ethical considerations. Participants may get caught up in competition that causes them to focus only on the bottom line or on winning at all costs. They may feel the need to please others, without stopping to think about the implications of the decisions and their long-term effects. They may tend to shove problems under the rug to avoid tarnishing the organization's reputation or to avoid causing conflict in the group.

We need to learn to slow the process down and reflect on the ethical and moral aspects of actions and decisions. If you are used to resolving ethical dilemmas quickly, then it might be a challenge for you to stop, reflect on the situation, involve others in helping to address it, and weigh all possible alternatives of action. The key is to allow yourself and others some time to work through complex problems and engage in a process that includes reflection before action. Consider the inclusive, process, and empowering components of the Relational Leadership Model. By including group members in resolving ethical dilemmas, they will feel empowered. The process of engaging them can lead to more informed decisions and solutions.

Chapter Overview

In Chapter Three, we introduced the ethical component of the Relational Leadership Model, emphasizing the importance of ethics in the leadership process. In Chapter Four we explored essential elements of personal values and character, and Chapter Five covered concepts related to leading with integrity, such as understanding others, conflict resolution, and the cultural influences of leadership. This chapter includes (1) a discussion of the process of creating and sustaining ethical organizational environments, (2) an analysis of the moral dimensions of transforming leadership theory, and (3) an examination of the ethical influences that participants have on their organizations through behavior modeling. Practical applications of ethics and leadership are highlighted, using ethical decision-making models.

Creating and Sustaining an Ethical Organizational Environment

Understanding and applying ethical theories and models that operate from organizational values or codes of conduct, as well as being aware of your own moral development and that of others in your organizations, helps to create and sustain ethical organizational environments. Nash (1990) proposes four qualities that are necessary for participants to advance ethical standards in an organization:

1. Critical thinking skills to analyze and convey the ethical components of a problem or dilemma

2. A high degree of integrity to stand up for your personal and professional ethics

3. The ability to see situations from others' perspectives (showing concern for others)

4. Personal motivation to do the right thing

It is important, when using these ethical decision-making models and principles, that you be prepared to receive criticism, see members revolt, and perhaps experience a decline in membership. Not everyone in an organization has a moral orientation or is prepared or willing to do the right thing. Some would prefer to take the easy way out, do what is more economical, or take the path of least resistance. Nash's idea of having personal courage is of utmost importance when trying to make the right decision for the good of an organization in the face of opposition from the membership. Part of the leadership process is to fully explain to others the problem at hand and the basis for the action or decision.

These four qualities of leadership, when translated into behavior and action, help create an ethical organizational environment. When you identify a problem as having moral or ethical implications and involve others in the decision-making process, you provide another example of how an ethical environment is established. Several strategies and interventions can be used to create and maintain an ethical climate in a group or organizational setting. The process of doing so should be intentional and include all the elements of the Relational Leadership Model and the dimensions of knowing-being-doing.

All participants—positional leaders and members alike—should be equally empowered to set a tone in the organizational climate that will foster and support ethical and moral actions and sensitivities. The organization's mission or the group's common purpose should be the driving force for identifying its values. Participants should identify and operate from a shared set of core values that guide the organization's activities, actions, and decisions. These core values will enable individuals to work toward a common purpose and provide a common understanding of the organization's principles and standards. Members are empowered to hold each other accountable, participate in moral talk or dialogue, and work together to sustain an ethical environment. Appointing one person to be the group's ethicist or standard bearer will not achieve the same ethical climate as when all participants are concerned with doing what is right. In fact, it may be counterproductive for a leader to handle ethical dilemmas alone or in isolation from other members of the organization.

Contrast this with the organizational climate of Enron—a corporation whose detailed sixty-four-page code of ethics document was eventually sold on e-Bay with this one-word description: "Unopened" (Kidder, 2005, p. 203). In the early 2000s, the Enron board waived many of its ethics policies, including allowing Andrew Fastow, its chief financial officer, to work for Enron and another entity in what was clearly a conflict of interest for the company. After the collapse of Enron, the board noted that that exception should have been "a red flag the size of Alaska" (p. 203).

As the Enron case demonstrates, not all leadership is "good"— our learning about leadership can come from both positive and negative exemplars. Kellerman (2004) and Lipman-Blumen (2005) address the notion of bad or toxic leaders and their resulting negative consequences. Kellerman divides bad leadership into two categories: "bad as in ineffective and bad as in unethical" (p. 32). Her definition of ineffective leadership includes the failure to achieve a desired change, whereas "unethical leadership fails to distinguish between right and wrong" (p. 34). Someone can be an ineffective leader but be considered an ethical leader; although the goals were not accomplished, the person still led with integrity. Ideally, leaders and followers are effective *and* ethical as they work to achieve a shared vision or a common agenda.

Lipman-Blumen describes toxic leaders as those "who engage in numerous destructive behaviors and who exhibit certain dysfunctional personal characteristics. To count as toxic, these behaviors and qualities of character must inflict some reasonably serious and enduring harm on their followers and their organizations" (p. 18). In some cases, followers can bring nontoxic leaders into the toxic realm of behaviors or, at a minimum, they can support the actions of toxic leaders. Here are a few examples of behaviors and traits associated with toxic leaders:

- Leaving their followers worse off than they found them
- Violating the basic standards of human rights of their own supporters, as well as those of other individuals and groups they do not count among their followers

- Consciously feeding their followers illusions that enhance the leader's power and impair the followers' capacity to act independently (e.g., persuading followers that [the leader is] the only one who can save them or the organization)

- Playing to the basest fears and needs of the followers

- Misleading followers through deliberate untruths and misdiagnoses of issues and problems

- Insatiable ambition that prompts leaders to put their own sustained power, glory, and fortunes above their followers' well-being

- Enormous egos that blind leaders to the shortcomings of their own character and thus limit their capacity for self-renewal

- Reckless disregard for the costs of their actions to others as well as to themselves

- Cowardice that leads them to shrink from the difficult choices (pp. 19–22)

What is rewarded and recognized often teaches others about what is acceptable and unacceptable behavior within an organization. Creating awards and recognition for members who help sustain an ethical environment by taking risks to do the right thing is a powerful way to publicly acknowledge and promote ethical behavior.

On the other side of the award continuum, unethical behavior should be addressed, but in a different manner. Public humiliation was a practice commonly used in the past to confront and punish violators of the law or ethical standards. Some cultures continue this practice today. Participants have the shared responsibility of confronting individuals who violate the organization's standards and practices. Although we do not condone public humiliation as a motivational method, members need to know that they will be held accountable for such breaches. Participants have an obligation under the principle of "doing no harm" to protect an individual's right to confidentiality when addressing a violation of rules or standards and ensuring that due process is provided and safeguarded.

"I think being ethical is absolutely necessary when talking about leadership. You have to have some moral code from which your ideals come. If you act unethical in any way, you are hurting not only yourself but those who look up to you. In the 'real world,' not everyone operates in an ethical manner, but I truly believe that those who do end up being the winner in the long run."—Tim Slaughter was vice president of Leadership Development and a former member of the Student Senate at Texas A&M University.

Some organizations lack a positive ethical environment because leaders and participants are not committed to a moral orientation. These types of organizations may, in fact, reward unethical behavior because it is seen as "improving" the organization. An example of this would be an organization that uses unethical practices during membership recruitment to increase its membership. This type of organizational environment would support shortcuts, poor-quality work, cover-ups, and a lack of personal responsibility for mistakes or problems.

A 2003 Gallup Poll on moral values in the United States showed that only 22% of Americans believe moral values in this country are "excellent" or "good" and 77% describe them as "poor" or "fair" (Gallup Poll Social Series, 2003, p. 6). When respondents were asked if moral values in this country were getting better or getting worse, 67% commented that they were getting worse (p. 7). These indicators point to the growing number of Americans who believe that the moral climate in the United States is deteriorating. In a survey conducted by the Ethics Resource Center in 2005, over

50% of American workers observed unethical conduct in their workplace (Ethics Resource Center, 2005).

We witness or learn of hundreds of examples of leaders who lack personal courage or a moral orientation in their dealings with people, money, laws, policies, and other matters. They set a climate in their organizations that rewards unscrupulous behavior. We read of their actions in the newspaper and say, "What were they thinking?!" These examples contribute to a sense of deteriorating moral values in society. A frequent outcome of these breaches is what Rushmore Kidder (1995) calls "CEMs"—career-ending moves (p. 38). Engaging in morally questionable or unethical behavior often results in CEMs. Martha Stewart, CEO of Omni Living, severely damaged her company over the cover-up of an insider trading scheme and received a federal prison sentence. The late Ken Lay, former CEO of Enron, duped shareholders and others and destroyed his company; just before his sudden death in July 2006, he had been convicted of conspiracy and fraud and faced a maximum sentence of 45 years in prison on those charges and 120 years in a separate case. Lobbyist Jack Abramoff received $82 million from Indian tribes he represented, funneling the money to political leaders, including Congressman Tom DeLay. Benjamin Ladner, the president of American University, was forced to resign for spending more than $500,000 of University funds on questionable expenses such as a lavish engagement party for his son. These examples of ethical lapses produced career-ending moves for each of these leaders. Although Martha Stewart has made a comeback since she was released from prison, her image and reputation were tarnished.

"Integrity is connected with respect. Without integrity, you cannot gain the respect of your fellow members and without that respect, organizational goals are not attained. The integrity of leaders also reflects the integrity of the organization and it members. Because the leaders are the most visible people in the organizations, their actions and values reflect on all of those who are involved."—Melissa Schlotterer, an accounting major at Kent State University, is president of Students of Scholarship and a member of Beta Alpha Psi Accounting Honorary.

Individuals committed to leading with integrity face their own dilemma of what to do when their values and principles clash with the organization's standards. This is a very difficult situation and offers only three choices: (1) ignore or put up with the situation, (2) address the situation and work to change the organizational climate into one that is ethical in nature, or (3) leave the organization. Leaders struggle with such decisions every day. Kidder (2005) describes ethical fitness as "getting in shape to tackle the tough ethical dilemmas as they arise. That same fitness applies to our ability to express moral courage" (p. 157). Being ethically fit means being mentally engaged—thinking about the dilemma you are facing, reasoning through it, and grappling with the tough issues. All of this requires practice—thinking through potential ethical dilemmas so you are used to this process when faced with a real dilemma. This is one way to prepare for the ethical fitness test.

Moral Purpose as an Act of Courage

It takes personal courage to do the right thing. Sherron Watkins, a former executive of Enron, displayed personal courage when she exposed breaches of conduct by her boss Ken Lay. In doing so, Watkins risked losing her high-level, high-paying job. She showed both personal courage and integrity in taking a stand against the unethical practices of Enron. In an interview, Watkins described her efforts as "symbolizing that individual actions matter and that you have to take ownership for your actions when you are in a position of leadership" (Lucas & Koerwer, 2004, p. 44). Gregg Levoy (2000), former reporter for the *Cincinnati Enquirer*, uses the metaphor of stone sculpting to illustrate integrity and personal courage: "To tell if a stone is 'true,' you bang on it with a hammer. A dull tone indicates a fault; the stone will crack when you work on it. But a clear ring, one that hangs in the air, means the stone is true. It has integrity. It will hold up under repeated blows" (p. 22).

More in-depth examination is needed of leaders and participants who are ethical in their dealings and who model good leadership—leadership that is moral, courageous, and responsible. Usually, we start searching for ethical leaders who were national or historical figures. But we know leaders like that in our everyday lives—local business leaders, faculty and administrators, religious leaders from the local community, committed citizens of a neighborhood organization, your peers, family members, and nonprofit leaders who often work quietly and with humility to serve others.

Kidder (2005) describes moral courage as "the quality of mind and spirit that enables one to face up to ethical challenges firmly and confidently, without flinching or retreating" (p. 72). Moral courage can be viewed as the intersection of three conceptual fields: principles, danger, and endurance (Kidder). It took moral courage for Nelson Mandela to be imprisoned for 18 years for his opposition to apartheid in South Africa. Having an awareness of danger is key in possessing moral courage. A willingness to endure some type of hardship, such as risking losing friends or a job, is a component of moral courage. The opposite would be doing or saying nothing or turning away when faced with ethical dilemmas. Upholding one's principles and putting them into action allows leaders to operate with moral courage.

Assumptions About Ethical Leadership

There are many myths and misunderstandings about "good" leadership—leadership that is both ethical and effective (Ciulla, 1995). Lucas and Anello (1995) propose eight assumptions about ethical leadership, which are central themes in the study and practice of ethical leadership:

★ 1. *Ethics is the heart of leadership.* It is the central issue in leadership (Ciulla, 1995). You cannot have a complete discussion about leadership without including the ethical components associated with leadership processes. "Good leadership" means leadership that is effective, in that goals were achieved, and that follows a sound and ethical process. The means do justify the ends when leading with integrity.

★ 2. *All leadership is values-driven.* We need to reframe leadership so that it represents values that reflect good (ethical) leadership. Participants and leaders bring to the organization their own values and beliefs about how people should be treated, notions of what is right versus what is wrong, and ideas about what is just and fair. Organizations and communities are values-driven as opposed to values-neutral.

★ 3. *Personal values intersect with organizational values.* The journey to ethical leadership begins with an examination of personal values, as well as ongoing reflection of personal core values and how these values are related to the values of an organization or community. Your personal moral compass will guide you in wrestling with ethical dilemmas and eventually will point you in the direction of making a decision based on ethical analysis, consideration of opposing viewpoints, your personal values, and the values of your organization.

★ 4. *Ethical leadership can be learned.* Ethical learning is a process involving experience, reflection, conceptualization, and application. Trial-and-error experiences can sharpen your ethical analysis as well as your reflection about notions of what is just and fair in a given situation. You can learn this before you must act or make a decision. The life experiences you gain over time will affect your development as an ethical leader.

★ 5. *Ethical leadership involves a connection between ethical thought and action.* Linking moral reasoning with values and action is imperative in leadership. The point of this chapter is not to have you memorize dozens of ethical theories. The goal is to engage you in ethical analysis and insights based on theories and concepts applied to real-life experiences.

 6. *Character development is an essential ingredient of ethical leadership.* A leader's character is defined by his or her actions and behaviors, not simply by the values that are espoused. Leaders can be popular yet not be respected by the public because they lack congruency between their values and actions. In other words, they don't walk their talk.

7. *Ethical leadership is a shared process.* Members at all levels of an organization or community have the opportunity and responsibility to participate in the process of exercising ethical leadership. Ethical leadership is a shared process, not just the responsibility of a positional leader. Leaders and participants share the responsibility of advancing core organizational values and of doing the right thing. Members often are called upon to be courageous and to advocate for what is right, despite risks such as losing a job or alienating friends. Organizations that are empowering and inclusive involve members in wrestling with ethical dilemmas and seek their advice on how to resolve problems.

8. *Everything we do teaches.* Role modeling is a powerful way to influence the ethical climate in families, organizations, and communities. We learn by watching others, and we make judgments about what is acceptable and unacceptable behavior in organizations. If any member (including the positional leader) routinely discriminates against other students in a membership recruitment process, then others in the organization might believe it is acceptable to exclude students of color in extending invitations to join the group. Conversely, if a leader values diversity and decides to increase the number of minorities on her senior staff by 50%, then other managers of the company will most likely follow her strategy.

Leading with moral purpose calls for an examination of your assumptions about what is ethical and what is unethical, what is good leadership versus bad leadership, what are toxic behaviors versus nontoxic behaviors and traits, how far you are willing to go to advance your core values and do the right thing, what you are willing to risk to achieve the values of justice and fairness, and how you will wrestle with an inconsistency between your values and the values of your organization. The goal is not to discover easy answers or quick fixes to these issues but to engage in an ethical analysis and to use your moral imagination in solving problems and dilemmas.

"Some of the values that I try to live by are respect and responsibility. When it comes to respect, I believe that you should respect everyone no matter what. Our wants or needs are no more important than anyone else's. Also responsibility is a major ethical value that I live by. I take seriously everything that I get involved with. I put my heart into it all and I take responsibility for everything that comes my way. One of the sayings that I have grown up with is that you must walk your talk. If you're going to say you're going to do it, then you better take action and do it. I think it is very important to stick and live by your ethical values. An active leader has to have a clear message about his or her ethical views and use these to lead others. With this view of what they plan on striving for, their true leadership will shine."—Joanna Caldarulo is a member of Delta Delta Delta Sorority and a peer mentor for the freshman class at the University of Tennessee.

Cultural Assumptions

Ethics exist in a cultural context; they are culturally bound or culture-specific. There is no universal agreement on what behaviors or practices are considered appropriate, legal, ethical, or moral across cultures (Henderson, 1992; Toffler, 1986). For example, the intentional oppression of and discrimination against women in Saudi Arabia is considered ethical, legal, and moral in that country but unethical, illegal, and immoral in the United States. Ethics are also temporal in nature, especially in light of changing laws and legal norms. What was considered by many to be an ethical and legal standard practice until the 1960s—having separate water fountains and other facilities for Blacks and Whites—is considered illegal, unethical, and immoral today. Laws and regulations influence the changing nature of ethical practices and behaviors, especially in the business world.

Some might argue that there are universal moral values (Kidder, 2005). Kanungo and Mendonca (1996) assert that "morally good acts are based on moral laws that are universal because they incorporate fundamental values such as truth, goodness, beauty, courage, and justice. These values are found in all cultures, although cultures may differ with regard to the application of these values" (p. 35). From interviews with twenty-four leaders from sixteen different countries, Kidder (2005) identified eight common values among them: love, truthfulness, fairness, freedom, unity, tolerance, responsibility, and respect for life (pp. 43–44). Seligman (2002) identified six virtues common to more than two hundred religious and philosophical traditions: wisdom and knowledge, courage, love and humanity, justice, temperance, and spirituality and transcendence (p. 133). Although different cultures may provide varying definitions of these virtues, the basic ideals of these virtues are similar from culture to culture.

Anthropological studies have documented divergent moral views and practices interculturally and intraculturally (De George, 1986). Notions of right and wrong or justice and injustice are validated by the values and attitudes of a given culture (Donaldson, 1989). To place worth on moral concepts through intercultural comparison is futile. For example, many American women believe the veil worn by Muslim women constitutes sexist behavior and practice. What is socially practiced and acceptable in one culture may be repudiated in another. This brings up the painful or perhaps sobering reality that there is no moral consensus in international affairs. Ethics and morals differ not only among various countries, but among individuals in the same country.

Cultural tolerance implies that differences in practices are recognized, but not for the purpose of imposing or changing the practices to suit a particular cultural belief (Donaldson, 1989). Cultural relativism is germane to a specific culture, society, or community. The goal in comparing cultural practices is to understand them, not to judge them as good or bad. For example, leaders of multinational business organizations must follow the local laws, norms, mores, and practices associated with the country in which they are conducting business.

Corruption is a culturally constructed behavior, with varying degrees of tolerance and therefore varying frequencies of occurrence across countries. The Corruption Perceptions 2001 Index, published by the world's leading nongovernmental organizations fighting corruption, ranks ninety-one countries on a scale from 1 to 10, with 10 being a clean score. The index is a poll of polls, reflecting the perceptions of business people and country analysts. Examples of corruption include parents bribing underpaid teachers to receive educational benefits for their children or large amounts of public funds wasted or stolen by public officials. Out of the 91 countries, 56 scored 5.0 or below (Amarl, 2001, p. 6). Countries that received a score of 2 or less were Azerbaijan, Bolivia, Cameroon, Kenya, Indonesia, Uganda, Nigeria, and Bangladesh (p. 7). Finland was the least corrupt country, with a score of 9.9, followed by Denmark, with a 9.5 score. The United States received a score of 7.6. This same ranking was conducted in 2003 with 146 countries (*Transparency International Annual Report*, 2004). Sixty countries scored less than 3; the five countries with the lowest scores were Slovakia, Brazil, Belize, Colombia, and Cuba.

In 2003, Transparency International partnered with Gallup International to conduct a public opinion survey called the Global Corruption Barometer. The Global Corruption Barometer assessed people's perceptions, experiences, and attitudes toward corruption (*Transparency International*, 2004). When people were asked to rate which sectors in their respective countries were affected by corruption, their responses showed that political parties were perceived to be the most affected, followed by parliament or legislature, the police, and the legal system or judiciary (p. 11).

Many of these ethical assumptions emanate from various leadership and ethical theories and models. The following section provides an overview of ethical theories and foundations in leadership.

Ethical Theories and Moral Purposes

The study of human behavior as it relates to ethics and ethical development reaches back to the philosopher kings (Aristotle, Plato, Socrates), as well as to eighteenth- and nineteenth-century philosophers and scholars such as Immanuel Kant and John Stuart Mill. Ethical theories provide a glimpse into how human judgments are made and the thought processes individuals engage in to solve ethical dilemmas and other problems. In the next section, transforming leadership theory is described as the foremost theory that incorporates a moral component as its foundation for leadership.

Transforming Leadership Theory

The leadership theory that includes a strong component of ethics and morals is James MacGregor Burns's transforming leadership theory. As noted in Chapter Two, transforming leadership is a process in which "leaders and followers raise one another to higher levels of morality and motivation" (Burns, 1978, p. 20). Transforming leadership reaches moral dimensions when the leaders' and participants' behavior and ethical aspirations are elevated by mutual influences on one another (Burns). Transforming leadership involves persuasion, a desire to change something, and multidirectional influence relationships between leaders and participants (Rost, 1991). In any leadership situation, participants can, and often do, influence leaders to higher ethical ends.

Values or ideals such as peace, justice, fairness, liberty, equal opportunity, and people's general welfare are expressed by transformational leaders. Burns labeled these ideals as "end values" (p. 43). Leaders, superiors, participants, peers, followers, and others influence these values through specific behaviors. "The leader's fundamental act is to induce people to be aware or conscious of what they feel—to feel their true needs so strongly, to define their values so meaningfully, that they can move to purposeful action" (p. 44).

Transforming leadership theory is about the relationship and influence between leaders and followers. Burns (1978) describes this symbiotic relationship as an interaction of power and shared values. "It is the power of a person to become a leader, armed with principles and rising above self-interest narrowly conceived that invests that person with power and may ultimately transform both leaders and followers into persons who jointly adhere to modal values and end-values" (p. 457). The moral purposes of both leaders and participants are the key factors in the transforming leadership process. Change results from these shared moral purposes.

"Some of the core ethical values by which I live and lead are to be honest, to be fair, and to be kind. Honesty is always important. If people cannot trust you, they will not respect you. It is a challenge to be a leader that people do not respect. Fairness is also important. If you treat everyone you come into contact [with] in the same way, you will rarely face interpersonal problems in your organizations or groups. This also illustrates to people with whom you are working that you believe in them just as much as anyone else, that you respect them as a person, and that you value their contribution to the group. Kindness is a third value by which I live and lead. While it is important to be firm, it is also important to 'lead with heart.' Most people will be more invested in the organization or group if they know the people in that group care about them and what is going on in their lives. By

Of the seven characteristics Tichy and Devanna (1986) use to
characterize transforming leaders, two relate to ethical and moral
dimensions of leadership: courageous and value-driven. Transforming leaders have the courage to "confront reality even if it is painful"
(p. 30) and have healthy egos to withstand peer pressure. Possessing positive self-esteem (not needing to please others to win their
favor) is a necessary element of leading with moral purpose. This
contrasts with leading to win a popularity contest (needing to be
liked by others). For example, the president of the Senior Council
decided to follow her school's alcohol policy and not permit members to take cases of beer on the spring break trip, despite the fact
that the membership had unanimously voted to take alcohol on the
trip. In this case, the president decided to do what was right despite
popular sentiment and knowing that most people would be upset
with her decision.

Transformational leaders also are value-driven. They have a core
set of values that are consistent with their actions. There are several ways in which a leader can inspire others to higher levels of
morality—through influence and through modeling behaviors that
become the standards for others to follow.

Modeling a Moral Purpose

If participants admire or identify with another member or leader,
they will be more likely to imitate that person's behavior. Social
learning theory provides a framework for understanding how indi-

viduals learn from others (Sims & Lorenzi, 1992). Bandura (1977), the pioneer of social learning theory, postulated that people can learn indirectly from observation or by vicarious learning (Bandura, 1977; Manz & Sims, 1981; Rosenthal & Zimmerman, 1978; Sims & Manz, 1981). Observational learning has its history in the practices of ancient Greeks, who referred to this concept as imitation or mimesis. Greek scholars selected the best models in Greco-Roman literature to teach their young students (Rosenthal & Zimmerman, 1978, p. 33). Behavioral modeling by leaders and participants offers a type of vicarious learning stimulus in organizational settings.

"I handle ethical dilemmas by examining the situation, weighing the pros and cons, and evaluating the situation against my personal ethics, morals, and values. I believe the most helpful thing in handling ethical dilemmas is to know yourself well. Know what your morals, values, and ethics are and gain some 'practice' in handling ethical dilemmas . . . that way you will have the courage to stand by what you believe in when ethical dilemmas occur."—Andrew Ho graduated from the University of Maryland with a degree in finance and received a citation in the College Park Scholars Public Leadership Program. He was involved in the Intervarsity Christian Fellowship organization on campus.

Models in organizations are capable of eliciting ethical or unethical behavior. Exemplars or models significantly influence the ethical decision making in organizations. For example, a student president of the Latino Student Union who wants everyone in the organization to feel empowered will practice sharing power and authority with leaders and members and will create opportunities for members to make meaningful contributions to the organization. Through observing the president, other organizational leaders empower committee chairs and members and involve them in the decision-making process.

Vicarious learning or behavioral modeling has important implications for the leadership process. Organizational and community members can learn ethical practices by observing those who model these practices in their leadership approaches. For example, members of the marching band who substituted a new activity for their traditional fundraiser—showing an X-rated movie—because such movies are degrading and offensive to women modeled social responsibility to other members of the campus community. They took a stand against that tradition and replaced it with another venue.

Another illustration of behavioral modeling by leaders occurs when a football coach benches the star player for violating an NCAA rule, even though the coach needs that player to clinch the final playoff game. Organizational and team members learn, by observing how a peer is treated, that negative consequences result from such behavior. Sims and Lorenzi (1992) refer to this phenomenon as "outcome expectation" (p. 143). Participants also might infer that the leader possesses a high degree of integrity and is motivated to do the right thing. The behavior of the leader, or the coach in the example, then influences team members to act ethically because that is what is reinforced or because they want to avoid punishment for unethical behavior—or both.

Participants also model behavior that inspires leaders' ethical awareness (Chaleff, 1995). For example, the members of a student-owned food co-op influenced the student-manager to use empathy in deciding whether to dismiss an employee who missed work three days in a row to care for his ill, elderly grandmother. The members asked the manager to consider the fact that the employee was putting himself through school and that he was the only relative who could care for his grandmother. They suggested that the manager revise the work schedule to allow the employee time to help his grandmother and still maintain some hours at the co-op. In this example, the members were modeling how empathy could be used by putting themselves in the employee's situation and realizing what the impact of dismissal would be.

Modeling also can have external effects that extend beyond organizational boundaries. Ben Cohen and Jerry Greenfield, of Ben & Jerry's Ice Cream, modeled a type of socially responsible behavior in the business world when they donated pretax profits to social programs. By doing this, Ben and Jerry attempted to model a moral standard for other business leaders to follow (Howell & Avolio, 1992). Since Ben and Jerry's initiative, many other companies have committed to socially responsible efforts. Examples include The Body Shop, Honeywell Inc., and Bell Atlantic Corp (Kurschner, 1996). The Dell computer company is known as a leader in its industry for its recycling initiatives; General Mills provides significant resources and services to initiatives focused on community development, women, and minorities. We also witness examples of corporate irresponsibility from companies like Wal-Mart that have a record of using discriminatory practices based on race and sex in hiring and promoting employees, or Nike and others whose goods are manufactured in sweatshops that employ child laborers in developing countries.

These examples, both positive and negative, illustrate that modeling by leaders and participants affects the ethical climate of organizations. Another form of modeling is when leaders or participants engage in discussions of ethical issues or bring up ethical dilemmas that can be resolved through an exchange of multiple perspectives.

Moral Talk

How often have you found yourself in an organizational meeting or in a classroom in which someone raises ethical or moral questions around a particular issue your group is working on? It is often hard to know how to approach a conversation about moral questions. Leaders and participants would benefit by engaging in conversations that allow people to explore the moral complexities and dimensions of problems or dilemmas. Bird and Waters (1989) provide an interesting notion of modeling or influencing ethical behavior through verbal exchanges or "moral talk" or "dialogic leadership" (Neilson, 1990, p. 765).

The dialogic leader initiates discussions with peers and members about what is ethical and what the material interests of individuals are. Dialogic leadership or moral talk can be used in student organizations as a way to model ethical approaches and to help create and sustain an ethical environment. For example, a student president of an honor society includes on the meeting agenda a discussion of the nature of the group's test files. A member speaks up at the meeting about her concern that a few of the exams in the files have been stolen. She then asks members if maintaining those files is the kind of activity the group should engage in, knowing that this is a violation of the college's honor code. A discussion ensues about whether or not the activity is counter to the organization's mission and the organization's values of academic excellence and integrity.

A real-life example of how a student government member used dialogic leadership to inspire leaders and members of the group to discuss values and ethics occurred when the student used the game of Scruples at a retreat. Although it appeared as if the members were just playing a game, in reality they were participating in conversations about how they would approach a series of dilemmas posed by questions on the cards. At the end of the game, the student government member asked others to reflect on what had just happened and how they, as a group of elected officials, should work together to confront complex issues back on campus.

Unfortunately, individuals often hesitate to participate in moral talk or discussions about ethical dilemmas (Bird & Waters, 1989). Although the topic of ethics is encountered by individual leaders and participants, little discourse about ethics takes place among group members. This lack of discussion about ethics is referred to as "moral muteness" (Bird & Waters, 1989). Reasons for this include avoidance of complex problems with moral overtones, protection of the positional leader's own managerial flexibility in solving problems, and avoidance of dealing with varying ideological or moralistic perspectives—all of which potentially inhibits the problem-solving process. Group members may also avoid discussion of ethics and morals due to their own ethical illiteracy. The potential harm caused by not modeling this through conversations or discussions is the neglect of moral abuses or an environment that is indifferent to moral considerations. It is the shared responsibility of members and leaders to initiate moral talk and to avoid moral muteness.

Moral expressions have the potential to arouse feelings of connection with moral action. For the modeling effect to occur, the language in moral talk has to be connected with experiences and expectations of people involved in the organization. Moral talk can be used as a type of modeling influence when the dialogue is used to identify problems, consider issues, advocate and criticize policies, and justify and explain decisions (Bird & Waters, 1989; Pocock, 1989). Leaders and participants can use moral talk to influence others to carefully consider their perspectives and positions on issues.

Ethical Decision-Making Models

The leadership process is filled with daily ethical dilemmas and problems that do not have readily identifiable solutions and that leaders and participants need to confront and resolve. It is not solely the responsibility of the leader to address these dilemmas or confront unethical behavior. The Relational Leadership Model, with its emphasis on inclusive and process-oriented leadership to achieve results for the common good, suggests that leaders and members both be included in addressing ethical dilemmas. Leaders and participants together need to be reflective, challenging, caring, purposeful, and consultative when working through ethical issues.

There are several approaches you can use to resolve ethical dilemmas. Some situations might call for using a professional code of conduct. For example, the professional conduct of lawyers and physicians is guided by standards upheld by their respective professional associations. Religious and counseling professionals are guided by a strict adherence to client confidentiality unless a client is a potential harm to self or others. Many campuses have sexual harassment and nondiscrimination policies that also guide behavior. Fraternities and sororities have rituals that serve as statements of organizational standards and values. Students may follow an honor code in classroom testing practices. Student governments are often bound to constitutions and by-laws that assist in decision-making processes related to funding and student organization recognition.

Like leadership, ethics is not a neat and tidy concept. Not all situations can be resolved by the application of professional codes or organizational standards (Beauchamp & Childress, 1979; Kitchener, 1984). It requires human judgment and analysis to even determine whether a situation represents an ethical dilemma or something else, like a personality conflict between two members.

Although one of several models could be used to guide ethical decision making, the following section includes models that can be used as practical tools in resolving ethical dilemmas. All of these models should be used by leaders and participants together to collaboratively work through problems. The models should be applied with careful analysis rather than with a rigid application of any particular model; reflection and a careful consideration of other factors are needed. These models call for the use of your moral imagination—visualizing new alternatives to old or unsolved problems. Otherwise, these frameworks cannot stand on their own.

Practical Applications

Imagine this scenario. You attend a college that has a strict academic honor code calling for community members to turn in anyone who violates the code. You are also the president of the

Interfraternity Council. During an exam, you notice a fraternity brother, who is also one of your best friends, cheating from another classmate. How do you go about confronting this situation? Do you follow the code and turn your fraternity brother in to the judicial office? Or do you try after the exam to persuade him not to cheat in the future because you will have to turn him in and it would look bad for your fraternity? Or do you begin to initiate a decision-making process that will guide you from the stage of interpreting the situation—if I respond in a certain way, how will it affect others?—to the final stage of acting with your convictions and moral purpose in mind? Or do you do nothing, acting without moral purpose?

Ethical decision-making models encourage people to work through dilemmas with a moral purpose in mind and provide frameworks with which to guide decision making and analysis. Rather than react quickly to dilemmas, you should carefully consider various steps, including ethical analysis, toward making sound decisions.

Kidder (1995) defines tough choices as "those that pit one 'right' value against another" (p. 16). "The really tough choices, then, do not center upon right versus wrong. They involve right versus right. They are genuine dilemmas precisely because each side of the problem is firmly rooted in one of our basic, core values" (p. 18). An ethical dilemma, then, is one of those right-versus-right situations in which two core moral values come into conflict—to distinguish such dilemmas from the right-versus-wrong issues that produce moral temptations. Kidder (2005) provides a framework for examining right-versus-right choices using a four-dilemma paradigm model:

1. Justice versus mercy: fairness and equity conflict with compassion, empathy, and love
2. Short term versus long term: immediate needs run counter to future goals
3. Individual versus community: self versus others or small group versus larger group

4. Truth versus loyalty: honesty competes with commitment, responsibility, or promise-keeping (pp. 18–23)

These dilemma paradigms represent values that collide with each other. The 2005 death of Terry Schiavo, who was kept on life support for nearly fifteen years after collapsing in her home and never regaining consciousness, represented a legal case in which the values of justice and mercy clashed. This dilemma raged into a public debate about the moral and legal rights of life and death. Another type of dilemma paradigm was present in the Elián Gonzalez case that began on Thanksgiving Day in 1999. Elián was a native Cuban boy whose mother attempted to bring him to the United States in a boat. She died at sea, but Elián survived. His relatives in Florida fought to keep him there against the wishes of his biological father, who was not the legal custodian of Elián since his parents had divorced. The values of justice and mercy, individual and community collided as this dilemma snowballed into political complications between Cuba and the United States.

An example of a truth-versus-loyalty dilemma occurred in April 1996 when David Kaczynski turned his brother, Theodore Kaczynski, in to the authorities because he suspected him of being the Unabomber—the man who plagued the country for more than two decades by sending bombs through the mail, killing or permanently harming several innocent victims. David Kaczynski is an example of a courageous individual who did what he believed was right and honest. He did so at the painful expense of knowing that his brother, if found guilty, would be given a severe sentence, perhaps even the death penalty. David Kaczynski acted with emotional agony because he wanted to believe that his brother was not the Unabomber. This incident illuminates the difficult human struggle that occurs when the values of truth and loyalty are in conflict or when the values of individual and community collide. The higher right value influenced David Kaczynski's action. Under this cir-

cumstance or a similar one, ask yourself, Would you turn one
siblings or your best friend in to the FBI if you thought he or she
was the Unabomber? Would you turn your father in to the police if
he robbed a bank? Or your mother, if she hit a pedestrian and fled
the scene of the accident? Which value would you choose and act
upon?

Kidder (1995) provides three principles for ethical decision-
making (pp. 24–25):

1. *Ends-based thinking*: Philosophers refer to this as utilitarian-
ism, best known by the maxim, *Do whatever produces the greatest good
for the greatest number*. Based on cost-benefit analysis, determining
who will be hurt and who helped. At the heart of this principle is
an assessment of consequences, a forecasting of outcomes.

2. *Rule-based thinking*: Kant's *"categorical imperative*: follow only
the principle that you want everyone else to follow." Ask yourself, "If everyone in the world followed this rule of action I am
following, would that create the greatest good or the greatest
worth of character?" Rule-based thinking is based firmly on
duty—what we ought to do rather than what we think might
work. This is deontological thinking, meaning based on moral
obligation.

3. *Care-based thinking*: putting love for others first. The Golden
Rule is an example of care-based thinking—*do to others what you
would have them to do to you*. Care-based thinking puts the feature
of "reversibility" into play: test your actions by putting yourself in
another's shoes and imagining how it would feel if you were the
recipient, rather than the perpetrator, of your actions.

These three principles can be applied in examining dilemmas as
you begin to work through their complexities and then decide the
right course of action. An effective approach is to use each of the
three principles before making a decision or taking an action. Kidder further provides nine checkpoints to use when faced with an
ethical dilemma.

Consider the following situation. You are the president of the college's Young Democrats or Young Republicans Club. Your group has discovered that an unflattering article about the club will be printed in the next day's campus newspaper. Club members begin planning a scheme to steal all the newspapers before students get them in the morning. Using the examples of ethical decision-making models, how would you approach this situation? What are the moral dimensions of this situation? Is it a violation of a constitutional right to freedom of the press, or a violation of the school's honor code? Would you convince members not to execute their plan because they might get caught and the club might lose its charter? Or would you threaten to turn them in if they proceed? Or would you urge them not to do this because it is wrong to steal these papers and an obstruction of the constitutional right of freedom of the press? If the group proceeds to steal the newspapers, would reporting them to the campus judicial office result in their expulsion from school and possibly prevent them from ever having the chance to complete their college degrees? If you did nothing, would you be modeling behavior to others that condones an illegal act? What should you do? What are all your alternative courses of action? How will your decision affect the ethical environment of your organization? What would you do if members actually stole the papers?

Ethical Principles and Standards

In the helping professions, several scholars have adapted Aristotle's ethical principles, which serve as the foundation for living an ethical life and as principles or standards to guide physicians, psychologists, and counselors in particular (Beauchamp & Childress, 1979; Kitchener, 1984). Beauchamp and Childress (1979) proposed five principles of biomedical ethics, which were later adapted by Karen Strohm Kitchener, a professor of education, for the counseling psychology field. These five ethical principles are (1) respecting autonomy, (2) doing no harm, (3) benefiting others, (4) being just, and (5) being faithful. As a leader or member, you can use these five principles, illustrated in Exhibit 6.1, as a critical evaluative approach to moral reasoning and ethical decision-making processes (Beauchamp & Childress, 1979). Using the critical evaluative approach allows leaders and members "to illuminate our ordinary moral judgment and to redefine the bases for our actions" (Kitchener, 1984, p. 45).

There are many applications of these five ethical principles in leadership and in organizational settings. Using these principles should help you determine the correct course of action and should have a bearing on how your decisions will affect others. Using the five principles, imagine that you are the chair of the homecoming committee and that the promotions subcommittee designed a homecoming T-shirt that you find to be offensive to ethnic groups. The committee spent $10,000 on the shirts, which are being sold by organizational members. The $10,000 must be replaced in the budget by the T-shirt sales. Which of the five principles would you use in working through this dilemma? Do any of the principles clash with one another, such as respecting the autonomy of the committee and doing no harm to others who might be hurt by the symbolism on the T-shirt?

Professional associations have codes of ethics that are standards used to guide professionals' decision making and actions. The Center for the Study of Ethics in the Professions has gathered over 850 codes of ethics for a wide range of professions including law, governments, engineering, the health care industry, sports, fraternal social organizations, and the media, to name a few (http://ethics.iit.edu/). There is a debate on the usefulness of professional codes of ethics, yet codes can protect professionals from pressures that could lead to questionable conduct. They are a unifying document of the common values and ethics associated with any given profession.

Exhibit 6.1. Five Ethical Principles in Decision Making.

Respecting Autonomy: providing leaders and members with freedom of choice, allowing individuals to freely develop their values, and respecting the right of others to act independently. Autonomy, like constitutional rights and liberties, has conditions and does not imply unrestricted freedom. A major assumption of autonomy is that an individual possesses a certain level of competence to make rational and informed decisions.

Doing No Harm or Nonmaleficence: providing an environment that is free from harm to others, both psychological and physical. Leaders and members refrain from "engaging in actions which risk harming others" (Kitchener, 1984, p. 47).

Benefiting Others or Beneficence: promoting the interests of the organization above personal interests and self-gain. The notion of promoting what is good for the whole of the organization or community and promoting the growth of the group is upheld in the principle of beneficence.

Being Just or Justice: treating people fairly and equally. This principle is traced to Aristotle's work on ethics.

Being Faithful or Fidelity: keeping promises, being faithful, and being loyal to the group or organization. Being faithful is a principle premised on relationships and trust. If you as a leader or member violate the principle of fidelity, it is difficult or impossible for others to develop a trusting relationship.

They can be used as a decision-making tool when confronted with professional dilemmas.

A quick and informal decision-making model, commonly referred to as the "newspaper test," can influence your actions and decisions. Consider this—before you act or decide, think about whether or not you would be comfortable with your actions or behaviors appearing in the newspaper. Will your decision pass the newspaper test?

These ethical decision-making models can help you reach a more informed and carefully analyzed decision before you take any action. Too often, we are tempted to quickly put out fires or react to pressing dilemmas without engaging in a process that would provide some assurance that the right decision was made. These models alone will not necessarily help you resolve every dilemma you encounter. They provide a framework to guide your decision making. They do not provide the moral imagination and creative thinking that are needed to address complex situations.

Chapter Summary

Leading with integrity is a complex process that includes the moral development of an individual, the influence of role models, values-driven leadership, and the organizational environment. The process of developing into an ethical participant and creating ethical environments does not occur overnight. Groups and organizations are made up of humans who can and do make mistakes, which is part of the learning process. Raising questions around ethical issues is a fundamental component of leading with integrity. People who lead with moral purpose often have as many questions as answers. Leading from the Relational Leadership Model means leading with moral purpose: empowering others to lead by example, including other participants in resolving ethical dilemmas, acting ethically to positively affect the public good, and using a process to approach problems that do not offer clear solutions.

Our society is calling for leaders and participants alike who can be trusted and who are committed to doing the right thing. Despite the turbulent and fast-paced nature of our world, leading with a moral purpose is central to the leadership process. Imagine what an organization, community, or the world would look like if everyone would strive to create and sustain an ethical environment by rewarding ethical acts, to engage in moral talk, and to carefully work, as a group, toward resolving dilemmas by using decision-making models?

What's Next?

The preceding chapters have shown how important the nature of relationships is in leadership and how complex it is to lead with moral purpose. In Part Three, you will learn about the complexities of teams, groups, organizations, and communities. Understanding yourself and others is a key component of leading with integrity. We challenge you to integrate this knowledge with the interdependent nature of working with others in various types of settings to facilitate positive change.

Chapter Activities

1. Think of a national, historical, or local person who you believe is an ethical leader. What skills, behaviors, attitudes, or characteristics does that person exhibit? Now think of a national, historical, or local person you believe is an unethical leader—a person who practices bad or toxic leadership. What skills, behaviors, attitudes, or characteristics does that person exhibit? How have both leaders' behaviors influenced or impacted followers or others in the organization?

2. Think of a person who has served as a role model to you. Why did you choose that person? What skills, behaviors, attitudes, or characteristics does that person exhibit?

3. How can or do you serve as a role model to others in your group or community?

4. How would you approach someone in your group or community who is behaving unethically or violating the group's standards?

5. Think of an ethical dilemma you have faced or somehow were involved with. Work through that dilemma using one of the three ethical decision-making models. How would you initiate moral talk with others in your group?

6. Think of a time when you or someone else served as a transforming leader. What was that experience like? How did the leader and members inspire each other to higher levels of morality?

7. Think about an organization in which you are currently a member and answer the following questions. How would you describe the ethical climate in this organization? What does the organization do to encourage members to do what is right?

8. What does the organization do that may encourage inappropriate behavior? What happens when someone violates the ethical standards of the organization? How could the organization become more supportive of ethical behavior? List the ways you could reward ethical behavior in your organization. Develop an action plan to put these ideas into place.

9. List the ways you could reward ethical behavior in your organization, residence hall, place of employment, and so forth. Develop an action plan to put these ideas into place.

Additional Readings

Chaleff, I. (1995). *The courageous follower: Standing up to and for our leaders*. San Francisco: Berrett-Koehler.

Ciulla, J. B. (1995). Leadership ethics: Mapping the territory. *Business Ethics Quarterly, 5*, 5–28.

Kellerman, B. (2004). *Bad leadership*. Cambridge, MA: Harvard Business School Press.

Kidder, R. M. (1995). *How good people make tough choices: Resolving the dilemmas of ethical living*. New York: Fireside.

Kidder, R. M. (2005). *Moral courage: Taking action when your values are put to the test*. New York: William Morrow.

Lipman-Blumen, J. (2005). *The allure of toxic leaders*. Oxford: Oxford University Press.

Transparency International 2004 Annual Report (pp. 1–24). Retrieved February 8, 2006, from http://www.transparency.org/publications/annual_report

Initiate Excitement
Focus attention

share

Part III

Context for the Practice of Leadership

Any leadership setting can be viewed as a community of people working together for shared purposes. Relational leadership is best practiced by framing any kind of group or organization as a community.

In the *Tao of Leadership*, Heider (1985) interprets,

> *The leader who understands how process unfolds uses as little force as possible and runs the group without pressuring people.*
>
> *When force is used, conflict and argument follow. The group field degenerates. The climate is hostile, neither open nor nourishing.*
>
> *The wise leader runs the group without fighting to have things a certain way. The leader's touch is light. The leader neither defends nor attacks.*
>
> *Remember that consciousness, not selfishness, is both the means of teaching and the teaching itself.*
>
> *Group members will challenge the ego of one who leads egocentrically. But one who leads selflessly and harmoniously will grow and endure. (p. 59)*

This part explores how groups develop through stages, how they can be enhanced by attention to process, and how they can become building blocks for complex systems and organizations. Leadership in groups and committees is substantially different from the complexity of leadership in organizational systems (for example, a college, a company, a hospital, a church).

Groups and organizations are best understood as communities of people working together to accomplish their shared purposes. Viewing all contexts in which leadership happens helps identify the important interdependence of people working together. The section ends with a chapter on the importance of organizations being self-renewing entities, able to stay adaptable, nimble, and developmental for their members.

7

Interacting in Teams and Groups

Your university is celebrating its one-hundredth anniversary and your student organization, the chemistry club, was asked to sponsor an activity or program as part of the celebration. Your group decided to put a planning team together with ten members. Juan volunteered to be the team leader and began calling meetings. When the group met for the first few times, members brainstormed ideas like conducting a fundraiser to buy a bench to place at the entrance of the student union or putting on a concert open to the campus and local community. With the anniversary celebration one month away, the group decided to put on a concert.

At the following meeting, Juan told the team members that their organization did not have the funds to do this. Members were disappointed and confused about their role in planning this event. A few questioned the purpose of hosting this anniversary activity when their mission was to sponsor educational outreach and peer tutoring to chemistry majors. Juan tried to facilitate another brainstorming activity, but the group members got frustrated and started to leave. At the following meeting, now two weeks before the celebration, only three members showed up, and there was great concern about not having an event identified and not knowing what resources they had to carry out their task.

What are some of the reasons why this team failed?

Chapter Overview

This chapter explores the characteristics of groups, the way groups develop, and the dynamics among group members in order to emphasize how leadership in groups is process-oriented. The chapter presents concepts of teamwork and collaboration in group work and applications of the Relational Leadership Model.

Understanding Groups

In an average week, you experience many types of groups. Some of these are highly structured, with clear roles and processes. Examples are a class or a student government senate meeting. Other groups are loosely structured and informal, like a discussion at a dining hall table or a pick-up softball game. However, the kind of group that is pertinent to this discussion of leadership is not just any gathering of people. For our purposes, a group is considered to be three or more people "interacting and communicating interpersonally over time in order to reach a goal" (Cathcart, Samovar, & Henman, 1996, p. 1).

There are many different dimensions to how groups are structured, and each has implications for the leadership dynamics in that group. Three key dimensions that help us understand different types of groups are purposes, structure, and time.

1. *Purposes:* Groups exist for very different purposes; they range from friendship support groups to highly focused task groups to groups like a staff that delivers a service or a product over time. The architectural maxim that form follows function applies to groups as well. The purpose of a group should lead to the structures and processes needed to help the people in the group accomplish their purposes.

2. *Structure:* Structure relates to the mechanisms for how the people in the group relate to each other. Some groups are highly structured, with hierarchical roles or positions; others are undefined

and evolve. Leadership roles in groups range from leaderless groups in which a group of people get together to do something but no one is the formal leader, to highly structured groups with a person in position as the formal leader—the president, chairperson, or director. In the informal setting, participants share needed roles, and leadership emerges or is all around in the group. In the formal, structured setting, the positional leader may be accountable but may use diverse styles ranging from highly autocratic (making all the decisions and directing or controlling the followers) to engaging group members and empowering them through the relational leadership elements presented in this book. Even in hierarchical organizations, there are informal leaders who influence the group or decision-making processes because of their seniority, their past stature in the organization, or their personalities. In campus student organizations, seniors who have been in the group for three or four years might exhibit this type of influence without holding a formal position.

3. *Time:* Groups exist over varying lengths of time. The group may be time-limited (meeting once to discuss a specific issue or completing a task in three meetings), or it may meet for a specified amount of extended time. Members may have a specified term of appointment, as would a representative from your major to the student senate for a year or in a class for a semester. The group may be an ongoing group (like staff members at work, your family, or a fraternity). Time-limited groups are often called a *task force* or *ad hoc committee*. Ongoing groups use such names as *committee*, *board*, or *council*. The duration of the group raises different challenges. Time-limited groups with a short time frame must quickly establish rapport and common purposes and engage members to be active and focused on their role. Ongoing groups must deal with member motivation over time, establish processes to welcome and bring new members into the group, and keep the group focused on its purposes.

Think for a minute about the groups you are involved with. What are the purposes for which the groups were created? What structures help them accomplish those purposes? What roles do group members assume? How do these groups vary in time commitment? How does the length of time change the dynamics of the relationships? Those groups clearly develop differently. One challenge to leadership is to attend to the process of group development in order to facilitate the most involvement of the most members in the most effective way to make the best decisions.

Group Development

Robert is visiting his friend Sean before spring break and attends a meeting of Sean's Business Entrepreneurs Club. Sean is a cofounder of this group. Robert is puzzled at what he sees. The group argues for most of the meeting about whether they should (1) engage in designing a logo for boxer shorts to sell and use the profits for a group party or (2) design a T-shirt to raise money as a service for a local youth recreation league. There are two loud factions, with several people competing for attention and trying to be seen as leaders. Robert is puzzled by this and realizes that the group has some problems.

It would help Robert to realize that most groups, whether formal or informal, go through fairly predictable stages of development as a group. One classic model labels these group development stages *forming, storming, norming,* and *performing* (Tuckman, 1965). If the group can handle the important issues at each stage, it can stay vibrant and healthy. If the group is struggling, it can revisit a stage to intentionally relearn together how to be effective. Sean's group is struggling with the storming process, which is characterized by differing opinions and goals.

Forming

Forming is the group's initial stage of coming together, which includes such tasks as member recruitment and affiliation. What information do people need? When will the group meet? How will the group communicate? What protocol needs to be put in place for the response time to members' e-mails? What will the type of commitment mean? What are the purposes and mission of the group? What agreement is needed to make this group functional? The forming stage of development is when team building initially occurs and trust is established. Successful strategies of this forming stage include building open, trusting relationships that value inclusion.

Storming

Storming is the stage in which the group starts to get in gear and differences of opinion begin to emerge. If the group is not clear about its purposes and goals, or if the group cannot agree on shared goals, then it may collapse at this stage. Members of Sean's Business Entrepreneurs Club have vastly different expectations of what the group should do: service or profit or both. They need to revisit some of the processes of the forming stage and resolve that issue so they can deal with the decisions of what projects to select. In this stage, individuals engage in self-assertion to get their needs recognized and addressed.

Storming can be a short process, in which the group comes to pretty clear direction, or it can be destructive. Some groups establish such trust in each other and in their process that the storming process is resolved quickly. Indeed, some members who feel like storming may never raise their issues because they are strongly connected to shared purpose and know their assertions would not be useful. Some groups exist in this storming phase and develop adversarial models of operating. They may depend on it so much that it becomes the way of getting their work done. The two-party political system and the check-and-balance processes of government are examples. Other groups have become accustomed to adversarial processes but would do better to develop more effective ways of relating. Examples include the constant conflict on some campuses among faculty and administrators or between the Greek and independent leaders in the student senate.

Norming

Norming follows storming. Once the group resolves key differences, it establishes patterns of how it gets work done. The group sets up formal or informal procedures for which things come to the whole group, which reports are needed, who is involved in what, and how people interact. At this stage, individuals in the group deal with both intimacy and identity. Members of the group begin to understand the group's culture. For example, do meetings always start ten minutes late so people can visit with each other for a few minutes first? Do members understand whether they should volunteer for new projects or wait to be invited? The group practices that evolve in the norming stage are often more obvious to outsiders than to those in the group. These practices and characteristics might also describe the personality of the group.

Performing

Performing is the fourth stage of group development. Built on the strong foundation of the previous three stages, the group now cycles into a mature "stage of equilibrium"—getting its work done (Lippitt, 1973, p. 229). Time-limited groups may need to quickly get to the performing stage to get their work done in a timely way. They need to intentionally and effectively work through the previous stages and not skip right to performing without the foundational processes. Time-limited groups still need the team-building steps so essential in the forming stage; in the storming stage they need to encourage diversity of opinion and wrestle with common purpose, and in the norming stage they must clearly establish group processes to effectively perform their task. Ongoing groups with a longtime duration will have to stay renewed (see Chapter Ten) and continually recycle to be effective. Otherwise, they risk becoming dysfunctional or even terminating. Even the most successful groups have to revisit this cycle when new members join (forming), when new issues challenge the group's purposes (storming), or when new processes are needed because old ones no longer work (norming).

Exhibit 7.1. Relational Leadership and Stages of Group Development.

When the group is . . .	Relational leadership philosophy would encourage participants to . . .
Forming	Be inclusive and empowering. Make sure all the shareholders and stakeholders are involved. Seek diverse members to bring talent to the group. Model the processes of inclusion and shared leadership. Identify common purposes and targets of change.
Storming	Create a climate in which each person matters and build commitment to the group as a community of practice. Be ethical and open. Be patient, to give divergent views a full hearing. Be aware when you may be biased or blocking the full participation of another. Handle conflict directly and openly, encouraging participants to identify their biases. Revisit the purposes of the group and targets of change.
Norming	Be fair with processes. Practice collaboration. Keep new members welcomed, informed, and involved. Clarify the individual's responsibility to and expectations of the group and the group's responsibilities to and expectations of individuals.
Performing	Celebrate accomplishments and find renewal in relationships. Empower members to learn new skills and share roles in new ways to stay fresh. Revisit purposes and rebuild commitment.

Exhibit 7.1 illustrates the aspects of the Relational Leadership Model that might help the group successfully deal with each stage of its development (Tuckman & Jensen, 1977).

Adjourning

The fifth stage, adjourning, is the final stage of group development. Tuckman and Jensen (1977) amended their stage model to accommodate the closure stages that groups experience. Groups exist over different time frames. All short-term groups, like task forces or ad hoc committees, need to plan on their eventual termination. This is a difficult stage for groups to enter because it marks a period of closure and finality (Smith, 2005). Some members experience a sense of loss at this stage. The adjourning stage should include a celebration and recognition of the group's accomplishments as well as a reflection on the lessons learned about what was effective and what was ineffective. Groups that have experienced longevity also can face the adjourning stage if their mission or purpose becomes irrelevant. In this case, the sense of loss is heightened, and some might experience anger about the organization's closure. Even so, it is important for the group to go through the adjourning stage as a learning experience and as a time to acknowledge the members' contributions.

Groups that do not engage in a continual revisiting of the cycle to stay active and vital may find themselves moving toward this final stage of group development. If a group does not maintain new members or keep up with current issues and needs, it may find itself unable to perform and may need to dissolve. It may be necessary for a new group to be formed, with new purposes and new members. Groups that intend to exist for a long time, often with no planned end in sight, need to stay vibrant and healthy if they are to continue effectively.

We visited a campus where the former Black Student Union (BSU) took the bold step of voting itself out of existence. Its programs had developed into social events with dwindling attendance. Most members felt that they could do social events through other avenues and that this group needed a broader scope. The circumstances on campus led many of the African American student leaders to think they needed a group with a more active educational and campus advocacy role. The key members decided to involve other non-Black student leaders in a planning session and formed a new group named Umoja—a Swahili word for unity. They sought a more diverse membership around their new purposes and were widely credited on that campus for strong programs and events that attracted a wide range of participants and benefited the whole campus. Although it would have been perfectly fine for this BSU to evolve into a social organization, it was not the intent of the leaders or members that the focus be social, so they boldly reorganized to accomplish social action and campus change around racial and ethnic unity. This was indeed a strong and courageous action; few groups would vote themselves out of existence or go through such a transformation, yet many groups need to do so.

Active participants need to continually assess their group's development. We have a colleague who encourages group members always to ask, "Should we, could we, are we?" "Should we?" leads a group to clarify their purposes and direction. "Could we?" asks the group to anticipate the storming and norming stages to see if they are up to the task. "Are we?" is the constant formative evaluation cycle in the performing stage to see if the group is truly doing what it sets out to do. Evaluation is both formative and summative. Formative evaluation—Are we?—is asked at various times for the purpose of reshaping plans and directions. Summative evaluation might ask, Did we? at the end of a task or event to see if it met original plans. When the cook tastes the soup, it is formative evaluation. But when the customer tastes the soup, it is a summative evaluation.

Dynamics in Groups

Groups engage in various processes that are often called group dynamics. Group dynamics is the study of the group's life (Johnson & Johnson, 1994). Group dynamics include such processes as how the group makes decisions, how the group handles its conflict, and how the group meets its leadership needs.

Group Roles

One of the foundations for understanding group dynamics is to recognize that in any interactive setting, individuals engage in communication patterns that may signal roles they are adopting in the group. Groups depend on two kinds of roles: group-building roles and task roles. Participants engaging in both kinds of roles are absolutely essential to effective group dynamics. Group-building roles are actions that focus on the group as people, including the relationships among members. Group-building roles attend to the process of the group. These have also been called group maintenance roles. Task roles focus on accomplishing the purposes of the group, including giving information and opinions and moving the group along on tasks by summarizing and by using various decision-making strategies. Task roles are focused on the content of the group discussion.

On occasion, group members may demonstrate some individual dysfunctional roles that actually hamper the group's progress. Someone may doggedly push his or her point like a broken record, even if the group is ready to move on. A person like this is called a *special interest pleader* and may have a secret reason for saying things—a hidden agenda. A member may resist or block any group action by being negative and disagreeable about everything. A person like that is called a *blocker.* We should stress that dysfunctional roles are those that truly hamper a group's goals or progress; participants who express negative opinions because they are truly concerned about a course of action are helpful to the group and should not be confused with someone who is a blocker. Someone who effectively uses humor (no matter how goofy) to relieve tension or create harmony should not be confused with someone who acts like a clown and never takes the group seriously—the latter may be exhibiting a dysfunctional role. Someone who is quiet at meetings, but is actively engaged in listening and thinking and who is willing to support the group's decisions is an active member (who might typically be called a follower), whereas someone who sits in the back reading a newspaper and not even listening is a nonparticipant.

Examples of common roles that help us understand group dynamics are presented in Exhibit 7.2. These roles have evolved from the early group dynamics research in the 1940s and 1950s

(Benne & Sheats, 1948; Knowles & Knowles, 1959). Think of examples you use or see others using. Describe the various roles you have played in different groups. Are there any similarities between groups? Do you find yourself playing the same role no matter what the group? Or do your roles vary? Do the roles you play give you any insights into how you act as a member of a group?

Each of us has a preferred set of practices we are most comfortable with in a group. This might be called our role set. You may find it more comfortable or easier in a group to seek opinions from others, make sure people have a chance to share their ideas, or summarize what was discussed before a vote. Someone else might like to share an opinion or give information. To perform effectively, the group needs participants to practice both task and group-building roles. You may prefer to do mostly group-building functions or mostly task functions.

Although any individual participant or positional leader may not perform in all roles comfortably, it is useful to know which roles the group needs and to ask someone to engage in them. For example, you may be terrible at summarizing discussions because it all seems a jumble to you, but if you know that a summary is needed before the group makes its final decision, you can intervene. In this case, you might say, "It would help me if someone would summarize the key points on both sides of this issue so I can fully understand before I vote." Someone who is comfortable with that role will provide that needed process. It is empowering for participants to be asked to contribute their preferred roles to the group process.

Group Norms

Imagine attending your first meeting of an ongoing group. You walk into the room and begin observing other group members for a clue to what is acceptable or expected. Does the group stay focused on its agenda or wander into other discussions? Do members seem friendly and social or distant and isolated? Do people sit formally and wait to be called on by the chair or is there a more open

Exhibit 7.2. Examples of Common Roles in Groups.

Task Roles	Role Description	Example of Role in Use
Information seeker	Aware that the group needs more facts or data before proceeding.	"We cannot vote on this yet; we need more information first, so let's ask Sharon to brief us at the next meeting."
Opinion seeker	Aware that the group needs more insight, ideas, or opinions before proceeding.	"What do you think, Roger? You have had a lot of experience with this topic."
Opinion giver	Sharing one's views, feelings, or ideas so the group has the benefit of one's thinking.	"I strongly think we must increase the budget for this project if we intend to serve more students."
Summarizer	Condensing the nature of the opinions or discussion in a capsule format for clarity.	"Before we go further, is it accurate to say that while some of us think we should not spend much money, we all agree we should do this project?"
Clarifier	Elaborating or explaining ideas in new words to add meaning. Showing how something might work if adopted	"Jim, did you mean we need *more* involvement, meaning quantity, or *better* involvement, like quality?"

discussion? All of these kinds of practices are the norms or rules of conduct that lead to consistent practices in a group.

Some norms are explicit and clearly seen by all participants. When you play cards you expect to follow suit; when you play baseball, you expect to bat in order. When your group uses Robert's Rules of Order, you know you must make motions, seek a second to the motion, speak in turn, and plan to vote on the motion eventually. Other norms may have evolved through the cultural practices of the group—arranging the chairs in a circle, starting each meet-

Group-Building Roles	Role Description	Example of Role in Use
Gatekeeper	Inviting those who have not yet spoken or who have been trying to say something into the conversation.	"Tanya has been trying to say something on this for a while—I'd like to hear what that is."
Encourager	Welcoming all individuals and diverse ideas. Responding warmly to promote the inclusion and empowerment of others.	"What the sophomores just said about this issue was really enlightening. I am really glad you took some risks to tell us that. Thanks."
Mediator	Harmonizing conflict and seeking to straighten out opposing points of view in a clear way.	"You two don't seem as far apart on this issue as it might seem. You both value the same thing and have many points of agreement."
Follower	An active listener who willingly supports the group's actions and decisions.	"I haven't said much, but this has been a great discussion and I feel really informed. I am comfortable with the decision."

Note: For other descriptions of roles in groups, see Benne & Sheats (1948) and Knowles & Knowles (1959).

ing with introductions of new members and guests, congratulating group members on their accomplishments, or celebrating birthdays.

Group norms contribute to the concept of group climate. Climate is like the group's personality. Just as individuals have personality, so do groups. Perhaps one group you are in is open, flexible, and supportive, uses humor often, and views each person as important, whereas another is formal, guarded, distrusting, impersonal, and stuffy. If you want your group to have a distinct personality, it is useful to consider what group norms will lead to those desired outcomes. The Relational Leadership Model is designed to create a group in which members feel highly engaged.

Creative Conflict

The storming stage of group development can paralyze a group's progress. Unresolved conflict at any stage can create a group climate that is tense and hostile, but it can also be an effective method for improving the group's outcomes.

What words or emotions come to mind when you think of the term *conflict?* For most people, the idea of conflict is uncomfortable and creates a knot in the stomach; most of us would prefer harmony. In many earlier leadership books, the term *conflict* does not even appear in the index, or the topic is handled in a power dynamics model, or in a section on how to win your own way.

Conflict can result from such things as clashes in personalities, differing expectations of roles (role conflict), or disagreement over ideas. Personality conflicts can often be understood by returning to personality preferences and learning preferences (presented in Chapters Four and Five) and being more focused on listening to and understanding others. Role conflicts are best handled by thinking of what assumptions you may be bringing to the conflict about your own role or your expectations of others that clash with their assumptions. Conflict in ideas is often called controversy, and a full airing of differences of opinions and ideas is essential for a group to make the best decisions. Such controversies need to be handled with civility and open dialogue (Higher Education Research Institute, 1996). Exhibit 7.3 illustrates some of the advantages and liabilities of conflict in groups.

It is not uncommon for people to want to avoid conflict, so they often ignore it or pretend it does not exist. Some say it is like having an elephant in the room. Everyone is aware of the tension that a huge conflict creates—like an elephant standing in the corner—but no one talks about it. Still others diffuse conflict by acting as if it is unimportant or can be handled at another time. True commu-

Exhibit 7.3. Understanding Conflict.

Advantages of Conflict	Liabilities of Conflict
1. Can increase motivation and energy.	1. Can be debilitating.
2. Clarifies issues and positions.	2. Can distract from goal achievement.
3. Can build internal cohesiveness and esprit de corps	3. Can cause defensiveness and rigidity.
4. Can lead to innovation and creativity.	4. Can cause distortions of reality.
5. Can increase self-awareness.	5. Often becomes a negatively reinforcing cycle.
6. May be a means of dealing with internal conflicts.	6. Tends to escalate (more serious) and to proliferate (more issues).
7. Can lead to a new synthesis of ideas or methods.	7. Efforts to resolve are often not reciprocated.

Source: Reprinted with the permission of Simon & Schuster Adult Publishing Group, from *The Art of Leadership* by Lin Bothwell. Copyright © 1983 by Prentice-Hall, Inc.

nities resolve conflicts rather than avoid them. That is often the best way. When conflict is confronted, it is usually best to employ negotiation and mediation strategies instead of power strategies.

The resulting different conflict resolution outcomes have been described as win-win, win-lose, and lose-lose. In win-win outcomes, both sides are heard and are satisfied with the resolution of their differences. The group often emerges as stronger for the discussion, and the decisions made may be significantly better than they would have been without the dialogue. In win-lose outcomes, one side uses power strategies to win by out-talking, putting down, or rushing to a premature vote. But in the process, a loser is created. The participants who lost (and their potential allies) feel marginalized, angry, and even resentful. The group's harmony is jeopardized and participants are not empowered or included. In lose-lose outcomes, both sides use power strategies and get so entrenched, rigid, or hurtful that no effective resolution is reached, even in compromise.

"I like a saying I heard, 'Find the truth in what you oppose; find the fault in what you espouse!"—Peter Tate was president of the Black Greek Association and majored in biology and public health at the University of Michigan.

Reciprocal and relational models of leadership know that some conflict is natural and inevitable. The Relational Leadership Model encourages processes to handle conflict that will promote inclusivity and empowerment. By anticipating that when great people get together they will have differences of ideas and approaches, the group can set some ground rules (that is, group norms) to guide the openness and honesty with which they will raise issues of possible conflict. These ground rules can "create an environment 'safe' for differences" (Lappé & Du Bois, 1994, p. 251). Such ground rules might include agreeing that everyone will have a chance to be heard who wants to speak and that the group will look for points of agreement as well as disagreements. Handling all these disagreements with civility is essential. Each person should commit to making "no permanent enemies" in the group (Lappé & Du Bois, 1994, p. 255) in order to be inclusive of all members' opinions.

Conflicts are useful when they raise perspectives that need attention before the group moves to resolution. The more homogeneous a group is, the more essential it is to think through an issue from multiple perspectives. Even if there is little diversity in the group, someone might say, "If there were freshman students here, how would they see this policy, and should we reconsider any parts of it?" or "If older students were here, would they see any issues we have not yet addressed?" In this way, at least decisions are informed by the broadest possible thinking, even if no person is physically present who holds a divergent view.

Group Decision Making

Traditional views of leadership often assume that a group or organization has a formal leader with the authority and responsibility for making final decisions. Indeed, on many occasions the positional leader has to make a decision on behalf of the group. Some possible reasons for this are that there may be no time to hold a group meeting or consult with group members, or the leader may be representing the group in another meeting and need to speak for the group, or the leader may judge that the decision is not a major one and not worth group time and energy. Whenever a positional leader is faced with making an individual decision, the Relational Leadership Model will be useful in guiding the decision process. The leader should ask herself these questions:

- Does this decision support our vision and mission? (purposeful)

- What opinions do my group members have about this issue? (inclusive)

- Will this decision heighten our involvement or limit involvement? (empowering)

- Is this the right thing to do? Is it principled? (ethical)

- Should I slow down making this decision so that others can get involved? (process-oriented)

In formal organizations with positional leaders, participative leadership is often thought to involve "the use of decision procedures intended to *allow* other people some influence over the leader's decisions" (Yukl, 1989, p. 83 [emphasis added]). The values in participative leadership acknowledge that a better decision is made and receives greater acceptance when those involved are part of that decision process. Group members may be empowered, learn more effective leadership skills, and sustain a higher commitment to the process when others are involved. You will see a profound philosophical difference when you examine the word *allow* in the definition of participative leadership. Allow correctly identifies who—the positional leader—has responsibility and who can involve or not involve others, as that leader chooses. In most work settings and in volunteer organizations, for the leader to presume that she should make the decision or "allow" the involvement of others is a conventional way of looking at the situation. A more useful perception would be to assume instead that the unit (the organization, the work unit, the group) must be involved with key decisions—has the right to be and should be. Now the question becomes *how* they should best be involved, not *whether* they should be. Clearly, there is tension in formal settings about the authority and role of participants in the decision-making process. We sense a shift in people's expectations—that they want, indeed often demand, a role in decision making. Examples include parent involvement in school-based management and employee involvement in selecting benefits packages.

Yukl (1989) identifies a continuum of four possible decision-making procedures: autocratic → consultation → joint decision → delegation or participation. They range, in the amount of influence others have on the decision, from no influence (in which an autocratic decision is made) to high influence of others in the process (in which complete delegation has occurred).

Johnson and Johnson (1994) describe five methods of decision making: (1) decision by authority without discussion, (2) expert member, (3) average members' opinions, (4) decision by authority after discussion, and (5) majority control. Each of the decision-making methods may have its own purpose, but relational leadership would promote consensus models whenever possible. When a trusting group climate exists, groups may select other models and be comfortable using minority control or majority control.

In our view, some decisions are best made by an authority or expert. However, most groups would benefit by shifting important decisions that affect the entire community to a discussion and consensus model. More and more participants in groups expect to be involved in decision making, and, indeed, involvement is essential to a relational, empowering approach. Positional leaders who make important decisions in an autocratic manner find that they alienate workers and group members, even when they, as leaders, have the authority to make those decisions.

"I think decisions should be made democratically in a group situation. Making decisions in this way allows input from all members without domination of the leader. The group can assess all options together in a creative environment. The leader is involved in the decision-making process, but does not control it. The group comes to a final decision as a whole and implements the course of action with guidance from the leader.

Challenges facing this type of leadership include a desire for control and conflicting viewpoints. The leader or one of the followers may desire to control the decision-making process and may insist on his or her own ideas. Conflicting viewpoints also cause controversy, for the group must generally go with the overall consensus. This could cause a detachment of conflicted group members who feel that their input was not incorporated into the final decision."—Forrest Harrison studies biology at East Tennessee State University. He is a member of the Leadership House and Venture Scouts. Forrest plans to pursue a career in medicine.

Consensus does not mean that every single decision is made by the entire group, nor does it mean that a majority vote equals reaching consensus. An important task of teams is to make decisions, and most teams prefer to reach consensus on critical issues. Rayner (1996) provides the following definition of consensus: "Consensus does not mean that everyone on the team thinks the best possible decision has been reached. It does mean that no one is professionally violated by the decision and that all team members will support its implementation" (p. 74). Achieving consensus is not always easy and can be a time-intensive process, taking much longer than making a decision by voting or giving feedback and asking the leader to make the decision. Rayner offers the following guidelines for reaching consensus within a team:

1. Clearly define the issue facing the team
2. Focus on similarities between positions
3. Ensure that there is adequate time for discussion
4. Avoid conflict-reducing tendencies (e.g., voting) (p. 76)

Not all decisions warrant the attention of the entire group. It would be absurd to waste group members' time or resources by meeting on everything. It is useful to think of two dimensions of decisions: the need for quality in the decision and the need for acceptance of the decision. Quality of the decision refers to its importance and accuracy. The art festival committee may decide to hold a film festival, but the particular films selected may not matter. A committee or individual can decide. Any decision that needs high acceptance by those involved usually has to be handled in an open and inclusive manner. The art festival committee might need help staffing the event, but to assign committee members to time slots could be a mistake. The approach to staffing requires high acceptance; these members may need to be involved in the scheduling.

Consensus brings the highest commitment among participants, is the most informed by the diverse knowledge bases in the group, and takes the most time. Consensus requires that the group become comfortable with handling conflict and be informed by the rising controversies that can lead to a good decision. Groups that are uncomfortable with controversy or who do not handle it in a civil manner may move prematurely to vote just to get the group to move on. Consensus requires that the group be willing to use strategies like active listening, compromising, and working in a collaborative manner. Encouraging divergent points of view, listening for understanding, and allowing people to disagree with each other with civility are important hallmarks of consensus-building processes.

When teams fail to reach consensus, it is often because they do not allow enough time for members to discuss perspectives and opinions to discover common ground, or because conflict is mismanaged or reaches a level that erodes trust among individuals. Mutual respect and trust among group members is a critical component to successfully achieving a decision by consensus.

Teamwork

Many look to the sports metaphor of a team to illustrate how individuals need to work together toward a common purpose. "We can no longer afford the luxury of even a few individualists working in isolation from the rest of the organization. . . . Strength is not in the individuals, but in the team. Put a group of superstars together on any team, whether baseball, hockey, football or soccer, and they will still lose if they operate as individual superstars. But once they start operating as a team, they become unbeatable" (Taylor, 1989, pp. 124–125). Many organizations have adopted that metaphor and reconceptualized the work unit as a team. Hospitals have a team for each patient, with a primary care nurse as team coordinator, and businesses have cross-functional teams that bring together staff from shipping, marketing, and manufacturing to do product advancement. This metaphor has implications for morale, motivation, support, common purpose, diverse roles, and inclusion. Previously, we have used the metaphor of jazz and referred to participants as an ensemble. For the purposes of this book we also use community as a metaphor for groups of participants.

Whatever the metaphor, participants in the same group should share the goal of working toward being an effective team. Strong ensemble casts on popular TV shows often show the reciprocity of collaborators working together for shared purposes. Think of the appreciation of differences among the television characters of *Grey's Anatomy* or *Will and Grace* or of Harry Potter and his buddies at Hogwarts.

Teams and Groups

Just as collections of people do not automatically constitute groups, all groups are not teams. Kotter and Cohen (2002) observe that a powerful group has two characteristics—it is made up of the right people and it demonstrates teamwork. Teams are, however, one kind of group. Teams are more than just a group of people working together. Hughes, Ginnett, and Curphy (1993) distinguish between groups and teams, noting that although both have the characteristics of mutual interaction and reciprocal influence, teams have a stronger sense of identity and common goals or tasks; in addition, task interdependence is higher within a team than in a group, and team members usually have more distinctive roles than group members.

Types of teams range from those that function like working groups, in which individual accountability is high (such as a golf team), to true teams that couldn't accomplish their goals individually (such as a football team or the homecoming committee). Exhibit 7.4 shows the distinction between working groups and teams.

Quinn (1996) defines a team as "an enthusiastic set of competent people who have clearly defined roles, associated in a common activity, working cohesively in trusting relationships, and exercising personal discipline and making individual sacrifices for the good

Exhibit 7.4. Working Groups Versus Teams.

Working Groups	Teams
A strong, clearly focused leader is appointed.	Shared leadership responsibilities exist among members.
The general organizational mission is the group's purpose.	A specific, well-defined purpose that is unique to the team.
Individual work provides the only products.	Team and individual work develop products.
Effectiveness is measured indirectly by group's influence on others (e.g., financial performance of business, student scores on standardized examinations).	Effectiveness is measured directly by assessing team work products.
Individual accountability only is evident.	Both team and individual accountability are evident.
Individual accomplishments are recognized and rewarded.	Team celebration. Individual efforts that contribute to the team's success are also recognized and celebrated.
Meetings are efficiently run and last for short periods of time	Meetings have open-ended discussion and include active problem solving.
In meetings members discuss, decide, and delegate.	In meetings members discuss, decide, and do real work together.

Source: From Johnson & Johnson (1994), p. 504. Published by Allyn and Bacon, Boston MA. Copyright (c) 1994 by Pearson Education. Reprinted by permission of the publisher.

of the team" (p. 161). Much has been written about when teams unravel or fail at accomplishing their goals, but here is a visualization of what it is like when teams achieve synergy and reach their potential. Dee Hock, the former CEO of Visa International makes the following observation about teams:

In the field of group endeavor, you will see incredible events in which the group performs far beyond the sum of its individual talents. It happens in the symphony, in the ballet, in the theater, in sports, and equally in business. It is easy to recognize and impossible to define. It is a mystique. It cannot be achieved without immense effort, training, and cooperation, but effort, training, and cooperation alone rarely create it. Some groups reach it consistently. Few can sustain it. (Quinn, 1996, p. 162)

Parker (2003) defines a team as "a group of people with a high degree of interdependence, geared toward the achievement of a goal or the completion of a task" (p. 2). Three common types of team are functional, self-directed, and cross-functional (Parker). Functional teams tend to resemble hierarchical organizations, in which power and authority are contained at the top. The self-directed team is typically a group whose members possess all the technical knowledge and skills to accomplish a task or goal, with a certain degree of power delegated to it from a leader or manager. Cross-functional teams usually are composed of individuals from a variety of skill sets, departments, or areas that combine skill sets that no one person possesses. For example, a company like Apple Computer might form a cross-functional team that consists of a software engineer, marketing and sales specialist, project manager, and applications designer to invent a new product.

Teams must have clear goals to achieve success. Often, teams either do not take the time to formulate goals or set goals that are unclear and unattainable. The SMART rubric provides a framework for teams to use as they establish their goals (Parker, 2003, p. 94):

1. Specific – the goal must be clear to everyone
2. Measurable – it is quantifiable
3. Attainable – the goal must be realistic and possible to achieve
4. Relevant – the goal is in alignment with the direction of the organization and its overall strategy

5. Time-bound – there is a set time frame by which
   the goal will be achieved (e.g., within a semester or
   within a year)

An example of a SMART goal is responding to all e-mails that the team receives about its upcoming event on April 2 within twenty-four hours.

Teams are more than a combination of skill sets or functional roles carried out by individual members. Teams are a blending of people with diverse backgrounds, histories, styles, talents, and personalities.

The following are some factors that are critical for a team's success (Parker, 2003, p. 260):

- Disregard organizational boundaries in an effort to arrive at the best solution
- Be sensitive and responsive to the concerns and considerations of other team members in the design of projects
- Understand that common goals and targets are mandatory of all team members
- Provide open and frequent (risk free) communications
- All team members pull their own weight and share a common objective
- Capitalize on team members' strengths
- Develop a sense of trust among all team members
- Be willing to accept and try ideas that are different from the norm, even if it means modifying the established process
- Use a bit of humor when discussions get tense and the pressure to complete a task is high

Team Learning

Individual learning is the conventional norm for a college student. Only you can read that book, write that computer program, or take that test. However, learning occurs in many other ways—through group projects, in experiential settings, and in study groups. Whenever a team has a shared responsibility, it has to find a way to learn together, not just learn separately. "The learning unit[s] of organizations are 'teams,' groups of people who need one another to act" (Senge, 1993, p. 134). Approaches to team learning include accumulating the learning preference of the majority of members (for example, a scientific research group in which everyone prefers facts and details or a friendship group in which most are flexible and casual). However, intentional team learning requires intentional practices.

Team learning happens in dialogue with each other and through reflection on shared experiences. Dialogue is a "sustained collective inquiry into everyday experience and what we take for granted" (Senge, Kleiner, Roberts, Ross, & Smith, 1994, p. 353). Dialogue is far more than the mere words used to share meaning. It includes the tone of voice, laughter, pauses, difficulty in finding the right words, and amount of discussion needed to come to some meaning. When a team is in dialogue, participants are aware of the process of their communication as well as its content. For true understanding to result, it is important that both teams and groups establish ground rules or norms to handle their inevitable controversies with civility (Higher Education Research Institute, 1996).

Dialogue and discussion are two slightly different processes. Some groups mistakenly engage in discussion in which members share their own views with minimal attempts at true understanding. This can lead to debate, which only beats down opposing views or leads to a deterioration of relationships that can unravel a group. Groups that value learning together will establish true dialogue methods, the goals of which are to learn together while engaging in change. Dialogue is built into the processes of reflection, which involves thinking together. Perhaps the best lesson for dialogue is "Don't just do something, stand there" (Isaacs, as cited in Senge et al., 1994, p. 375). Your obligation as a listener is to understand and connect. Dialogue encourages you to clarify your points, not prove them. We encourage you to refer to Chapter Five to review how different individuals learn to truly listen to each other.

Leadership Implications

"In a productive work community, leaders are not commanders and controllers, bosses and big shots. They are servers and supporters, partners and providers" (Kouzes & Posner, 1993, p. 7). Leaders in teamwork settings are also facilitators of team learning. Facilitating team learning requires individual participants to understand their motivations, to advocate for their own interests while being open to hearing others' points of view, and to find common ground (Ross, 1994b).

Participants and leaders must all share the responsibility of processing any shared group experience to make it a conscious process as a team. Successes need to be understood as well as failures. Too often, groups do not reflect on why something worked really well but spend hours and hours finding errors in failures.

Team Leadership

Team performance and team development are two critical functions of leadership. The Relational Leadership Model underscores the importance of both of these functions, with its emphasis on process-oriented (team development) and purpose (team performance). Team performance means accomplishing the group's goals, making decisions and plans, achieving results, and solving problems. Team development includes establishing effective relationships, creating an environment in which individuals feel valued, and facilitating cohesion within the team. Research conducted on teams shows that productivity, innovation, creativity, decision making, quality, problem solving, and use of resources are all increased or enhanced as a result of people working in team structures. Why teams fail is also widely documented; it is often a result of poor leadership (Hill, 2004).

"Leaders do not always have to be the ones selected to lead in a group. Sometimes leaders are those who sit back, listen, and help the group move forward without having to be in charge. I know that I personally appreciate those team members who work hard and contribute. When I am not in the team leader position I too try and take on a role of leading behind the scenes in order to get the job done most effectively. It is a pleasure to work with people who are not afraid to speak out and challenge the norms especially when I am confident that they are really listening and working toward a common goal. Leaders in a group are those that lead by their actions. To set an example and then have others follow, a true leader is made."—Marissa Evans is a teaching assistant in the Collaborative Leadership Course at Cornell University and a Judicial Board member. She is a manager of Campus Promotions and participated in a study abroad program at the London School of Economics.

While balancing the ongoing activities of the team or group, leaders also face both internal and external demands. Leaders shift between the behaviors of monitoring, taking action, and paying attention to internal and external group issues. Team members can also take on these functions, which is typically the case with more experienced and mature groups. In these cases, leaders would do well to step aside and let the team take on those responsibilities and tasks. It is a delicate balancing act of determining which problems to intervene in and which to let team members resolve as a whole.

Several researchers and scholars on team leadership have found the following characteristics of team leadership (Hill, 2004, p. 211):

1. Clear, elevating goal – the group believes the goal is worthwhile and it is clear enough to tell when the objectives have been met
2. Results-driven structure – the group's purpose needs to drive the structure of the team
3. Competent team members – the group members must possess appropriate technical knowledge and interpersonal skills to work collaboratively as a team
4. Unified commitment – the group has a sense of identity and level of team spirit that has been intentionally facilitated and developed
5. Collaborative climate – all individuals contribute collectively to the success of the project and individual accomplishments are integrated into the whole team's efforts
6. Standards of excellence – standards of excellence are established and clearly understood by the team with the emphasis on everyone performing at the highest levels
7. Principled leadership – the leader establishes priorities and helps team members stay focused on the goals, sustains collaborative environments for the team, and manages performance
8. External support – the team is provided resources (money, equipment, supplies) to accomplish its goals and is given recognition for its successes

Team leaders are tasked with monitoring the group's progress and relationships and taking action when appropriate. Leaders are often called upon to take action when the group is stuck and unable to move forward or when internal conflict takes place that the team itself cannot resolve. It may require the leader to mediate conflict, assist the group in focusing on its goals, or coach the group on interpersonal skills. In some cases, the leader facilitates an external role for the team by networking with other alliances or sharing information from external sources with the team.

It's important to establish a team at the beginning before initiating the work to be accomplished. Based on research findings from effective teamwork, Hughes, Ginnett, and Curphy (1993) provide four design components needed to establish teams:

1. Task structure – the team understands its task and finds meaning in it; the team is given autonomy to accomplish the task

2. Group boundaries – the size of the team is just right (not too big and not too small); diversity exists within the team; and the team has sufficient knowledge, information, and interpersonal skills to accomplish the goals harmoniously

3. Norms – the team has a set of norms to guide the behaviors of the team members

4. Authority – there is a flexible rather than a rigid use of authority by the leader and team members that allows for open debate and instills a sense of empowerment and trust as well as a degree of command when compliance by group members is warranted

These four conditions are important at the beginning stages of team development to allow the team to work effectively and efficiently.

Chapter Summary

Groups are the building blocks of communities of practice. We function in many different kinds of groups that are at different stages of development. This chapter presented group development models and principles of group dynamics, including aspects of decision making, conflict resolution, and team learning that inform group practices. It is important to note the differences between groups and teams and the intentional process of developing working groups into effective teams.

What's Next?

Organizations are made up of multiple groups and teams. The next chapter explores how formal organizations function and the unique role of leadership in the organizational context.

Chapter Activities

1. Analyze several groups of which you are a member according to the key dimensions of purpose, structure, and time. How are the groups similar? How are they different?

2. Think of a group of which you were a member. Using Tuckman's model as a framework, describe what it was like to be a member of the group in each of the four stages. Did the group experience any problems? In which stage? What did you do to resolve the problems? Have you ever known a group to dissolve itself? If yes, what were the situations surrounding this decision? Identify a group that should dissolve itself. Why do you think they do not take this final step?

3. Think about your personal style in conflict situations. Now read the descriptions that follow and assign a percentage to each conflict style based on how often you use it. Your total percentages should add up to 100%.

> Style 1: I avoid conflict and stay away from issues involving conflict.
>
> Style 2: I want to be the winner in conflict situations.
>
> Style 3: I want to be liked, so I avoid conflict.

Style 4: I believe in compromise.

Style 5: I view conflict as an opportunity to identify and solve problems.

What are the advantages and disadvantages of each style? Consider your most preferred styles and identify circumstances in which these styles are most and least effective for you.

4. Identify a team that you are or have been affiliated with (sports, within an organization, class project, and so on). Analyze the leadership of that team using Hill's eight characteristics of team leadership. How well did your team perform on each of those eight dimensions? What improvements could be made to strengthen the effectiveness of your team?

5. Think of the best team of which you have ever been a member. This could be any kind of team (newspaper staff, student government, club or organization, scouts, 4-H, sports team). What made this team special? Was there ever a time when this team had to learn something? Describe that experience.

6. Using the SMART rubric for establishing clear goals, create a goal statement using each of the five elements of SMART. Check your goal statement to ensure that it meets the SMART test.

Additional Readings

Hill, S.E.K. (2004). Team leadership. In P. G. Northouse (Ed.), *Leadership: Theory and practice* (pp. 203–225). Thousand Oaks, CA: Sage.

Howard, V. A., & Barton, M. A. (1992). *Thinking together.* New York: Morrow.

Johnson, D. W., & Johnson, F. P. (1994). *Joining together: Group theory and group skills* (5th ed.). Boston: Allyn & Bacon.

Kotter, J. P., & Cohen, D. S. (2002). *The heart of change: Real-life stories of how people change their organizations.* Boston: Harvard Business School Press.

Parker, G. M. (2003). *Cross-functional teams: Working with allies, enemies, and other strangers.* San Francisco: Jossey-Bass.

8

Understanding Complex Organizations

Consuela and Martin are newly elected leaders of the new multicultural student union. Both are second-year students who had a great deal of leadership experience in high school and in various community organizations. As they meet to begin developing a plan for the coming months, Consuela and Martin begin to feel overwhelmed. Their university is huge and their organization is new and small. The questions come quickly: How do we get others excited about the mission of our new organization? How are we going to recruit new members? What do we want our meetings to be like? What other officers will we need to make this work? How are we going to make decisions and handle conflict that we know is going to emerge? They end their first meeting with more questions than answers but excited about the challenges ahead.

You, as a student, see and experience numerous organizations every day. You may get up in the morning and read the campus newspaper or tune in to the student radio station—both are important student organizations. You have undoubtedly visited some campus administrative office and had the frustrating experience of trying to work with a bureaucratic organization.

Different types of student government organizations represent student views and help protect student rights. Student programming boards work closely with administrative offices to provide educational, cultural, social, and recreational activities for the campus.

Campus service organizations like Habitat for Humanity or Circle-K are local branches of larger, international organizations; they provide opportunities for students to help those in need. ROTC units contain student organizations, are an academic unit in a college, and are a part of a bigger governmental military structure. Various forms of business organizations provide opportunities for students to make money by working on and off campus. Other organizations provide fellowship, programs, and support for students who are members of different cultural groups. Organizations of all kinds exist everywhere in and around campus and add to the quality of life for everyone. Leadership in organizations is both prevalent and common in our everyday lives, both on and off campus.

Learning to work successfully in organizations gains you a skill set you will use throughout your life. Teachers work in schools; engineers and lawyers work in firms; social workers operate in human service agencies and interact with the legal system. We live in towns with governance processes, worship in religious institutions, and have surgery in hospitals. No matter what your major, you encounter organizations on a regular basis.

Chapter Overview

In the previous chapter, we explored leadership within team and group settings. In this chapter, we expand the scope of the environment and discuss leadership in an organizational context. In this context, the importance of focusing on the five aspects of the Relational Leadership Model (purpose, inclusivity, empowerment, ethics, and process) becomes even more evident.

Groups and Organizations

It can be difficult to differentiate between groups and organizations. Some of the differences are obvious; some are more subtle. One way to get a sense of the difference can be shown by answering the who,

Exhibit 8.1. Groups and Organizations.

	Groups	Organizations
Who?	Small-to-medium (3+ participants)	Large (20+ participants)
What?	Collection of individuals	Collection of groups
When?	Continuous interactions	Continuous interactions
Where?	Close proximity	Proximity unimportant (ranges from close to far away)
How?	Simple structures	Complex structures
Why?	Purpose	Purpose

what, when, where, how, and why questions (Exhibit 8.1). Organizations are large collections of groups of people that interact in a continuous manner within a complex structure to accomplish a specific purpose. Organizations are inherently social entities. Although proximity of location has traditionally been a determining factor for organizations, we will see that this is not always the case.

Organizations have many participants. Remember when you were growing up and you played with your best friend? Although you sometimes had problems or difficulties with each other, it was relatively easy to work them out. As your friendship group expanded, things got more difficult. All of a sudden, you realized that not everyone wanted to play the same game you did or that they wanted to play the game differently. Then your world expanded even further to your high school or places of employment. Being associated with more and more people meant being exposed to different values, ideas, and ways of doing things. This probably made life more interesting, as well as more complicated.

Again, think about organizations as collections of groups of people. Imagine a college or university with students, professors, administrators, alumni, parents, a board of trustees, legislators, and others, all working together to try to accomplish basically the same thing: to educate students. Yet each of these groups views the education of students in a different way. What groups participate in the life of *your* organization?

Interactions within organizations are continuous. The success of any organization depends on the various groups within it staying connected so they can work together easily and effectively. Becoming isolated or separated can have a negative impact not only on the specific group that has become separated but also on the entire organization.

Proximity—being physically close to other participants—is certainly helpful but not absolutely necessary in organizations. This is contrary to our conception of an organization as people working in the same room or at least in the same building. As we will discuss later in the section on virtual organizations, there are a growing number of organizations that are physically separated yet remain connected through technology and the strong belief in a mission or purpose.

Organizations are complex in their structures. There are usually many layers and departments in the organizational structure and many people involved in leadership and decision making. Think again of the college or university example. To successfully involve all of the different groups in the educational process, different roles, policies, and procedures must be in place. There will also be a number of different leadership positions.

Organizations exist to accomplish a specific purpose. We have all been participants (and possibly leaders) in numerous organizations throughout our lives, but we probably have never stopped to ask, "I wonder how this organization got started?" Unless you were part of the core group that started an organization, it was probably just "always there." Your participation began with you showing up at a meeting and either continued or ended based on how your needs were met by the organization. If we try to formulate an answer to the question, Why do organizations exist? we probably come up with this: they exist to accomplish a specific purpose. This would be the correct response.

Organizations as Complex Systems

Organizations are also systems. A system is defined as an environment in which each interaction between members produces outcomes that affect each individual and subsequent interactions and outcomes (Tubbs, 1984). With more people and groups in the organization, interactions become more frequent, and life within the organization becomes more complicated because everything affects everything else.

In *Out of Control*, Kevin Kelly (1994) introduces "The Nine Laws of God," which he describes as "the organizing principles in systems as diverse as biological evolution and SimCity" (p. 468). Depicted in Exhibit 8.2, these "laws" also apply to organizations as systems. These qualities relate closely to the new paradigm material covered at the end of Chapter Two, yet they also apply directly (and indirectly) to organizational life. We believe that these qualities really describe life, both in and out of organizations, and will become even more visible to us in the coming century. Look at Kelly's list of principles (Exhibit 8.2); which ones resonate with you? Which ones have you seen operate in your life or in your organizations?

Organizations are tremendously challenging places in which to participate and lead. They are also places of great potential because of the large number and variety of talented people who are members with you. As a leader, you may find yourself wanting to return to the time in your life when things seemed simpler and less complicated. Try not to worry. You will probably find that those qualities that helped you be successful in your youth—enthusiasm, energy, honesty, willingness to work hard, and character—will serve you well as a leader in a complex organization.

Exhibit 8.2. The Nine Laws of God—Organizations as Systems.

Distribute being	Essence of the organization exists in all of its connected members.
Control from the bottom up	Empower members at all levels of the organization.
Cultivate increasing returns	Focus on what your organization does well and do it even better.
Grow by chunking	Organizations grow, not one piece at a time, but in bunches.
Maximize the fringes	Honor your creative members and their ideas, even if they're really "out there."
Honor your errors	It is only through trial and error that learning happens.
Pursue no optima, have multiple goals	There is no one "right" answer to complex problems, there are only many partial solutions.
Seek persistent disequilibrium	Disequilibrium brings energy into the organization.
Change changes itself	Change leads to more change, which changes the initial change.

Source: Adapted from Kelly, 1994, pp. 468–472. Copyright 1994 by Kevin Kelly. Reprinted by permission of Basic Books, a member of Perseus Books, LLC.

"Our organization meets once a week, we go over weekly plans and what's going on. Everyone knows what presentations are going on and what events are happening. We are also a very tight group. Very rarely does a day go by when we don't see each other or talk to one another. We let each other know what's going on and help each other to make sure nothing is missed."—Dean Porter is the vice president of Men Against Violence and member of the Network at the Texas State University. He is an international relations major.

Organizational Leadership

In the previous sections, we addressed the questions What are organizations? and Why do they exist? It is also interesting to ask, Why does leadership exist in an organization? Because organizations are widely considered to be structures in which a set of groups can engage with each other over time, leadership in an organization exists to help these groups work together to accomplish a specific purpose. Although this seems simplistic, how could leadership be anything else? Regardless of how it comes into being, leadership exists for only one reason: to help an organization accomplish its stated purpose. This purpose may shift over time, but leadership must always honor its inherent commitment to keep the organization on track to pursue its mission. By maintaining this focus on the mission, leadership helps the organization to be sustainable—to exist over the long term. This is a critical function of leadership. We believe that the Relational Leadership Model provides a usable framework from which leaders can work to accomplish an organization's purpose. By being inclusive, empowering, ethical, and process-oriented, while helping all of the organization's members be purposeful and work toward positive purposes, leaders and members can work together successfully to accomplish significant change.

Organizational Structures

Just as all organizations exist for some purpose, they also have a structure that makes their day-to-day operations easier. Max Weber (1924/1947) created the classic bureaucratic model for organizations, featuring a hierarchical structure, "divisions of labor," and clearly articulated rules and regulations to govern how the organization should operate. This structure was designed to promote order and accountability within the organization. In Figure 8.1 this structure has been adapted to show how it might look for a typical student organization. In this model, the power, authority, and responsibility for leading the organization is at the top, with the president, and flows downward in the structure through the other officers and committee chairs. This power and authority are delegated as needed. The "rules of the game" in the traditionally structured organization are that the members have little power, authority,

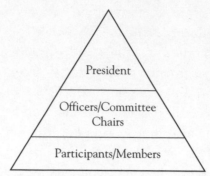

Figure 8.1. The Traditional Organizational Structure.

or responsibility. They simply do as they are told and have little, if any, input into the decision-making process. But things are changing. Now there is a call for organizations to be collaborative (Berry, 2004), compassionate (Hill & Stephens, 2003), and empathetic (Lei & Greer, 2003). Rather than the old "command and control" functions, leadership within these structures is being asked to connect people across the entire environment by involving the wants, needs, and talents of the organization's membership (Allen & Cherrey, 2000).

One new way of conceptualizing the organization proposed that the traditional pyramid be flipped upside down so that the members are at the top and the president is at the bottom (Figure 8.2). This reconceptualization means that the work of the president is to support the efforts of the other officers and committee chairs so they can better meet the needs and wishes of the members. This can be a powerful exercise for any organization. Turn your organizational pyramid upside down. How well does your leadership help the other members of the organization work toward achieving the purposes for which the organization exists? Who are your members, and what are you as a leader doing to meet their wants and needs? How are you using the talents of your members?

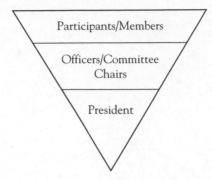

Figure 8.2. Inverted Organizational Structure.

Another organizational structure that has been proposed is the concept of a web (Allen, 1990; Helgesen, 1990, 1995). The web is defined both by its pattern (similar to a spider's web) and by the idea that the shape and pattern of the web will vary over time (this is called *series processes*) (Helgesen, 1995). New members easily connect to the structure at its outer edges where the web is looser and more permeable (Helgesen, 1995). This structure works well in an environment filled with change, as the pattern is "continually being built up, stretched, altered, modified, and transformed" (Helgesen, 1995, p. 20).

Our conceptualization of the web is shown in Figure 8.3. As you can see, common purpose is at the center of the web. We believe that the purpose of the organization—the reason it exists— is more important than its leadership and is the reason people become participants. The RLM (see Figure 3.1) also places purpose at the center of the model. This is a different interpretation than Helgesen's (1995), which has the leader at the center of the web—surrounded by other participants and at the center of the organization's activities.

Helgesen (1995) outlines six important processes that define these webs more clearly than the patterns define them. Within the

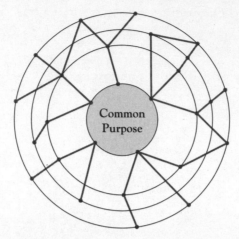

Figure 8.3. The Web Structure.

web, communication is open and happens across and among all levels of the organization. Thinking of what to do and actually doing it are not separated, because information and expertise are distributed all over the web. The strands of the web distribute the power throughout the network, so those who come up with creative ideas feel they have both the responsibility and the authority to follow through on implementation. Reorganization is easy, as the web can tighten around its center or become looser, and there is less emphasis on who is in what position or who holds how much power. The strands radiating out from the leader provide points of connection to the outside environment and allow new members to latch onto the organization. Finally, the web organization constantly reinvents itself through a process of trial and error. Processes that are successful continue and strengthen the entire web, whereas those that are not successful change into something new. This change is more easily accomplished because communication and decision-making power are distributed throughout the web (Helgesen).

One final form of organizational structure is labeled *nonhierarchical*. In nonhierarchical organizations, power and authority are shared throughout the membership. This organizational structure is flat with no levels. Decisions are often made by consensus, and leadership roles are shared by all. Many organizations use a nonhierarchical structure for philosophical reasons—the members believe in true equality.

A note of caution: whichever organizational structure you have already in place, it is important to remember that the structure is not the organization. The organization is the membership—the people—who have come together for certain purposes. The structure was created to help the membership achieve the purposes for which the organization was developed. Organizations also exist to connect people to each other. When the structure ceases to do either of these things, it must be changed. It is easy to convince yourself that a change in structure will remedy an organization's problems. We have found that this is not always the case. Changing your organization's structure may simplify things or make them operate more efficiently. It will not solve profound issues that exist between people.

"When I was younger, I believed that leadership was hierarchical; the leader had the power at the top and all the followers were below them. I suppose this was taught to me through my classroom experience where the teacher possessed all of the information and was the leader of the class. We, as students, were followers who were told what to do and what was expected of us. As I got older, I began to realize that this was not true. Experiences as an officer of various student organizations have taught me that leadership can come from many different places. The leader(s) must depend on others to accomplish anything. Just recently I have learned about the importance of followership through my President's Leadership Program class. It has been important to my leadership career to realize that without followers, there would be no one to *lead*."—Hannah Brown is a participant in the President's Leadership Program, Peer Contact

Coordinator of Asian/Pacific American Student Services, president of Ramnime (CSU anime club), and Student Leadership Coordinator of Student Leadership and Civic Engagement at Colorado State University.

Organizational Mission, Vision, and Core Values

Organizations exist for a specific purpose: to represent the views of the membership, to produce some product, to provide activities for its members, or for countless other reasons. This is what causes people to want to join and participate in organizations. A critical aspect of the success or failure of any organization will be how its purpose (or mission) comes to life in its vision and actions. The importance of mission, vision, and core values of an organization cannot be overestimated.

The mission of the organization is, quite simply, why it exists. Jones and Kahaner (1995) collected the mission statements of fifty corporations; these make for interesting reading. Checking out the web sites of most major corporations, it is easy to find their mission statements. Southwest Airlines vows, "The mission of Southwest Airlines is dedication to the highest quality of Customer Service delivered with a sense of warmth, friendliness, individual pride, and Company Spirit" (http://www.southwest.com/about_swa/mission.html). Google sets an incredibly high standard with their mission statement, "Google's mission is to organize the world's information and make it universally accessible and useful" (http://www.google.com/corporate/index.html). Dell Computers describes their corporate philosophy as the "Soul of Dell," which includes descriptions of the core elements of customers, the Dell team, direct relationships, global citizenship, and winning (http://www1.us.dell.com/content/topics/global.aspx/corp/soulofdell/en/index?c=us&l=en&s=corp). United Parcel Service has a simple purpose statement, "We enable global commerce" (http://www.pressroom.ups.com/mediakits/factsheet/0,2305,792,00.html).

From the values and vision statement of Levi Strauss, it would be difficult to identify them as a maker of jeans:

Our values are fundamental to our success. They are the
foundation of our company, define who we are and set us
apart from the competition. They underlie our vision of
the future, our business strategies and our decisions,
actions and behaviors. We live by them. They endure.
Four core values are at the heart of Levi Strauss & Co.:
Empathy, Originality, Integrity and Courage. These four
values are linked. As we look at our history, we see a
story of how our core values work together and are the
source of our success.
(http://www.levistrauss.com/about/vision/)

Apple Computer has become well known for its innovative
products. Through July 1, 2004, Apple included the following statement in all press releases:

Apple ignited the personal computer revolution in the
1970s with the Apple II and reinvented the personal
computer in the 1980s with the Macintosh. Apple is
committed to bringing the best personal computing
experience to students, educators, creative professionals
and consumers around the world through its innovative
hardware, software, and Internet offerings.
(http://www.apple.com/pr/library/2004/jul/01itunes.html)

Beginning with a press release on July 7, 2004, announcing the
international availability of the iPod, that statement changed to the
following:

Apple ignited the personal computer revolution in the
1970s with the Apple II and reinvented the personal
computer in the 1980s with the Macintosh. Today,
Apple continues to lead the industry in innovation with
its award-winning desktop and notebook computers,
OS X operating system, and iLife and professional

applications. Apple is also spearheading the digital music revolution with its iPod portable music players and iTunes online music store.
(http://www.apple.com/pr/library/2004/jul/07ipod-mini.html)

An organization's mission statement should answer the question, Why does this organization exist? The mission statement must be written in clear, concise language and include input gathered from throughout the organization so that it reflects the personality of the organization. Once written, the statement should be shared widely in as many forms as possible so that it can be used to truly guide the actions of the organization (Jones & Kahaner, 1995).

The mission statement should do something else. It should offer a compelling reason for the organization's existence. The contribution the organization makes to the campus, community, or world needs to be articulated in a way that is enticing to potential participants and motivational to those who have already joined the organization. The mission of your organization could be social, service-related, programmatic, political, or any combination, but the effectiveness of your organization will be determined by how well it moves toward its mission.

As you might imagine, many definitions could describe the vision of an organization. Kouzes and Posner (1995) call a vision "an ideal or unique image of the future" (p. 95). Albrecht (1994) terms it "an image of what the people of the enterprise aspire for it to be or become" (p. 150). The vision answers the questions, "What do we want to be? What is the best we can be?" (Jaffe, Scott, & Tobe, 1994, p. 146). We believe that the vision answers the question, What is the ideal future for this organization? As such, it must motivate and inspire, be a stretch, be clear and concrete, be achievable, reflect high values, and be simple (Jaffe, et al). The vision that the organization embraces challenges both the leader and the membership to do their very best—sometimes even more than believed possible—to move toward the mission for which the organization exists.

Getting the members of your organization to share this vision can be very challenging, but unless it is shared and owned by the members, nothing of significance will ever happen. The vision must tap into the motivational systems of the people in your organization. This is why it is so important for the mission and vision statements to be clearly stated and inspiring. It is also the reason why these two statements must constantly be in front of all leaders and members and used to guide the actions of the organization. As Margaret Wheatley (1992) notes, "We need to be able to trust that something as simple as a clear core set of values and vision, kept in motion through continuing dialogue, can lead to order" (p. 147). In other words, the mission and vision need to come alive and be kept constantly alive through the actions of the leaders and members of the organization.

"For a group to remain coherently 'focused,' each individual must be aware of what it is their gaze is focused upon. In times of ambiguity it has been helpful to together redefine the goal, and to reestablish the team's commitment to reaching this goal. Once an objective has been defined and the team has set their eyes upon this common aim, the group often feels a greater connection and drive which empowers them to explore steps to solidify this vision."—Michelle Peterie studies English at University of Wollongong and is a participant of the Black Opal Leadership Program, member of the Snowy River Shire's Youth Council (Youth Action Committee), and is a tutor with SCARF (Strategic Community Assistance for Refugee Families).

The final concept we explore in this section is that of core values. Without core values, any behavior would be justifiable as long as it moved the organization toward its mission or vision. We have all seen examples of this when people say that the ends justify the means. In their examination of visionary companies, Collins and Porras (1994) described core values as "The organization's essential and enduring tenets—a small set of general guiding principles; not to be confused with specific cultural or operating practices; not to be compromised for financial gain or short-term expediency" (p. 73). These core values are small in number (usually three to six values) and "so fundamental and deeply held that they will change or be compromised seldom, if ever" (p. 74). Core values answer the question, How do we, as organization members, agree to treat ourselves and others as we pursue our mission and vision? Although core values are important to the success of any organization, they are seldom discussed or shared among the membership. We encourage you to take some time, both individually and as a group, to reflect on the core values for which your organization stands. It will be time well spent.

Organizational Culture

Many people believe that organizations are so powerful and influential that they take on a culture of their own. Edgar Schein, in his classic work *Organizational Culture and Leadership* (2004) defines this form of organizational culture as

> a pattern of shared basic assumptions that was learned by a group as it solved its problems of external adaptation and internal integration, that has worked well enough to be considered valid and, therefore, to be taught to new members as the correct way to perceive, think, and feel in relation to those problems. (p. 17)

James Carse (1986) defines culture in a slightly different manner. "Culture . . . is an infinite game. Culture has no boundaries . . ." (p. 53) and "for this reason it can be said that where society is defined by its boundaries, a culture is defined by its horizons" (p. 69).

Schein (2004) proposes that culture has three different levels. The most visible level is the artifacts—the "structures and processes" of the organization. The espoused beliefs and values of the organization make up the next level. These are the "strategies, goals, and philosophies" that the organization claims it embraces. At the final, deepest level are the underlying assumptions. These are the "beliefs, perceptions, thoughts, and feelings" that are assumed to be true by members of the organization. These underlying assumptions drive the values and actions of the organization. He asserts that the most important job the leader has is to manage the culture (p. 26).

Terrence Deal and Allan Kennedy (1982) offer a different framework from which to examine organizational cultures. They stress the importance of the organization's values, heroes, rites and rituals, and communications network. Values are important because they provide the core of the organization and a guide for the behaviors of the members. Ordinary individuals who are heroic in their actions are critical because they make success more possible to achieve, provide role models, symbolize the organization to outsiders, preserve what makes the organization special, set a standard of performance, and motivate members (Deal & Kennedy). The rites and rituals provide the formal and informal guidelines for how the everyday occurrences within the organization are to proceed. They include how members should communicate, socialize, work, and play, as well as what actions should be recognized and how they will be rewarded. The rites and rituals also govern the intricacies of how the organization operates—for example, how its meetings are conducted. Finally, Deal and Kennedy analyze the organization's communications network by examining how information is gathered and disseminated, both formally and informally. As they note, "The whole process depends on people, not on paper" (p. 87).

Deal and Kennedy (1982) describe various characters within the organization and outline how they contribute to the communications network. Storytellers interpret what is going on in the organization; what they say may or may not be the truth, because it reflects their perception of what is happening. Priests see themselves as guarding the values of the organization's culture; another of their roles is to keep the membership of the organization together. Whisperers work behind the scenes and have power because of their close connection to the leadership of the organization. Gossips can provide detailed information about what is currently happening within the organization; sometimes the facts they provide are correct, sometimes they are not. Administrative support sources can tell members what is really going on in the organization because of their access to important information. Spies are loyal to the leaders of the organization and provide information to them about what is happening. Finally, cabals are groups of two or more people whose main purpose in joining together is to advance themselves within the organization; their alliance is often kept secret.

Another way to view organizations is offered by Bolman and Deal (2003b) who use four "frames" of organizations: structural, human resource, political, and symbolic. As you might imagine, the structural frame focuses on formal processes like organizational charts, roles, and job descriptions. The human resource frame emphasizes the people in the organization—their feelings and motivations. The political frame operates from the perspective that there will always be a scarcity of resources, so organizations are inevitably in conflict with each other and must operate in ways, such as forming coalitions, that will enable them to gain more. The symbolic frame focuses on the ceremonies, stories, and heroes that help define the organization and reveal or reflect its values. Paying attention to how these different frames are operating within your organization can provide clues to why some parts may be doing well while other aspects are struggling.

Geert Hofstede (2003) adds to our understanding of organizations and cultures through his studies of societies around the world. He proposes that people differ in five broad dimensions: the Power Distance Index (the degree to which the particular society supports inequality or equality), Individualism (how much individual work is emphasized over collective action), Masculinity (the degree to which traditionally male values are embraced over traditionally female values), Uncertainty Avoidance Index (the degree to which ambiguity and uncertainty are tolerated), and Long-Term Orientation (how much a long-term perspective is favored over a short-term view). Compare this work with the dimensions of culture identified by Project GLOBE that appeared in Chapter Five. Considering Hofstede's dimensions can help us understand our own organizations by reminding us that people have different beliefs and preferences for how the world should work. For example, imagine that a group of students wants to join your organization and that they believe strongly in equality and that all opinions should be given equal consideration (Power Distance). Unfortunately, for them at least, your organization has a long history of being hierarchical, with preference given to the ideas of long-standing members (Long Term). This is simply how you operate, and you've been effective with this method of operation. As a leader in such a situation, you may have a difficult time convincing the group of students that they will be able to make a contribution to your organization.

It is important to have a sense of the culture of your organization because it provides insight into how your organization *really* operates. This may seem trivial because we all think we know how it operates. But veteran members' experiences in an organization can be very different from those of new or prospective members. Consider the general concept of change. In some organizations, "If it ain't broke, break it" could define the culture, whereas in other organizations, "If it ain't broke, don't worry about it" may be the way things operate. Being a new member of a change-oriented organization can be very exciting because your opinions may be listened to more closely than in the organization that embraces the status quo. Veteran members, however, may think things are just fine the way they presently are and see no need for much change at all.

An organizational culture can also negatively affect life within an organization. As Stacey (1992) notes, "Strongly shared cultures inevitably block new learning and cut down on the variety of perspectives brought to bear on an issue" (p. 143). In other words, "The more norms we strongly share, the more we resist changing them" (143). Although the development of a culture that supports the pursuit of the organization's mission, values, and goals is very important, everyone must be aware of how the culture may also be inhibiting the organization. People must also realize that trying to change the mission, vision, and values of the organization without paying attention to changing the culture may meet with resistance. Think about how something as "simple" as eliminating hazing from the initiation process of an organization should be. Hazing is against the law, causes harm, and does little to benefit the organization. Yet the culture of many organizations strongly embraces the need for such rites of passage in order for new members to show their dedication to their new organization. Changing the mission and values of the organization to embrace nonhazing principles is often relatively easy. Changing the culture of the organization so that individuals in it do not haze is often more difficult. Planning a rewarding substitute activity to celebrate the transition of new members to full membership can enrich the culture.

Organizational Networks

The importance of networks has received much attention in recent years (Barabási, 2002; Watts, 2003). Networks even made it into the popular culture when people played the game "Six Degrees of Kevin Bacon." How many links would it take to connect Kevin Bacon to Will Smith? Probably two links. Bacon was in *JFK* with Tommy Lee Jones, who was in *Men in Black* with Will Smith—get the idea? Jessica Lipnack and Jeffrey Stamps (1993) define networks as "where disparate groups of people and groups 'link' to work together based on common purposes" (p. 7). These groups of people may be participants in your organization and may also include others from outside the organization. The keys are that they work together and have a common purpose. Networks are important because they provide the chance to bring together a wide range of individuals. The network either may address a specific issue, such as when a wide range of students, faculty, and staff members are brought together to plan an institution's one-hundredth birthday celebration, or it may work on an ongoing concern like student retention. Student ethnic or cultural groups may network for diversity programs on campus or take on advocacy issues. Key issues in the formation of a network include agreement on the network's purpose, creating as many links as possible among members of the network, and making sure that multiple leaders exist within the network (Lipnack & Stamps).

Life Cycles of Organizations

Although the emerging paradigm described in Chapter Two would suggest that organizations cannot be controlled, we believe that a critical point in the success of any organization is its ability to adapt to change—changing conditions, changing membership, and changing leadership. This ability to adapt enables an organization to renew itself and maintain its vibrancy. A small group of skilled and determined individuals can move an organization into greatness by their focused actions. This sometimes happens with new organizations. A group of students gets excited about an idea and, with the help of a few other students, forms an organization dedicated to a specific purpose. The energy, excitement, and dedication of this small group often helps them accomplish powerful outcomes. However, this success can be short-lived unless the organization makes plans for what will happen next—specifically, who will be recruited as new members and who will be groomed for future leadership positions. This is one of the most critical, and often overlooked, responsibilities of leadership—to identify, recruit, prepare, and mentor the future leaders of the organization. Feeling this obligation to sustain the organization into the future is called generativity.

John W. Gardner (1990) and Ichak Adizes (1988) present the concept of "lives" of organizations. Gardner uses the terms *infancy* and *maturity* to differentiate organizations that are in their early lives from those that have evolved into something more orderly and with more of a sense of direction. Adizes goes into more detail and uses the terms *courtship, infancy, go-go, adolescence, prime, stable, aristocracy, early bureaucracy, bureaucracy,* and *death* to describe a similar change process. As Gardner notes, "At each stage something is gained and something is lost" (p. 122). When organizations are young, they are very flexible and motivated, are willing to try new things, and have the ability to respond quickly to new challenges. Yet they may expend much energy to accomplish relatively little. As organizations mature, this flexibility lessens, and they become more orderly and are more satisfied with slow, steady advances (Gardner). These stages in the life of organizations are similar to the stages of group development presented in Chapter Seven.

It has been said that when asked about the early days of the Peace Corps, Sargent Shriver, its director, noted that the leadership of the organization didn't meet—they were too busy doing things. This dedication is often felt early on in new organizations and is exciting—even intoxicating—but it will always end. The model of Adizes (1998) is critical for student leaders to understand because of its focus on how an entire organization changes. Take a hard look at your organization. How would a random sample of students on your campus describe the student government? Would they be positive? Negative? Indifferent? Could they identify any recent accomplishments of the group?

Your organization needs to ask itself two questions on a regular basis: What have we accomplished recently? and How does what we've accomplished reflect our organization's mission? If you are having trouble formulating answers to either of these questions, you may need to reexamine what you are doing and how you are doing it. Remember that the purpose of meetings and standard operating procedures is to help your organization do things in the most expedient manner. They are not designed to become ends unto themselves. As a leader, you must identify and describe significant accomplishments that you helped your organization achieve—not the fact that you attended or ran a lot of meetings.

Multicultural Organizational Development

To remain vibrant and viable over an extended period of time, an organization needs to be willing to remake itself. One way to approach organizational transformation is through the concept of multicultural organizational development (Armour & Hayles, 1990; Jackson & Holvino, 1988; Pope, 1993). This process emphasizes the full participation of members from all cultural and social groups and a commitment to end all forms of social oppression that may exist within the organization that blocks the meaningful, inclusive involvement of all members. This emphasis on diversity and social justice offers a fresh perspective from which to approach organizational transformation. Because the Relational Leadership Model emphasizes being inclusive and empowering, it is essential to understand how an organization might transform itself to be multicultural. What do you think the impact would be if every organization on your campus made a commitment to end all forms of social oppression? This would clearly be a transformation, and the campus would become a better place for all its students, faculty, and staff.

Armour and Hayles (1990) and Jackson and Holvino (1988) offer similar models for multicultural organizational development. Their models show the organization moving from a perspective that is monocultural and exclusionary to one that is compliant and nondiscriminatory, through a redefinition process, and finally to a multicultural perspective. Of particular importance in Jackson and Holvino's (1988) work is their elaboration of the assumptions that change agents make, depending on whether they come from a monocultural, nondiscriminatory, or multicultural perspective (Exhibit 8.3). Whereas those coming from a monocultural

Exhibit 8.3. Change Agent Assumptions in Multicultural Organization Development.

	Monocultural	Nondiscriminatory	Multicultural
Nature of Society	Harmonious		Conflict
	Similar interests		Different interests
	Needs to improve, but basically OK		Oppressive, alienating, needs radical change
Oppression	Dominance	Desegregation	Pluralism
Liberation Model	Assimilation	Integration	Diversity
Self-Interest in Change	Survival and social acceptability	Adaptation and full use of human resources	Equity, empowerment, collective growth
Values and Ideology	Basic rights of individual		Interdependence
	Best person is rewarded		Ecological survival
			Development of human and societal potential
	Efficiency and economic survival		

Source: Adapted from Jackson & Holvino (1988), p. 18.

perspective view society as basically harmonious and doing all right, those having a multicultural perspective see society as filled with conflict and in need of radical change. You may already see examples of these two opposing perspectives on your campus. Learning to understand, respect, and work effectively with others who have strongly held views that differ from your own is one of the great challenges of being a leader. It is also absolutely necessary as you work to make your organization and campus a better place for all people.

Learning Organizations

Peter Senge (1990), Watkins and Marsick (1993), and others have proposed a way to conceptualize organizations that will help them operate successfully in the chaotic world described in Chapter Two.

They used the label *learning organizations* to describe organizations that have the capacity to grow, change, and develop in order to adapt to the challenges of their constantly changing environments. In his conceptualization of the learning organization, Senge (1994) included the modules of personal mastery, mental models, shared vision, and team learning. These modules make up a framework of systems thinking; each is interrelated with the others. We believe that the concept of the learning organization and its guiding principles of the primacy of the whole, the community nature of the self, and the generative power of language have much to offer in our discussion of organizations.

Personal mastery involves individuals doing the best possible job. For a treasurer in an organization, this might include knowing how to use new financial software, being able to follow the steps needed to purchase something, and having budgeting skills. For a vice president, this might include skills in working with committee chairs so that their respective groups can get organized and be productive. Everyone in an organization—officers and members—has skills and abilities that can be contributed to the organization. It is important for leaders to work with the group's membership, not only so that individuals can gain the skills needed to be effective in their current roles within the organization, but also as a way of preparing them for future positions. When members are skilled and empowered to use these skills, the whole organization benefits.

Mental models are the assumptions that people make about the various aspects of the world. For instance, when someone says the words *leader, conflict, diversity,* or *meeting,* what images pop into your head? These mental models are often difficult to grasp and, therefore, are sometimes difficult to change. But these models must be changed if any real positive change is to occur in the world. Disagreements sometimes arise because these differing mental models are not brought to the surface so they can be examined and, if necessary, changed. Consider for a moment the concept of *adviser.* If your organization has an adviser, you may assume that this person will make sure details do not fall through the cracks when you are planning a big event. When this turns out not to be true, everyone loses. It is important to compare the mental models that you have with others in your organization. In this way, false assumptions can be minimized. Mental models can also be empowering for a whole organization. Consider what would happen if, when members thought about your organization, the concepts of inclusion, empowerment, process, ethics, and common purpose immediately came to mind. These images could do a lot to guide the organization in a way that would help make it strong and successful.

Shared vision focuses on the idea that the mission, vision, and purpose of an organization must be shared by all members. Shared vision—or common purpose—is especially important given the current emphasis on empowerment. People can be empowered and their personal mastery level high, yet without some shared sense of direction, everyone will be pushing hard in different directions. The result will be an organization that moves haphazardly, if at all. Although vision is certainly important, Helgesen (1990) notes that feeling confident in one's "voice" may be just as critical because this is how the vision is related and shared with others.

The concept of team learning is also vital in any learning organization. As Senge (1990) and others (Kline & Saunders, 1993; Watkins & Marsick, 1993) note, learning at the individual level (Senge's concept of personal mastery) must be supplemented by learning at the team, organizational, and societal levels if any true learning is to occur. This might include learning how to make decisions, how to really communicate, and how to disagree—aspects of organizational life that we usually take for granted, yet perform very poorly. The concept of team learning also underscores the need to consider leadership as an ongoing process rather than an end result or product. Just as team members are constantly engaged with each other in learning new approaches or methods, leaders must be continually engaged in dialogue with members of their organizations.

Finally, a systems approach governs the thinking in a learning organization. When people think systematically, they share responsibility for the good and bad things that are happening. Rather than looking for someone else to blame, members of a learning organization hold up the mirror and ask what they have done to contribute to the problem. Think of how many problems we blame on someone or something else rather than accepting responsibility for them ourselves and working toward a solution. Senge (1990) calls this specific "learning disability" a belief that "the enemy is out there." As in our earlier example of the organization as a weather system, all aspects of a system are constantly working together to create the reality of the system. All of these aspects—personal mastery, mental models, shared vision, team learning, and systems thinking—combine to create a learning organization.

We have gone into so much detail about the learning organization because the capacity for an organization to continuously learn enables it to continuously recreate itself as it faces new challenges. Consider the following example: A student government organization needs to appoint a student member to its college's board of trustees. What qualities should such a representative have? How should that person be selected? What issues should this representative bring to the board? All of a sudden, the student government has moved from being an organization that may have a programming emphasis to one that gives students a voice in the group that makes the major decisions regarding campus life. This is a major change in focus. To take advantage of this opportunity, the organization must be able to learn how the board operates, what issues will be of most interest to the board, and what approaches will be most successful. Much of this learning will have to be "on the hoof" (Stacey, 1992). Only an organization that is truly open to and embracing of learning new approaches will make optimal use of this opportunity.

Virtuality and the Impact of Technology

Understanding the essential role of technology and its impact on organizational life is crucial (see Oblinger & Oblinger, 2005; Postman, 1992). The growth of virtual teams and organizations has been chronicled in a number of publications (for example, Avolio & Kahai, 2003; Davidow & Malone, 1992; Davis, 2004; Grenier & Metes, 1995; Handy, 1996; Hart & McLeod, 2003; Kissler, 2001; Lipnack & Stamps, 1993; Petersen, 1994; Pickover, 1991; Rheingold, 1993; Zaccaro & Bader, 2003; Zigurs, 2003). Charles Handy defines virtual organizations as "organizations that do not need to have all the people, or sometimes any of the people, in one place in order to deliver their service. The organization exists but you can't see it. It is a network, not an office" (p. 212). Zigurs notes that we should think in terms of "virtuality" as a continuum. The more the team is separated in terms of geography, time, or culture, or organizationally, the more virtual it is.

So what will these virtual organizations be like? Handy (1996), Zigurs (2003), and Zaccaro and Bader (2003) believe that trust will be extremely important—and very difficult to develop when people do not often see each other face-to-face. He also stresses the need for a common purpose and values to be shared by all the organization's members. Davidow and Malone (1992) note that organizations will certainly be flatter (multiple layers of hierarchy will be a thing of the past) and built on the need for the organization's members to believe and trust in each other, and that they will involve members at all levels more and more in the decision-making process.

Leadership within these virtual environments is described by Avolio and Kahai (2003). "At its core, leadership is about the development of relationships. Whether connected via information technology or not, leaders have to build relationships in order to lead effectively" (p. 331). Among the associated "major changes and future trends" identified by Avolio and Kahai are the following:

"leaders and followers have more access to information and each other . . . leadership is migrating to lower and lower organizational levels . . . [and] leadership creates and exists in networks" (p. 333). Kissler (2001) identifies a number of e-leadership attributes for success; among other traits, successful leaders "revel in complexity, ambiguity, and uncertainty; [and are] incredibly curious and insatiable life-long learners; courageous due to deeply-held values and unwavering beliefs; able to build and retain talent" (p. 132). Zaccaro and Bader (2003) note a number of e-team leader roles that lead to e-team effectiveness, including "enhancing cohesion, nurturing trust, promoting sharing of information and ideas, moderating team conflict, facilitating team coordination and integration, and developing social and human capital" (p. 382).

Your organization may already seem a lot like a virtual organization, with members coming and going at all hours of the day or night and spending very little time together in the same place. You may already be involved in other examples of virtual organizations on your campus. Your student government organization may also be a member of a state, regional, or national coalition with other student government groups. You might plan a leadership conference with students on other campuses via e-mail, phone, and fax and never actually meet face-to-face in the same room until the conference begins. On your campus, you may find that you communicate more often with the members of your own organization through the use of cell phones, e-mail, text messaging, Yahoo! Groups, or other technologies than in face-to-face meetings.

The impact of all this technology cannot be overstated. We now have the ability to communicate and share information with anyone, anytime, anywhere. So what does this mean for your organization? What will it mean for organizations in the future? We have already seen how this technology can be used to organize people (Rheingold, 2003). In what other ways will it fundamentally change how organizations operate? Does more communication always make better organizations? At what point does having access to all this information become overwhelming? At this point, we cannot predict how organizations will change as a result of the use of technology. All we know is that they will change.

New Paradigm Leadership in Conventional Paradigm Cultures

One of the most challenging results of reading a book like this is realizing that you might embrace the principles of new paradigm leadership but find yourself mired in a conventional culture. This can present a dilemma, but you can take actions toward continuing to use this information. First of all, share what you know with other leaders, members of your organization, advisers—anyone who will listen. By sharing, you do two things: you learn the information better yourself, and you may find some other interested people with whom you can continue to connect. Accept personal responsibility for finding ways to use the information rather than always saying, "Well, so-and-so won't let me do that." Maintain a positive outlook and try to find areas in which you can use this information rather than focusing on areas that seem out of bounds. Continue to try new things, even in small ways. You will find a number of different exercises and thought pieces in *The Fifth Discipline Fieldbook* (Senge, Kleiner, Roberts, Ross, & Smith, 1994) that you can use in a variety of settings, both in and outside of your organization. Volunteer to do programs or activities with other organizations or to be a guest speaker or teacher. Finally, continue to read and explore. A number of resources are listed in this book. Continue to develop your own leadership library. It will serve you well for your entire life (Allen, 1990).

Chapter Summary

In this chapter we have discussed complex organizations. We have discussed why organizations exist and how they are structured. We have stressed the importance of mission, vision, and core values.

We also have presented what the virtual organization of the future might be like. Throughout this chapter the importance of the Relational Leadership Model has been evident. It is only by being inclusive that an organization can creatively use the talents and abilities of all of its membership. By being empowering and process-oriented, the organization encourages all members to take an active role in the life of the organization. By being ethical, the organization ensures that members can hold each other to a higher standard of behavior that is more closely aligned with the organization's mission, vision, and core values. Finally, it is only when this vision or common purpose is truly shared by the entire membership that an organization can reach its potential and be purposeful.

Organizational life need not be an endless series of meetings run by *Robert's Rules of Order*. There can and should be excitement and energy there. We hope you will find it.

What's Next?

So far in this part we have presented leadership in the context of groups and organizations. In the next chapter we introduce the community context. The term *community* can be used to describe a spirit that encourages a collection of people to work and act collaboratively (sense of community). It can also be used to identify the population of a geographic area (the community of Smallville). The spirit of community and the principles of community development are explored further in the next chapter.

Chapter Activities

1. *Groups and Organizations:* Identify a group and organization in which you are currently a participant. Now look at Exhibit 8.1. How do your experiences support the way we differentiated among these three concepts? How do your experiences differ from our framework?

2. *Organizational Mission:* Find your organization's mission statement or an example of a mission statement not described in this chapter. Does it meet the criteria suggested by Jones and Kahaner? What are your statement's strengths? Where does it fall short? How could you change it to make it more reflective of both the purpose and the personality of your organization? How compelling is it? If you don't have a mission statement, write one now. How did you do? Would you be inspired by your statement if you knew nothing of your organization?

3. *Organizational Vision:* Imagine an ideal future for your organization. Try to capture this image on paper. Be creative. You can make a collage or a drawing or use words—whatever works for you. When you are finished, look at your image. Is it inspiring? Would it motivate your members? How could it be improved?

4. *Core Values:* Reflect for a couple of minutes on the core values of your organization. Write down what these values are. Do not worry about the number you have, but try to come up with at least ten. Do not worry about putting them into any order. Once you have your list, pick the top five—the five most important core values. Again, do not worry about prioritizing your choices. From this list of five, pick the three most important values. Finally, pick the most important core value for your organization. Repeat this exercise with all members of your organization.

5. *Organizational Culture:* Answer the following questions about your organization:

    Values: What basic values do the members of your organization embrace?

    Heroes: Who are the heroes of your organization? Why are they famous or infamous? What qualities do they exemplify?

6. *Rites and Rituals:* How do members of your organization work together? How do members of your organization play

together? What actions or behaviors are recognized? How are they rewarded?

7. *Four Frames of Organizations:* Identify an organization of which you are a member. Describe your organization using each of the four frames of organizations in Bolman and Deal's four-frame theory.

8. *Multicultural Organizational Development:* Think about the concept of multicultural organizational development. How committed is your organization to full participation by members of all cultural and social groups? How committed is your organization to ending all forms of social oppression that might exist within the organization? What could you do to increase this commitment?

9. *Virtual Organizations:* Think about your organization. How virtual are you? How do you use technology to interact? If you use technology in your organization, how do you use it? What has been the effect of its use? What have been the benefits and challenges associated with its use?

Additional Readings

Allen, K. A., & Cherrey, C. (2000). *Systemic leadership: Enriching the meaning of our work.* Lanham, MD: University Press of America.

Avolio, B. J., & Kahai, S. S. (2003). Adding the "E" to e-leadership: How it may impact your leadership. *Organizational Dynamics, 31*(4), 325–338.

Barabási, A.-L. (2002). *Linked: The new science of networks.* Cambridge, MA: Perseus.

Handy, C. (1996). *Beyond certainty: The changing worlds of organizations.* Boston: Harvard Business School Press.

Helgesen, S. (1995). *The web of inclusion: A new architecture for building great organizations.* New York: Currency/Doubleday.

Hofstede, G. (2003). *Culture's consequences: Comparing values, behaviors, institutions and organizations across nations* (2nd ed.). Thousand Oaks, CA: Sage.

Oblinger, D. G., & Oblinger, J. L. (Eds.). (2005). *Educating the net generation.*

Educause. (http://www.educause.edu/content.asp?PAGE_ID=
5989&bhcp=1#copyright)

Rheingold. H. (2003). *Smart mobs: The next social revolution*. New York: Basic
Books.

Schein, E. (1992). *Organizational culture and leadership* (2nd ed.). San Francisco:
Jossey-Bass.

Watts, D. J. (2003). *Six degrees: The science of a connected age*. New York:
Norton.

9

Being in Communities

Denise is at home not feeling well. She is sorry to have missed the commencement committee meeting this morning. The phone rings and Jason is on the line. He has Stacy and Carl in his room, and they are worried because Denise did not come to the meeting.

> JASON: Denise, it's Jason and I'm here with Stacy and Carl. Our committee was really worried when you didn't show up this morning. Dean Jacobs asked if anyone knew if you were OK, since you are always right there. You sound terrible! Are you OK?
>
> DENISE: [clearing her throat] Thanks, Jason. It feels really good to know you all noticed. I have a killer cold. It hit me late last night. Sorry I didn't call so you wouldn't worry.
>
> JASON: That's OK, Denise. Hope you feel better. Stacy says she'll drop some résumés of the possible commencement speakers by your house tonight because we are all supposed to be ready to vote on one of them as our recommendation to the senior class council for Friday—oh, Stacy says to ask if you need anything she can bring when she comes by?

This committee appears to be a healthy community. Denise's absence was noticed by committee members and by the adviser.

They cared enough to check on her and to pick up copies of materials in her absence. Denise knows from this encounter that she matters.

Community is a compelling feeling, whether on a smaller personal level or on a macro or national level. Remember all the ways in which communities pull together in times of crises: the families who opened their homes to strangers after the 2005 hurricanes, the colleges that took in displaced students after Hurricane Katrina, and how America reunited following the terrorist attacks on September 11, 2001.

Chapter Overview

Envisioning each group or organization you are in as a community provides a mental model that will respond to the relational needs of these rapidly changing times. Individuals function concurrently in many different kinds of community. Thinking of each of your formal and informal groups as a community provides a frame for the interdependence of relational leadership. This chapter discusses the nature of communities, principles of community development, and your role as an active member of your communities of practice.

The Importance of Community

Knowing about community, philosophically believing in the worth of community, and being skilled at developing and sustaining community are essential aspects of relational leadership. Ideal, perfect communities do not exist in reality. We all live, work, and learn in imperfect communities, which, if they are striving to be better, become supportive environments for individual and group growth. Any group of people that come together for a purpose (such as a neighborhood, an office, a class, or a city experiencing a natural disaster) "continually participate in conversations about the questions

'Who are we?' and 'What matters?'" (Wheatley & Kellner-Rogers, 1998, p. 17).

Gardner (1990) asserts that "*skill in the building and rebuilding of community is not just another of the innumerable requirements of contemporary leadership. It is one of the highest and most essential skills a leader can command*" (p. 118, emphasis in the original). Relational leadership calls for attending to community as a discipline. The term "discipline" in this case refers to a concept to be studied, learned, and practiced, as one would learn academic disciplines such as biology, English, or history (Gozdz, 1993). It is not enough to understand self and others; understanding is essential to creating and nurturing the context in which the group or organization functions. Thinking of the relationships in that setting as a community focuses participants' attention on the responsibilities, the processes, and the spirit of working together.

Think of the most effective and meaningful classes, clubs, committees, or groups you have experienced. You probably felt a commitment to the whole and felt like you mattered and were meaningful to others in that setting. Not all groups feel that way. You can probably recall or imagine a group you had to be a part of but which held little value for you or in which you felt little in common with others or little commitment to the task in that setting. That group may have accomplished its goals, but few members would say they enjoyed working together; they probably would not want to work together again if given a choice. Relational leadership asks you to envision the context of the setting as a healthy community, which leads to a whole paradigm of expectations and norms for working together effectively as participants in shared leadership.

"I feel part of a community within a family group at church camp. Each group I have been a part of has been characterized by the formation of a group covenant, a common purpose, trust, acceptance of people's emotional levels, willingness to share, security to reveal emotions, thoughts, and opinions without criticism, strong role models within the surrounding group, and time for both fun and serious activities."—Trisha Fields was chair of the Spring Leadership Trip at Texas A&M University.

Elements of Community

A community is most often described as "a social group that not only shares an identity and structured pattern of interaction, but also a common geographical territory" (Goodman, 1992, p. 48). However, community is not just a place where interaction occurs, but also an attitude of connection and commitment that sustains relationships and purpose. Sharing that community commitment is the essence of relational leadership. The phone call to Denise might not seem to illustrate leadership on the surface, but imagine a small committee or class whose members matter so much to each other and to the adviser or professor that someone's absence is not only noticed but becomes a matter of concern, and whose members look out for the person's needs. In that environment, each participant feels a sense of ownership and shared leadership.

Communities know they are a collection of individuals who accomplish their goals through trust and teamwork. Teamwork requires processes to make decisions, methods of communication, and a commitment to some level of participation by community members. Gardner (1990) extends the traditional definitions of community to refer to effective communities as those that practice these eight elements:

1. Wholeness incorporating diversity
2. A shared culture
3. Good internal communication
4. Caring, trust, and teamwork
5. Group maintenance and governance

6. Participation and shared leadership tasks
7. Development of young people [or new members]
8. Links with the outside world (pp. 116–118)

Through their work together, community members develop a shared culture that is concerned about new members. Effective communities realize they are not insular but are in a constant, dynamic interaction with their broader environment. Binding all of this together is the awareness that a group is a community—the shared culture may reflect that spirit of community. The spirit of community makes many other relational processes possible.

Many traditional views of community are changing. Conventional views present communities as homogeneous groupings of people who have much in common and may even resemble each other in ideology, race, or class. Those may indeed be communities, yet "cultural and ethnic diversity (and all other forms of diversity, as well) are necessary resources for building community. A true community cannot exist without diversity" (Gudykunst, 1991, p. 146). Diversity of ideas, diversity of skills, diversity of experiences, and diversity of worldviews bring to a group's shared goals the many talents of people gathered as a community. If all community members saw things the same way, had the same skills, and had the same life experiences, their ability to be resilient and face change would be limited. "Community is that place where the person you least want to live with always lives. And when that person moves away, someone else arises to take his or her place" (Palmer, 1981, p. 124).

Other traditional views have held that communities need face-to-face interaction, which is possible only through close geographic proximity. Increasingly, however, the term *community* also describes those with common identity and interaction but without geographic proximity. References to "the medical community" or "the spiritual community" reflect their common frame or perspective and not their physical daily interactions. Many members of these communities do find ways to meet and think together. Professional society meetings through associations and conventions provide a forum for the development of community connections.

Electronic networks have provided a creative way for communities of common interest to interact. Internet chat rooms, blogs, message boards, online discussion groups, and sites such as MySpace.com are linking people across the globe into selective communities in which minds meet. There are those who express concern that electronic communications like e-mail, text messaging, and chat rooms diminish community; indeed, it is possible to become isolated from face-to-face interaction when using the computer for most of your interactions. But the effective and responsible use of electronic communication can facilitate community. Think of how you feel closer to the community of your high school friends when you can text message them wherever they now live—like at other colleges, in the military, or at work. Cyber communities have provided support connections for gay and lesbian students and students with disabilities. Although many remain cautious of Internet relationships, studies demonstrate that off-line and on-line relationships do not differ in depth or breadth and may even be associated with social well-being (Bonebrake, 2002).

You can also find identity and feel a sense of community with others without interacting. For example, if you are an avid environmentalist, you feel a close connection to the struggles of Greenpeace or the Sierra Club when you read about them in the news. If you are concerned about poverty, you feel a sense of community watching the worldwide Live Aid–style concerts attempting to influence the G8 summit. If you participate in community service concerned with abused children, you feel anguish over the latest tragedies reported on the radio and can empathize with social workers struggling to find solutions. If you are a member of a national organization like a sorority, you may feel immediate kinship with a sister from another chapter whom you met while you were both on vacation. You might even seek out certain communities when you move to a new town because you know you will be welcomed as a new member.

As human beings, we all want meaningful connection to others. Settings that are inclusive and empowering, in which there is purposeful change being accomplished through ethical and collaborative processes, are the epitome of effective communities. Relational leadership flourishes in settings that value the elements of community.

A Common Center

In his 1958 classic *I and Thou*, Martin Buber contends that in our life together, some form of community is what makes life worth living. He describes community as a group of people who have made a choice around a common center. A true community is not a collection of people who all think alike but people with differing minds and complementary natures.

We participated in a group of leadership educators who struggled with the role and importance of community in shared leadership. This group eventually defined community as the "binding together of diverse individuals committed to a just, common good through shared experiences in a spirit of caring and social responsibility" (National Invitational Leadership Symposium, 1991, p. 19). Developing communities like this depends on relational leadership that deeply values the inclusion of all members, empowered to work together toward common purposes.

In these communities, openness is a central practice. True dialogue requires listening and being willing to give up the need for control, even when your ideas and thoughts are in conflict with those of another. Without the willingness to give up control, you engage in monologue that cannot promote community. Being in community requires the realization that a member's own needs will not always prevail. Buber (1958) reminds us that this does not mean accepting views of others just to create a false peace; rather, it means keeping in mind the commitment to greater values. "Communities speak to us in moral voices. They lay claims on their members. Indeed, they are the most important sustaining source of moral voices other than the inner self" (Etzioni, 1993, p. 31). Stop and think of how authentic and genuine you are as a supporting member of the communities that matter to you. Communities are where we exhibit the values to which we are committed. The difference between our espoused values and actual behaviors becomes transparent in communities. Indeed, "communities are the mirrors in which we see our true selves" (Hesselbein, Goldsmith, Beckhard, & Schubert, 1998, p. xiii).

"John Donne said, 'No man is an island unto himself.' I believe these immortal words to mean that while we can and often must function individually to achieve personal goals and self confidence, we must interact with our friends, our family and our community. Through working with a community of people one can learn acceptance and equality. There is a necessary sharing of ideas and technologies. By working as a team and building on each other's ideas, plans and ideas are not just created but are evolved into better, clearer plans. Enthusiasm and success are contagious—you can't spread it to yourself."—Christopher Mowbray is a management cadet and works in a finance division of a corporation while attending the University of Wollongong.

Communities of Practice

It is not sufficient to think of yourself as being a mere member of multiple communities; membership may mean having only a passive connection or being a name on a roster. You may be highly involved and committed to the success of your fraternity, the senior class council, an ethnic or religiously affiliated group you are a part of, or the service organization you colead. However, because of limited time, disinterest, or shifting priorities, you may become affiliated with only one of those communities and not highly active in the others.

No one has enough time or energy to be highly involved in every community with which they identify. Being a member of a community of practice, however, implies an engagement with others who are working toward some action. The people in that community are doing something, and you are a part of that in some meaningful way. "Each person belongs to many communities of practice but with varying degrees of centrality. In some communities of practice we are only peripherally involved; in others we are centrally involved" (Drath & Palus, 1994, p. 11). You may have intentionally decided that this is the time to devote more time and energy to your family, to some special needs in your job, or to your senior thesis project, so you cannot do as much as you might like in your worship community or in your other organizations.

Just as there are residence hall floors where residents keep their doors shut and do not even talk on the elevators going down to classes in the morning, there are also floors where residents are in and out of each other's rooms, gather in the floor lounge to watch a favorite reality TV show, and cluster in the same section of the dining hall for dinner each evening. A person can lead an isolated life while surrounded by people in classes, in the snack bar, or at work—or a connected life when meaningfully involved in a community. Even within the larger environment, one can find what Harvard sociologist Herbert Gans calls "urban villages" (cited in Etzioni, 1993, p. 120). Urban villages are the many small communities within larger systems. The giant lecture class can become an urban environment of small villages through the use of such class structures as discussion groups and team projects.

The social networks we form in these communities of practice are critical to accomplishing shared goals as well as to our personal identification and satisfaction. A high level of people's involvement in their diverse communities characterizes the nature of American democracy. Robert Putnam (1995) focused attention on this aspect of American life when he studied the involvement of people in civic life and saw declines in indicators like labor unions, church attendance, and PTA meetings. These symptoms are captured in his observation that "between 1980 and 1993 the total number of bowlers in America increased by 10%, while league bowling decreased by 40%" (p. 70)—so he concluded that Americans were now "bowling alone." New kinds of organizations and issues have grown to capture Americans' attention, such as environmental groups like the Sierra Club, book clubs, and hobby clubs—and support groups have grown to the point that 40% of all Americans claimed to be part of a group that cares for and supports members (Wuthnow, as reported in Putnam). Most Americans have replaced socializing with neighbors with socializing with friends and colleagues from the workplace (Putnam). This shift from being involved in groups that work for civic outcomes to groups that promote more personal outcomes deserves attention. Noting the importance of social networks, Putnam describes the value of social capital, "by analogy with notions of physical capital and human capital—tools and training that enhance individual productivity—'social capital' refers to features of social organization such as networks, norms, and social trust that facilitate coordination and cooperation for mutual benefit" (p. 67).

Focusing on communities of practice also raises the question How can those communities best function to fully engage community members? The policies, behaviors, expectations, norms, and other structures may promote or may prohibit your meaningful involvement in that community. Assume that you are very committed to the community of practice that is the office of your part-time job. An office culture that includes you in decision making, supervision that promotes your personal development, reward systems that show your work is valued, coworkers who support and trust each other, and office celebrations of work successes all create an environment that bonds people to this community. Assess the environment of any of your communities of practice to determine how their structures and processes may be blocking meaningful identity and involvement with that culture. Addressing that information can help it become a more effective environment.

"A community I enjoyed being part of is the Student Activities Office. I am able to learn from as well as interact with the professional and student staff in a way that empowers me as an individual as well as a leader. This has exponentially increased my skill sets/levels in areas of leadership, listening, time and stress management as well as many others. The core characteristics that I was able to pick up on and adapt to my current leadership and teamwork styles were account- ability and responsibility. These proved to be vital to the success of any organization."—Robert Elam was the vice president of the Black Student Alliance and Student Funding Board chair at George Mason University. He majors in finance and marketing and plans to pursue a career as a consultant in the marketing or management field.

Being "in community" requires an awareness of reciprocal processes. An individual has to decide to be part of the larger com- munity, and the community has to involve and welcome individ- uals. Harvard sociologist Charles Willie (1992) asserts that in any community (that is, work group, classroom, neighborhood, or vol- unteer organization) there are concurrent obligations of con- tributive justice and distributive justice. Each individual in the community must practice contributive justice. Individuals con- tribute to the group's belief that it is fair and reasonable for each to do his or her part in the greater whole, uphold obligations, and feel a commitment to shared purposes. Conversely, the commu- nity must practice the distributive justice of caring for all com- munity members and ensuring that each is included, is heard, and is not hurt or disadvantaged through community membership. Some people in communities do not uphold their responsibilities nor share the transcendent values that bind a community together. Communities sometimes act to remove members who are not willing to uphold shared values. The student who persis- tently pulls false fire alarms may not be an appropriate member of a residence hall community, nor is the member of a lab team who sabotages other teams' experiments appropriate for that community.

Communities thrive on "serial reciprocity" (Ulrich, 1998, p. 161). This means that on his residence hall floor, Chris will help Mary move her refrigerator, and Mary repays that kindness, not necessarily by helping Chris back, but when she helps floormate Dianne put up flyers in the hall; Dianne likewise pays Mary back when she picks up the trash that has spilled out of the trash can at the end of the hall (Ulrich). The responsibility each floor resident feels toward the others in the community of the floor creates the civic culture of the floor to generate and regenerate its sense of community.

Arun Gandhi (1998) shares many lessons he learned as a small boy from his grandfather, Mohandas Karamchand Gandhi. Among those lessons were his grandfather's reflections on what caused violence in human life:

- Wealth without work
- Pleasure without conscience
- Knowledge without character
- Commerce without morality
- Science without humanity
- Worship without sacrifice
- Politics without principle
- Rights without responsibilities (p. 90)

Learning to feel responsible for others in our communities of practice is critical for our human connection.

The Development of Community

On the first day that you and thirty other residents move into your new residence hall floor, or fifty students come to a first class, or a committee of twelve convenes its first meeting, community does not magically happen. The development of a spirit of community must happen intentionally.

Scott Peck (1987) has identified four stages of developing true authentic community. The first stage is *pseudocommunity*. In this stage a group may feel like things are just fine, people seem to be getting along, relationships are courteous, but it is in reality a superficial, underdeveloped level of community. For example, "pseudocommunity is conflict-avoiding; true community is conflict-resolving" (p. 88).

The second stage of community building is *chaos*. During this stage there is a noisy din of different views. Different people or factions are asserting their perspectives from which to set the community's agenda or determine important processes. Committee members promote individual agendas; cliques form on the residence hall floor. This stage can be dangerous because some give up and retreat instead of working through this stage. It is important to find meaning in the idea that even "fighting is better than pretending you are not divided" (Peck, 1987, p. 94). This stage is similar to the storming stage of group development presented in Chapter Seven.

Peck (1987) observes that groups take one of two paths out of chaos: *organization* or *emptiness*. Organization leaves the source of fighting untouched, by establishing structures and systems to manage and handle the differences of opinion. For example, the residence hall floor group makes a new policy to rein in those who are misusing the floor lounge; or a committee, frustrated with long debates, decides to vote on decisions and let the majority rule. The structures may solve the immediate problem, but the source of tension and disagreement may fester. Although it is counterintuitive to think of the term *emptiness* as good, emptiness is Peck's term for the process of community members emptying themselves of their barriers to true communication; thus emptiness becomes a stage in community building.

This third stage is the realization that many personal feelings, assumptions, ideas, stereotypes, or motives become barriers to truly listening and understanding (and being understood). Again, emptiness refers to emptying oneself of the assumptions and preconceived notions that may block one from truly listening. It may mean someone saying, "Wait a minute. This argument is beginning to sound like the freshmen think all the seniors are money-hungry, selfish egoists, and the seniors think the freshmen are unrealistic idealists. We need to let go of those assumptions and look at the good thoughts each group is raising."

In the fourth stage of true, authentic community, conflict still arises, but there are ways to be heard, and the community members usually know they cannot reach consensus or any level of agreement without dissensus or disagreements to create truly better decisions. Building community is creating a feel of "we" out of lots of "I's." Many groups never get past pseudocommunity and find ways to courteously interact and get their work done. That may be sufficient for their purposes, but ongoing groups that are doing difficult work would benefit from recognizing Peck's stages and working toward authentic community.

Communities that engage in this developmental process and reach a stage of authentically functioning as a community often err by not recognizing that being a community is a process, not an end state. Communities are not static—they constantly change. New members join the group, external crises cause new levels or types of conflict, and key members, who had been instrumental to nurturing community, leave. Communities must recognize when they need to attend to the cycle of rebuilding a genuine community.

Participants who want to be highly engaged in the work of any community need to assess the ways in which they can become effective community members. Gudykunst (1991) proposes that individual participants practice these seven community building principles:

1. *Be Committed*: Commitment to others is prerequisite for community to exist.

2. *Be Mindful:* Think about what we do and say.
   Focus on the process, not the outcome . . . be contemplative in examining our own behavior.
3. *Be Unconditionally Accepting:* Accept others as they
   are; do not try to change or control them . . . minimize expectations, prejudices, suspicion, and mistrust.
4. *Be Concerned for Both Yourself and Others:* Engage
   in dialogue whenever possible . . . consult others
   on issues that affect them and be open to their
   ideas . . . fight gracefully.
5. *Be Understanding:* Strive to understand others as
   completely as possible.
6. *Be Ethical:* Engage in behavior that is not a means
   to an end, but behavior that is morally right in and
   of itself.
7. *Be Peaceful:* Do not be violent [or] deceitful, breach
   value promises, or be secretive . . . strive for internal harmony . . . and harmony in relations with
   others. (pp. 147–148)

If each participant has the mental model of their organization as a community and practices community-building skills, the group will be enriched. Participants will listen more keenly, respect each other even when there are disagreements on specific issues, seek resolution of differences, and learn more in the process. Etzioni (1993) challenges us to "lay claims on others to be similarly involved in, and dedicated to, community" (p. 142).

Modeling and practicing this kind of participation is essential to being a contributing community member. Relational leadership is directly linked with building community. Exhibit 9.1 illustrates the connections among the elements of relational leadership, with the understandings of the elements of community from Gardner (1990) and the advice on community-building principles from Gudykunst (1991).

Exhibit 9.1. Connecting Relational Leadership to Elements of Community.

Relational Leadership (See Chapter Three)	Elements of Community (Gardner, 1990; *Gudykunst, 1991*)
Inclusive	Wholeness incorporating diversity; links with the outside world; *Be Committed; Be Unconditionally Accepting*
Empowering	A shared culture; group maintenance and governance; development of young people [or new members]; *Be Understanding; Be Concerned for Both Yourself and Others*
Ethical	Caring, trust, and teamwork; *Be Ethical*
Purposeful	Participation and shared leadership tasks
Process-Oriented	Good internal communication; *Be Mindful; Be Peaceful*

College Communities

For hundreds of years, college campuses have been described as communities of scholars or as learning communities. Yet in reality, a sense of true community is not always a shared experience. Hate crimes happen on campus, incivility can be found in senate meetings, some organizations devalue the purposes of other organizations, and not all people know or care about each other. The Carnegie Foundation for the Advancement of Teaching (1990) conducted a major study of what students, faculty, and staff would like to change about their campuses. All groups agreed that they need a renewed sense of community—not a return to an older, homogeneous model, but a kaleidoscopic community that embraces differences and finds common purpose. The Foundation promoted the concept that healthy college communities would be purposeful, open, just, disciplined, caring, and celebrative. Campuses can take purposeful steps to valuing being together in community.

As a microcosm of the society, the entire college campus is a community and includes multiple communities. There are communities within the various positions on campus (for example, students, faculty, administrators, staff, alumni). Within those groups are smaller community clusters (for example, seniors, the Asian Student Association, graduate students); each cluster has unique needs and shares community issues. There are communities by departments and by the programs of functional units (for example, the history department, the engineering college, the student activities office, the intercollegiate athletics program, the women's center). All of these communities are bound together by the common goals of being a community of people committed to learning and to advancing their own education and the education of others.

"Serving as president of the student body and also president of the disabled student organization, I have had the opportunity to see both sides. Administration is concerned with cost-effectiveness, being politically correct, community support, and a positive representation of the college at a community level. The student is concerned with pursuing and fulfilling the needs of fellow students, environment, community, and dealing with issues. Working together allows results that benefit both sides."—Dawn M. Roberts was a returning adult learner at Gulf Coast Community College majoring in social work.

Different organizations have different purposes and focus. Higher education communities emphasize such elements as collegiality, learning, scholarship, academic freedom, and student development. A social organization might emphasize friendship, fun, and enriching experiences. A sports team stresses competence, teamwork, and responsibility. Regardless of the special mission and focus of those groups and organizations, the people in them will experience healthy communities if they intentionally practice the discipline of community.

Our smaller communities become a fractal of developing global communities. "Identifying our common interests and broadening our relationships will be the defining elements of twenty-first century communities" (Morse, 1998, p. 230).

The global community of the future will be, at best, a series of communities that are interdependent and diverse, embracing differences, releasing energy, and building cohesion. The broader global community will be enhanced by the health of the many smaller communities that constitute the whole. Those living within each community define all community (Hesselbein, Goldsmith, Beckhard, & Schubert, 1998, p. xi).

Committing to promote and develop community in the places you function on campus is a key way of building and supporting the larger campus community.

Chapter Summary

Framing any group or organization as a community of people working together for shared purposes enhances relational leadership. Thinking of that group as a community connects participants to a shared paradigm of expectations and obligations. To flourish, communities require relational leadership. Relational leadership practices value community as the context in which meaningful change can occur.

What's Next?

All organizational entities can get stale, lose focus, or fail to bring in new members in productive ways. Organizations benefit from intentional strategies to stay renewed and vital. The last chapter of this part discusses strategies for groups, organizations, and communities to stay renewed.

Chapter Activities

1. Think about a particular community of which you are or have been a member. Which of Gardner's eight elements of community were especially visible in this community? Which were missing and why?

2. Describe a community of which you were an active member. Try to relate this community to the four stages of community development as outlined by Peck. Did you experience each stage? If not, why not? What was each one like? How were they similar? How were they different?

3. To what degree is some kind of community awareness essential for the Relational Leadership Model? Can the model still be a helpful frame to guide your leadership role (as a participant or as a positional leader), even if a sense of community does not exist in your groups or organizations?

4. Think about a healthy community that you are or were associated with and identify its characteristics. Now think about a community you know of that is unhealthy or is in the early stages of community development. What has contributed to the status of this community? How would you go about strengthening this community?

5. Communities sometimes are strengthened during times of crisis. Provide an example not already mentioned in this chapter of a community in crisis that became stronger as a result.

Additional Readings

Chinn, P. L. (2004). *Peace and power: Creative leadership for building community* (6th ed.). Boston: Jones and Bartlett.

Etzioni, A. (1993). *The spirit of community*. New York: Crown.

Peck, M. S. (1987). *The different drum: Community-making and peace*. New York: Simon & Schuster.

Rheingold, H. (1993). *The virtual community: Homesteading on the electronic frontier*. New York: HarperCollins.

10

Renewing Groups, Organizations, and Communities

Aaron and Michael are the newly elected president and vice president of their fraternity. Their organization has a long and distinguished history of service to the university, high grade point averages, and being considered excellent representatives of the Greek system. Lately, however, there has been slippage. Participation in service activities is not at previous levels, grades have dropped, and conduct-related incidents have occurred. Aaron and Michael are concerned, but when they share their concern with some of the current members they are told, "It's no big deal, don't worry about it." When they approach the outgoing officers about their observations, they are told "It's your problem now. Take care of it!"

No matter how effective or exciting a group or organization may be for its members, it will inevitably find itself in need of renewal. Renewal must be an ongoing function but may be an obvious need in periods of inactivity when the organization seems stagnant or in times of frenzied activity when the members seem stressed. It may be needed during times, like the fraternity noted above, when there needs to be a recentering around purpose and values. This is natural and is not something to fear. It is, however, something that must be addressed. As a participant, you have the obligation to recognize when things are not going right and to work to change them.

Richard Farson (1995) discusses organizational renewal in *Management of the Absurd*:

> Most often what gets organizations into trouble are faulty leadership styles, poor internal relationships, and managerial blind spots. The delusional hope of a troubled organization is that it will be saved without having to make changes in these highly personal areas. (p. 86)

Farson (1995) goes on to note, "Individuals are very strong, but organizations are not" (p. 90). With these prophetic words, he focuses on one of the basic issues facing groups, organizations, and communities as they try to remain healthy and productive—that relationships ultimately determine the actions taken. These relationships, when broken or never fully formed, can lead groups, organizations, and communities to a point of being unproductive and even destructive to their members.

Chapter Overview

We begin this chapter with the concepts of generativity and transition and how they can be used to help leaders and members renew themselves and their organizations. We then address the issues that can cause problems for groups and organizations as they attempt to continually renew themselves. These issues include a lack of attention to mission, vision, and core values; poor relationships; not taking responsibility for actions; lack of involvement by members; lowering of ethical standards; and lack of attention to process. As we explore these various concerns, we show how the Relational Leadership Model, with its stress on the role of purpose, inclusion, empowerment, ethics, and process, can serve as a useful guide in your renewal efforts. We end the chapter with a discussion of the impact of the human spirit.

Generativity

Erik Erikson made the concept of "generativity" famous in his 1963 book *Childhood and Society*. By generativity, he meant "the concern in establishing and guiding the next generation" (p. 267). This idea is important to our discussion of renewal because it relates to the obligation that falls on the older, more experienced leaders and members of organizations. We believe that they have a responsibility to leave the organization better than they found it; this means they need to help coach, mentor, and prepare the less-experienced members to take on leadership roles within the organization. Developing the talents and abilities of *all* members within the organization is a challenge that must not be overlooked.

"You may be a mentor and not even realize it. Actions can speak louder than words. Your manner in which you act, conduct yourself and approach everyday situations is a reflection of who you are. Set high standards for yourself and others will follow. It's important to be a mentor because the strength you provide sets a foundation for others to grow from."—Lauren Smith is a senator-at-large, Senate Campus Advancement Committee chair, Senate Judicial Committee member, Senate Executive Committee member, Public Affairs Committee chair, peer mentor academic advisor, and global ambassador at Drake University.

The Concept of Transition

In his book *Transitions: Making Sense of Life's Changes*, William Bridges (1980) explores the concepts of transition and change. Change is localized in time and space. It is easily identifiable; it begins when something old ends and something new begins. Transition is the psychological process that accompanies the change. It is difficult to identify, and it begins with an ending—people letting go of old attitudes and beliefs. Bridges notes that changes require people to make transitions, and it is the transitions that make life difficult. These concepts will be explored in detail in Chapter Eleven.

Transitions have three components: ending, neutral zone, and beginning (Bridges, 2003). The ending is a time of disengagement, disidentification, disenchantment, and disorientation. This is followed by the neutral zone—the most difficult period because it is a time of emptiness, disorganization, and despair. Only by being in this psychological state, however, can we prepare ourselves for a new beginning, but it is often difficult to decide how long to stay in it. New beginnings will be successful only if you have stayed long enough in the neutral zone. Because new beginnings take physical and psychological energy, they will often be troublesome. Bridges (1988) has also applied these ideas to corporations and organizations (see Exhibit 10.1).

As a leader, you can use this information in a number of ways. If you have recently taken a new position, realize that it might take the group or organization (and you) a while to get used to your being in the role. This will be especially true if there are many others who were officers or members under the previous leadership.

You may also find that you were much more productive (and a better student) when you were busier. Many students find that their grades are best when they hold offices or positions of responsibility. This makes sense when you think about it. If you only have two hours a night to do your homework, you will be productive and will stay focused. If you have all night to do the same amount of work, you may find that what begins as an hour of watching television turns into an all-night marathon. This makes no sense intuitively, but many former leaders have found it to be true. If you monitor your time, you can use it in ways that benefit you.

Groups and organizations go through a similar process when they are undergoing a change or transition. The psychological

Exhibit 10.1. Organizational Transition.

Ending	Neutral Zone	Beginning
Loss of attachments	Create temporary procedures and policies	What is the new idea that lies at the heart of the new beginning?
Loss of turf	Create temporary lines of authority and responsibility	What is the new organization that is going to put this idea into place?
Loss of structure	Do whatever is possible to encourage cohesion within the organization as a whole and within its component units	Who is going to make the decisions?
Loss of a future	Expect old issues to resurface and try not to choke them off as irrelevant to the present situation	What is your vision for the new organization?
Loss of meaning	Take care to keep the reasons for the organizational ending in people's minds so that the anxieties and confusions of the neutral zone do not lead them to try to escape from the chaotic present back into the simpler past	How is that vision going to be realized?
Loss of control		What is going to happen?
		When?
		In what order?
		How are present activities going to be coordinated with new activities?
		What training will be needed to staff the new roles, and how is that going to be provided?
		Where is everyone going to fit?
		What are the new roles going to look like?

Source: Adapted from Bridges (1988). Used with permission.

process of understanding and accepting change can range from easy to difficult. Knowing that there will be a time of uncertainty as the new way of doing things gets established is an important concept for leaders. Change and transition can certainly renew a group or organization. In fact, from a systems perspective, any act of renewal really does change everything. Understanding how these processes work can help a leader be effective in these kinds of situations.

"My organization has just recently gone through a major change. We have just transitioned from one advisor to an interim advisor. What our organization learned is that we have to be independent and flexible. We cannot rely on one person, whether it be an advisor or a fellow member, to see that the organization is successful. The organization must be a stable unit on its own. If the organization cannot survive change, the organization will not last."—Alexis Harrison is the Rebel Connection Student Chair of the Rebel Pride Council, Rebel Pride Council Representative of the Leadership Advisory Board, and member of the Phi Eta Sigma National Honors Fraternity, National Society of Collegiate Scholars, and Honors College at the University of Nevada, Las Vegas.

The concept of transition has much to offer all participants in groups, organizations, and communities. By considering the psychological processes outlined by Bridges (2003), new and old officers can gain a better understanding of their feelings as they enter into or leave their offices. These feelings—joy, anxiety, excitement, nervousness—are all natural reactions to being placed in new situations. In addition, knowing about the transition stages of ending, neutral zone, and beginning can help participants feel more comfortable in their current situation and help them anticipate what might be coming next.

The Renewal Process

Gardner (1990) notes that continuous renewal is necessary in groups and organizations in order to renew and reinterpret values, liberate energies, reenergize forgotten goals or generate new goals, achieve new understandings, and foster the release of human potential. Gardner notes further that "leaders must understand the interweaving of continuity and change" (p. 124). Continuity means taking the best of how the group or organization is currently and carrying it forward under conditions that require new approaches.

According to Gardner (1990), the most critical step in the renewal process is "the release of talent and energy" (p. 136) from within the members. As he notes, "Nothing is more vital to the renewal of an organization than the arrangements by which able people are nurtured and moved into positions where they can make their greatest contribution" (p. 127). This process begins with the recruitment of new members and continues with their ongoing development. What do you do to tap into the talents and energy of the members of your groups, organizations, and communities? How could you do this even better?

Gardner (1990) makes a number of other suggestions that can help the renewal effort for organizations. We believe these suggestions can also apply to groups and communities. Groups, organizations, and communities can reassign their leaders to expose them to new challenges; take steps to increase the motivational level of leaders and participants alike; foster at least some diversity and dissent, to encourage the development of new ideas; refocus on the original reasons that the groups and organizations were formed; ensure that both internal and external communication are easy and open; keep focused on the vision of a desired future; and, finally, reorganize. Some of these steps may require the use of an outside evaluator, because people become used to the status quo and can find themselves resistant to any significant change efforts.

Gardner's ideas are important because they give us some ideas about where we need to go when things are going poorly. His work also reflects the relevance of the basic concepts of the Relational Leadership Model. By paying more attention to issues of purpose, inclusion, empowerment, ethics, and the process orientation, groups, organizations, and communities can remain productive places for all members. When things are going poorly, returning to these basic principles can provide an excellent starting point for efforts aimed at renewal.

Common Purpose and Renewal

In Chapter Eight we explored the importance of mission, vision, and core values, which combine to form the common purpose component of the Relational Leadership Model. The concept of being purposeful plays a critical role in the renewal of groups and organizations. In fact, we believe that when things are going badly, going back to the basics of mission, vision, and core values is a great place to begin your renewal efforts.

James Collins and Jerry Porras (1994) examined eighteen extraordinary companies—extraordinary in their longevity and in their productivity. Collins and Porras found that these great companies did not do things as you might expect. Instead of relying on charismatic leaders, they had leaders who were concerned more about building great organizations than about being visible and out front. Instead of complex strategic planning, they tried a lot of different things and kept doing what worked. Instead of changing constantly, they relied on a set of core values that had remained relatively constant over the years. And although these organizations might sound like great places to work, the authors found that a good fit was needed for a member of the organization to thrive. This emphasis on strong core values and on action, experimentation, risk taking, and "big hairy audacious goals" (Collins & Porras, p. 9) is something that groups, organizations, and communities need to constantly keep in mind.

"I have engaged others in creating and supporting a vision. I have to believe in the vision. The vision has to be positive and beneficial to the members and the campus population-at-large. Motivation and passion are the keys to obtaining the support of others as well as engaging them in the organization's vision."—M. J. Giammaria majors in business administration at the University of North Carolina, Wilmington. She serves on the auditing committee of the State Employees Association of North Carolina and is a member of Toastmasters International.

The importance of vision is also articulated by Albrecht (1994); Jaffe, Scott, and Tobe (1994); Senge (1990); and others. Albrecht encourages leaders to do some scanning: scan the environment to discover what is going on, and scan the various opportunities that are available to determine what the possibilities are. Jaffe, Scott, and Tobe cite the importance of self-responsibility, empowerment, purpose, commitment, and partnership. Senge notes the necessity of a "shared vision," of empowerment accompanied by members pulling in the same direction.

This connection between common purpose and renewal is especially evident in student groups, organizations, and communities; members need to know why they are doing what they are doing. When things are not going well, it is often because members have lost touch with what has made their group or organization unique or special. In essence, they no longer remember why the organization exists. Renewal requires members to reaffirm their common purpose.

Getting experienced members to re-embrace this common purpose can be very challenging. A retreat can be a powerful opportunity for renewal. On leaving for a weekend retreat, some members will complain about having to give up a weekend when they could be socializing and having fun back on campus. But often, at the end of a well-designed retreat with a focus on renewal, members will return uplifted, energized, and glad they spent their weekend on this growth-producing activity. The challenge then becomes how to maintain back home the momentum that was developed at the retreat. In any event, a retreat is a popular method for reconnecting to the common purpose that brought the participants together originally.

Retreats and other structured opportunities that are created for the purpose of renewal provide a forum for all members to come together to share their thoughts and feelings about the group or organization: where it is now and where they would like it to go. Revisiting the vision through this kind of "group conversation" is necessary to keep it fresh for the membership. Meetings like this can also reveal that the vision needs to be changed or shifted. Knowing when to maintain a current vision and when to change the vision is a critical aspect of leadership and renewal. Having a vision that is meaningful to the members is absolutely necessary if it is to guide their plans and actions.

Another way to maintain a vision that works well with new members is an exercise called The Five Whys, developed by Rick Ross (1994a, p. 108). Ask yourself the most simple of questions, such as, Why does your organization (or group or community) exist? This question is relevant whether it is asked about student government, a service organization, the chess club, a residence hall floor or house government, a fraternity or sorority, or a club related to your major. Probe deeply. Now take the reason you have given and ask why that answer is important. Take the answer to that second Why? and ask Why? again. Do this until you have asked Why? a total of five times. Doing this helps you get closer to the essence of why the group exists. See Exhibit 10.2 for an example of the way this technique would apply to an organization.

Although the final line in Exhibit 10.2 about working for the development office is humorous, the conversation does get us to a deeper understanding of why we have campus entertainment—to

Exhibit 10.2. The Five Whys.

Consider this imaginary conversation with the
chair of a campus entertainment committee:

Why does your organization exist?	To provide campus entertainment for students.
Why is that important?	So they'll have something to do and have fun.
Why is that important?	So they'll enjoy going to school here and stay out of trouble.
Why is that important?	If they like going to school here and stay out of trouble, they'll stay in school and hopefully graduate.
Why is that important?	If they graduate, hopefully they'll go out and be successful, make a big salary, and contribute money to the school.
So you really work for the Development Office?	I guess so!

Source: Adapted from Ross (1994a), pp. 108–112. Used with permission of Rick Ross.

retain students. With this as a reason for the existence of such an organization, the activities they sponsor must appeal to a broad range of students.

Consider the differences between a student government group whose primary reason for existence is to provide social, recreational, and physical activities for the campus community and another student government group whose purpose is to be the voice of student opinion to the campus administration. These two groups have very different focuses. No one group or organization can be all things to all people. Decide what is at the core and return to this core at every opportunity. The core defines why your group or organization exists. It is why people originally started it and why others decided to join. As leaders and active participants, it is your duty to help make this core come alive for the membership.

Inclusion: Tapping Into the Energy of Others to Renew the Organization

As we outlined in Chapter Three, inclusion involves developing the talents and ideas of all members in the group or organization, then building on differences and commonalities. Although embracing this perspective presents a challenge for leaders, it provides valuable information as we consider the renewal process. Of particular importance in this process is developing the talents of members and using the energy that new members can bring with them.

An obvious way to make any group or organization better is to help its members become more aware, knowledgeable, and skilled. By developing the talent of the people who are already members, tasks can be accomplished in a more timely and efficient manner. Knowledgeable members such as these will also provide an experienced core of individuals who have a historical perspective and know about past accomplishments. This will also provide a solid foundation of individuals who are committed to the common purpose, vision, and core values.

When people realize that a group or organization has helped them become more knowledgeable and skilled, they usually feel a reciprocal allegiance. We see this all the time in groups of students. For instance, many RAs, student government leaders, and members of volunteer agencies will talk at great length about what they have gained both personally and professionally from their experiences. These same students are also very loyal to other members and dedicated to the common purpose, vision, and core values. They should be selected to play an active role in any renewal effort.

One way to continually renew the group or organization is to invest in developing the talents of all of your members. This can take on a variety of forms: providing workshops on various topics; encouraging attendance at conferences; discussing a pertinent article; asking people to perform a task or duty they have not previously done; and developing the leadership potential in new members.

These, and countless other methods, can be used to develop the awareness, knowledge, and skills of the members. Your efforts on behalf of the members will be returned many times over.

Remember to focus your efforts on the members who are on the fringes—people who are sometimes viewed as outside the core group. There may be great energy and creativity in these often-ignored individuals (Kelly, 1994). Such students may be so thrilled at the new-found attention that they become active, involved members.

Empowerment: Helping Members Become Involved

Albert Bernstein and Sydney Rozen (1994) address the concept of empowerment in *Sacred Bull*. In this book, they identify ten "sacred bulls" that prevent people from reaching their potential as members of corporate organizations. The sacred bull is a metaphor for an assumption we make and do not question. "They are the ideas that nobody checks or questions because 'We've always done it this way'" (p. 7).

Many of us would note that denial, blame, and excuses are relatively immature ways of coping with mistakes or with results that did not turn out as you had hoped. These ways of coping are examples of sacred bulls. But some of the other examples are less obvious. In fact, they include aspects of our lives that we may define as being very positive, such as being nice, being a perfectionist, and always viewing our way of doing things as the right way. Being nice can mean avoiding conflict. Being a perfectionist can mean seeing your efforts, or the efforts of others, as either being perfect or being nothing. Being right can mean that others never have the right answer or approach.

These sacred bulls can be lethal in that they encourage us to avoid taking responsibility for our actions and for the result of our actions. As such, they can keep us in the quagmire of organizational life, in which mistakes are always someone else's fault. Leadership is about the task of solving problems—big problems and little

problems, significant problems and seemingly insignificant problems—so that the group or organization can better meet its core
purpose and be a good place for its membership.

Think for a moment how this concept of empowerment and
taking responsibility is essential for renewal. When things go
wrong, our first inclination is to say something like, "Well, it wasn't
my fault. I did what I was supposed to do." We try to find the person responsible so blame can be placed and our lack of responsibility can be proven. Yet "there is no blame" (Senge, 1990, p. 67).
In a group, organizational, or community system, we are all
involved in every aspect of the system—in all of its successes and
failures. Just as on a true team, winning and losing are treated as
outcomes shared by the entire group. The group dynamic changes
in amazing ways once we quit trying to lay blame. This can be a
key step in renewal.

"A leader is a person who clears the path and empowers others to
respond to a changing environment and meet prospective goals. A
leader works diligently to accomplish his or her end, but never for-
gets that his or her most important job is to empower teammates to
work to their utmost capacity. Leadership is a team exercise. It is
about delegating responsibilities based on who can do a job best. It
is about recognizing team members' talents and capitalizing on their
experiences. Leadership grows and evolves as a team changes and
different needs are presented."—Lisa Plush is a pilot member of the
Leadership Initiative for the College of Human Ecology, a teaching
assistant, and academic development chair of Delta Delta Delta at
Cornell University. She has also worked in a second-grade classroom
and at the Second Circuit Court of Appeals.

Let us look at a familiar organizational example. In any organization, recruiting new members is everyone's responsibility. However, the reality of the situation may be quite different. Many times,

recruiting may be viewed as the job of a specific officer. Sure, other members are willing to "do their part," but they may see their part as simply being friendly to prospective members who may come to visit. If membership decreases, members may blame the officer because they, having done their part, could not possibly deserve blame. This is a very different dynamic from that of members who see their part as bringing prospective members to meetings, making sure they feel welcomed, and engaging them in conversation. These members are truly sharing the responsibility of recruitment and are much less likely to lay the blame for declining membership on any one officer. They understand the role that all participants have in making the recruitment of new members a success. They know that for an event to be a success, everyone must share responsibility and feel a need to make it work.

When this becomes an organizational reality and a "web of shared responsibility" is developed among the membership, dynamic results can occur. But this is far easier said than done. A good way to begin the process is to forge a strong sense of connection among the members. This helps each person feel like a part of the whole, a part of something bigger than herself or himself. Next, involve as many different people as possible in the various aspects of the life of the group or organization. When asked to participate in something meaningful and important, and given some sense of input into how the situation is to be approached, most people will respond with their best efforts. People like to be part of something that is successful and believe that success now will lead to success later. As you can see, all of this begins with shared responsibility—from the leader taking the responsibility of helping the individual members be part of something important, to the individual members taking responsibility for doing their very best to make the group or organization successful in everything it does.

As a leader, taking responsibility for your actions is essential. Encouraging others to take responsibility for their own actions can be an essential part of renewal. Once members agree to take on more responsibility for various activities and functions, they inherently become more involved and feel a greater sense of commitment to themselves and to the other members. Taking responsibility can also help members receive compliments for jobs well done and help them realize that those efforts that lead to less-than-anticipated outcomes are not the end of the world.

Being Ethical: How Doing the Right Thing Can Help Renew the Organization

Being ethical is a proud commitment to justice, care, and socially responsible actions. Maintaining a high standard of ethical behavior helps create a proud membership and provides some guidelines to help leaders do the right thing. Being ethical is not easy. It involves hard work, ongoing conversations, introspection, and dedicated organizational leaders and members. Yet all of these efforts will benefit the group or organization in the long term by making it attractive to new members.

Consider two different Greek chapters. The first Greek organization truly embraces its founding principles and the policies of the institution, even when these policies create tensions within the membership. Leaders of this group take the time to explain policies to new members and do everything they can to hold the membership to the high ideals upon which the group was founded. Scholarship, service, and sisterhood or brotherhood are stressed, and every effort is made to encourage the membership to be ethical in every way. The second Greek organization has realized just how difficult it is to truly embrace the ideals of scholarship, service, and sisterhood or brotherhood and has chosen to take the easy way out by lowering the expectations they have of each other. Although this may seem beneficial in the short term, it will hurt the organization dramatically in the long term. Each organization will attract new members with goals, beliefs, and interests similar to those of the present membership. The group that stresses ethical behavior in its members will attract new members who have similar beliefs and standards. The group that has lowered its standards will attract new members whose behavior may be questionable. Which organization will grow stronger over time and experience longevity?

Although this example may seem simplistic, we all know of organizations that fall into each of these two categories. We also have seen that in the long run, the group or organization that treats its membership well and holds its members to a high standard of ethical behavior will continue to grow and develop, whereas the other organization will struggle to survive. An organization that has ethical leaders and is committed to justice, care, and socially responsible actions will attract a membership that is committed to similar ideals. These new members will both renew and strengthen the organization in an ongoing manner.

Being Process-Oriented: Using the Concept of Appreciative Inquiry to Renew the Organization

Being process-oriented means that individuals and the group or organization as a whole are reflective, challenging, collaborative, caring, and communal. The main way of accomplishing this is to create opportunities for ongoing dialogue and discussion about what is happening within the organization. Appreciative Inquiry, a method for identifying the positive aspects of an organization or entity, is a process that can aid in renewal efforts.

The process of Appreciative Inquiry has recently received attention from educators, organizational consultants, human resource professionals, and those who study organizational behavior (Cooperrider, Sorensen Jr., Whitney, & Yaeger, 2000; Cooperrider & Srivastva, 1987; Cooperrider, Whitney, & Stavros, 2003; Watkins & Mohr, 2001; Whitney, Trosten-Bloom, & Cooperrider, 2003). Appreciative Inquiry is "a collaborative and highly participative, system-wide approach to seeking, identifying, and enhancing the 'life-giving forces' that are present when a system is performing optimally in human, economic, and organizational terms" (Watkins & Mohr, p. 14). Its basic premise is that every organization is doing something right, and the key to creating positive change is to identify and work from those positive aspects.

The Appreciative Inquiry process involves identifying a topic and then proceeding through four stages of inquiry—discover, dream, design, and destiny (Figure 10.1). The topic can be anything of importance to the organization—"anything the people of an organization feel gives life to the system" (Cooperrider & Whitney, 2000, p. 9). Although using slightly different terminology, Charles Elliott (1999) offers succinct descriptions of the four stages of inquiry:

- *Discovering periods of excellence and achievement.* Through interviews and storytelling, participants remember significant achievements and periods of excellence.

- *Dreaming an ideal organization or community.* In this step people use past achievements to envisage a desired future. . . . [I]mages of the community's future that emerge are grounded in history, and as such represent compelling possibilities.

- *Designing new structures and processes.* This stage is intended to be provocative—to develop, through consensus, concrete short- and long-term goals that will achieve the dream. . . . Provocative propositions should stretch an organization or community, but they should also be achievable because they are based on past periods of excellence.

- *Delivering the dream.* In this stage, people act on their provocative propositions, establishing roles and responsibilities, developing strategies, forging institutional linkages and mobilizing resources to achieve their dream. (pp. 3–4)

Gervase Bushe (2000) describes an applicable use of an Appreciative Inquiry approach focused on teamwork. The group begins

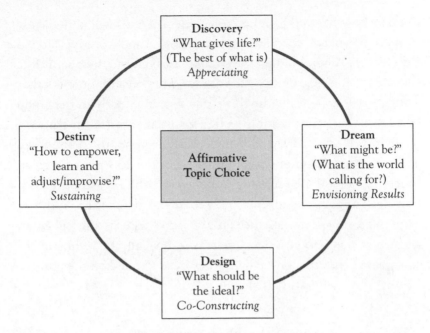

Figure 10.1. Appreciative Inquiry 4-D Cycle.
Source: Cooperrider, Sorensen Jr., Whitney, & Yaeger (2000), p. 7. Reprinted with permission.

by talking about the best team experience they have ever had, with each member sharing his or her story while the rest of the group listens attentively, engaging in dialogue when appropriate. Working together, the group then creates a consensus list of attributes that would describe "best teams." Finally, members are asked to share any experiences they have had with other group members that embodied any of these attributes. Just imagine the power of this relatively simple experience.

Both of these process models have much to offer leaders. Rituals have been developed that encourage members to speak about what is in their hearts and minds and to share what they appreciate about their organization and its members. Groups may hold informal or formal sessions in which members share their thoughts and feelings about the group. Some organizations will periodically invite all members to form a circle and pass a candle or gavel around the group. When holding the candle or gavel, the member is free to say anything she or he wishes to say. Other organizations ask that members comment on one thing that is going poorly in the group and one thing that is going well. This is an excellent method of soliciting feedback from all members of the group, including those who are usually quiet. Communities hold open forums or town meetings for a similar purpose. Whatever method is used, the leaders need to be sure that they know what the membership is thinking and feeling. They also need to strive to create an atmosphere in which members feel free to express their thoughts and feelings without fear of repercussions. Finally, they need to build on the positive things the organization is already doing.

The Importance of the Human Spirit

An aspect of leadership and organizational life that is receiving increased attention is the importance of the human spirit. In *Leading with Soul: An Uncommon Journey of Spirit*, Lee Bolman and Terrence Deal (1995) take readers on an interesting journey, describing the trials and tribulations of a corporate executive named Steve who is having trouble finding fulfillment in his work. Maria, the woman who acts as Steve's guide on this journey, helps him explore his leadership style in an unconventional manner. She poses questions instead of providing answers. Through this experience, Steve learns the importance of spirit and soul in leadership, that is, of leading from the inside out—from the core of who you are. He also learns the importance of giving and sharing.

Although this may sound like another form of religion, it is not. The human spirit is the core of your being that gives life its meaning. It is what helps you get out of bed in the morning and look forward to the new day. As such, it needs to be nurtured. This approach is certainly different from what you would expect from a leadership book, yet is found in a growing number of books addressing this topic, including the recent work of Margaret Wheatley (2005), Parker Palmer (2000, 2004), and others (Conger & Associates, 1994; Fox, 1994; Hawley, 1993; Lewin & Regine, 2000).

The soul-searching that is the basis of Bolman and Deal's book is as important as, and probably even more important than, all the how-to-run-a-meeting books you will ever encounter. Certainly, knowing how to run a meeting is important. You probably have some experience doing that or have seen others do it. But have you ever asked yourself why you want to be a leader or what motivates you to want to make a difference? You may not have done that before nor ever seen others try to answer the question. By exploring questions like this, you will find out a lot about yourself. The best leaders know themselves very well—their strengths and the areas in which they need work. You will find that exploring the tough questions and tough issues can be difficult, but it is necessary if you are to find meaning in life and, by doing so, renew yourself and your organization.

Although renewing your own spirit is important, helping members of your organization renew their spirit is essential if you are to be a successful leader. You must help others identify their own reasons for being associated with this particular group or organization and then try to strengthen these reasons. You can also help provide an environment in which people feel passionate about being members. Being upbeat, positive, and optimistic is infectious. If you do not believe it, just try it. The human spirit is a renewable resource that can prove to be invaluable in all forms of renewal efforts.

Chapter Summary

Groups and organizations are like human beings—they need continual sources of energy to fuel their minds, bodies, and spirits. We know that we need nutritious food and liquids to sustain our bodies, that we need new ideas and information to stimulate, challenge, and intrigue us and keep our minds sharp and flexible, and that we need something to love and something that will give our existence meaning. Without those things, it is difficult to remain upbeat. Groups and organizations are similar in that having a common purpose provides a reason for being. Having a purpose stimulates new ideas, new thoughts, and new approaches to old issues and provides a guide toward greater achievement.

Energy comes with something new; without this energy, groups and organizations become complacent. They begin to value style over accomplishment. It takes participants with foresight and good judgment to see things that may be wrong but appear to be right, and vice versa. Groups and organizations will not automatically renew themselves. They become renewed when their members become renewed. This sounds simple and maybe it is. Maybe it is as simple as asking, What would it take to make this organization great?—then joining with the other participants and running with the answers as far as you can go.

What's Next?

Part Four of this book addresses the concept of change—first, understanding responses to change, and second, strategies for facilitating change. Change is a desired result of most leadership processes. Chapter Eleven examines frameworks and models for understanding change and how to initiate change processes. Chapter Twelve outlines strategies that can be used to produce change.

Chapter Activities

1. *Things Were Going Well:* Think back to a time when things were going very well for your group or organization. Get a good strong mental image of this time. Make it vivid in your mind's eye. Now jot down some answers to these questions:

   What was your group or organization doing?

Why were you doing these things?

With what other groups, organizations, communities, or individuals were you doing things?

What was your group or organization doing to take care of its members? (for example, recognition or awards)

Compare your group or organization now to how it was when things were going very well. How are things different? How are they similar? What changes could you make to help return to the time when things were going well?

2. *A Retreat:* Design a retreat for a group or organization that is in need of renewal. What will be your goals for the retreat? Where will you go? What activities will be included? Design a town meeting for a community. What will be your goals for the town meeting? How will you plan, advertise, and run it?

3. *Recruiting New Members:* Design a plan to recruit new members. Make it a priority to enlist persons from underrepresented campus populations. Try to incorporate several different approaches.

4. *Cross-Functional Teams:* Identify an important issue that is a major concern on your campus. To address this issue would obviously involve a number of different groups, organizations, and individuals working together effectively. Design a plan to address this major issue. Who would be involved? How would they all work together? What problems do you anticipate? How could you overcome these problems?

5. *Transition:* Identify a major transition that your group or organization has experienced. Describe it in terms of Bridges' model. What was each phase—ending, neutral zone, beginning—like? What was difficult about each phase? What was exciting about each phase?

6. *Spirit:* Plan a way to renew the spirit of your group or organization. What will you do? Who will do it? How will you do it?

7. *Appreciative Inquiry:* Imagine facilitating an Appreciative Inquiry process in your organization. What would you identify as the discover, dream, design, and destiny of your organization?

Additional Readings

Bridges, W. (2003). *Managing transitions: Making the most of change.* Cambridge, MA: Perseus Books.

Bridges, W. (1988). *Surviving corporate transition.* New York: Doubleday.

Cooperrider, D. L., Sorensen, P. F., Jr., Whitney, D., & Yaeger, T. F. (Eds.). (2000). *Appreciative inquiry: Rethinking human organization toward a positive theory of change.* Champaign, IL: Stipes.

Jaffe, D., Scott, C., & Tobe, G. (1994). *Rekindling commitment: How to revitalize yourself, your work, and your organization.* San Francisco: Jossey-Bass.

Palmer, P. J. (2000). *Let your life speak: Listening for the voice of vocation.* San Francisco: Jossey-Bass.

Wheatley, M. J. (2005). *Finding our way: Leadership for an uncertain time.* San Francisco: Berrett-Koehler.

Whitney, D., Trosten-Bloom, A., & Cooperrider, D. L. (2003). *The power of appreciative inquiry: A practical guide to positive change.* San Francisco: Berrett-Koehler.

Part IV

Making a Difference with Leadership

Futurist Alvin Toffler (1970) observes that "change is the process by which the future invades our lives" (p. 1). It is our assertion that *leadership is the way we invade the future*. Observing the trends around us, making meaning out of the perspectives of diverse shareholders and stakeholders on any topic, and seeking to continuously improve ourselves and our organizations, leads us to be people who want to shape the future and not just have it happen to us. In times of permanent white water, we need to work collectively smarter, reflectively smarter, and spiritually smarter (Vaill, 1991). In this part we return to Vaill's concepts, first discussed in Chapter One, to explore the creative dynamic of individuals and groups working together to make a difference.

Leadership is inherently about people working together toward change. People providing leadership are often called change agents; they seek to be effective in improving their organizations and addressing social issues. The two chapters in this part explore the nature of change and the challenges for change agents. Chapter Eleven, Understanding Change, explores processes for change. Chapter Twelve, Strategies for Change, explores the social change model of leadership. This model advances a perspective on socially responsible leadership and the importance of collective action, coalitions, and civic engagement. This part will focus on the purpose element of the relational leadership model, illuminated by how the process orientation makes that purpose happen.

11

Understanding Change

Laura just took office as president of the Young Entrepreneurs Club, a student organization affiliated with the business school. She was excited to move this 300-member organization forward with an ambitious agenda of raising $100,000 to go toward student scholarships for entering business majors. Laura could see the benefits of such a scholarship in attracting academically talented students to the college. Laura wanted to use the mission of the club to make a difference in other students' lives. Applying what she learned in one of her courses, she put together a detailed business plan to share with other members at the first meeting of a new semester. Laura knew not every member would come to the first meeting, so she made only 150 copies of the business plan.

The first meeting drew only 30 members. After Laura presented her plan and asked for feedback, the members were silent and stared at Laura. Finally, a senior member spoke up and said that he doubted they would get enough of the membership to get behind this good idea because they had never done anything like this before. He feared that fewer members would come to meetings if they were expected to put this much time and energy into this plan. Another member added that she believed the college expected the club to carry out its traditional activities of sponsoring a car wash to raise money for the year-end banquet.

Laura was stunned at their reactions, because she'd expected the members to be excited about the new idea. After all, they were aspiring business majors who surely would want to gain this type of experience and successfully accomplish this goal.

Chapter Overview

This chapter provides an overview of a major component of leadership—change. Understanding and facilitating change is a major task in the leadership process. Facilitating change is complex, fragile, exhilarating, and rewarding. This chapter provides a conceptual framework for understanding change and introduces various models of implementing change processes.

Understanding Change

We can see change all around us—we embrace some change, and we fear other types of change. How we learn and how we acquire information have changed dramatically over the last decade—with first the Internet, then the advancement of web sites and e-mail communications, and now blogs. These and other changes have impacted how change is facilitated at organizational and community levels. In the scenario at the beginning of this chapter, Laura did not foresee or plan for the challenges of introducing change, including the resistance her idea might receive.

We no longer simply manage change, we now pursue change (Conner, 1992). Today, change cannot be characterized along cultural dimensions—change strategies that are implemented in Hong Kong look very similar to change processes in Moscow. How individuals react to change may take on distinct cultural characteristics, but our ideas of how to facilitate change within organizations vary little across cultures (Conner). Losing control is a common fear of human beings and a common concern when change is introduced in organizational environments. A critical leadership task is to understand this tension and transform it into what Senge (1993) refers to as "creative tension" (p. 142). Effective leaders approach change processes with sensitivity and the assumption that people may perceive even the smallest of changes to be monumental. Thomas Edison understood this human phenomenon well when he unveiled the electrical light bulb in 1879. He fashioned the look and intensity of these new lights after the familiar gaslights used in that era, diminishing people's fear of this unfamiliar invention (Conner, p. 101).

Change is a complex concept in the leadership process. Even the smallest of changes can be difficult to introduce and manage. Many people resist change or are fearful that a change in their work, their environment, their job, or their personal life will negatively affect them. Simply changing someone's office space can evoke feelings of uncertainty and resentment. Making personal transitions in your life can involve some type of change and often results in feelings of insecurity or disequilibrium. Moving away from home to go to college or changing your major can be exciting and scary at the same time. We often fear the unknown or are unsettled in changes to our patterns and way of life. Anthropologists who studied primitive tribes concluded that resistance to change was required to sustain social order and cohesion in groups (O'Toole, 1996). Facilitating change in the leadership process can trigger those same reactions. Change can also bring about exciting possibilities, renewed energy and enthusiasm, and a deeper commitment to the goals and future of an organization.

"Our group's purposes are to increase others' awareness about health and wellness and to reduce the frequency and severity of violent acts—both speak to the core of necessary social enlightenment and change far beyond the aspiration of any one member."—Emily Swanzy is pursuing a master's degree in professional counseling at Texas State University. She is an assistant advisor of the Network and Men Against Violence.

Understanding Change from an Individual Perspective

To fully understand how organizations change, it is important to first explore how change is experienced by individuals. William Bridges (1980) and Nancy Schlossberg (1989a) offer models that are helpful in this regard. As discussed in Chapter Ten, Bridges notes a difference between change and transition. A change occurs at a specific time and involves something beginning or ending. A transition cannot be pinpointed to a particular time and always begins with an ending. Transitions are much more difficult because they are psychological processes that take time to complete. A commonly experienced example involves someone leaving an important leadership position, such as the presidency of an organization. There is a specific time when the change occurs—such as when the new president is elected or is ceremonially placed in office. For the outgoing president, the transition process of not being president any longer can be more difficult and lasts longer. This will be especially true if the person was very engaged in the leadership position. It is difficult to give up an office, especially one that has been important. The person may feel lost at first—unsure of how to spend free time, unsure of the new role in the organization, and missing the feeling of importance that goes along with being a leader. This can be a difficult time, and the person needs to spend time there before being able to move on to a new beginning. The new beginning will also be difficult because it involves a great expenditure of physical and psychological energy. Likewise, members of the group have to get used to new leadership. They may regret the transition of the seasoned leader and be wary of new leadership. They may wait to see how the new position leader will fulfill the role before they fully engage in new directions.

Nancy Schlossberg (1989a) notes that a life change is difficult because it impacts one's roles, relationships, routines, and assumptions about oneself. To illustrate, we will use the example of two students who care passionately about an issue and join a student organization to try to address this issue. Certainly their lives as students are impacted because this new activity has been added. New relationships are formed with other members of the organization, and their daily routines will be changed as they get more involved in the cause. Finally, their assumptions about themselves can change as they begin to make an impact.

Schlossberg also identifies four potential resources that can be used to help manage change—the situation (how you feel about the change, the timing), yourself (how you view change, your previous history of change, and so on), supports (people and resources that can be of assistance), and your strategies for coping (the steps taken to proactively engage the change). Understanding how change impacts you and others around you will help you be a more successful leader of change.

Every leader faces challenges and obstacles in facilitating and managing change, yet change processes are not rule bound, and there is no single tested approach that can guarantee successful change efforts. To understand how change is facilitated is to understand how human transformations take place (Bridges, 2003; Conner, 1992). As you prepare to facilitate change, you will be well served if you reflect on patterns of human behavior and how to respond to people's reactions to change. Understanding others is a primary step in any change management approach. Human beings, in general, want to control their environments, and some experience an even greater need to be in control of their surroundings. Connor comments that "the single most important factor to managing change successfully is the degree to which people demonstrate *resilience*: the capacity to absorb high levels of change while displaying minimal dysfunctional behavior" (p. 6).

Understanding those expectations is a part of understanding how to facilitate change. O'Toole (1996) offers a few hypotheses as to why people are resistant to change:

1. *Satisfaction:* Being satisfied with the status quo. You might hear this often in your organizations: "We've never done it

that way before, so why do we need to change?" That is a
clear sign of a change-resistant organizational response.

2. *Fear:* People fear the unknown. Risk-taking behaviors, like
   doubling your membership dues without knowing what
   impact that will have on recruiting new members, raises fear
   of unknown consequences or the fear of failure.

3. *Self-Interest:* Even if the change benefits others, it may alter
   their status or perks, so they resist. Sometimes change means
   giving up power or authority to achieve a particular result. For
   example, an individual interested in running for chair of an
   organization might resist a proposed change to create a
   cochair structure.

4. *Lack of Self-Confidence:* Change makes us vulnerable and
   requires confidence to inspire others to see the possibilities.
   Lack of confidence can deter a group from charting a new territory.

5. *Myopia:* Not being able to see beyond the present. Historian
   John Lukacs describes myopia this way: "when people do not
   see something, this often means that they do not wish to see
   it—a condition that may be comfortable and profitable to
   them" (as cited by O'Toole, 1996, p. 163).

6. *Habit:* Habits can be positive, but they can also inhibit
   change, causing groups to be driven by traditions, customs,
   and patterns. For example, it might be a habit for the Latino
   Student Organization to recruit new members in the spring,
   but it might be a better practice, yielding more members, if
   recruitment took place in the fall.

Borrowing from the work of Kübler-Ross (1970) (as noted in
Chapter Four), who studied human reactions to the death and dying
process, we can understand people's reactions to negative change
or to changes they cannot control, such as discontinuing a popular
product, downsizing an organization, or changing the name or iden-

tity of an organization (Conner, 1992). Conner expanded Kübler-Ross's five-stage model by adding three phases (pp. 132–134):

Phase 1 – *Stability:* the present state

Phase 2 – *Immobilization:* shock or paralysis to initial change

Phase 3 – *Denial:* change-related information is ignored or not accepted as reality

Phase 4 – *Anger:* frustration and anger as a reaction to change and often directed to those most supportive of the change effort

Phase 5 – *Bargaining:* negotiation to avoid pending change, signifying that the person can no longer deny the change process

Phase 6 – *Depression:* a typical response to negatively perceived change, including disengagement and a decrease in physical and emotional energy

Phase 7 – *Testing:* regaining a sense of control and seeking out new ways to redefine goals

Phase 8 – *Acceptance:* change is responded to realistically, even though individuals may still be adverse to the change

Here's a scenario of a change effort with corresponding responses. The Liberal Arts School at State University decided that holding two commencements each year, one in December and one in May, was expensive and inefficient, so the dean announced a plan to eliminate the December ceremony. Twice as many students graduated at the end of the spring semester as at the end of fall semester. Alumni, parents of current students, the Liberal Arts Parents' Club, graduating students, and some faculty were stunned when they received the information about this change (immobilization). They wanted to see the fall graduation tradition continue (stability). Members of each of these groups e-mailed the dean saying that it would be impossible to expect the fall graduates and their families to come back to campus for the spring semester graduation after they had been gone for a semester (denial). Others wrote e-mails and letters in protest to the president (anger).

The Parents' Club banded together and offered to write other parents and alumni asking them to consider making financial dona-tions to help pay for the fall graduation ceremony (bargaining). After several attempts to organize these and other efforts, the par-ents gave up because the dean's office was not responding to their proposals and they began to feel like they were wasting their time and energy (depression). Two months later, the leadership of the Parents' Club began to plan a separate fall reception for the gradu-ates as a way to give those seniors special recognition at the time of their graduation (testing). The Dean's Office collaborated with the club members to sponsor the reception, which was less expensive and involved less staff effort. At the end of the first reception, sev-eral parents and graduating seniors commented on how they enjoyed the smaller, intimate environment while still having the opportunity to participate in the annual spring event (acceptance).

These eight phases represent human reaction to perceived neg-ative changes. These phases are fluid and elastic—they are not lock-step and rigid. Effective change agents pay attention to the negative reactions to change and help others move through these stages to regain control and restore engagement and productivity.

Although it is normal to respond to negative change with phases that mirror a death and dying process, some may initially respond to a perceived positive change, then later resist this change. For example, some may initially perceive a company's merger with another as positive, based on little knowledge or facts. Then con-cern or doubt begins to emerge in the informed pessimism level. If this level of tolerance is exceeded, then "checking out" behavior begins to emerge and people withdraw from the change.

Conner (1992) offers five phases of positive response to change, illustrated in Figure 11.1:

Phase 1: Uninformed optimism

Phase 2: Informed pessimism

Phase 3: Hopeful realism

Phase 4: Informed optimism

Phase 5: Completion

Starting a new organization sometimes can evoke a positive response to change (uninformed optimism). Initially, individuals are excited about the possibilities of simply creating something new; then reality begins to sink in (informed pessimism) as people begin to wonder if the idea will attract enough interest. Once individuals begin to see the opportunities and benefits this new organization can offer, they become more confident (hopeful realism). The founders of the group may begin to test the idea for launching the new entity by doing some focus groups and web surveys. The results show that a majority of people are interested and would join such

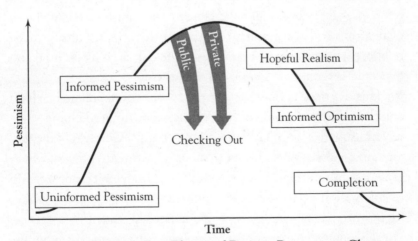

Figure 11.1. Conner's Five Phases of Positive Response to Change.

Source:Managing at the Speed of Change by Daryl R. Conner, Copyright © 1993 by O. S. Resources, Inc. Used by permission of Villary Books, a division of Random House, Inc.

an organization, motivating the founders to move forward with excitement and energy (informed optimism). The planning group remains focused on setting up the structure for the new organization and recruiting new members (completion).

Change also can be understood by examining the dimensions of depth and pervasiveness of the intended change (Eckel, Hill, & Green, 1998). As shown in Figure 11.2, "*Depth* focuses on how profoundly the change affects behavior or alters structures. The deeper the change, the more it is infused into the daily lives of those affected by it" (p. 4). A deep change results in changing patterns, behaviors, culture, and attitudes. When an organization decides to transform its mission from a social and recreational one to a service-based organization, deep change will follow. The values, patterns, behaviors, and culture will be transformed if the change effort is effective. "*Pervasiveness* refers to the extent to which the change is far-reaching within the institution. The more pervasive the change, the more it crosses unit boundaries and touches different parts of the institution" (p. 4). For example, if a university or college decides to require all professors and instructors to administer student course evaluations and also requires that those evaluation results be made public, pervasive change in the academic culture is a potential and expected outcome.

This matrix identifies four types of institutional change, which could overlap with each other: adjustment, isolated change, far-reaching change, and transformational change. Changes of the first type, in quadrant one, are described as adjustment changes, which are minor alterations. If an organization changed its membership requirement in its recruitment policy from a 3.0 GPA to a 3.1 GPA for prospective members, that would be an adjustment type change. If a subcommittee of an organization wants to change its fundraising activity, which only the subcommittee participates in, that is a type of isolated change because it does not impact the rest of the organization. An example of a far-reaching change might be when an organization decides to change its name. The impact will be per-

Depth

		Low	High
Pervasiveness	Low	Adjustment (I)	Isolated Change (II)
	High	Far-Reaching Change (III)	Transformational Change (IV)

Figure 11.2. The Typology of Change.

Source: Reproduced with permission of the American Council on Education from Eckel, Hill, & Green (1998), p. 5.

vasive in that a new identity will develop, with marketing implications, but the name change most likely will not result in deep change. The fourth quadrant of transformational change is significant and includes both deep and pervasive changes. Transforming the Multicultural Student Organization into a Multicultural Student Union with a building, staff, and academic programs is an example of transformational change.

Change occurs at different rates and sometimes not at all. Competition in the marketplace influences a more rapid pace of change, whereas some organizations work hard to maintain the status quo, slowing the rate of change. Our world is more accustomed to continuous change. In the 1970s, only 5% of those surveyed in corporate America viewed a successful future characterized by continuous, overlapping change, compared with 75% in the early 1990s who viewed continuous, overlapping change as vital to the organization's success (Conner, 1992, p. 44). "For example, John Sculley, the former chairman of Apple Computer, Inc., says that more than half of Apple's revenues comes from products that were not even invented three years ago" (p. 46). Ten years later, in view of the marketing of the iPod, Sculley's observation seems understated.

Some changes can be incremental, finite, and temporary; others are transforming, widespread, and monumental. Changes that usher in new fads, impact demographics, introduce new phenomena, or result in contagious behaviors can have a dramatic tipping effect. Malcolm Gladwell (2002) uses social epidemics to examine tipping points, which he defines as "that moment in an epidemic when everything can change all at once" (p. 9). The tipping point happens when something unique or unknown becomes common. Gladwell describes the tipping point of change using three characteristics: (1) the emergence of a trend, idea, a crime wave, and the like is contagious—these spread like viruses do; (2) little changes can have big effects; and (3) change happens in one dramatic moment rather than gradually. In 2006, the world was wondering whether or not the avian flu—originating in wild birds and spread to domesticated fowl, from which its mutations have infected humans—would reach a tipping point, causing a pandemic that could strike millions of people around the world. Although as of July 2006 only 131 people had died from this strain of flu (small event), could it take on Gladwell's three tipping point characteristics and reach pandemic proportions (big change)?

Sudden change is at the core of the tipping point concept (Gladwell, 2002). The concept of "sudden change" was first introduced in the 1970s during White flight to the suburbs in the American Northeast. For example, sociologists predicted that a White neighborhood would tip when enough African Americans had moved into it to make up approximately 20% of households, causing Whites to begin moving out. "The tipping point is the moment of critic mass, the threshold, the boiling point" (Gladwell, p. 12). The tipping point is "where the unexpected becomes expected, where radical change is more than possibility" (p. 14). Technology is a powerful example for understanding the tipping point phenomenon. For example, in 1984, Sharp produced the first low-budget facsimile machine, and by 1987 there was a critical mass of people who owned a "fax," making it possible for almost any organization to receive a fax. That was the tipping point for fax machines (Gladwell). Cell phones followed, resulting in many people no longer having land lines in their houses. In recent years, the television industry has experienced the tipping point with plasma and LCD televisions.

You can use the tipping point to understand the moment in time when schools lose control or when crime breaks out in cities or when a virus reaches epidemic proportions. The tipping point can result in positive outcomes, like when the school basketball team at a university with a regional reputation begins having a winning streak that leads to a national championship title. All of a sudden, the campus repeatedly is spotlighted on the national news, admissions applications double that year, more alumni make financial donations to the school, and student attendance at campus functions increases.

An epidemic tips when something happens, causing a phenomenon to move from an equilibrium state. You will understand the tipping point more fully if you can think about life as an epidemic (Gladwell, 2002). Use this analogy and you might begin to see tipping-point changes all around you—think about the well-known breast-cancer awareness and antismoking campaigns. These are types of social change epidemics. Epidemics can be influenced and controlled using the leadership process. Leaders have intentionally facilitated change using a tipping-point strategy.

Gladwell (2002) describes three agents of change that can tip an epidemic: (1) the law of the few, (2) the stickiness factor, and (3) the power of context. Often, student organization leaders reflect that 20% of the members do 80% of the work. You may think this same effect occurs in group projects in academic courses. This is the law of the few—a disproportionate number of people cause a tipping point change to occur.

Marketing messages illustrate the importance of the stickiness factor—how to create a lasting message so that people will buy your product. Jingles on the television or radio are designed to create the stickiness factor. Commercials during the Super Bowl game are dependent upon this to the point that they are now analyzed during post-game commentaries: Which commercial did you like the best? Universities and colleges create their own marketing messages—the University of Maryland at Baltimore Campus markets itself as an honors college, while New Century College at George Mason University uses the motto "Connecting the classroom to the world." They use this strategy as a way to brand their identity so that the general public will associate a motto with their institution, making that message unforgettable.

The power of context, Gladwell's third agent of change, points to understanding the smallest of details in people's immediate environment. Franklin D. Roosevelt's famous fireside chats are an example of the power of context. During that era, in the early 1930s, families valued gathering around the radio to listen to music and receive the news of the day. FDR understood that environment well and exploited it as a way to reach out to the American public and deliver his message. College and university web sites offer that same common medium of disseminating information and messages to constituencies. Major renovations of student union buildings often are designed with the power of context in mind—a design that will consistently attract students to the building for educational, recreational, cultural, and social purposes.

Facilitating Change

Core values are a fundamental driving factor in leading successful change efforts. Social movement leaders focused on great values such as equality and freedom as the ultimate goal of effecting change (O'Toole, 1996). Their leadership was tied to deep beliefs in greater ideals, and their focus on change was founded on those same core values. Introducing change for the sake of change is contrary to facilitating change based on fundamental values. In the movie *Brubaker* an ambitious warden attempted to transform a corrupt prison by making deep changes that threatened internal and external political coalitions. He was met with resistance at every stage until finally his most trusted ally came to him with a proposition that if he stopped, he would get the resources to change the physical conditions inside the prison. Brubaker responded, "Every warden puts new paint on the walls" (Quinn, 1996, p. 122). He went on to argue that compromising on principles or core values would not lead to deep change for this troubled prison. The same is true in student organizations. Organizations that struggle with retaining members think that if they change their logo, give everyone free T-shirts, or serve food at meetings that will result in a more committed membership. Following the *Brubaker* example, members will want to stay involved in a group if they find meaning and purpose or feel a sense of affiliation beyond a T-shirt or free food at an event.

"As the world becomes more and more fast-paced, student leadership is vital. Without dedicated students who are committed to creating a better place for all, the future is left up in the air. Student leaders hold the keys to creating a more just and humane world to live in; it is through the efforts of hard-working and devoted student leaders that change really begins to happen. The power that student leaders hold in changing the future is truly amazing and is something that keeps me focused through some of the most challenging times, either within the University or in the world. My leadership skills give me much hope and power as I strive to make a more just and humane world."—Julia Barr is president of the Campus Activities Board, co-president of the Education Club/Kappa Delta Pi, treasurer of Sigma Tau Delta, and class senator, and participates in University Ministry at Dominican University.

A challenge for leaders as they facilitate major change is to help others cope with their uncertainties and fears (Quinn, 2004).

Facilitating deep change means helping people out of their comfort zones and supporting them as they try out new behaviors. It also requires leaders and members to provide support for each other as they make these transitions. Some will feel a sense of loss when a new change is introduced and an old practice or tradition is put to rest. Others may feel that they will lose status or will feel less significant as a result of a new arrangement. In Chapter Ten we presented similar concepts to support the concept of organizational renewal. Bridges (1991) offers seven approaches that can be used to assist organizations and people through transitions:

1. Explain that this is a time to think outside of the box and to let go of old assumptions and ways of thinking about the organization. Facilitators of change processes should model this behavior by talking about how they too will be affected by changes and how they will think differently about their roles and practices.
2. Create opportunities or settings for everyone involved to engage in thinking differently about the organization or activity. Organize a retreat or focus group meetings to involve others in the initial stages of the change process before decisions are made.
3. Provide information or training on how to think outside of the box and how to facilitate innovation. Asking members or individuals to make changes does not assume that they are prepared for the creative process that follows.
4. Model and encourage risk taking and experimentation. People will need to feel secure and supported when they test new ideas or put new practices in place.

5. View mistakes and losses as learning opportunities and as a time for innovation. Facilitators of change will encourage people to stretch their thinking when they experience failure.
6. Encourage everyone to break through barriers or ruts by brainstorming new solutions, new ideas, or new ways of thinking about existing problems.
7. Persuade the group to be comfortable with ambiguity and uncertainty while explaining that they are in a temporary state until more clarity and direction can be achieved. Otherwise, people might have a tendency to move too quickly to solutions or closure in the process as a way to maintain their comfort zone of equilibrium and security. (pp. 43–44)

"As new member educator for Alpha Sigma Tau national sorority, I held meetings with the group to ease in a change in the new member program. In the meetings, I stressed the benefits of changing the program and how it would be more efficient and effective for everyone."—Roxanne Hudson is treasurer of the Marketing Club and New Member Educator of Alpha Sigma Tau Sorority at Frostburg State University. She is a math tutor on campus and assistant buyer at the Frostburg State University Bookstore.

Any type of major or deep change does not come easy and does not happen overnight, at least in those changes where change has been successful. John P. Kotter, a management professor and scholar at Harvard Business School, has studied change processes in major companies and nonprofit organizations. Kotter (1996) formulated an eight-stage, sequential change model based on his research and insights of organizations who successfully achieved organizational transformations. Kotter's model is presented in Figure 11.3.

This model is sequential, but multiple phases can occur at the same time. The steps in this model build on one another, so it is important not to skip stages or phases when they become too time-consuming or challenging. Kotter and Cohen (2002) adapted this model based on new research about these eight stages. These researchers found that the core factor of organizational change is about changing people's behavior and not simply the structures, rules, systems, or culture. What they gleaned from their study of 130 organizations and 400 people is that "people change what they do less because they are given analysis that shifts their thinking than because they are shown a truth that influences their feelings" (p. 1). The four major lessons learned were:

1. Successful organizations know how to seize opportunities and avoid hazards. They recognize that taking bigger risks is associated with bigger wins and that small, gradual improvements are not enough.

2. Successful change processes flow in the eight-stage model until a culture is created that allows new behaviors to stick.

3. The core challenge and focus in each of the eight stages is changing people's behavior—what people do.

4. Change agents need to help others see and feel the emotions associated with a change effort. "The flow of see-feel-change is more powerful than that of analysis-think-change" (p. 2). This pattern of see-feel-change allows people to see the problems when they are presented vividly and visually, feel the negative emotions that are getting in the way and increase the positive feelings that change can create, and change or reinforce new behaviors (such as being less complacent, devoting more effort to achieve the vision, and so on).

1. Establising a Sense of Urgency
- Examining the market and competitive realities
- Identifying and discussing crises, potential crises, or major opportunities

2. Creating the Guiding Coalition
- Putting together a group with enough power to lead the change
- Getting the group to work together like a team

3. Developing a Vision and Strategy
- Creating a vision to help direct the change effort
- Developing strategies for achieving that vision

4. Communicating the Change Vision
- Using every vehicle possible to constantly communicate the new vision and strategies
- Having the guiding coalition role model the behavior expected of employees

5. Empowering Broad-Based Action
- Getting rid of obstacles
- Changing systems or structures that undermine the change vision
- Encouraging risk taking and nontraditional ideas, activities, and actions

6. Generating Short-Term Wins
- Planning for visible improvements in performance, or "wins"
- Creating those wins
- Visibly recognizing and rewarding people who made the wins possible

7. Consolidating Gains and Producing More Change
- Using increased credibility to change all systems, structures, and policies that don't fit together and don't fit the transformation vision
- Hiring, promoting, and developing people who can implement the change vision
- Reinvigorating the process with new projects, themes, and change agents

8. Anchoring New Approaches in the Culture
- Creating better performance through customer- and productivity-oriented behavior, more and better leadership, and more effective management
- Articulating the connections between new behaviors and organizational success
- Developing means to ensure leadership development and succession

Figure 11.3. The Eight-Stage Process of Creating Major Change.

Source: Reprinted by permission of Harvard Business Review from "Leading change: Why transformation efforts fail" by J. Kotter, 73, 1995. Copyright 1995 by the President and Fellows of Harvard College; all rights reserved.

The following chart of the eight-step model of change (Exhibit 11.1) illustrates the importance of new behaviors at every stage (Kotter & Cohen, 2002, p. 7). These eight action steps are embedded in the dimensions of the Relational Leadership Model (RLM).

Before a change effort can be realized, it is critical to make a commitment to understand both change and the human responses to change. Too often, facilitators of change skip this important step and launch right into action. What can result from that omission is a chaotic state that may not allow an organization to achieve its results. The message is to be thoughtful and reflective as you plan a change effort. Anticipating and understanding human responses to change can lead to healthier and more meaningful processes. This approach calls for initiators of change to be empathetic, compassionate, and thoughtful while also acting with clarity, purpose, and vision.

What's Next?

The following chapter will describe various strategies for change, moving from understanding change to implementing change. You will learn about the importance of engaging others outside your organization through coalition building and how the Social Change Model of Leadership can influence change processes.

Chapter Activities

1. Why is change important in the leadership process? What are the challenges of facilitating change?

2. What are some obstacles you might face in facilitating change? What are some reasons why some people are resistant to change?

3. Think of an experience in which a successful change effort took place. What factors in the organization or community environment led to successful change? What did the leaders

Exhibit 11.1. The Eight Steps for Successful Large-Scale Change Related to the Relational Leadership Model.

Step	Action	New Behavior
1	Increase urgency	People start telling each other, "Let's go, we need to change things!" (RLM – Purpose)
2	Build the guiding team	A group powerful enough to guide a big change is formed, and they start to work together well (RLM – Inclusive, Process)
3	Get the vision right	The guiding team develops the right vision and strategy for the change effort (RLM – Purpose and Ethical)
4	Communicate for buy-in	People begin to buy into the change, and this shows in their behavior (RLM – Purpose)
5	Empower action	More people feel able to act, and do act, on the vision (RLM – Empowering)
6	Create short-term wins	Momentum builds as people try to fulfill the vision, while fewer and fewer resist change (RLM – Process)
7	Don't let up	People make wave after wave of changes until the vision is fulfilled (RLM — Purpose)
8	Make change stick	New and winning behavior continues despite the pull of tradition, turnover of change leaders, and the like (RLM – Process)

and members do to prepare for change efforts? How were people aligned with the change?

4. Consider an organization you're involved in. What one major change can be made and why? Describe how you could use each of the components of the RLM to facilitate change.

5. Why is it important for organizations to be flexible and open to change? What happens to organizations that are resistant to change?

6. What are the root causes of inertia in organizations?

7. Why is it that some ideas or behaviors or products start epidemics and others don't? What can you do to start a social epidemic of your own?

Additional Readings

Conner, D. R. (1992). *Managing at the speed of change: How resilient managers succeed and prosper where others fail*. New York: Villard Books.

Gladwell, M. (2002). *The tipping point: How little things can make a big difference*. Boston: Little, Brown.

O'Toole, J. (1996). *Leading change: The argument for values-based leadership*. New York: Ballantine Books.

Quinn, R. E. (2004). *Building the bridge: A guide for leading change as you walk on it*. San Francisco: Jossey-Bass.

12

Strategies for Change

Meredith is a first-year biology major interested in environmental issues. She recently became concerned about how chemicals used in th labs are disposed of, and she began reading about the concept of "green biology," a more environmentally friendly approach to the discipline. She shared her concerns with a few classmates—some who were receptive and others who were not concerned at all. She approached her introductory biology course instructor about it, and he said that, although interested, he didn't have time to work on the issue. Meredith is becoming more and more concerned about this issue but is unsure what to do next. She's just a student—what can she do? Where can she go? Who can she talk to? How can she get others interested in this issue?

Consider, too, any of the following situations:

- Jun and her suitemates have become concerned about a recent rise in the number of assaults against women on campus. One was in the parking lot behind their residence hall. They have decided to do something about it.

- Samuel decided to become active in the upcoming national election and has joined an on-campus group supporting the candidate of his choice.

- Tamela has worked twenty hours a week at the same accounting firm since she was a junior in high school. The firm is located a block from an elementary school with a growing proportion of children on the free or reduced-price lunch program and increasing numbers being raised by grandparents. She thinks the firm has an obligation, as a community neighbor, to partner with the school in some way to support those children.

In short, these students have gotten excited about an issue and want to do something to make the situation better. It could be an environmental issue, political issue, or social justice issue. What do you do? Where do you begin? How do you get others excited about this issue? What strategies might you use to make this change happen? What does it mean to be a change agent?

Chapter Overview

In Chapter Eleven you learned about the change process. In this chapter we will build on that change material and introduce strategies you can use to implement change. The chapter begins with a discussion of issues involved in individual change and moves on to present different perspectives on organizational change. The Social Change Model of Leadership Development is also presented in this chapter.

Introduction

The situations just described are examples of the many change efforts that are happening every day on campuses throughout the world. As Raelin (2003) notes, "An organization or a community is always in motion" (p. 155). Political issues, environmental issues, curricular issues, social justice issues, and numerous other issues are being engaged in from all sides; no single perspective has a monopoly on student support or action.

We believe that change is an essential part of leadership. Recall the definition from Chapter Three: *Leadership is a relational and ethical process of people together attempting to accomplish positive change*. From our perspective, maintaining the status quo is not leadership because it does not involve change or movement toward a shared purpose.

Yet, if we know anything about change, we know that change is difficult. Change is hard at any and every level—individual, team, organizational, institutional, societal. As labor organizer Saul Alinsky said, "Change means movement; movement means friction; friction means heat; heat means controversy" (Chambers & Cowan, 2004, p. 31). Teams, organizations, and institutions, like individuals, are the way they are for a number and variety of complicated reasons. These reasons may or may not make sense to persons within the groups and will make no sense at all to some outsiders. Leading change can seem impossible, yet it must be done. Raelin (2003) describes it this way: "Change inevitably translates into letting go of old and safe ways of doing things. People and groups react differently to this transition process, often depending upon their psychological security. Helping people overcome the losses typically associated with change can serve as an important contribution on the part of change agents" (p. 160). We explored some of those issues of transition in Chapter Eleven.

Margaret Mead said, "Never doubt that a small group of thoughtful, committed citizens can change the world; indeed it is the only thing that ever has" (cited in Mathews, 1994, p. 119). Individuals who decide to engage fully in their group or communities and join with others around common needs can make a difference. As Morton (1995) notes, "Change . . . comes about when otherwise ordinary people find way(s) to bring their values, their actions, and their world into closer alignment with each other" (p. 28). Making a difference may require that several groups form coalitions and work together toward shared outcomes. In this chapter we will outline strategies that will help you lead or participate in change processes.

Students as Change Leaders

Students are involved in change efforts all over the country and the world. For example, Campus Compact is a national coalition of nearly 1,000 college and university presidents—representing some five million students—dedicated to promoting community service, civic engagement, and service-learning in higher education (Campus Compact, n.d.). On your campus, students may be involved in change efforts related to campus life policies, curriculum initiatives, recycling, or various funding issues. In the community, students may be involved in change efforts in schools, agencies, and nonprofit organizations.

The focus of each change may call for different change agents—people who are able to facilitate the change. Consider the following categories of change agents listed by Conner (1992):

- Those who influence personal change: parents for their families, counselors for the troubled, individuals for friends in need

- Those who influence organizational change: executives, managers, and union leaders for work settings; administrators and teachers for educational systems; clergy for religious institutions; administrators, doctors, and nurses for health-care systems; students for the campus culture; consultants for their clients

- Those who influence large-scale social change: politicians for the general public; civil servants for government; political action groups for special interests; researchers for the scientific community; opinion leaders for the media (p. 9)

As a shareholder or a stakeholder in many arenas, purposeful participants can be change agents that do help accomplish shared goals.

"Social change begins in the grassroots, with those willing to make a difference in society, no matter how small or inefficient the change might seem. It is important if those who effect the change believe it is important to their society. A leader's role in effecting social change is to establish a definitive need for society through the ideas and thoughts of others and then to bring those people together to act upon that need."—Elise Burmeier is a member of the Great Beginning Orientation Team and the building representative on the Resident Student Association at St. John Fisher College. She is pursuing a major in American studies while working at the St. John Fisher College Library.

Within any change efforts, there are those who are working directly with an issue, called *advocates*, and those who support those working directly with an issue, called *allies* (Edwards & Alimo, 2005). There are many lists of ally characteristics. Wijeyesinghe, Griffin, and Love (1997) offer one that includes "Acts against social injustice out of belief that it is in her/his own self-interest to do so" and "Is committed to taking action against social injustice in his or her own sphere of influence" (p. 108). In Exhibit 12.1, we offer a slightly different perspective, taken from *Real Change Leaders* (Katzenbach, Beckett, Dichter, Feigen, Gagnon, Hope, & Ling, 1996).We believe these attributes apply to advocates (those working directly with an issue) and allies (those who support those working directly with an issue). As Katzenbach et al. go on to say, "A critical mass of such leaders seems to be essential in every institution striving for major change" (p. 15).

This all sounds great, but trying to initiate change is very difficult, challenging work that usually causes leaders to be filled with self-doubt. It can be easy for students to come up with many reasons to not get involved in change efforts, but it is not just students who hesitate. In *Leadership Reconsidered: Engaging Higher Education in*

Exhibit 12.1. Common Characteristics of Real Change Leaders.

1. *Commitment to a better way.* They share a seemingly inexhaustible and visible commitment to a better way.

2. *Courage to challenge existing power bases and norms.* They develop the personal courage needed to sustain their commitment in the face of opposition, failure, uncertainty, and personal risk.

3. *Personal initiative to go beyond defined boundaries.* They consistently take the initiative to work with others to solve unexpected problems, break bottlenecks, challenge the status quo, and think outside the box.

4. *Motivation of themselves and others.* Not only are they highly motivated themselves, but they have the ability to motivate, if not inspire, others around them.

5. *Caring about how people are treated and enabled to perform.* They really care about other people, but not to the extent of blind self-sacrifice. . . . They do not knowingly manipulate or take advantage of others.

6. *Staying undercover.* They attribute part of their effectiveness to keeping a low profile; grandstanding, strident crusading, and self-promotion are viewed as sure ways to undermine their credibility and acceptance as change leaders.

7. *A sense of humor about themselves and their situations.* This is not a trivial trait. A sense of humor is often what gets them through when those around them start losing heart.

Source: Higher Education Research Institute (1996). Copyright 1996, Developed by the Higher Education Research Institute. Printed with permission from the National Clearinghouse for Leadership Programs, College Park, MD 20472.

Social Change, Alexander Astin and Helen Astin (2000) outline a number of beliefs that can both constrain and empower students and faculty to action (see Exhibit 12.2). Notice how similar the beliefs are for these two groups—both constraining and empowering. This can be helpful as you enlist the assistance of faculty, staff, and administrators in your campus change efforts.

In Chapter Eleven, we explored the impact of the change process on individuals and some of the constraining and empowering beliefs you may be experiencing. The Social Change Model of Leadership Development shows the relationship between the individual and the group that is seeking a positive change to benefit the community.

Exhibit 12.2. Constraining and Empowering Beliefs of Students and Faculty

Constraining Individual Internal Beliefs		Empowering Individual Internal Beliefs	
Students	*Faculty*	*Students*	*Faculty*
I don't have time to get involved	I don't have time to get involved in change efforts	I can manage multiple roles and tasks so that I can make a difference on campus	I help create the institutional culture through my daily individual decisions
Faculty don't value my contributions	My colleagues will never change their way of doing things	As a campus citizen, I have a responsibility to help shape matters that affect me	Leadership is not a separate activity; it is an integral part of what I do
I can't "lead" because I don't hold a formal leadership title	I'm not a leader because I don't have a leadership position	Individual students have the ability to shape their futures	Learning is an activity that I can model daily
	My role is to transfer disciplinary knowledge	Each student has the capacity to engage in leadership processes without formal titles	I can model leadership in every class
	Students are not motivated, interested in, or capable of mature action		I have the freedom and autonomy to initiate inquiry or action
	My role is to criticize, not to initiate		Students have the capacity, and therefore should be given the opportunity, to engage in decision making that affects them

(Continued)

Exhibit 12.2. Constraining and Empowering Beliefs of Students and Faculty *(continued)*

Constraining Group Internal Beliefs		Empowering Group Internal Beliefs	
Students	*Faculty*	*Students*	*Faculty*
This campus doesn't care about students	Faculty expertise is not valued in running the institution	Students are viewed as major stakeholders	Faculty are the stewards of the institution
Students do not have enough experience to lead major campus-change efforts	Nothing can be changed because of administrative attitudes	Students are viewed as change agents	Everyone in the institution directly contributes to student development
The senior campus leaders (president and vice president) are not responsible for making major decisions	Faculty and administrators could never work together	Student leadership can make a difference on campus	Change initiatives can start with anyone
	All learning occurs in the classroom		We make change through collective action
	Student Affairs can't be trusted in academic matters		
	Faculty and staff have nothing in common		

Source: Astin & Astin (2000), pp. 25, 26, 42, 46. Used with permission.

The Social Change Model of Leadership Development

In the mid-1990s, a group of college and university educators (including two of this book's authors, Komives and Lucas), supported by a grant from the Dwight D. Eisenhower Leadership Development Program of the U.S. Department of Education, met and developed the Social Change Model of Leadership Development (Astin, 1996; Higher Education Research Institute, 1996). The "7 Cs" model (see Exhibit 12.3), as it soon became known, describes the values that are necessary for a leader to embody as she or he works at the individual, group, and society or community levels. As you review the values embraced by the Social Change Model you will notice similarities with the Relational Leadership Model described in this book. (For examples of how the Social Change Model has been used, see *Developing Non-Hierarchical Leadership on Campus: Case Studies and Best Practices in Higher Education* by Outcalt, Faris, and McMahon, 2001.)

In Figure 12.1, the arrows show the feedback loops between the various aspects of the model. Arrows a and b indicate how the Individual and Group Values influence each other; c and d, how the Group and Society/Community values impact each other; and e and f indicate how the Society/Community and Individual Values mutually shape each other. Each arrow has specific meaning (Higher Education Research Institute, 1996).

> *Arrow a.* Consciousness of self is a critical ingredient in forging a common purpose for the group as its members ask, What are our shared values and purposes? Similarly, the division of labor so basic to true collaboration requires an understanding of each group member's special talents and limitations. Likewise, the civil controversy that often leads to innovative solutions requires both congruence (a willingness to share one's views with others even when those others are likely to hold contrary views) and commitment (a willingness to stick to one's beliefs in the face of controversy).

> *Arrow b.* Feedback from any leadership development group is most likely to enhance the individual qualities of consciousness of self, commitment, and congruence when the group operates collaboratively with a common purpose and accepts controversy with civility.

Exhibit 12.3. The Social Change Model of Leadership.

Personal (Individual) Values

Personal values are those that an individual strives to develop and exhibit at the group activity level. As personal qualities that support group functioning, they are essential in leadership for social change.

Consciousness of Self. Consciousness of self means knowledge of yourself, or simply self-awareness. It is awareness of the values, emotions, attitudes, and beliefs that motivate one to take action. Self-awareness implies mindfulness, an ability and a propensity to be an observer of one's current actions and state of mind. A person with a highly developed capacity for consciousness of self not only has a reasonably accurate self-concept but also is a good observer of his or her own behavior and state of mind at any given time. Consciousness of self is a fundamental value in our model because it constitutes the necessary condition for realizing all the other values in the model.

Congruence. Congruence is thinking, feeling, and behaving with consistency, genuineness, authenticity, and honesty toward others. Congruent persons are those whose actions are consistent with their most deeply held beliefs and convictions. Developing a clear consciousness of self is a critical element in being congruent. Being clear about one's values, beliefs, strengths, and limitations, who one is as an individual, is essential.

Commitment. Commitment implies intensity and duration in relation to a person, idea, or activity. It requires a significant involvement and investment of self in the object of commitment and in the intended outcomes. It is the energy that drives the collective effort. Commitment is essential to accomplishing change. It is the heart, the profound passion that drives one to action. Commitment originates from within. No one can force a person to commit to something, but organizations and colleagues can create and support an environment that resonates with each individual's heart and passions.

Group Values

Group values are expressed and practiced in the group work of leadership activity. Group values are reflected in such questions as, How can the collaboration be developed in order to effect positive social change? What are the elements of group interaction that promote collective leadership?

Collaboration. Collaboration is a central value in the model that views leadership as a group process. It increases group effectiveness because it capitalizes on the multiple talents and perspectives of each group member, using the power of that diversity to generate creative solutions and actions. Collaboration underscores the model's relational focus. Collaboration is about human relationships, about achieving common goals by sharing responsibility, authority, and accountability. It is leadership for service.

Common Purpose. A common purpose develops when people work with others within a shared set of aims and values. Shared aims facilitate group members' engagement in collective analyses of the issues and the task to be undertaken. Common purpose is best achieved when all members of the group build and share in the vision and participate actively in articulating the purpose and goals of the group work.

Controversy with Civility. Controversy with civility recognizes two fundamental realities of any group effort: first, that differences in viewpoint are inevitable and valuable and, second, that such differences must be aired openly and with respect and courtesy. Disagreements are inherent in almost any social interaction or group process. They bring valuable perspectives and information to the collaborative group, but eventually, they must be resolved. Such resolution is accomplished through open and honest dialogue backed by the group's commitment to understand the sources of the disagreement and to work cooperatively toward common solutions.

A Societal and Community Value: Citizenship

A commitment to social change connects individuals and their collaborative groups to their communities. The societal and community value of citizenship clarifies the purpose of the leadership. Toward what social ends is the leadership development activity directed?

Citizenship names the process whereby the self is responsibly connected to the environment and the community. It acknowledges the interdependence of all involved in the leadership effort. Citizenship thus recognizes that effective democracy requires individual responsibility as well as individual rights. Citizenship, in the context of the Social Change Model, means more than membership; it implies active engagement of the individual and the leadership group in an effort to serve the community. It implies social or civic responsibility. It is, in short, the value of caring about others.

Source: Higher Education Research Institute, 1996, pp. 6–7. Copyright © 1996, Developed by the Higher Education Research Institute. Printed with permission from the National Clearinghouse for Leadership Programs, College Park, MD 20472.

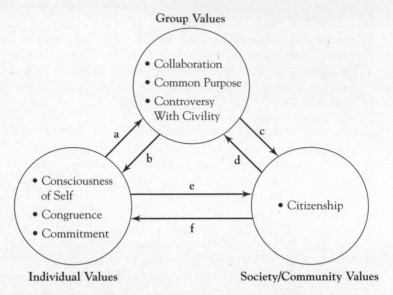

Figure 12.1. The Social Change Model of Leadership Diagram.

Source: Higher Education Research Institute (1996). Copyright 1996, Developed by the Higher Education Research Institute. Printed with permission from the National Clearinghouse for Leadership Programs, College Park, MD 20472.

Arrow c. Responsible citizenship and positive change are most likely to occur when the leadership group functions collaboratively with a common purpose and encourages civility in the expression of controversy.

Arrow d. Conversely, the group will find it very difficult to be an effective change agent or to fulfill its citizenship or community responsibilities if its members function competitively, if they cannot identify a common purpose, or if they pursue controversy with incivility.

Arrow e. The community is most likely to respond positively to an individual's efforts to serve if these efforts are rooted in self-understanding, integrity, and genuine commitment. Responsible citizenship, in other words, is based on self-knowledge, congruence, and commitment.

Arrow f. An individual learns through service, and his or her consciousness of self is enhanced through the realization of what he or she is (and is not) capable of doing. Commitment is also enhanced when the individual feels that he or she can make a difference. Congruence is enhanced when the individual comes to realize that positive change is most likely to occur when individual actions are rooted in a person's most deeply held values and beliefs. (Higher Education Research Institute, 1996, p. 7)

Let's return to the opening scenario of Meredith's concern about green biology (commitment). She has become keenly aware that she does not want to dispose of chemicals in a harmful way (congruence). She is not sure how to go about making a change (consciousness of self) and knows she needs to reach out to others for assistance (consciousness of self, common purpose). Her lab instructor is too busy (consciousness of self), and although he has some sympathy for the cause (commitment), it does not seem to be enough to motivate him to get involved (lack of congruence). Meredith decides to approach the Society of Student Environmental Engineers (commitment, citizenship). The president agrees to put the topic on the agenda of the next meeting (common purpose, collaboration) for the awareness raising (consciousness of self, commitment) and possible action of the group (common purpose).

At the meeting, Meredith knows she is nervous (consciousness of self), but the issue is important to her (congruence, commitment), so she brings a handout with information she has pulled from the Internet. The group has a lively discussion (common purpose, controversy with civility). One member even says, "This is the kind of thing we should have been talking about all year!" and there are nods of agreement from many members (commitment, common purpose). As the discussion proceeds, the president observes, "Seems like we want to take this on as an issue, right?" (common purpose, collaboration). The group discussed possible actions (common purpose, citizenship), like asking the department chair to come to the next meeting. Several members volunteer (commitment, collaboration) to check into different aspects of the issue (citizenship) for the next meeting. Meredith thanks the group and takes her seat, amazed that so much might now happen from bringing this to the meeting.

Comparison of the Relational Leadership Model and Social Change Model

As you are undoubtedly seeing, the Social Change Model and the Relational Leadership Model have much in common, with a few important differences. Both view leadership as a relational and collaborative process. Both are values-focused, with an emphasis on being ethical and creating positive change for the greater good. The main difference between the models is their differing focus. Leadership, according to the Relational Leadership Model, involves the components of process and purpose by being ethical, empowering, and inclusive. The Social Change Model proposes a dynamic interplay between the sets of personal, group, and societal values. The models can be used together—in fact, we are encouraging you to do this, to help you better understand leadership in a given situation. Meredith, for example, knew she needed to involve others (inclusive) and that she had every right to raise this important issue (empowering). She wanted to address a problem that was causing harm to the environment (ethical, purpose). The way to do this was to find an advocate (process) or a group or coalition that would take on the issue with her (process). Educating the student group members was going to be critical (process) and she knew that the information would be compelling (empowering).

As you think about your own leadership development or the development of your organization and members, use the individual values portion of the Social Change Model in combination with the components of the Relational Leadership Model to identify areas of strength and areas you want to further strengthen. The connection between the two models is shown in Exhibit 12.4.

To accomplish change, you must work with other individuals and groups of individuals. In the following sections, we will explore how to do that through the development of coalitions.

Building Coalitions for Community Action

Today's organizational and societal problems are complex and thus require community-based solutions. "If there is no sense of community, it stands to reason that it will be difficult to solve community problems. . . . People in a community have to have a public spirit and a sense of relationship" (Gudykunst, 1991, p. 128).

Whether these are campus community problems, problems in your apartment building, or problems facing the athletics department, they need the involvement of several groups, not just one. Rarely is one group or one organization solely responsible or does it possess sufficient resources (including information) to create, implement, or sustain a complex change. This reality necessitates a commitment to coalition building. "Coalitions are often a preferred vehicle for intergroup action because they promise to preserve the autonomy of member organizations while providing the necessary structure for united effort" (Mizrahi & Rosenthal, 1993, p. 12). The approach to changing campus parking policies would not be nearly as meaningful if, for example, a residence hall government complained that change was needed instead of joining with the Commuter Student Union and Graduate Student Housing to work together toward that change.

Joining with other interested groups and organizations can cre-

Exhibit 12.4. Comparison of the Relational Leadership Model and the Social Change Leadership Model.

Relational Leadership Model	Social Change Model
Purposeful	Individual Values: Commitment
	Group Values: Common Purpose
	Societal Values: Citizenship
Ethical	Individual Values: Congruence and Consciousness of Self
	Group Values: Common Purpose and Controversy with Civility
Empowering	Individual Values: Consciousness of Self and Commitment
	Group Values: Collaboration and Common Purpose
	Societal Values: Citizenship
Inclusive	Individual Values: Consciousness of Self and Commitment
	Group Values: Collaboration and Controversy with Civility
	Societal Values: Citizenship
Process-Oriented	Individual Values: Commitment
	Group Values: Collaboration and Common Purpose
	Societal Values: Citizenship

ate impressive change. "Through coalitions, separate groups can develop a common language and ideology with which to share a collective vision for progressive social change" (Mizrahi & Rosenthal, 1993, p. 12). They define a social change coalition as "a group of diverse organizational representatives who join forces to influence external institutions on one or more issues affecting their constituencies while maintaining their own autonomy. It is (a) an organization of organizations who share a common goal; (b) time limited; and (c) characterized by dynamic tensions" (p. 14).

"In order to facilitate social change, a leader must have the courage to stand against the norm. A saying I have coined in trying to help others understand the need for change is, "Just because you've 'always' done it, that does not mean it was 'always right.' But, that does not mean doing something different is wrong." Social change is not always a bad thing, though it is often given a negative connotation. I believe social change means guiding others to adopt a new idea concerning an old belief, and implementing that change so that those affected can experience life in a better way. Basically, it opens the minds and hearts of others to believe in things that were once deemed impossible or unbelievable, until that belief eventually becomes an action, and then a pattern."—Jamii Ng is a moderator for the South Peer Leadership Council and budget coordinator for the Church of Jesus Christ of Latter-Day Saints. She is a psychology major at Salt Lake Community College.

Mizrahi and Rosenthal (1993) have identified four distinct types of goals and time durations of coalitions: "specific goal, short-term groups (e.g. organizing demonstrations or forums); specific goal, long-term (e.g. banishing domestic violence, housing court reform); general goal, short-term (fighting crime or drugs); and general goal, long-term (neighborhood improvement coalitions, anti-racist networks)" (pp. 14–15). Imagine some examples of what this might look like regarding campus issues (see Exhibit 12.5).

Coalitions are not easy to build. Mizrahi and Rosenthal (1993) propose that each of these types of coalitions experiences a cooperation-conflict dynamic; four dynamic tensions arise to varying degrees.

1. The tension of mixed loyalties; this results from the dual commitment the members feel, to both their own sponsoring organization and the coalition. For example, a member of the Campus Safety Committee may come to learn the logistical and financial realities of improving campus lighting and see the need to have a

Exhibit 12.5. Campus Coalitions.

	Time Frame	
Goals	*Short Term*	*Long Term*
Specific	Homecoming; Thanksgiving canned food drive	Reducing incidents of date rape
General	Freshman community building	Diversity initiatives Revising general education requirements

phased program, but be pressured from the women's group she is representing to make it all happen at once.

2. The tension between autonomy and accountability; the coalitions need the independence to act, yet each member needs to connect back to their organization to maintain organizational commitment and endorsement. The Campus Environmental Action Coalition just discovered a state grant they can apply for, but they must set a focus for the grant and meet a one-week deadline. There is not time to fully consult with other organizations; this could cause those organizations to feel excluded.

3. The tension of determining the amount of emphasis to place on the coalition; should the group be seen as a means to achieve a specific goal or as a model of cooperation? Tension arises between those who support the coalition as a means for achieving desired results and those who want to preserve relationships regardless of the results. The coalition probably needs to be both. It needs to be the way in which some goal is actually addressed and also serve as a model of how various groups can work effectively together. For example, think of a coalition of Asian American Student Associations on campus who have come together to work for an Asian studies program. Some in the group will see the potential of working together for other purposes as well and be hopeful that the various

Asian American student groups are in dialogue. Others in the group just want this one goal accomplished and see no need to preserve the coalition.

4. The tension between unity and diversity; members of the coalition need to find ways to act with common purpose, recognizing the differences they bring to the goal. "The more one favors strengthening communities . . . the more one must concern oneself with ensuring that they see themselves as parts of a more encompassing whole, rather than as fully independent and antagonistic" (Etzioni, 1993, p. 155). The homecoming committee might work hard to keep a balance among the athletic emphasis, social reunions, cultural events, current student celebrations, and academic updates that are planned, even if those behind any one kind of event think it should be preeminent.

Bobo, Kendall, and Max (2001) note that "Coalitions are not built because it is good, moral, or nice to get everyone working together. Coalitions are about building power. The only reason to spend the time and energy building a coalition is to amass the power necessary to do something you cannot do through one organization" (p. 100). There are distinct advantages and disadvantages to working in coalitions (Exhibit 12.6).

Coalitions face unique challenges when forming alliances between groups that differ in fundamentally different approaches or worldviews that are reflected in their sex, race, sexual orientation, or class. "Minority groups have many reasons to mistrust majority groups who have historically exploited, co-opted, and dominated them" (Mizrahi & Rosenthal, 1993, p. 31). Majority groups (those who have been in the dominant culture) have been used to being in control and have most often seen decisions made and problems approached in ways they are comfortable with. For marginalized group members to follow the methods of the dominant culture, leadership may feel like it's being co-opted; to bring up issues of interest may seem like having a special agenda; and

Exhibit 12.6. Advantages and Disadvantages of Working in Coalitions.

Advantages	Disadvantages
Win what couldn't be won alone.	Distracts from other work.
Build an ongoing power base.	Weak members can't deliver.
Increase the impact of an individual organization's efforts.	Too many compromises.
Develop new leaders.	Inequality of power.
Increase resources.	Individual organizations may not get credit.
Broaden scope.	Dull tactics.

Source: Bobo, Kendall, & Max (2001), pp. 101–102. Used with permission.

teaching the dominant culture about the issues salient to those who have not been heard in the past takes energy and can build resentment. The dominant culture may be administrators, those with resources, or the White culture. Marginalized culture may be students, lower socioeconomic groups, or historically peripheral groups. Although this may not be true of the group experiences of all those who have been underrepresented, marginalization should be addressed as if it is indeed a problem in the coalition. This will help build sensitive coalitions. The RLM elements of inclusion, empowerment, ethics, and process are all involved in building such coalitions.

Building effective coalitions among diverse members is important to producing successful results. A critical question is posed by Pascale, Millemann, and Gioja (2000, p. 203): "If conversation is the source and soul of change, the first concern is: Who should be included in it?" Mizrahi and Rosenthal (1993) recommend that all coalition members (notably what they identify as the minority groups) be involved in the design of the coalition goals and methods from the beginning and not brought in at a later point, which can be seen as tokenism. Further, the coalition must continuously make it a top priority to enhance diversity and must insist on the involvement of those who will be affected by the change outcome. Relational leadership values doing things *with* people, not *to* them.

Civic Engagement

We all have a responsibility to be civically engaged in all the communities that matter to us. This engagement can take various forms and will exist to varying degrees. Association of American Colleges sand Universities vice president Caryn Musil (2003) shares the belief that "students need to be prepared to assume full and responsible lives in an interdependent world, marked by uncertainty, rapid change, and destabilizing inequalities" (p. 4). She envisions a range of different "expressions of citizenship" (summarized in Exhibit 12.7). It is important to note that each face or phase describes a different form of campus engagement with the outside world and contains "different definitions of community, values, and knowledge" (p. 5).

The Relational Leadership Model—with its emphasis on the change process, purpose, empowerment, and being ethical and inclusive—relates directly to Musil's work, especially the Reciprocal and Generative Faces or Phases. Musil's view of citizenship is decidedly relational in nature—note how Musil defines community with the concepts of empowerment and interdependence. This theme is carried through in the "levels of knowledge" that are seen through "multiple vantage points." There are many examples of how this could work on campuses. When you say "We're going to do something," ask yourself "How big is our *we*?" (Bruteau, 1990, p. 510). Partnering with other organizations in forming coalitions expands your sense of perspective, especially if those organizations are ones with which you do not typically interact.

Exhibit 12.7. Faces or Phases of Citizenship.

Face or Phase	Community is . . .	Civic Scope	Levels of Knowledge	Benefits
Exclusionary	. . . only your own	Civic disengagement	One vantage point (yours) Monocultural	A few and only for a while
Oblivious	. . . a resource to mine	Civic detachment	Observational skills Largely monocultural	One party
Naïve	. . . a resource to engage	Civic amnesia	No history No vantage point Acultural	Random people
Charitable	. . . a resource that needs assistance	Civic altruism	Awareness of deprivations Affective kindliness and respect Multicultural, but yours is still the norm center	The giver's feelings, the sufferer's immediate needs
Reciprocal	. . . a resource to empower and be empowered by	Civic engagement	Legacies of inequalities Values of partnering Intercultural competencies Arts of democracy Multiple vantage points Multicultural	Society as a whole in the present
Generative	. . . an interdependent resource filled with possibilities	Civic prosperity	Struggles for democracy Interconnectedness Analysis of interlocking systems Intercultural competencies Arts of democracy Multiple interactive vantage points Multicultural	Everyone now and in the future

Source: Musil, 2003, p. 8. Reprinted with permission from *Peer Review*, vol. 5, no. 3. Copyright 2003 by the Association of American Colleges and Universities.

Service as Change-Making

Service is one way in which many college students help bring about change in their communities and in the larger world. Service on a college campus can take many forms. It can be done because of an individual's commitment to a cause or program, or it can be part of an organizational effort to "give back" to the community. It can be one aspect of a course or can even be used as part of a conduct sanction. From volunteering for one-time service projects to being a participant in ongoing service efforts, you can learn a lot about yourself, about others, and about policies that inhibit or promote change through service of all kinds. Whether the service involves schools, hospitals, environmental agencies, or numerous other human services agencies or projects, good things generally happen.

For these good things to happen, the service program needs to contain certain factors. The program must place students within an agency or community that provides (1) real learning for students and a real benefit to the community, (2) an application of what students are learning in the classroom, (3) opportunities for reflection, and (4) chances for students to hear and experience the voice of the community (Eyler & Giles, 1999). It is important to remember that service does not benefit just those being served; it also benefits those doing the serving. Eyler, Giles, Stenson, and Gray (2001) summarize a number of studies in highlighting the benefits of service for students:

- Service-learning has a positive effect on interpersonal development and the ability to work well with others, leadership and communication skills.

- Service-learning has a positive effect on reducing stereotypes and facilitating cultural and racial understanding.

- Service-learning has a positive effect on sense of social responsibility and citizenship skills.

- Service-learning has a positive effect on commitment to service. (pp. 2–3) (Used with permission)

How someone engages in service makes all the difference. Although it might seem that the experience of service itself would be enough, this is not always the case. Imagine someone grudgingly participating in a service project as part of a course or because it is required of all members of an organization. How often have you heard someone say something like this: "I'm paying tuition to do this!? I don't know why we have to do this stuff—it doesn't make any difference. It's just glorified charity work. It's sure not academic. I could be spending my time studying." Contrast that with another student who is a willing participant: "I'm learning so much about myself from this experience—more than I ever learned in a class! I'm learning skills I can use in the real world. I'd rather do this than be stuck in a classroom." Certainly this student will have a different kind of experience. Still, without reflection, learning from the experience is minimized and, one could argue, personal growth as an individual and as a leader is limited.

Morton (1995) addresses this situation by describing service in terms of distinct paradigms: charity, project, and social change. Charity is "the provision of direct service where control of the service (resources and decisions affecting their distribution) remain with the provider" (p. 21). The project paradigm is a "focus on defining problems and their solutions and implementing well-conceived plans for achieving those solutions" (p. 22). The social change paradigm emphasizes "process: building relationships among or within stakeholder groups, and creating a learning environment that continually peels away the layers of the onion called 'root causes'" (p. 22–23). Using terminology taken from Geertz (1973), Morton goes on to note, "Each paradigm has 'thin' versions that are disempowering and hollow, and 'thick' versions that are sustaining and potentially revolutionary" (p. 24).

Morton (1995) sums up the potential of service in the following way:

> Certainly, students need to understand that several forms
> of service exist; that they can all be meaningful; and that
> they have choices about what they will do and how they
> will do it. And they need to be challenged to make those
> choices consciously, based on experience and reflection.
> The irony is that unless we can adequately describe the
> range of service that exists, students will continue to
> work with a narrow and artificial definition of service
> that polarizes into a limited domain of service and an
> expansive domain of non-service. (p. 29)

These paradigms of service offer much to help us broaden the concept of leadership. The critical nature of the "thin" and "thick" versions is important to keep in mind. The thin versions involve maintaining power and control of the processes, of doing things to and for others. The thick versions respect the agency of those populations with which the service group is working. Just as the Relational Leadership Model emphasizes empowering others, so does service when it is done in a thoughtful, respectful, reciprocal, reflective manner.

Identifying Critical Issues

When you take a critical look at the organizations, institutions, communities, nation, and world in which you live, there is much that needs to be changed. But where to begin? This can be a very difficult question to consider because it can lead one to a sense of hopelessness—there is so much that needs to be changed, and you are only one person, so the task can seem overwhelming and impossible. One result is that we give in to that hopelessness and decide to not engage in any serious change efforts. Or we jump right into the fray—but once we have decided to try to make a difference, how do we select from the many areas that could use our attention? Here are some questions to ask yourself as you consider where to devote your leadership efforts and energy. You can relate these questions back to the Social Change Model.

- About what issues am I the most passionate? (Change takes energy.)

- Am I willing to take the time and make the sacrifices to work on this issue? (Change is not easy.)

- Am I willing to face the challenges associated with this issue? (Change takes courage.)

- For which issues am I most likely to be able to recruit others? Who are the shareholders or stakeholders who might join me in working with this issue? (Change involves others.)

- With which issues can I (and interested others) really make an impact? (We want our change efforts to accomplish something.)

Once you have answered these questions, you'll need to make the difficult choice of the one issue on which to focus. Although we all know students who have been able to juggle involvements in multiple change efforts, the time and energy needed for such efforts usually prohibits them from being successful. This can seem like a cop-out at first, but one successful change effort can lead to even more changes happening in the future. It is also important to remember the critical nature of working with others and being ethical while identifying critical issues. Without involving those stakeholders immediately in the situation, something important is being missed and the change efforts will have less chance of success. The ethical component of leadership also comes into play when working on important issues. Critical questions come to the forefront: To what lengths are we willing to go when working on this issue? Do the ends justify the means? The identification of critical issues can be a test of the leadership of a group, organization, or community.

Joining with Others

Once you have identified a single issue, the challenge becomes joining with others to work on the change effort. Jeffrey Luke (1998) helps us with this next step by providing a set of common questions used to identify potential stakeholders (Bryson & Crosby, 1992; King, 1984):

- Who is affected by the issue?
- Who has an interest in or has expressed an opinion about the issue?
- Who is in a position to exert influence—positively or negatively—on the issue?
- Who ought to care? (Luke, 1998, p. 69)

Encouraging others to care about an issue as much as you do is difficult. Something that seems critical to you may seem like a non-issue to others. As you are considering different issues, it can be helpful to differentiate between a condition, a problem, and a priority issue (Luke, 1998) (see Exhibit 12.8).

Relatedly, Luke (1998) notes that issues rise to priority in the policy agenda due to the convergence of four elements, which do not necessarily occur in a predictable time frame or sequential order. The four elements are

1. Intellectual awareness of a worsening condition or troubling comparison

Exhibit 12.8. The Issue Attention Cycle.

A "condition"	A "problem"	A "priority issue"
(an existing situation or latent problem)	(a problem captures the public's attention)	(an issue rises to priority status for key decision makers)
Not every condition will surface as a problem or be defined as a problem.	A societal concern becomes salient and important, and thus captures public attention through increasing awareness, visibility, and emotional concern.	The issue is felt as urgent and pressing, coupled with some optimism that it can be addressed, and thus displaces other problems on the policy agenda.
Example: Residential students complain that there is "nothing to do on the weekends."	Example: The student newspaper prints an article detailing the consumption of alcohol by under-age students at a student government retreat that was financed from student fees.	Example: Membership on key all-campus committees is composed of very similar students. You and a group of concerned peers decide to try to broaden this group to be more representative of the entire student body.

Source: Adapted from Luke (1998), p. 44. Used with permission.

2. Emotional arousal and concern regarding the conditions
3. Sense that the problem is urgent
4. Belief that the problem can be addressed (p. 54)

In thinking about who you might be able to recruit for your change effort, some individuals may immediately come to mind. These could be like-minded friends or acquaintances, peers who are members of organizations to which you belong, or others in groups that would be directly impacted by the changes you are interested in proposing. Luke (1998) offers questions to ask yourself as you consider who you might try to recruit:

- Who are the stakeholders, knowledgeholders, and other resources?

- Who can make things happen in this issue area? Who can block action?

- Who are appropriate newcomers or outsiders with unique perspectives?

- What is an appropriate critical mass to initiate action?

- Who should be invited to participate in the effort to address the issue?

- How can core participants once identified, be motivated to join the collective effort?

- What other forms and levels or participation could generate quality ideas?

- How can first meetings be convened to create a safe space and legitimate process for problem solving? (p. 88)

(Used with permission.)

Conflict

Conflict is inevitable, even among and between individuals who want to create similar changes. Dealing with conflict is one of the most challenging aspects of leadership. It is difficult to keep from labeling those who disagree with us as "bad," "wrong," or "not caring enough." As we have noted previously, groups that are able to work through the storming stage of group development find themselves stronger and better able to work together than they were before the conflict began. It is also important to remember that the Relational Leadership Model defines leadership as a process, and conflict is certainly one aspect of this process. What is important to remember is the need to maintain focus on the purpose of what you are trying to accomplish as you also maintain the relationship with others who are involved. The Social Change Model presents the idea of "controversy with civility." Certainly disagreement is to be expected, and even invited, as you are trying to accomplish almost any sort of meaningful change. Luke (1998, p. 198) helps us understand this conflict and provides typical causes and possible interventions (see Exhibit 12.9).

Conflict most likely is inevitable when you are involved in change. Dealing, or not dealing, with that conflict can determine the success of the change effort. Conflict, in general, involves relationships and goals. When people are involved in a stressful change effort, our feelings become heightened, so anything can take on added importance. Obviously it is better to address conflict earlier rather than later and to do so in a respectful manner while maintaining an open mind. Working with conflict can be one of the most challenging aspects of leadership.

Navigating Environments

The college environment can be difficult to navigate. As in any complex hierarchical system, there are many layers. As with any bureaucratic organization, it can be tough to figure out who is responsible for what areas. You encounter deans, directors, coordinators, and all other levels of staff positions. Although there are similarities from campus to campus, each institution retains its own way of doing things. Figuring out who to contact in order to begin working for change is not always easy.

Some questions to ask yourself:

- What do I want to accomplish? Be able to state clearly and succinctly what you are trying to do. Try explaining this to someone who knows nothing about the particular topic or area. This will force you to state things in simple terms that are easy to understand.

- Who else might be interested in this project? What other individuals or organizations might I contact? No matter how committed or talented you are, you cannot do it alone.

- Where can I begin? What person or office should I contact first? The key thing is to begin—starting any project may be frustrating at first.

- What persons or offices can this first contact refer me to? People are generally helpful—you will undoubtedly grow your list of contacts.

Conclusion

We began this chapter with a well-known quote by Margaret Mead, "Never doubt that a small group of thoughtful, committed citizens can change the world; indeed it is the only thing that ever has" (cited in Mathews, 1994, p. 119). We end it with a short but powerful quote by Paul Loeb (1999), who writes about a call to action in his book, *Soul of a Citizen:* "We can never predict the impact of our actions" (p. 1). When you engage in leadership in your organization, your community, your school, your neighborhoods, your state, your nation, and the world, you are working to make changes. Through these changes, the world becomes a better place for all of us.

What's Next?

Your reactions to engaging with others to accomplish change may signal how you have developed as a leader or how renewed you feel to engage in new challenges. The last part of this book examines how leadership develops over time, your leadership identity, and how you stay renewed in your leadership commitments.

Exhibit 12.9. Sources of Conflict on Action Strategies.

Source of Conflict	Typical Causes	Possible Interventions
Underlying value differences	Different ways of life, ideology, or religions Strong emotional beliefs	Rely on superordinate goal or outcome that all members share Avoid defining criteria in terms of underlying values Do not require the divergent strategies to adhere to the same underlying values Seek shared interests, not shared values
Differing priorities	Perceived or actual competing interests "Zero-sum" or "fixed-pie" assumptions (additional allocation of resources for one cause/person means that another cause/person will receive less) Scarce resources will force the selection of only a few strategies to pursue	Facilitate interest-based bargaining Agree on criteria for selecting strategies

Chapter Activities

1. Revisit the Social Change Model. What personal values guide your leadership? How does your thinking, feeling, and behaving around these values show congruence? How do you demonstrate your commitment to those values?

2. Again, consider the Social Change Model as it relates to an organization in which you are a participant. What happens

Source of Conflict	Typical Causes	Possible Interventions
Relationship issues	Historically created distrust	Deal with past relationship issues
	Stereotypes and misperceptions	Control expression of negative emotions through procedural ground rules
	Poor communication and listening	
		Allow appropriate venting of emotions as part of strategy-development process
		Improve the quality and quantity of communications
Data conflicts	Lack of information	Agree on what data are important
	Different interpretations of data	Use third-party experts to gain outside opinion and clarify data interpretations

Source: Luke (1998), p. 198. Used with permission.

when you are faced with a difficult issue? How do you demonstrate "controversy with civility"? How might your organization improve in this area?

3. Consider a recent change you have made or tried to make within an organization. What role did conflict play in this change process? Who was involved in the conflict? What did you try that was unsuccessful in working with the conflict? What was successful?

4. Being an effective change agent means knowing key decision makers within the community (Kahn, 1991). What campus

officials do you need to know better? How might you go about becoming better acquainted with them?

Additional Readings

Astin, A. W., & Astin, H. S. (2000). *Leadership reconsidered: Engaging higher education in social change.* Battle Creek, MI: W. K. Kellogg Foundation.

Bobo, K. A., Kendall, J., & Max, S. (2001). *Organizing for social change: Midwest Academy manual for activists* (3rd ed.). Santa Ana, CA: Seven Locks Press.

Higher Education Research Institute (HERI). (1996). *A social change model of leadership development: Guidebook version III.* Los Angeles: University of California Los Angeles Higher Education Research Institute. (Guidebooks are available from the National Clearinghouse for Leadership Programs; http://www.nclp.umd.edu/.)

Kahn, S. (1991). *Organizing: A guide for grassroots leaders* (Rev. ed.). Washington, DC: National Association of Social Workers.

Katzenbach, J. R., Beckett, F., Dichter, S., Feigen, M., Gagnon, C., Hope, Q., & Ling, T. (1996). *Real change leaders: How you can create growth and high performance at your company.* New York: Random House.

Loeb, P. R. (1999). *Soul of a citizen: Living with conviction in a cynical time.* New York: St. Martin's Griffin.

Luke, J. S. (1998). *Catalytic leadership: Strategies for an interconnected world.* San Francisco: Jossey-Bass.

Wijeyesinghe, C. L., Griffin, P., & Love, P. (1997). Racism curriculum design. In M. Adams, L. A. Bell, & P. Griffin (Eds.), *Teaching for diversity and social justice: A sourcebook* (pp. 87–109). New York: Routledge.

Part V

Leadership Development and Renewal

The leadership journey presented in this book started with the inward journey into yourself. Having a consciousness of yourself is the most essential step toward relating effectively to others (Higher Education Research Institute, 1996). Throughout the pages of this book, you have explored leadership as a process engaging you and others in communities, groups, and organizations.

It would be a mistake to end with something like "six steps to becoming an effective leader" or "ten principles of leadership for all times." Such postulates would be suspect, even ludicrous. Although we have promoted your thinking about relational leadership and strongly emphasize the importance of people working together, we encourage you to develop a personal philosophy of leadership grounded in the principles and values that will work for you in your uplifting relationships with others toward shared, positive purposes. Heider (1985), in sharing the reflections of Lao Tzu, offers this:

> *Beginners acquire new theories and techniques until their minds are cluttered with options.*
>
> *Advanced students forget their many options. They allow the theories and techniques that they have learned to recede into the background.*
>
> *Learn to unclutter your mind. Learn to simplify your work.*

As you rely less and less on knowing just what to do, your work will become more direct and more powerful. You will discover that the quality of your consciousness is more potent than any technique or theory or interpretation.

Learn how fruitful the blocked group or individual suddenly becomes when you give up trying to do just the right thing.
(p . 95)

We want to end this journey by exploring how you are constructing a life you want to live, including how you view yourself working with others toward shared purposes. Now that you are at the end of the book, your leadership identity development may be an important part of your other social identities. Seeking to understand yourself as a leader might now be an important personal goal. Engaging in leadership can be hard work. It can add pressure and stress and can require you to work hard to balance all aspects of your life. We, as individuals, must connect our mind, body, and soul to stay renewed.

Renewal literally means to "make new again." To "re-new" through a process of individuals and their groups and organizations learning together is a dynamic undertaking. No matter how busy, no matter how stressed, no matter how discouraged, no matter how joyous, no matter how satisfied, no matter how happy, no matter how effective—individuals, groups, and organizations regain balance and stay fresh by making renewal processes an essential focus.

13

Developing a Leadership Identity

A True Story

Jenn was excited to be appointed yearbook editor her senior year in high school, only to discover that the yearbook from the year before was not finished. Inwardly she groaned. She would have to finish putting out that book, then work on her class yearbook as well. Initially working with a small group of other seniors, she eventually found it easier to just do it all herself, as she knew what she wanted done.

It seemed to take all her waking hours getting the yearbooks completed. Eventually no one else even came to yearbook meetings. Looking back on this time, she observed, there are "those who see leadership as shared, participatory, or transforming—there was *none* of that in me as yearbook editor!" She acknowledged that her view of leadership at that time was that she had to get the job done, so she just did it.

For one-half day every week throughout high school, Jenn worked with a boy, Tony, who had severe disabilities. Among other developmental disabilities, Tony could not hear or see. From working with Tony, Jenn was inspired to consider speech therapy as a career. She said, "I came to realize how many gifts and skills an individual can bring to a situation. He amazed me with all he could create and how his sense of touch and smell were so powerful!" Initially she saw this service as shaping her career goals, but gradually her time with Tony began to teach her bigger life lessons.

By the time she was a college sophomore, she was enjoying being one of three cochairs of the university tour guides in the admissions offices. She enjoyed working with others to share the responsibilities, and she liked the system, in which one of the cochairs was always new so that others could mentor and coach that person. She valued the development of this pipeline of leaders among the ambassadors and enjoyed mentoring others.

As a junior tapped to be in a leadership honor society, Jenn took on chairing a major committee assignment with a bit of anxiety. After all, to be a leader of leaders felt a bit intimidating. She came to the first committee meeting of all these leaders with an agenda and specific goals and ideas about what the group might do. She was really organized. To her relief, the group wanted it to be a full group process of consensus on how the group approached their tasks. On Senior Council she found she did not like the class gift idea that was getting support, but she also knew her idea did not have as much support and it would be important to get behind the decisions of the group. She decided to stop pushing for her idea and joined with the group in endorsing this gift idea that was emerging with great support.

Chapter Overview

Jenn's story was adapted from the story of a student in a study on leadership identity development, presented in this chapter. How did Jenn go from wanting to get everything done by herself to enjoying shared leadership and valuing working with others in collaborative settings? Her perception of leadership and her identity as a leader changed over the course of her high school and college experiences. This chapter will discuss what identity is and specifically how leadership identity develops.

This chapter helps conclude your study of yourself and of leadership. The chapter gives you an opportunity to reflect on how you have developed leadership. As you read this chapter, think about these questions:

1. What is identity and how does one's identity impact leadership development? Can identity change over time? What influences the development of identity, and is it a permanent state? How does leadership identity relate to other identities?

2. How do components of the relational leadership model influence the development of interdependence and identity?

3. Why is interdependence important in leadership and in relationships with group members?

Developing the Capacity for Leadership

College is a time of expanding your individual capacities. Many colleges profess to develop a set of student learning outcomes that include individual development (to find these for your college, look at the mission statement of the college or the student affairs division). Colleges seek to develop cognitive complexity; they want you to be able to acquire, integrate, and apply knowledge; develop humanitarianism; expand your interpersonal and intrapersonal skills; and build practical skills; and they want to help you commit to being engaged in communities and be effective in leadership (National Association of Student Personnel Administrators & American College Personnel Association, 2004). Although each institution has a different emphasis in those possible outcomes, students consistently report that they attend college to expand their capacities to be more complex and effective individuals. College graduates want to be people who can make a difference in their families, their professions, and their communities.

Self-Authorship

Constructing a life for yourself is a dynamic process of self-assessment, reflection, and self-confidence in the context of your interests and relationships. The maturation process leads to knowing oneself well, building a personal life plan, learning to make good decisions, and acknowledging the capacity that one can learn and develop over time; in other words, it leads to being comfortable in your own skin. "Adult life requires the capacity for self-authorship— the ability to collect, interpret and analyze information and reflect on one's own beliefs in order to form judgments" (Baxter Magolda, 1998, p. 143).

Building on the work of Robert Kegan (1994), Marcia Baxter Magolda (1998) conducted a longitudinal study of college students into their young adult years. This study connected with students during college and on a regular basis over nearly twenty years. According to the participants in her study, self-authorship "involves learning how to make knowledge claims, gaining confidence in doing so, learning to balance external forces with one's own perspective and knowledge, and developing an internal identity that supports acting on one's knowledge and priorities" (p. 153). Although most of her participants were White students, the lessons are compelling for all of us. Self-authorship begins with trusting yourself and deepening and enriching your self-awareness. The social change model presented in Chapter Twelve emphasized the values of consciousness of self, commitment, and congruence to support the concept of self-authorship.

Self-Efficacy

Another college outcome is to develop the self-confidence that you can engage in the tasks that are important to your life and career. Self-efficacy is the confidence to know that you can do something specific. You may have absolutely no self-efficacy that you could stand in front of two hundred people and give a speech, but a high level of self-efficacy that you could run a marathon. You may have self-efficacy that you can relate well to diverse people but no self-efficacy that you could sing. Self-efficacy is developed primarily through meaningful experience (Bandura, 1997). When you have done something before and did it well or learned to do it better, you have a higher self-efficacy the next time that you could handle a similar task. Each time you engage with a task or practice a new skill, you get better at it.

Bandura (1997), who writes about social learning theory, asserts that there are four sources of information that shape whether we think we have the efficacy to handle a specific task. The first is meaningful experience or performance accomplishments; it is the most powerful of these sources of information. If you have done something before and handled it well or learned from it, you have more confidence you could do it or something like it again. In addition, you may have the second source: affirmations, or verbal persuasion, from others that you can handle the task. Your resident assistant, your faculty advisor, your supervisor at work, or your brother may say, "You are really good at this, you should go out for that position." Their affirmation gets your attention and provides an external validation of your capacity, giving you the confidence to try. The third source of information is modeling or vicarious experiences. When you see someone like yourself succeeding, you begin to think *I could do that too*. Modeling is one reason it is so important to see people like you in key positions on campus and in the community. The fourth source of information is the emotional cues that you experience when confronting a task. You may be fearful but challenged and even energized to try something new, or you may be fearful, feel threatened, and decide not to take a risk.

In addition to individual self-efficacy, Bandura (1997) also presents the concept of collective efficacy. Collective efficacy is the confidence a group has that it can handle a task. Individuals in the group may know they could not do it individually, but together the group works effectively to use their shared talents, and they can handle a task creatively and well. Conversely, individuals may be quite self-confident but they have no confidence the group can work well together. They may dread working with some individuals or not have group processes for information sharing or decision making. Their past experience together may have proved they cannot handle shared problems and they do not want to try. Saying "I can do something" is individual self-efficacy; saying "we can do something" is collective efficacy.

Learning from Experience

If the most powerful contributor to developing self-efficacy is experience, then examining how we learn from experience is critical to developing self-authorship. The seeking of meaningful experiences must become intentional. However, things that happen to us do not become experience without reflection.

Kolb's experiential learning model was presented in Chapter One. Revisit it now and think about the leadership learning you have done. The Kolb model is a cycle of experience → reflection → abstract conceptualization → experimentation. Although you can enter this circle from any point, imagine that you are working with a group of other students on a class project. The group is bogged down and seems stuck (concrete experience). Someone might then say, "Let's figure out why we are stuck. What is really happening here?" (reflection). After some discussion, someone might then form a working hypothesis and say, "We seemed to get stuck because we got attached to one idea that was not going to work. The next time we get stuck, it would be beneficial for us to shift into a brainstorming mode so we could generate ideas that would help" (abstract conceptualization). Sure enough, when the group bogs down again someone quickly says, "Let's try to brainstorm again now about what we might do next, because that helped last time" (active experimentation).

On a personal level this model helps us understand how we learn and integrate our learning with our personal experience. Something happens and you either think it through with a friend or journal about it to figure it out. You then speculate about why this happened or what you could do about it, and then you try that solution and see what happens. Whatever your learning style, making meaning out of experiences is an essential step to learning something from them. In this case, processing your experiences in groups and in other leadership situations lets you learn and practice in ways that increase your self-efficacy and work toward self-authorship. This process is essential to developing a personal identity.

Personal Identities

Erikson (1968) asserted that identity is a sense of a continuous self. He argued that people discover, more than they create, their identities, and they do it within a social context that is in interaction with others. Identity is "not just a private, individual matter [but] a complex negotiation between the person and the society" (Josselson, 1996, p. 31). Each person discovers and uncovers their identity through a continual process of observation and reflection. "Identity development models describe a process of increasing differentiation in the sense of self and the integration of that growing complexity into a coherent whole" (Pascarella & Terenzini, 2005, p. 23). Differentiation means observing how you are different from others and seeing the complexity of all your parts, whereas integrating means making a whole unique self out of those parts that is your own distinct identity.

Each of us has many important identities. For example, we have a gender identity, a sexual orientation identity, and a racial or ethnic identity. Those with normative identities such as White identity may never have reason to question it until it is challenged and the consciousness process starts to make them aware of White privilege (that is, the unearned advantages of being White as the dominant cultural group) and begin the identity exploration and development process (McIntosh, 1988, 2000). For more on this, revisit some of the concepts in Chapters Four and Five.

These multiple identities intersect, and at times one of our identities may get more of our attention than another. Some identities can conflict or cause tension, such as establishing a gay identity within an ethnic group or religious group that may not be accepting of that identity.

Social Identity

In addition to identities based on gender or ethnicity, we also establish a social identity by taking on the norms and expectations of a role such as an athlete identity, a fraternity identity, a graduate student identity, an air force officer identity, or a lawyer identity. Being a leader can also be a social identity. A social identity of being a leader is very connected to one's philosophy of leadership; indeed

> leadership identity is the cumulative confidence in one's ability to intentionally engage with others to accomplish group objectives. Further, a relational leadership identity appears to be a sense of oneself as someone who believes that groups comprise interdependent members who do leadership together (Komives, Owen, Longerbeam, Mainella, & Osteen, 2005, p. 608).

We view others through an identity lens and make attributions based on our expectations of some identities. Ruderman and Ernst (2004), for example, describe how the expression of emotion from a leader might be viewed. For many people, a White male pounding his fist on the table to make a point might be seen as assertive; however, if a woman did the same, they might perceive her as out of control or emotional, and if an African American male did the same thing, some might see it as aggressive. These kinds of stereotypes and attributions of social identities were discussed in Chapter Five.

We also bring our own social identities to how we view our interactions with others, both in what we expect of ourselves and as a basis for how we form our judgments of others. Our personal leadership identity shapes how we view the expressions of leadership in others. For example, Josh and Jessica walk out of a meeting together. Josh complains about Deana, the group's president. "Deana isn't a very good leader; she wants us all to talk about the decisions and I wish she would just be decisive!"

Jessica quickly responds, "Oh, I don't agree. I think she is an excellent president. She cares about all of us sharing what we think and agreeing on what we want to do. I love coming to these meetings." Josh and Jessica may have different reactions to Deana's behaviors because they have come to hold different views of what "good" leadership is.

The Leadership Identity Development Study

Researchers have studied how students' leadership identity changes over time. This Leadership Identity Development (LID) study may help you integrate your reading of the previous chapters in this book with aspects of your personal experience and college experience (Komives et al., 2005). This study found that at different points in their college experience, students felt differently about themselves working with others and took on different leadership identities. Understanding the development of a leadership identity can provide a framework to understand yourself and others.

Komives et al. (2005) were interested in how leadership identity developed, specifically in terms of how one comes to the self-acceptance of knowing one can work effectively with others to accomplish shared goals from any place in an organization—that is, to engage in leadership and see oneself as a leader. This interest led to a qualitative research study to address this "how" question. Using a grounded theory methodology (Strauss & Corbin, 1998), the researchers spent extensive time interviewing a diverse group of mostly juniors, seniors, and recent graduates who were nominated by campus faculty and student affairs staff as being people who practiced relational leadership, as described in this book. The researchers (Komives et al.) asked students to think back to their earliest life experiences and describe how they became the person they are now. Additional questions explored such things as the students' experience with others in groups. This kind of study does not seek to be generalizable, as do studies from quantitative methodology, but it is rich in meaning and therefore may be transferable to others. As you read about this theory, examine how it connects with your own experience and with that of others you know.

Developing a Leadership Identity

A key element in the findings of developing a leadership identity was developing the self. Developing oneself included deepening self-awareness, building self-confidence, establishing interpersonal efficacy in working with others, applying new skills, and expanding one's motivations—from joining groups just to make friends to being involved in groups to make a valuable contribution. Students in the study developed themselves in their interaction with others in groups. Group influences included engaging meaningfully in groups, learning from the continuity of group membership, and sticking with a group over time. In addition, their perceptions of groups changed over time, from seeing groups as a collection of friends to seeing them as organizations with structure and purpose. They eventually saw groups as part of a larger system of organizations.

As participants interacted with others in groups, these students changed their view of themselves in relation to others. They initially saw themselves as *dependent* on others, then also being *independent* from others, and eventually they came to a realization of being *interdependent* with others. As that view of self in relation to others changed, it broadened their view of what leadership was. Initially they saw leadership as something external to oneself—often a national figure or a teacher. They then began to see leadership as a position, believing that the person in a positional role is the leader and the leader leads while others follow. Their view then broadened to seeing that leadership can be nonpositional and anyone can lead in a group, and eventually they saw that leadership is a process among people in a group. James, a student in the study, realized, "I can be a leader without a title." This broadening view could be seen in the shift from saying, "I am *the* leader" or "I am not *the* leader" to "I am *a* leader" or "I can do leadership." One of our participants, Joey, said "I see leadership now as an everyday thing."

The processes of developing self, changing one's view of self in relation to others, and broadening the view of leadership were facilitated by various developmental influences in the students' environments. Adults and peers played a significant role as affirmers and sponsors and became coaches and mentors. Students sought meaningful involvement opportunities in their campuses and communities that fit their interests and goals. Throughout their leadership development, students were thoughtful about what they were learning and found ways to reflect with experienced adults, older peers, friends, and others. Leadership courses and other leadership development programs were critical to many participants in teaching the language of leadership, to help them differentiate their leadership views as they grew in leadership complexity.

The LID Stages

Looking at the student life span, the LID study identified six stages that students experienced over time (Komives et al., 2005; Komives, Longerbeam, Owen, Mainella, & Osteen, 2006). These stages were Awareness, Exploration/Engagement, Leader Identified, Leadership Differentiated, Generativity, and Integration/Synthesis. Each stage reflects a new way of thinking, with new tasks and challenges. Exhibit 13.1 briefly describes these stages, with an example of what an identity statement might be at that stage.

The students in this study came to college well into stage three, Leader Identified. Students had functioned in organizations for years—in high school, church, part-time jobs, clubs, choir, and schools. They recognized that those organizations had a purpose and a structure, with formal designated leaders to get the job done. In this stage, the predominant philosophy was that the leader is the one who exercises leadership. Students in the study held a hierarchical

Exhibit 13.1. Leadership Identity Development Stages

LID Stages	Stage Description	Sample Identity Statement
(1) Awareness	Becoming aware of how some people lead and influence others. Usually an external other person, like the U.S. president or a historic figure like Martin Luther King, Jr. *[feels dependent on others]*	A leader is someone out there, not me.
(2) Exploration/ Engagement	Immersion in a breadth of group experiences (e.g., Scouts, youth group, swim team) to make friends and find a fit. *[feels dependent on others]*	Maybe I could be a leader.
(3) Leader Identified	Fully involved in organizations and groups. Holds a belief that the positional leader does leadership whereas others do followership. *[may be independent from others (being a leader), dependent on others (being a follower), or hold both views]*	If I am the leader, it is my responsibility to get the job done. If I am a follower, I need to help the leader get the job done.

Source: Adapted from Komives, Longerbeam, Owen, Mainella, & Osteen (2006.)

view of organizations and leaders. Some students saw themselves as leaders (what the researchers call an independent view). Others preferred to be group members or followers (called a dependent view). Many students practiced both; they could be positional leaders in some groups and were also comfortable being involved group members or followers helping the leader in other groups.

As the consciousness developed that people in groups are interdependent, students transitioned to stage four, Leadership Differ-

LID Stages	Stage Description	Sample Identity Statement
(4) Leadership Differentiated	Recognizes that leadership comes from all around in an organization; as a positional leader, seeks to be a facilitator and practices shared leadership; as a member, knows one is engaged in doing leadership. *[feels interdependent with others]*	I can be *a* leader even if I am not *the* leader and I see that leadership is also a process. We do leadership together.
(5) Generativity	Is concerned about the sustainability of the group and seeks to develop others; is concerned about personal passion to leave a legacy and have one's actions make a difference. *[feels interdependent with others]*	We all need to develop leadership in the organization and in others. I am responsible to serve the organization.
(6) Integration/ Synthesis	Leadership capacity is an internalized part of oneself and part of the perspective one brings to all situations. *[feels interdependent with others]*	I can work with others to accomplish shared goals and work for change.

entiated. Their leadership identity began to shift. Those who were the positional leader of a group recognized in this stage that the group needed everyone to accomplish the group's goals, and they saw themselves as facilitators practicing shared leadership. They valued being a community builder in a group and valued team leadership. If they were members of a group, they now saw the member role as also engaging in leadership. Many students said, "I can be a leader without a title." In this stage it becomes important to learn such things as teamwork, listening skills, and collaboration. The participants began to see their organizations as part of a bigger picture and saw the benefit of forming coalitions with other organizations or collaborating with other organizations. This reflects a systems view of organizations. They began to see leadership as a process that people engage in together.

"Since high school I have learned that being a leader doesn't always mean being president of an organization. I have found ways to be a leader in the fulfillment of responsibilities on a variety of organizational levels. I have learned that as a leader, it is most important to me to inspire my peers to serve those around them. I know now that leaders don't always have official titles and don't always spend the majority of their time in the spotlight. There are leaders in every walk of life who are leaders by the character, selflessness, and integrity that they display in their personal lives"—Jacquelyn Knupp attends the University of Richmond and is a biology and leadership studies major. She volunteers at the Pediatric Intensive Care Unit and is a research coordinator for brain tumor cell research.

As the students began to face leaving college, it became important to make sure their organizations had a leadership pipeline; it was important to bring others into leadership positions. This Generativity stage found them intentionally affirming younger members, sponsoring others into leadership roles, and being a peer mentor to others.

"Being a mentor and a friend to someone is the most rewarding experience I have ever known. Having this opportunity to explain your philosophies and ideas to another, and in return watching their eyes light up as you see them come to new understandings about life, is an incredible feeling. It's important to be a mentor because I enjoy passing on the gift of knowledge to another individual. To be the catalyst for more advanced forms of thought is rare, but gratifying."—Ryan Roberts was an advertising/history major active in the Delta Chi fraternity, the Interfraternity Council, and the Hall Government Association at Marquette University.

The students also realized they had a passion for something important to them; this passion led them to focus their commitments on a core organization (like doing service work with youth with disabilities or being a resident assistant helping floor residents have a good college experience). Several of them wanted to leave behind a legacy of improving something for others. Their personal character and integrity became an essential part of their being. Those who moved into the full Integration/Synthesis stage knew how to assess organizations and had a philosophy of working with others effectively toward change. They now saw leadership capacity as part of their personal identity.

Look back, now, at the opening example of Jenn going into the meeting of a new committee of seniors she was chairing with a fairly structured agenda and several ideas about group projects. The group slowed her down and said that they really wanted to play an active role in deciding what the group would do and how to go about it. She was relieved, because that approach mirrored her new personal views of shared facilitative leadership, but she had thought the group might expect something else. The group's climate valued a philosophy of interdependence and shared leadership. So in the earlier scenario, when Josh criticized Deana's leadership he likely held stage three views (Leader Identified), whereas Deana may have been practicing a stage four philosophy (Leadership Differentiated). Jessica may have resonated well with Deana's approach because she also valued stage four thinking. Perhaps some organizations value one of the four stages as a predominant way of functioning.

Transitions

A classic psychology question is, "Do attitudes change behavior or does behavior change attitudes?" The answer is just "yes." How does this work for you? Some people need to think differently about something before they can act differently; others start acting differently and then stop to think about why. At some point in experiencing each LID stage, students started to feel some dissonance with the experience and knew that they needed to see things differently or act differently. This signaled the transition between stages. For example, in the Exploration/Engagement stage they may realize that they want to change something, or an advisor may affirm that they have great potential and could take on more of a role in the group. The idea gets planted that they could be leaders, and they think about taking on those roles, signaling a transition into stage three. The support of that advisor was critical: "If he thinks I can do this, maybe I can!" The transition between Leader Identified and Leadership Differentiated, for example, may be triggered when the task to be done is too big and complex for one leader to do it alone. It may be triggered when students learn the language of leadership, through leadership courses or retreats, and begin to realize there are other approaches and strategies that fit their view of themselves and how they want to work with others versus feeling that they were bossing others around. This transition is facilitated by experienced adults and older peers who can affirm the struggle of change and make meaning out of the students' growing awareness about themselves through their experience with others in groups.

Recycling

This type of stage-based theory asserts that a person experiences each stage before moving into the next one. As consciousness is raised and complexity is encountered, new ways of thinking about self and others emerge. Kegan (1994) calls these stages of consciousness. One becomes able to look back and see oneself objectively and can say, "I used to think only the leader could provide leadership, but now I see leadership as something we all do from any place in the organization." One knows what the thinking is like at an earlier stage and can be effective with that, even if one is thinking now in a more interdependent or complex way. For example, John can work in an office with a commanding boss who wants things done her way and be able to function in that environment, but may also feel some dissonance that his own talents are not being used to the fullest when he is treated that way. In a new situation (like moving into graduate school or a new job), one might recycle back to the task of an earlier state and explore and engage with the new environment while trying to find out what is a good fit. One does not go back and think at that stage, but returns with a higher level of complexity about why that exploration is happening.

The Relational Leadership Model and Leadership Identity Development

The LID study sought to understand how a relational leadership identity develops (Komives et al., 2005). The findings of the study affirmed that across the stages of LID, students practiced increasingly complex and differentiated perspectives and behaviors of being purposeful, inclusive, empowering, ethical, and process-oriented. These five elements best describe the interdependent perspectives of working with others. Exhibit 13.2 depicts LID characteristics of RLM dimensions. The first two stages are not included in the exhibit because we assert that most college students arrive at college in at least stage three.

Interdependence

Perhaps the most critical and complex perspective to leadership identity is to truly understand one's interdependence with others. Based on years of research, theorist Arthur Chickering (Chickering

Exhibit 13.2. Relational Leadership Model Perspectives in Leadership Identity Development Stages.

	LID Stage Three *Leader Identified*	LID Stage Four *Leadership Differentiated*	LID Stage Five *Generativity*	LID Stage Six *Integration/Synthesis*
View of Self with Others	Independent or Dependent	Interdependent	Interdependent	Interdependent
RLM Dimension *Purpose*	Get the job done	Develop common goal or vision	Help others develop; commit to a personal passion	Be effective in any group or setting in which one may find oneself
RLM Dimension *Inclusive*	Effective member recruitment; delegate well	Welcome diverse ideas; form coalitions with other groups	Develop pipeline of emerging leaders	Seek out diverse views; function well in multicultural settings
RLM Dimension *Empowering*	Prepare members with good followership skills	Prepare people to share group leadership; develop team skills; build community in the group	Sponsor younger members into new experiences; mentor others; help peers make meaning from their experiences	See self as able to engage in diverse contexts with diverse people; internalize self-confidence

	LID Stage Three *Leader Identified*	LID Stage Four *Leadership Differentiated*	LID Stage Five *Generativity*	LID Stage Six *Integration/ Synthesis*
RLM Dimension *Ethical*	Treat people fairly; practice high personal standards	Expect the group to be ethical and fair in its practices	Seek shared positive interests with other groups	Integrate personal integrity as a way of being across all types of groups and involvements
RLM Dimension *Process-Oriented*	Have well-planned agendas; involve members in decision making	Develop group listening skills; use teamwork; build community in group; learn to act collaboratively and seek consensus	Prepare new members with information needed to fully participate; mentor younger members	Integrate self-development with group leadership

& Reisser, 1993) modified one of the vectors in his psychosocial theory from "developing autonomy" to "moving through autonomy to interdependence." Referencing the work of biologist Lynn Margulis, Wheatley and Kellner-Rogers (1998) observed that "*independence* is not a concept that explains the living world. It is only a political concept that we've invented. Individuals cannot survive alone" (p. 11).

"Over the past five years, my view on leadership has changed drastically. I used to think of leadership as a one-sided, dictatorial-type situation in which invariably more followers than leaders could exist. Through my experiences in various organizations, and as a member of the Women's Leadership Initiative in my college at Penn State, I have developed a more sophisticated perspective on leadership. Good leadership involves the collaborative effort of many individuals utilizing their skills, knowledge, and abilities toward a common goal. Above all, I have learned that good objective listening and communication skills are essential to any leadership role. One person (or a few people) may have more socially prominent roles than others, but ultimately the investment of individuals should be more distributed."— Faheemah Mustafaa was a member of the crew team, the Student Awareness Committee on Multicultural Affairs, and the Biobehavioral Health Society at Pennsylvania State University.

Interdependence brings a recognition of reciprocity, of community, and of connectedness with others in all we do. As leadership happens among and between people, it is a central principle of effective relational leadership. Interdependence is illustrated by the last question in the triad—"How am I like no one else here?" "How am I like some others here?" and "How am I like everyone here?"— that we posed in Chapter Five.

Nature models interdependence in marvelous ways. The symbiotic processes of people taking in oxygen and releasing carbon dioxide, which is taken in by plants, which release oxygen; the ecological movement to save wetlands and endangered species; indeed, "It seems that the world is trying to tell us something. Perhaps it hopes that demonstrating our intrinsic interdependence will stimulate us to consciously co-create positive forms of interdependence—mutuality, community, synergy and co-intelligence" (Interdependence, Interdependence Days and Declarations of Interdependence, n.d.).

Tensions in Reality

Interdependence is desirable, but not all positional leaders value others in their organizations, not all organizations function with that premise, and hierarchies can produce disempowering environments. What tensions might you expect if you believe in interdependence and Leadership Differentiated approaches to leadership?

The "I"/"We" tension. It is challenging to answer the question, How do we move from a perspective of "me" to "we"? From "my" and "mine" to "us" and "ours"? As individuals in a Western culture, we will always have a strong "I"; the need to keep our "I" in context of the settings and the others we engage with as we approach leadership tasks constantly stretches us to come to "we." Moving to value interdependence means understanding diverse worldviews, understanding the context of others in the group, and believing in the inclusive and empowering dimensions of the Relational Leadership Model. The move from dependence through independence to interdependence is common in most identity models. "Me" is about individualistic self-interest, whereas relational or mutual self-interest reflects a value of "you and me," and an interdependent self-interest acknowledges the bigger "us" (Goodman, 2000).

The hierarchical nature of organizational leadership. Although leadership in teams or project groups or among same-level staff in an office may not be hierarchical, most settings in which we experience leadership are in organizational structures with a hierarchical framework. Some amount of power, authority, and control is vested in the positional leader, who is held responsible for the outcomes of that unit. Classrooms have professors, committees have chairpersons, offices have directors, and divisions have vice presidents. Imagine a continuum depicting the collaborative intersection between the positional leader in a hierarchical structure and the members of the group. At one end of the continuum, the leader in an authoritarian role does not meaningfully involve group members and may even exclude them; when some collaboration is allowed, the leader identifies key tasks that the group can take responsibility for and supports that shift in power; in a shared leadership setting, the group members, including the positional leader, share responsibility, and the leader retains control of very little, choosing instead to support the direction set by the group.

Leader Development or *Leadership* Development?

Much of the attention on how leadership is developed has focused on expanding the capacity of an individual to be more effective in leading others or in being a good follower. Educational systems are designed to help individuals expand their individual knowledge and skills, usually apart from the context of working with others. Higher education does little to focus on the leadership development of a group of individuals to expand their collective capacity to work effectively together, although opportunities to do so abound in project groups, committees, student organizations, lab teams, and collaborative class projects. Earlier in this chapter we shared the concept of collective efficacy (Bandura, 1997). Individuals in a group may be effective individual leaders but may not have developed as a group (see Chapter Seven). A different set of processes and skills is needed to build the leadership capacity of a group.

As shown in Exhibit 13.3, Day (2000) explains this difference by outlining the developmental targets of leader development or leadership development interventions. The contrast in these two targets is evident in the LID model between Leader Identified (stage three) and Leadership Differentiated (stage four). The awareness and skills that a positional leader or active follower may need in

Exhibit 13.3. Differences Between Leader Development and Leadership Development.

	Development	Target
Comparison Dimension	*Leader* *(LID Stage Three)*	*Leadership* *(LID Stage Four)*
Capital Type	Human	Social
Leadership Model	Individual	Relational
	Personal power	Commitments
	Knowledge	Mutual respect
	Trustworthiness	Trust
Competence Base	Intrapersonal	Interpersonal
Skills	Self-awareness	Social awareness
	Emotional awareness	Empathy
	Self-confidence	Service orientation
	Accurate self-image	Political awareness
	Self-regulation	Social skills
	Self-control	Building bonds
	Trustworthiness	Team orientation
	Personal responsibility	Change catalyst
	Adaptability	Conflict management
	Self-motivation	
	Initiative	
	Optimism	

Source: Reprinted from Day (2000), p. 584. Used with permission from Elsevier.

stage three have a more complex relational dimension, incorporating attention to context in stage four to work more effectively in a relational group context.

Summary

Each individual holds views of leadership based on feeling dependent on, independent of, or interdependent with others. A view that someone in a positional role is the leader (that is, only the leader provides leadership) gradually shifts to realizing that those not in positional roles also facilitate leadership and view leadership as a process among people in a group. One's leadership identity shifts from thinking "I am *the* leader" or "I am *not the* leader" to "I am *a* leader" and "I can engage in leadership with others." Acquiring the self-efficacy that one can engage in leadership with others is built on the self-confidence developed by experiencing others in group settings.

What's Next?

This exploration of leadership ends in the next chapter, focusing back on you. What personal renewal do you need to stay focused, engaged, and balanced?

Chapter Activities

1. Refer to the concept of self-efficacy. Identify the areas in which you have self-efficacy that enhances your own leadership. How would you describe those using the concept of self-efficacy?

2. When you were in elementary school, what did you think leadership was? What do you think it is now? What factors might have influenced your shifts in thinking?

3. What stages of the LID model have you experienced? What stage might be next for you and why? Build your own leadership developmental process model. Write the following words on separate small sticky notes (you can repeat or add any you wish): *listen, reflect, authority, influence, teamwork, values, independent, dependent, interdependent, follower, collaborator, mentors, sponsors, power, control, delegate, join, character, integrity, affirm.* Now arrange these notes on a large piece of paper to reflect the developmental process you went through to come to the views you now hold about yourself and leader-

ship. Use only those words that relate to your own views of leadership. Add any concepts not in this set that you think are important. Use a marker to connect any of these notes. How does this describe the process of building your own leadership identity?

Additional Readings

Bandura, A. (1997). *Self-efficacy: The exercise of control*. New York: Freeman.

Baxter Magolda, M. B. (1998). Developing self-authorship in young adult life. *Journal of College Student Development, 39*(2), 143–156.

Kegan, R. (1994). *In over our heads: The mental demands of modern life*. Cambridge, MA: Harvard University Press.

Komives, S. R., Owen, J. E., Longerbeam, S., Mainella, F. C., & Osteen, L. (2005). Developing a leadership identity: A grounded theory. *Journal of College Student Development, 46*, 593–611.

14

The Mind, Body, and Soul of the Leader

Any leadership process can be rewarding, exciting, and developmental as well as exhausting, challenging, consuming, and stressful. Most active participants would agree that others in their organizations expect a great deal from them, sometimes at the sacrifice of their personal time or commitments. Political leaders are challenged to meet the demands of dissatisfied constituents while maintaining personal balance in their lives. Students often are confronted with the demands of their leadership and membership roles, leaving them feeling like they are doing all the work—or everyone's work—on top of their academic responsibilities. How many times have you felt overwhelmed by all your responsibilities and tired by trying to juggle too many things, and said to yourself, "I can't wait until my obligations in this organization are over so I can have a life again!"

Many leadership publications and seminars talk about how leaders can provide renewal to their organizations, members, and communities, which was the focus of Chapter Ten. Equally important is the intentional renewal that leaders can bring into their own lives. Achieving renewal can be a challenge when leaders have a tendency to be preoccupied with the daily activities of leading a group or community balanced by school, family, employment, and other responsibilities. Self-renewal is a continuous way to reach your full potential. Too often, individuals seek renewal when it is too late or when they are burned out. We encourage you to view renewal as lifelong learning. John W. Gardner (1981) observed, "It is a sad but unarguable fact that most people go through their lives only partially aware of the full range of their abilities" (p. 10).

Chapter Overview

This chapter focuses on the renewal of the leader or participant and stresses the importance of being a healthy, renewed individual. Leaders can be more effective and beneficial to their respective organizations and groups when they are energized by what they are doing and balanced by finding personal time. They need to spend time in reflection and to do things unrelated to their organizations along with fulfilling their obligations and performing the tasks of leadership.

The health of a leader or participant is as important as the organization's goals and outcomes. A leader who is stressed, unbalanced, physically exhausted, or overwhelmed is not likely to be as effective as a leader who is balanced, renewed, and physically and mentally healthy. Being in a leadership position can be like living in a fishbowl—others seem to be watching what you do all the time. It is critical for all participants to pay attention to their mental and spiritual well-being. Leaders tend to take care of others and to put their personal needs aside as they advance the needs of their group and its members. Although this is noble, the leader's health is sometimes sacrificed or compromised for the good of others. A balanced approach suggests that organizational needs and priorities be balanced with the leader's needs—such as personal time away from the organization without feeling guilty, time to reflect, and other opportunities for personal renewal.

"Being a student leader means at times being a cheerleader for your group. Constantly being the motivator is draining. If I get burned out, I won't have the energy to give my group all that I have. I make sure that I do things to recharge. Sometimes that means taking a step back from all of my responsibilities like homework. I find if I just sit and watch a movie I feel 100% better. If I don't do this periodically, the quality of all my work suffers."—Karen Abruzzino majors in accounting at Lake Erie College. She is president of the Student Government Association and a member of Mortar Board. She serves as a student assistant at the Lake Erie College Human Resources Office.

Personal or individual renewal can be viewed as a proactive strategy, in that a person works intentionally to bring new perspectives and energy to a task or role. Conversely, renewal can be approached in a reactive way or as a means to correct an already unhealthy or unbalanced lifestyle. Some students, unfortunately, realize too late that working fourteen hours a day, six or seven days a week nonstop, results in burnout, broken relationships, serious health problems, and, ultimately, a negative effect on their organizations. These cases have been chronicled in our daily newspapers in stories of university presidents, congressional leaders, or athletes who step down from their roles because they need to spend more time with family or to pursue other interests. They may state that their jobs did not permit them to find balance in their lives. Women and people of color may also feel pressure to work twice as hard to achieve the same recognition and credibility as their male counterparts (Morrison, 1996), and they often are turned to by others for support. Although that adds to their impact on the organization, it also adds to their stress, which can lead to burnout, dissatisfaction, or disappointment.

We also have positive role models in leaders and members whose lifestyles enable them to be productive in their roles. Perhaps they learned the hard way that there is more to life than a career on the fast track or working harder to get more recognition and material rewards. This realization might have come from a personal shipwreck in the person's life—the sudden death of a family member or similar personal tragedies cause leaders to reflect on what is most important in life. Some leaders possess a philosophy that they need daily or regular time for personal or spiritual renewal, and they work to avoid leading a stressful, unhealthy life that can lead to burnout. Dr. Freeman Hrabowski, president of the University of Maryland, Baltimore County, enjoys "reading 19th century British literature to get out of this fast-paced period" (Lucas, 1999, p. 179). Wilma Mankiller, former chief of the Cherokee Nation, had regular conversations with a confidant who understood her and with whom she could be open and honest (Lucas). Martin Luther King III, son of the late civil rights leader Martin Luther King Jr. and former president of the Southern Christian Leadership Conference, "meditates and turns to God and prays as a way to gain strength" (p. 181).

"I think that I am lucky enough to have multiple mentors in my life. I feel as though I have many people to turn to in my life to help me when I have concerns regarding various leadership positions that I hold, and these mentors have come from a great network that I have found at Georgetown within the Student Programs administration. I have benefited from having the perspective of someone who knows me well but can see things that I sometimes miss in my actions or thoughts. My leadership has invariably gotten stronger through my relationships with my mentors, because they have had the opportunity to work with other leaders in the past who have had some of the same problems that I am having. It has also allowed me to meet challenges, in that they have at times helped me critically look at my position and allowed me to defend my position and helped me see the strengths in it through defense of it, or helped me see the flaws in it."—Kendra Jackson, majoring in international political economy at Georgetown University, was the new student orientation coordinator, executive board member of Hoya-Thon (dance marathon), and coordinator of Take Back the Night.

Personal renewal means different things to different people, but we understand renewal when we experience it. Some people escape or take a week or so away from their organization to recycle, be alone, rest, get refreshed, or simply have fun and enjoy the company of friends or family. Others regularly take long walks, exercise, garden, paint, dance, hang glide, listen to soothing music, take a bubble bath, or find quiet, uninterrupted time for reflection. To start each morning feeling rejuvenated, some people meditate or exercise, or engage in some other habitual, renewing activity; others find time later in their day for renewal.

Here is an example: A former president of Carlow College was about to retire, and her secretary of many years stepped into her office to ask a question that had been on her mind for quite some time. The secretary inquired of the president, "During all of these years that you've been president, you've had a standing appointment every day at four o'clock in the afternoon with someone named Mrs. Jones. In all my time as your secretary, not only have I never met Mrs. Jones, but I never once saw Mrs. Jones enter or leave your office. Now that you are getting ready to step down from the presidency, can you tell me who this mysterious Mrs. Jones is?" The president explained that Mrs. Jones was a fictitious person whom she scheduled every day on her calendar for one hour because if people knew that what she really was doing for that hour was reflecting quietly in her office, the hour would be frivolously taken up by appointments, phone calls, or meetings. The president went on to say that probably the most productive time of her day while she was in office was that time she had with Mrs. Jones.

This chapter is entitled "The Mind, Body, and Soul of the Leader" because we see these three entities as interrelated. Tending to your mind, body, and soul as a leader is a part of the renewal process. When your body is tired or you feel mentally exhausted, your spirit may lack enthusiasm. If you have overcommitted yourself by agreeing to do dozens of projects and tasks, you may drift aimlessly, not knowing where to begin. However, when you feel refreshed and energized and approach your work with spirit and zest, you achieve entirely different results. Your critical task as a leader is to pay attention to your "inner voices" (Bolman & Deal, 1995, p. 38), focus on your purpose or mission, continue your search, and find meaning in your endeavors. Like most aspects of the arduous work of leadership, this is easier said than done. The bottom line is that leaders must take good care of themselves physically, mentally, and spiritually in order to effectively lead with others.

As you approach all your communities of practice, learn to view the people and processes with new lenses, which is part of the renewal process. This book attempts to guide you to understand and accept a new meaning of leadership. To be an effective community member or leader, you need to continually develop your capacity to understand how the systems around you are "mutually related and interacting and continually changing" and how they affect you as a person.

Self-Renewal

One way to assess your self-renewal is to ask, Am I exhausted, existing, or excited? Which of these attributes describes you most of the time? Each of these three questions identifies a different status of renewal and describes various aspects of the mind, body, and soul of a leader.

Am I Exhausted?

Busy people who face many responsibilities and much stress may think they feel exhausted. Your body can give you physical signals that you have abused it. Like an engine, it will shut down until it gets the repairs it needs. You may indeed need to maintain some balance and set some priorities on your activities. If the source of your exhaustion is guilt, however, it may become a slippery slope, because you can never be good enough, or do enough, or work hard enough. This Superman-Superwoman syndrome can wear you down. We know a woman with a sign on her refrigerator door that reads "Don't should on yourself today." Think of all the "should" messages you deliver to yourself (I should be thin; I should be done with this paper; I should be cheerful when someone comes to my room at 3 A.M.). It is overwhelming, if not impossible, to try to be all things to all people all of the time. At the end of each day, do you find that you have spent the entire day doing for others to the extent that you are too exhausted to do anything for yourself?

You might also identify a source of your exhaustion as worry. You may live in the world of "what ifs?" and spend a great deal of energy worrying about things that might never happen. Even if they did (or did not) happen, it might not be so terrible. Life will go on. An excited person may also feel fatigued, but this is very different from mental depression or exhaustion. If you experience anxiety or depression to the degree that it becomes debilitating, you need some professional intervention or, at a minimum, self-renewal.

Constant stress can lead to high levels of exhaustion. Stress alone is not necessarily an unhealthy human response. Stress can be healthy if it is managed by periods of recovery (Buckingham, 2005). Prolonged stress is unhealthy and destructive to your mind, body, and soul. Successful athletes intentionally structure their regimens with periods of stress and recovery. The periods between stress and recovery make a difference in their achievement levels. In a study of athletes, the best ones had better recovery routines. "In the thirty seconds between points, the best players were able to slow their breathing and their heart rate dramatically, thus recovering the energy and the focus they would need during the subsequent point" (p. 228). The same is true in leadership. Leaders need a "disciplined process of stress and recovery. . . . So look at your life as a series of sprints, they say, rather than a marathon. Impose on your life a set of routines that allow you to stress yourself, then recover, stress, then recover, and you will find that over time, your capacity, your resiliency, and your energy will expand" (p. 228). It is not realistic to believe that you can lead a life totally free of stress.

"When you're a leader sometimes things can pile up and cause stress. Sometimes this is real stress and sometimes this is unnecessary stress, but either way it affects you the same way. The first step in working to rejuvenate yourself when stressed is to review the situation. If you cannot step back and see the things that may be holding you back from being your most effective then you cannot work to fix them. The next step is understanding what needs to be done and, most important, to realize that if you need help, it's OK to ask for it, because after all, though you're a leader you are still human, and in order to run your group effectively you have to stay that way."—Larissa DeMeo, an orientation leader at Bridgewater State College, majors in communication studies and is planning a career in television news production.

Am I Existing?

Perhaps you are pausing and need some time out. You may need some time to pull yourself back together after breaking up with someone close to you, to handle the death of a family member, or to manage some other energy-draining crisis. Pausing in this way—existing—can be a useful psychological state that allows you time to pull parts of your life back together. Your mind may be in need of developing new or positive perspectives.

But perhaps you feel like you are existing because you are plateauing (Bardwick, 1986). You are stressed—you have simply done all you can in the organizations of interest to you. Or perhaps you see your parents stagnating in their jobs because there is not enough newness to challenge them. Or maybe simply existing is a way for you to manage a very busy, stressful time in your life. Some people might say that they need to get recentered as a way to move from an existing state to a more focused and exciting existence. When you are in an existing state, it is important to return to, or refocus on, what makes you happy, what energizes you, and what brings meaning to your life.

Parker Palmer (2000) raises these reflective questions: "What am I meant to do? Who am I meant to be?" (p. 2). When our aspirations and purposes are out of alignment with what we are doing in our daily lives, we sometimes fall into a state of existence. Palmer's questions are meant to bring congruence between who we are and what we are doing. Using the Quaker saying, "Let Your Life Speak," Palmer reflects on what this means in his life: "Before you tell your life what you intend to do with it, listen for what it intends to do with you. Before you tell your life what truths and values you have decided to live up to, let your life tell you what truths you embody, what values you represent" (p. 3). This call to one's vocation can lead to a sense of wholeness, steering you away from a state of existence.

Am I Excited?

If you are an excited person, you are open to new experiences and seek out new opportunities. And not all excited people are outgoing and energetic. You may be low-key and thoughtful, but your friends can tell from the twinkle in your eye that you love what you do. Excited people are continuous learners; they can identify something they know this year that they did not know last year. They know they are always growing and learning. Excited people feel some control over their own sphere rather than completely powerless to do anything. They tend to initiate things instead of waiting for others to tell them what to do. Excited people may get very tired, but being a tired, excited person is different from being an exhausted one. Excited people draw on internal energy—they draw from their spirits—and they operate from a philosophy based on optimism and a focus on what is possible for a fulfilling future. Their souls are ablaze with their purpose or mission in life, which is the fuel that keeps their engines going. Being in touch with your personal values, seeking congruency between those values and actions, and being in touch with your inner core are ways to stay energized throughout your leadership journey.

Continuity and Transition

Self-renewal is not something you put off until Thanksgiving or wait to do after summer break starts. Renewal is the endless "interweaving of continuity and change" (Gardner, 1990, p. 124). It is the best of how you are now and what you want to be in the future, woven together with the new challenges and opportunities you face. Renewal is a way of viewing every day of your life so that you stay as fresh as possible. Renewal also means keeping your priorities in perspective and knowing when you need to do something differently to regain balance. It requires you to pay attention and tend to your mind, body, and soul.

Being reflective, noticing what is occurring in intense dynamics, and stepping back from the action taking place around you is an important renewal technique. The biggest challenge is to notice what you are doing at that moment. Heifetz and Linsky (2002) use the metaphor of being on a balcony as a way to see the whole picture versus getting caught up in the small parts. "Seeing the whole picture requires standing back and watching even as you take part in the action being observed. But taking a balcony perspective is tough to do when you're engaged on the dance floor, being pushed and pulled by the flow of events and also engaged in some of the pushing and pulling yourself" (p. 52). The move from action to reflection back to action will allow you to examine what is really going on in the organization or in your personal life.

Why is this a form of self-renewal? Self-reflection is a dimension of self-renewal. Understanding the dynamics between observation and action will give you a clearer perspective and more realistic view of any situation. "When you observe from the balcony, you must see yourself as well as the other participants. Perhaps this is the hardest task of all—to see yourself objectively" (p. 54). Find ways to practice moving from the dance floor (where the action is taking place) to the balcony (where observation is taking place) back down the dance floor (getting back into the action). Staying too long on the balcony or too long on the dance floor will tilt the balance between reflection and action. "If we want our world to be different, our first act needs to be reclaiming time to think. Nothing will change for the better until we do that" (Wheatley, 2002, p. 99).

As part of your leadership development, you will be making many transitions along the way—transitioning into a new role or position, transitioning out of a leadership role, graduating from college, starting a new career, going back to graduate school. The list goes on. At times, you may feel overwhelmed or stressed as you go through transitions in your life. Transitions can also be a source of renewal. In *Overwhelmed: Coping with Life's Ups and Downs*, Nancy Schlossberg (1989a) proposes a model of transition. In her model, the significance of a particular transition will depend on four factors: how it changes your roles, your relationships, and your routines, and how it affects your assumptions about yourself and the world. The more factors that the transition changes, the greater the impact of the transition. Think about the newly elected student government officer. Certainly that person's role, relationships, and routines will change dramatically. It is also quite possible, even probable, that the person's assumptions about self and the world will also change. Feelings of importance and significance may be enhanced, and the world may now be viewed as full of previously unseen opportunities.

As presented in Chapter Eleven, potential resources for helping a person deal effectively with these transitions are called the four S's model by Schlossberg (1989a); these include examining your overall situation, your self, your supports, and your strategies for coping. Again, consider the newly elected student government officer. The position itself will include many resources, such as other officers and advisors. Exhibit 14.1 illustrates that many of these strengths—including the ability to connect with other people, a sense of self-confidence, and a record of previous achievement—will also be helpful in working through the transitions being faced. Obviously, supports for a new officer are evident in the people found in and around the student government itself. Finally, the strategies the new officer develops for working through the transition will also be useful. These could include a new officer retreat away from the business of campus to plan what will happen during the first few days and weeks of the new administration.

The sources of support offered by Nancy Schlossberg (1989a) can assist you in identifying the various people, processes, and resources that may be useful. Another way of achieving renewal is by incorporating the four S's of support into your leadership approach.

Knowing and Cultivating Your Strengths as Renewal

Identify a time when you had a clear success. Think about the behaviors that you exhibited to achieve that success. What exactly did you do to cause this accomplishment to happen? (Buckingham, 2005). Now think of another success that you've had in your life. Reflect on your actions and behaviors. What did you do? What specific actions did you take? Describe your behaviors. Now think of a third and fourth success and ask yourself these same questions. Identify the common behaviors that cut across these different successes. These are your strengths. A focus on what you are good at doing—your behaviors—is a way to stay renewed. An obsession with your weaknesses and what you are not good at doing will you lead to a path of less productivity and less satisfaction.

Martin Seligman (2002), psychologist and author of the best-seller *Learned Optimism*, believes that people possess signature strengths. He defines signature strengths as "strengths of character that a person self-consciously owns, celebrates, and (if he or she can arrange life successfully) exercises every day in work, love, play, and parenting" (p. 160). Dr. Seligman's belief is that if you use your signature strengths every day, you will experience abundant gratification and authentic happiness.

Identify your top five strengths—the behaviors that you do well and that lead you to success in your life. Now, ask yourself if any of these criteria apply to each of your strengths:

- A sense of ownership and authenticity ("This is the real me")

Exhibit 14.1. Sources of Support.

Situation	Excited about new responsibilities; looking forward to new relationships you'll form; anxious to begin new activities; able to make plans in advance for assuming a new office; previous leadership experience; feelings of optimistic excitement; good timing.
Self-confidence	Challenging nature of new leadership role; based on previously successful leadership experiences; feelings of optimistic excitement.
Support	Staff advisors; other officers, previous officers, members; trusted friends; mentors; printed resources; teachers; family members.
Strategies	Take action; seek advice; assert yourself; create structures (such as meetings); practice relaxation skills.

Some ideas adapted from Schlossberg (1989), pp. 33–91.

- A feeling of excitement while displaying it, particularly at first
- A rapid learning curve as the strength is first practiced
- Continuous learning of new ways to enact the strength
- A sense of yearning to find ways to use it
- A feeling of inevitability in using the strength ("Try and stop me")
- Invigoration rather than exhaustion while using the strength
- The creation and pursuit of personal projects that revolve around it
- Joy, zest, enthusiasm, even ecstasy while using it (p. 160) (Reprinted with permission.)

"If one or more of these apply to your top strengths, they are signature strengths" (p. 161). Leading and living with your strengths will keep you on a path of feeling renewed, energized, motivated, and affirmed.

Leadership Development as Renewal

No matter what career you choose, you can make a difference by being effective with others in a leadership or group setting. Whether you become an engineer or a high school French teacher, professional and work-related issues will benefit from the relational leadership processes presented in this book. Whether the focus of your leadership activity is your work, your neighborhood, your team, your place of worship, or community services, you can be an effective agent of change in collaboration with others.

The relational leadership principles presented in this book emphasize being process-oriented, seeking common purpose with others, and being inclusive, empowering, and ethical. As we noted earlier, being the kind of person who practices this philosophy of leadership is being what Covey (1991) calls a principle-centered leader. Covey relates values and beliefs to leadership by identifying characteristics of principle-centered leaders. They are continually learning. They are service-oriented. They radiate positive energy. They believe in themselves and in other people. They lead balanced lives. They see life as an adventure. They are synergistic. They exercise for self-renewal (pp. 33–39). Consider several interventions or practices to keep you engaged in the opportunities of leadership while keeping yourself renewed:

1. Stretch yourself to learn and to do new things. Learning and confidence are built by experiencing new situations that require you to use your skills and values to adapt or to make changes. Fear of failure is an obstacle to your growth. The first woman commandant of the U.S. Naval Academy was asked about her experience and her advice to others in a similar situation. In describing how she best learned, her reply was "to find your comfort zone, and then stay out of it." Think of all the exciting possibilities for you and your organization with "a healthy disregard for the impossible" (LeaderShape Institute, 1996).

2. Develop the realization that what you are doing matters. People who know that their contributions make a difference somehow or that there is value in their work have a sense of purpose and con-

fidence that sustains them through many difficult times. In a study of sixty thousand Americans, Gail Sheehy (1981) sought to identify characteristics of well-being and life satisfaction. She found that the ability to say "My life has meaning and direction" was the most salient factor distinguishing happy adults from those who were not.

3. Keep a sense of personal balance. Find time to enjoy not only leadership endeavors but personal interests and pursuits that bring satisfaction and happiness to your life. It is important to avoid being consumed by your leadership or membership responsibilities or to become addicted to your organization or work. What you do to find and maintain balance in your life may change over time, which in itself is renewing. When you take time for yourself, do not let yourself feel guilty because you think you should be doing something for someone else or your organization. Your morale will be better when you feel balanced and renewed, which should positively affect the morale of your organization or group.

4. Make time for peaceful reflection and centering. Most major problems and dilemmas do not have easy and quick solutions. One of the best strategies for resolving a dilemma is to step back from the situation after you have gathered the necessary information and consulted with the appropriate people and to carefully think through all the dimensions of the situation. Reflect on what is actually happening and identify all your possible alternatives for action. On a personal level, constant reflection is needed to stay in touch with your inner core and to stay centered with your values and principles and with knowing what is really important to you.

5. Maintain healthy, supportive relationships. This means relationships within your group and outside of your group. Develop relationships with mentors. Leaders often mentor others in the organization. Leaders also need the rich support and empowerment that can be derived from a mentor—someone who has your best interests at heart and can help you stay centered, renewed, and balanced while leading others. "Pity the leader who is caught between unloving critics and uncritical lovers. Leaders need reassurance,

but just as important they need advisors who tell them the truth, gently but candidly" (Gardner, 1990, p. 135).

6. Prioritize your tasks and responsibilities. Use your judgment to determine what must be accomplished by the end of the day and what realistically can wait until tomorrow, or next week, or next month. If your daily to-do list goes on for pages, then you have to decide what is achievable in the time you have each day. And make sure that you build in time for yourself or time to take care of yourself, whether that means having a daily appointment with Mrs. Jones, exercising, or spending time with friends or family. Look at your day the same way that your body works—in ninety-minute increments. The human body works most effectively in such increments (Buckingham, 2005). Work yourself into the habit of taking a break from studying, from intense conversations, from e-mail correspondence every ninety minutes.

"I would consider a mentor someone who personally touched and changed my life, and that would give me motivation to continue to work hard and accomplish my goals. My brother would be an example of a mentor. I can look at the life he is leading and really take from the example he has set for me. He has accomplished so much and I would like nothing more than to follow in his footsteps. There are many things that make him a role model: his dedication to what he does in his life, the success he has had and that overall balance that he seems to have achieved. It's not just about his accomplishments, it's his ability to lead a life that embraces life, love, work, and friendship. The way in which my brother has influenced my life, and reached out to me as someone that would always be there for me in any way I needed makes him a role model. He has motivated me to do my best in life, and has always pushed me to never give up and always set my goals high. I feel that his motivation, advice, and encouragement have always helped me while I was down, and pushed me further while I was up."—Tori Charnl was the president of

the Inter-Residence Hall Council and president of the Rubin Residence Hall at New York University. Her major is political science, and
she plans to pursue a career in law and politics.

Your personal leadership development can be a source of
renewal-seeking opportunities to develop new skills and to find various avenues (careers, community service, recreational activities,
and so forth) for exercising your leadership.

Spirituality and Renewal

Parker Palmer (2000) uses the analogy of shadow and light in
describing the relationship between spirituality and leadership.
Leaders can "shine a light that allows new growth to flourish, while
others cast a shadow under which seedlings die" (p. 78). Paying
attention to both the light and the shadow sides of leadership (such
as the criticisms leaders often receive) brings an understanding of
their interplay rather than compartmentalizing them. It is a danger
to have the shadows go unchecked. "Leaders need not only technical skills to manage the external world but also the spiritual skills
to journey inward toward the source of both shadow and light" (p.
79). Casting more light and less shadows is a renewal strategy—for
personal benefit and for those in relationship with you.

Giving and receiving love in all kinds of relationships, not just
personal ones, are characteristics of self-renewed individuals (Gardner, 1981). "They are capable of depending on others and of being
depended upon. They can see life through another's eyes and feel it
through another's heart" (p. 15).

Chapter Summary

In Chapter One a few essential questions were raised: What is your
purpose? Who are you? What do you stand for? These questions are
central to the self-renewal process. Understanding yourself, being
aware of your inner core, paying attention to the signals your mind,

body, and soul give you, and being comfortable with yourself are elements of self-renewal. Your journey to self-renewal will have no end destination. The process of renewal is cyclical.

Be careful not to fall victim to thinking that you are renewed when in fact you are not. Renewal affects your entire being. On your journey to renewal, make sure your mind, body, and soul together benefit from this process. Gardner (1990) observes, "The consideration leaders must never forget is that the key to renewal is the release of human energy and talent" (p. 136). When your mind, body, and soul are in harmony, you will feel good about yourself as a leader or contributing member and become a greater asset to your organization.

Chapter Activities

Reflect on your renewal by considering the following questions:
1. What does self-renewal mean to you?
2. Right now, do you feel renewed? Why or why not?
3. Make a list of all the activities you are involved in currently. Then, next to each activity designate which activities you do for other people and which you do for yourself. Are you spending enough time on you?
4. What would you like to do every day that would cause you to feel renewed? How could you make this a habit?
5. Think of an individual who you believe leads a healthy life, is balanced, and intentionally seeks renewal. What does this person do that allows him or her to be balanced? (If possible, arrange an interview to ask questions to explore this.) What is there about this person that you can adapt to your life?
6. Identify your top five strengths. Think about all the behaviors you do currently in your leadership or membership role. Which ones are you doing that are in your top five strengths? Which ones are not? Within this same organization, which

members or leaders have strengths that you don't? How can you work as a team to more effectively maximize everyone else's strengths and your strengths?

7. Using the balcony and dance floor metaphor, think of a current situation that you are involved in. What do you observe when you move from the dance floor to the balcony? What do you see about yourself? What action will you take, using what you observed and learned, when you return to the dance floor?

8. Reflect on your aspirations and purpose in life. What are you meant to do? Who are you meant to be?

9. What self-renewal strategies or techniques can you use to reach your full potential in life or in your leadership?

A Final Reflection

Through fourteen chapters, we have taken a journey through the world of leadership. A theme throughout this book has been our belief that leadership means change—change for the greater good of the people in your group, organization, community, and world. We hope that you have found the Relational Leadership Model to be a useful guide when you work with others to accomplish change.

We have ended each chapter with a series of reflections and activities. The activities are over, but we did want to end with a few questions for you to reflect on as you consider what you have learned and what the future might hold for you as a leader.

- How have you been able to apply what you have learned about leadership?

- How are you more aware of yourself?

- What things do you now see differently? How are you changing?

- How will you continue your learning about leadership?

- What is your own philosophy of leadership?

As noted by Michael Sarich and Reena Meltzer—who were both students at the University of Maryland, College Park, when we wrote the first edition of this book—"While the theories and concepts included within this text do work, they are not a substitute for work." Now it is time for you to continue on this incredible journey—into your own world of people and ideas—into your own future. We hope you have been challenged and maybe even inspired to see how you can make a difference.

We wish you well in this hard work. We know there will be rough seas ahead, but we hope you will navigate the permanent white water successfully and with a sense of passion, joy, and wonder, and with a commitment to the relationships you will have along the way.

Additional Readings

Bolman, L. G., & Deal, T. E. (1995). *Leading with soul: An uncommon journey of spirit*. San Francisco: Jossey-Bass.

Gardner, J. W. (1981). *Self-renewal* (Rev. ed.). New York: Norton.

Gardner, J. W. (1990). *On leadership*. New York: Free Press.

Palmer, P. (2000). *Let your life speak: Listening for the voice of vocation*. San Francisco: Jossey-Bass.

Schlossberg, N. K. (1989a). *Overwhelmed: Coping with life's ups and downs*. Lexington, MA: Lexington.

Seligman, M.E.P. (2002). *Authentic happiness: Using the new positive psychology to realize your potential for lasting fulfillment*. New York: Free Press.

Vaill, P. B. (1996). *Learning as a way of being: Strategies for survival in a world of permanent white water*. San Francisco: Jossey-Bass.

Wheatley, M. J. (2002). *Turning to one another: Simple conversations to restore hope to the future*. San Francisco: Berrett-Koehler.

References

A person of character. (1993). *Character Counts Coalition*. Marina del Ray, CA: Josephson Institute of Ethics.

Adelman, L. (executive producer). (2003). *Race—The power of an illusion* (three-episode film). (Available from California Newsreel, Order Department, P.O. Box 2284, South Burlington, VT 05407)

Adizes, I. (1988). *Corporate lifecycles: How and why corporations grow and die and what to do about it*. Englewood Cliffs, NJ: Prentice Hall.

Alberti, R. E., & Emmons, M. L. (1974). *Your perfect right: A guide to assertive behavior*. San Luis Obispo, CA: IMPACT.

Albrecht, K. (1994). *The northbound train*. New York: AMACOM.

Alinsky, S. (1971). *Rules for radicals*. New York: Vintage Books.

Allen, K. E. (1990). Making sense out of chaos: Leading and living in dynamic systems. *Campus Activities Programming*, May, 56–63.

Allen, K. E., & Cherrey, C. (2000). *Systemic leadership: Enriching the meaning of our work*. Lanham, MD: University Press of America.

Amarl, L. H. (2001). A crisis of corruption (pp. 6–15). *World Press Review*. Retrieved on September 24, 2005, from http://www.worldpressreview.org

Andersen, P. A. (2003). In different dimensions: Nonverbal communication and culture. In L. A. Samovar & R. E. Porter (Eds.), *Intercultural communication: A reader* (10th ed.). Belmont, CA: Wadsworth.

Angelou, M. (1994). *The complete collected poems of Maya Angelou*. New York: Random House.

Armour, M., & Hayles, R. (1990, July). *Managing multicultural organizations*. Paper presented at the Summer Institute for Intercultural Communications, Portland, OR.

Astin, A. W., & Astin, H. S. (2000). *Leadership reconsidered: Engaging higher education in social change*. Battle Creek, MI: W. K. Kellogg Foundation.

Astin, H. S. (1996). Leadership for social change. *About Campus*, July/August, 4–10.

Avolio, B. J., & Gardner, W. L. (2005). Authentic leadership development: Getting to the root of positive forms of leadership. *Leadership Quarterly, 16*, 315–338.

Avolio, B. J., Gardner, W. L., Walumbwa, F. O., Luthans, F., & May, D. R. (2004). Unlocking the mask: A look at the processes by which authentic leaders impact follower attitudes and behaviors. *Leadership Quarterly, 15*, 801–823.

Avolio, B. J., & Kahai, S. S. (2003). Adding the "E" to e-leadership: How it may impact your leadership. *Organizational Dynamics, 31*(4), 325–338.

Bandura, A. (1977). *Social learning theory*. Englewood Cliffs, NJ: Prentice Hall.

Bandura, A. (1997). *Self-efficacy: The exercise of control.* New York: Freeman.

Barabási, A.-L. (2002). *Linked: The new science of networks*. Cambridge, MA: Perseus.

Bardwick, J. M. (1986). *The plateauing trap: How to avoid today's #1 career dilemma*. New York: Bantam Books.

Bass, B. M. (1981). *Stogdill's handbook of leadership: Theory and research* (2nd ed.). New York: Free Press.

Bass, B. M. (1990). *Bass & Stogdill's handbook of leadership: Theory, research, and managerial applications* (3rd ed.). New York: Free Press.

Baxter Magolda, M. B. (1998). Developing self-authorship in young adult life. *Journal of College Student Development, 39*, 143–156.

Beauchamp, T. L., & Childress, J. F. (1979). *Principles of biomedical ethics*. New York: Oxford University Press.

Beck, L. G., & Murphy, J. (1994). *Ethics in educational leadership programs: An expanding role*. Thousand Oaks, CA: Corwin Press.

Benne, K. D., & Sheats, P. (1948). Functional roles of group members. *Journal of Social Issues, 2*, 42–47.

Bennett, M. (1979). Overcoming the Golden Rule: Sympathy and empathy. In D. Nimmo (Ed.), *Communication yearbook 3* (pp. 407–422). New Brunswick, NJ: Transaction Books.

Bennis, W. G. (1989). *On becoming a leader*. Reading, MA: Addison-Wesley.

Bennis, W. G., & Goldsmith, J. (1994). *Learning to lead*. Reading, MA: Addison-Wesley.

Bennis, W. G., & Nanus, B. (1985). *Leaders: The strategies for taking charge*. New York: Harper & Row.

Bennis, W. G., & Thomas, R. J. (2002). *Geeks and geezers: How era, values, and defining moments shape leaders*. Boston: Harvard Business School Press.

Berman, S., & La Farge, P. (Eds). (1993). *Promising practices in teaching social responsibility*. Albany, NY: State University of New York Press.

Bernstein, A., & Rozen, S. (1994). *Sacred bull: The inner obstacles that hold you back at work and how to overcome them*. Hoboken, NJ: Wiley.

Berry, L. L. (2004). The collaborative organization: Leadership lessons from Mayo Clinic. *Organizational Dynamics, 33*, 228–242.

Bird, F. B., & Waters, J. A. (1989). The moral muteness of managers. *California Management Review, 32*(1), 73–87.

Block, P. (1993). *Stewardship: Choosing service over self-interest*. San Francisco: Berrett-Koehler.

Bobo, K. A., Kendall, J., & Max, S. (2001). *Organizing for social change: Midwest Academy manual for activists* (3rd ed.). Santa Ana, CA: Seven Locks Press.

Bok, D. (1982). *Beyond the ivory tower: Social responsibilities of the modern university*. Cambridge, MA: Harvard University Press.

Bok, D. (1990). *Universities and the future of America*. Durham, NC: Duke University Press.

Bolman, L. G., & Deal, T. E. (1995). *Leading with soul: An uncommon journey of spirit*. San Francisco: Jossey-Bass.

Bolman, L. G., & Deal, T. E. (2003a). Reframing ethics and spirit. In *Business leadership: A Jossey-Bass reader* (pp. 330–350). San Francisco: Jossey-Bass.

Bolman, L. G., & Deal, T. (2003b). *Reframing organizations: Artistry, choice, and leadership* (3rd ed.). San Francisco: Jossey-Bass.

Bonebrake, K. (2002). College students' Internet use, relationship formation, and personality correlates. *CyberPsychology & Behavior, 5*, 551–558.

Bothwell, L. (1983). *The art of leadership: Skill-building techniques that produce results*. Englewood Cliffs, NJ: Prentice Hall.

Bridges, W. (1980). *Transitions: Making sense of life's changes*. Reading, MA: Addison-Wesley.

Bridges, W. (1988). *Surviving corporate transition*. New York: Doubleday.

Bridges, W. (1991). *Managing transitions: Making the most of change*. Cambridge, MA: Perseus Books.

Bridges, W. (2003). *Managing transitions: Making the most of change* (2nd ed.). Cambridge, MA: Perseus Books.

Briggs, J., & Peat, F. (1999). *Seven life lessons of chaos: Timeless wisdom from the science of change*. New York: HarperCollins.

Broome, B. J. (1993). Managing differences in conflict resolution: The role of relational empathy. In D.J.D. Sandole & H. van der Merwe (Eds.),

Conflict resolution theory and practice: Integration and application (pp. 97–111). New York: Manchester University Press.

Brown, I. (1963). *Understanding other cultures.* Englewood Cliffs, NJ: Prentice Hall.

Brussat, F., & Brussat, M. A. (1996). *Spiritual literacy: Reading the sacred in everyday life.* New York: Touchstone.

Bruteau, B. (1990). Eucharistic ecology and ecological spirituality. *Cross Current, 40,* 499–514.

Bryson, J. M., & Crosby, B. C. (1992). *Leadership for the common good.* San Francisco: Jossey-Bass.

Buber, M. (1958). *I and thou.* New York: Scribner.

Buckingham, M. (2005). *The one thing you need to know . . . About great managing, great leading, and sustaining individual success.* New York: Free Press.

Buckingham. M., & Clifton, D. O. (2001). *Now, discover your strengths.* New York: Free Press.

Burns, J. M. (1978). *Leadership.* New York: Harper & Row.

Bushe, G. R. (2000). Appreciative inquiry with teams. In D. L. Cooperrider, P. F. Sorensen Jr., D. Whitney, & T. F. Yaeger (Eds.), *Appreciative inquiry: Rethinking human organization toward a positive theory of change* (pp. 183–194). Champaign, IL: Stipes.

Campus Compact. (n.d.). Retrieved July 28, 2006, from http://www.campuscompact.org/

Carnegie Foundation for the Advancement of Teaching. (1990). *Campus life: In search of community.* Princeton, NJ: Carnegie Foundation for the Advancement of Teaching.

Carse, J. (1986). *Finite and infinite games.* New York: Ballantine.

Cartwright, T. (1991). Planning and chaos theory. *APA Journal,* Winter, 44–56.

Cathcart, R. S., Samovar, L. A., & Henman, L. D. (Eds.). (1996). *Small group communication: Theory & practice* (7th ed.). Madison, WI: Brown & Benchmark.

Chaleff, I. (1995). *The courageous follower: Standing up to and for our leaders.* San Francisco: Berrett-Koehler.

Chambers, E. T., & Cowan, M. A. (2004). *Roots for radicals: Organizing for power, action, and justice.* New York: Continuum.

Chickering, A. W., Dalton, J. C., & Stamm, L. (2006). *Encouraging authenticity and spirituality in higher education.* San Francisco: Jossey-Bass.

Chickering, A. W., & Reisser, L. (1993). *Education and identity* (2nd ed.). San Francisco: Jossey-Bass.

Chinn, P. L. (2004). *Peace and power: Creative leadership for building community* (6th ed.). Boston: Jones and Bartlett.

Chrislip, D. D., & Larson, C. E. (1994). *Collaborative leadership: How citizens and civic leaders can make a difference*. San Francisco: Jossey-Bass.

Ciulla, J. B. (1995). Leadership ethics: Mapping the territory. *Business Ethics Quarterly, 5*, 5–28.

Clifton, D. O., & Nelson, P. (1992). *Soar with your strengths*. New York: Delacorte Press.

Cohen, M. D., & March, J. G. (1974). *Leadership and ambiguity* (2nd ed.). Boston: Harvard Business School Press.

Collins, J., & Porras, J. (1994). *Built to last: Successful habits of visionary companies*. New York: HarperCollins.

Conger, J., & Associates. (1994). *Spirit at work: Discovering the spirituality in leadership*. San Francisco: Jossey-Bass.

Conger, J. A., & Benjamin, B. (1999). *Building leaders: How successful companies develop the next generation*. San Francisco: Jossey-Bass.

Conner, D. R. (1992). *Managing at the speed of change: How resilient managers succeed and prosper where others fail*. New York: Villard Books.

Cooperrider, D. L., Sorensen, P. F., Jr., Whitney, D., & Yaeger, T. F. (Eds.). (2000). *Appreciative inquiry: Rethinking human organization toward a positive theory of change*. Champaign, IL: Stipes.

Cooperrider, D. L., & Srivastva, S. (1987). Appreciative inquiry in organizational life. In W. Pasmore & R. Woodman (Eds.), *Research in organization change and development* (Vol. 1, pp. 129–169). Greenwich, CT: JAI Press.

Cooperrider, D. L., & Whitney, D. (2000). A positive revolution in change: Appreciative inquiry. In D. L. Cooperrider, P. F. Sorensen Jr., D. Whitney, & T. F. Yaeger (Eds.), *Appreciative inquiry: Rethinking human organization toward a positive theory of change* (pp. 3–27). Champaign, IL: Stipes.

Cooperrider, D. L., Whitney, D., & Stavros, J. M. (2003). *Appreciative inquiry handbook: The first in a series of Ai workbooks for leaders of change*. Bedford Heights, OH: Lakeshore Communications.

Cormier, S., & Hackney, H. (2005). *Counseling strategies and interventions* (6th ed.). Boston: Allyn & Bacon.

Covey, S. R. (1989). *The 7 habits of highly effective people*. New York: Simon & Schuster.

Covey, S. R. (1991). *Principle-centered leadership*. New York: Summit Books.

Crum, T. F. (1987). *The magic of conflict*. New York: Simon & Schuster.

Cullinan, C. (1999). Vision, privilege, and the limits of tolerance. *Electronic Magazine of Multicultural Education, 1*(2), n.p. Retrieved July 28, 2006, from http://www.eastern.edu/publications/emme/1999spring/cullinan.html

Davidow, W., & Malone, M. (1992). *The virtual corporation: Structuring and revitalizing the corporation for the 21st century*. New York: HarperBusiness.

Davis, D. D. (2004). The Tao of leadership in virtual teams. *Organizational Dynamics, 33*(1), 47–62.

Day, D. V. (2000). Leadership development: A review in context. *Leadership Quarterly, 11,* 581–613.

De George, R. T. (1986). *Business ethics* (2nd ed.). New York: Macmillan.

De Pree, M. (1989). *Leadership is an art.* New York: Doubleday.

De Pree, M. (1992). *Leadership jazz.* New York: Doubleday.

Deal, T., & Kennedy, A. (1982). *Corporate cultures: The rites and rituals of corporate life.* Reading, MA: Addison-Wesley.

Donaldson, T. (1989). *The ethics of international business.* New York: Oxford University Press.

Drath, W. H., & Palus, C. J. (1994). *Making common sense: Leadership as meaning-making in a community of practice.* Greensboro, NC: Center for Creative Leadership.

Eagley, A. H., Karau, S. J., & Makhijani, M. G. (1995). Gender and the effectiveness of leaders: A meta-analysis. *Psychological Bulletin, 117*(1), 125–145.

Eckel, P., Hill, B., & Green, M. (1998). *On change I: En route to transformation.* Washington, DC: American Council on Education.

Edwards, K. E., & Alimo, C. (2005, April 3). *Social justice educator competencies.* Pre-Conference Workshop, ACPA National Convention, Nashville, TN.

Elliott, C. (1999). *Locating the energy for change: An introduction to appreciative inquiry.* Winnipeg, Manitoba, Canada: International Institute for Sustainable Development.

Eoyang, G. (1997). *Coping with chaos: Seven simple tools.* Cheyenne, WY: Lagumo.

Erikson, E. H. (1963). *Childhood and society.* New York: Norton.

Erikson, E. H. (1968). *Identity: Youth and crisis.* New York: Norton.

Ethics Resource Center. (2005, October 12). National Business Ethics Survey. Retrieved February 4, 2006, from http://www.ethics.org/nbes/nbes2005/index.html

Etzioni, A. (1993). *The spirit of community.* New York: Crown.

Eyler, J., & Giles, D. (1999). *Where's the learning in service-learning?* San Francisco: Jossey-Bass.

Eyler, J. S., Giles, D. E., Jr., Stenson, C. M., & Gray, C. J. (2001). *At a glance: The effects of service-learning on college students, faculty, institutions, and communities, 1993–2000* (3rd ed.). Providence, RI: Campus Compact. (http://www.campuscompact.org/resources/downloads/aag.pdf)

Fairholm, G. W. (1994). *Leadership and a culture of trust.* New York: Praeger.

Farson, R. (1995). *Management of the absurd: Paradoxes in leadership*. New York: Simon & Schuster.

Festinger, L. (1962). *A theory of cognitive dissonance*. Stanford, CA: Stanford University Press.

Fitzgerald, C., & Kirby, L. K. (1997). *Developing leaders: Research and applications in psychological type and leadership development: Integrating reality and vision, mind and heart*. Palo Alto, CA: Davies-Black.

Fox, M. (1994). *The reinvention of work: A new vision of livelihood for our time*. New York: HarperCollins.

French, J.R.P., & Raven, B. H. (1959). The bases of social power. In D. Cartwright (Ed.), *Studies in social power* (pp. 150–167). Ann Arbor, MI: Institute for Social Research.

Friedman, T. L. (2005). *The world is flat: A brief history of the twenty-first century*. New York: Farrar, Straus & Giroux.

Gallup Poll Social Series. (2003). Princeton, NJ: The Gallup Organization.

Gandhi, A. (1998). Lessons from Sevagram Ashram. In F. Hesselbein, M. Goldsmith, R. Beckhard, & R. F. Schubert (Eds.), *The community of the future* (pp. 83–90). The Drucker Foundation. San Francisco: Jossey-Bass.

Gandossy, R., & Effron, M. (2004). *Leading the way: Three truths from the top companies for leaders*. Hoboken, NJ: Wiley.

Gardner, J. W. (1981). *Self-renewal* (Rev. ed.). New York: Norton.

Gardner, J. W. (1990). *On leadership*. New York: Free Press.

Gardner, J. W. (1993). The antileadership vaccine. In W. E. Rosenbach & R. L. Taylor (Eds.), *Contemporary issues in leadership* (3rd. ed., pp. 193–200). Boulder, CO: Westview Press. (Original work published 1965)

Gardner, J. W. (2003). *Living, leading, and the American dream*. San Francisco: Jossey-Bass.

Gardner, W. L., Avolio, B. J., Luthans, F., May, D. R., & Walumbwa, F. (2005). "Can you see the real me?" A self-based model of authentic leader and follower development. *The Leadership Quarterly, 16*, 343–372.

Gardner, W. L., Avolio, B. J., & Walumbwa, F. (Eds.). (2005). *Authentic leadership theory and practice: Origins, effects, and development*. San Diego: Elsevier.

Gardner, W. L., & Schermerhorn, J. R., Jr. (2004). Unleashing individual potential: Performance gains through positive organizational behavior and authentic leadership. *Organizational Dynamics, 33*, 270–281.

Geertz, C. (1973). Thick description: Toward an interpretive theory of culture. In C. Geertz (Ed.), *The interpretation of cultures* (pp. 3–32). New York: Basic Books.

Gladwell, M. (2002). *The tipping point: How little things can make a big difference*. Boston: Little, Brown.

Goodman, N. (1992). *Introduction to sociology*. New York: HarperCollins.

Goodman, D. (2000). Motivating people from privileged groups to support social justice. *Teachers College Record, 102*, 1061–1085.

Gozdz, K. (1993). Building community as a leadership discipline. In M. Ray & A. Rinzler (Eds.), *The new paradigm in business: Emerging strategies for leadership and organizational change* (pp. 107–119). Los Angeles: Tarcher/Perigee.

Greenleaf, R. G. (1977). *Servant leadership: A journey in the nature of legitimate power and greatness*. New York: Paulist.

Greenwood, R. G. (1993). Leadership theory: A historical look at its evolution. *The Journal of Leadership Studies, 1*(1), 4–19.

Grenier, R., & Metes, G. (1995). *Going virtual: Moving your organization into the 21st century*. Upper Saddle River, NJ: Prentice Hall.

Gudykunst, W. B. (1991). *Bridging differences: Effective intergroup communication*. Thousand Oaks, CA: Sage.

Haas, H. G., & Tamarkin, B. (1992). *The leader within*. New York: HarperCollins.

Handy, C. (1996). *Beyond certainty: The changing worlds of organizations*. Boston: Harvard Business School Press.

Harriger, K., & Ford, M. (1989). Lessons learned: Teaching citizenship in the university. In S. W. Morse (Ed.), *Public leadership education: Preparing college students for their civic roles* (pp. 22–28). Dayton, OH: Kettering Foundation.

Hart, L. B., & Dalke, J. D. (1983).*The sexes at work: Improving work relationships between men and women*. Englewood Cliffs, NJ: Prentice-Hall.

Hart, P. D., & Associates. (1998). *New leadership for a new century: Key findings from a study on youth, leadership, and community service*. Washington, DC: Peter D. Hart Research Associates. Retrieved May 20, 2002, from www.publicallies.org/poll.htm (p. 6)

Hart, R. K., & McLeod, P. L. (2003). Rethinking team building in geographically dispersed teams: One message at a time. *Organizational Dynamics, 31*, 352–361.

Hawley, J. (1993). *Reawakening the spirit in work*. New York: Fireside/Simon & Schuster.

Heider, J. (1985). *The tao of leadership: Lao Tzu's Tao Te Ching adapted for a new age*. New York: Bantam.

Heifetz, R. A., & Linsky, M. (2002). *Leadership on the line: Staying alive through the dangers of leading*. Boston: Harvard Business School Press.

Heilbrunn, J. (1994). Can leadership be studied? *WQ*, Autumn, 65–72.

Helgesen, S. (1990). *The female advantage: Women's ways of leadership*. New York: Doubleday.

Helgesen, S. (1995). *The web of inclusion: A new architecture for building great organizations*. New York: Currency/Doubleday.

Helms, J. E. (1992). *A race is a nice thing to have*. Topeka, KS: Content Communications.

Henderson, V. E. (1992). *What's ethical in business?* New York: McGraw-Hill.

Hesselbein, F. (2002). *Hesselbein on leadership*. San Francisco: Jossey-Bass.

Higher Education Research Institute (HERI). (1996). *A social change model of leadership development: Guidebook version III*. Los Angeles: University of California Los Angeles Higher Education Research Institute. (Guidebooks are available from the National Clearinghouse for Leadership Programs; http://www.nclp.umd.edu/.)

Hesselbein, F., & Shinseki, E. K. (2004). *Be-know-do: Leadership the army way*. (Adapted from the Official Army Leadership Manual). San Francisco: Jossey-Bass.

Hesselbein, F., Goldsmith, M., Beckhard, R., & Schubert, R. F. (Eds). (1998). *The Drucker Foundation: The community of the future*. San Francisco: Jossey-Bass.

Hill, R. P., & Stephens, D. L. (2003). The compassionate organization in the 21st Century. *Organizational Dynamics, 23,* 331–341.

Hill, S.E.K. (2004). Team leadership. In P. G. Northouse (Ed.), *Leadership: Theory and practice* (pp. 203–225). Thousand Oaks, CA: Sage.

Hodgkinson, C. (1983). *The philosophy of leadership*. New York: St. Martin's Press.

Hofstede, G. (1980). Motivation, leadership, and organization: Do American theories apply abroad? *Organizational Dynamics,* Summer, 42–63.

Hofstede, G. (2003). *Culture's consequences: Comparing values, behaviors, institutions and organizations across nations* (2nd ed.). Thousand Oaks, CA: Sage.

Holland, J. (1998). *Emergence: From chaos to order*. Reading, MA: Helix/Addison-Wesley.

Hollander, E. P. (1993). Legitimacy, power, and influence: A perspective on relational features of leadership. In M. M. Chemers & R. Ayman (Eds.), *Leadership theory and research: Perspectives and directions* (pp. 29–47). San Diego: Academic Press.

Hoopes, D. S. (1979). Intercultural communication concepts and the psychology of intercultural experiences. In M. D. Pusch (Ed.), *Multicultural education: A cross cultural training approach* (pp. 10–38). Chicago: Intercultural Press.

Hoopes, D. S., & Pusch, M. D. (1979). Definition of terms. In M. D. Pusch (Ed.), *Multicultural education: A cross cultural training approach* (pp. 1–8). Chicago: Intercultural Press.

Horwood, B. (1989). Reflections on reflection. *Journal of Experiential Education*, *12*(2), 5–7.

House, R. J., Hanges, P. J., Javidan, M., Dorfman, P. W., & Gupta, V. (Eds.). (2004). *Culture, leadership, and organizations: The GLOBE study of 62 societies*. Thousand Oaks, CA: Sage.

Howard, V. A., & Barton, M. A. (1992). *Thinking together*. New York: Morrow.

Howell, J. M. (1988). Two faces of charisma: Socialized and personalized leadership in organizations. In J. A. Conger, R. N. Kanungo, & Associates (Eds.), *Charismatic leadership: The elusive factor in organizational effectiveness* (pp. 213–236). San Francisco: Jossey-Bass.

Howell, J. M., & Avolio, B. J. (1992). The ethics of charismatic leadership: Submission or liberation? *Academy of Management Executive*, *6*(2), 43–54.

Hughes, R. L., Ginnett, R. C., & Curphy, G. J. (1993). *Leadership: Enhancing the lessons of experience*. Homewood, IL: Richard D. Irwin.

Interdependence, Interdependence Days and Declarations of Interdependence. (n.d.) Retrieved June 8, 2005, from http://www.co-intelligence.org/interdependenceday.html

Jackson, B., & Holvino, E. (1988). Developing multicultural organizations. *Journal of Religion and Applied Behavioral Science*, *9*, 14–19.

Jaffe, D., Scott, C., & Tobe, G. (1994). *Rekindling commitment: How to revitalize yourself, your work, and your organization*. San Francisco: Jossey-Bass.

Javidan, M., & House, R. J. (2001). Cultural acumen for the global manager: Lessons from Project GLOBE. *Organizational Dynamics*, *29*, 289–305.

Jensen, G. H. (1987). Learning styles. In J. A. Provost & S. Anchors (Eds.), *Applications of the Myers-Briggs Type Indicator in higher education* (pp. 180–206). Palo Alto, CA: Consulting Psychologists Press.

Johnson, D. W., & Johnson, F. P. (1994). *Joining together: Group theory and group skills* (6th ed.). Boston: Allyn & Bacon.

Johnson, D. W., Maruyama, G., Johnson, R., Nelson, D., & Skon, L. (1981). Effects of cooperative, competitive, and individualistic goal structures on achievement: A meta-analysis. *Psychological Bulletin*, *89*(1), 47–62.

Jones, J. M. (Ed.). (2003). *Issues facing state, local governments affect public trust*. Gallup Poll Tuesday Briefing. Retrieved October 14, 2003, from http://www.gallup.com/poll/tb/goverpubli/20031014b.asp

Jones, P., & Kahaner, L. (1995). *Say it and live it: The 50 corporate mission statements that hit the mark*. New York: Currency/Doubleday.

Jones, S. R., & Lucas, N. J. (1994). Interview with Michael Josephson. *Concepts & Connections: Rethinking Ethics & Leadership, 2*(3), 1, 3–5.

Josselson, R. (1996). *Revising herself: The story of women's identity from college to midlife.* New York: Oxford University Press.

Jung, C. (1923). *Psychological types.* New York: Harcourt Brace.

Kahn, S. (1991). *Organizing: A guide for grassroots leaders* (Rev. ed.). Washington, DC: National Association of Social Workers.

Kanter, R. M. (1989). *When giants learn to dance.* New York: Simon & Schuster.

Kanungo, R. N., & Mendonca, M. (1996). Ethical dimensions in leadership motivation. In R. N. Kanungo & M. Mendonco (Eds.), *Ethical dimensions of leadership* (pp. 33–51). Thousand Oaks, CA: Sage .

Katzenbach, J. R., Beckett, F., Dichter, S., Feigen, M., Gagnon, C., Hope, Q., & Ling, T. (1996). *Real change leaders: How you can create growth and high performance at your company.* New York: Random House.

Kegan, R. (1994). *In over our heads: The mental demands of modern life.* Cambridge, MA: Harvard University Press.

Keirsey, D., & Bates, M. (1984). *Please understand me: Character and temperament types* (4th ed.). Del Mar, CA: Prometheus Nemesis Books.

Kellerman, B. (2004). *Bad leadership.* Cambridge, MA: Harvard Business School Press.

Kelley, R. E. (1988). In praise of followers. *Harvard Business Review, 66* (6), 142–148.

Kelley, R. E. (1992). *The power of followership: How to create leaders people want to follow and followers who lead themselves.* New York: Currency/Doubleday.

Kelly, K. (1994). *Out of control: The new biology of machines, social systems, and the economic world.* Reading, MA: Addison-Wesley.

Kets de Vries, M.F.R., & Florent-Treacy, E. (2002). Global leadership from A to Z: Creating high commitment organizations. *Organizational Dynamics, 30,* 295–309.

Kidder, R. M. (1993). Ethics, youth, and the moral barometer. *In The Public Perspective, 4*(6), 22–25.

Kidder, R. M. (1994). *Shared values for a troubled world: Conversations with men and women of conscience.* San Francisco: Jossey-Bass.

Kidder, R. M. (1995). *How good people make tough choices: Resolving the dilemmas of ethical living.* New York: Fireside.

Kidder, R. M. (2005). *Moral courage: Taking action when your values are put to the test.* New York: William Morrow.

Kiefer, C. F., & Senge, P. M. (1984). Metanoic organizations. In J. D. Adams (Ed.), *Transforming work: A collection of organizational transformation readings* (pp. 68–84). Alexandria, VA: Miles River Press.

King, W. R. (1984). Integrating strategic issues into strategic management. *OMEGA: The International Journal of Management Science, 12,* 529–538.

Kissler, G. D. (2001). E-Leadership. *Organizational Dynamics, 30,* 121–133.

Kitchener, K. S. (1984). Intuition, critical evaluation and ethical principles: The foundation for ethical decisions in counseling psychology. *The Counseling Psychologist, 12*(3), 43–55.

Kline, P., & Saunders, B. (1993). *Ten steps to a learning organization.* Arlington, VA: Great Ocean.

Knowles, M., & Knowles, H. (1959). *Introduction to group dynamics.* New York: Association Press.

Kohn, A. (1992). *No contest: The case against competition* (Rev. ed.). Boston: Houghton Mifflin.

Kolb, D. A. (1981). Learning styles and disciplinary differences. In A. W. Chickering & Associates (Eds.), *The modern American college: Responding to the new realities of diverse students and a changing society* (pp. 232–255). San Francisco: Jossey-Bass.

Komives, S. R. (1994). Increasing student involvement through civic leadership education. In P. Mable & C. Schroeder (Eds.), *Realizing the educational potential of college residence halls* (pp. 218–240). San Francisco: Jossey-Bass.

Komives, S. R., Longerbeam, S., Owen, J. E., Mainella, F. C., & Osteen, L. (2006). A leadership identity development model: Applications from a grounded theory. *Journal of College Student Development, 47,* 401–420.

Komives, S. R., Owen, J. E., Longerbeam, S., Mainella, F. C., & Osteen, L. (2005). Developing a leadership identity: A grounded theory. *Journal of College Student Development, 46,* 593–611.

Kotter, J. P. (1995, Mar./Apr.). Why transformation efforts fail. *Harvard Business Review,* p. 61.

Kotter, J. P. (1996). *Leading change.* Boston: Harvard Business School Press.

Kotter, J. P., & Cohen, D. S. (2002). *The heart of change: Real-life stories of how people change their organizations.* Boston: Harvard Business School Press.

Kouzes, J. M., & Posner, B. Z. (1987). *The leadership challenge: How to get extraordinary things done in organizations.* San Francisco: Jossey-Bass.

Kouzes, J. M., & Posner, B. Z. (1993). *Credibility: How leaders gain and lose it, why people demand it.* San Francisco: Jossey-Bass.

Kouzes, J. M., & Posner, B. Z. (1995). *The leadership challenge* (2nd ed.). San Francisco: Jossey-Bass.

Kouzes, J. M., & Posner, B. Z. (2002). *The leadership challenge* (3rd ed.). San Francisco: Jossey-Bass.

Kübler-Ross, E. (1970). *On death and dying.* New York: Macmillan.

Kurschner, D. (1996). The 100 best corporate citizens. *Business Ethics Magazine*, *10*(3), 24–35.

Labov, W. (1972). *Sociolinguistic patterns*. Philadelphia: University of Pennsylvania Press.

Lappé, F. M., & Du Bois, P. M. (1994). *The quickening of America: Rebuilding our nation, remaking our lives*. San Francisco: Jossey-Bass.

Latour, S. M., & Rast, V. J. (2004). Dynamic followership: The prerequisite for effective leadership. *Air & Space Power Journal*, *18*(4), 102–114. Retrieved April 14, 2006, from http://www.airpower.maxwell.af.mil/airchronicles/apje.html

Eagly, A. H., Karau, S. J., & Makhijani, M. G. (1995). Gender and the effectiveness of leaders: A meta-analysis. *Psychological Bulletin*, *117*(1), 125–145.

LeaderShape Institute Manual (1996). Champaign, IL: LeaderShape.

Lee, R. J., & King, S. N. (2001). *Discovering the leader in you: A guide to realizing your personal leadership potential*. Center for Creative Leadership. San Francisco: Jossey-Bass.

Lei, D., & Greer, C. R. (2003). The empathetic organization. *Organizational Dynamics*, *32*(2), 142-164.

Leppo, J., & Lustgraaf, M. (1987). *Student government: Working with special constituencies*. Programming, Leadership & Activities Network, Memorial Union. Grand Forks, ND: University of North Dakota.

Levine, A. (1993). *A portrait of college students in the 90s: Taking responsibility for educational management*. Paper presented at the Annual Conference of the National Association of Student Personnel Administrators, Boston.

Levoy, G. (2000). Character: Courage to follow your calling. *The Inner Edge*, *3*(3), 22–23.

Lewin, K. (1958). Group decision and social change. In E. E. Maccoby, T. M. Newcomb, & E. L. Hartley (Eds.), *Readings in social psychology* (pp. 197–211). New York: Holt, Rinehart & Winston.

Lewin, R., & Regine, B. (2000). *The soul at work: Listen . . . respond . . . let go*. New York: Simon & Schuster.

Lewin, R., & Regine, B. (2001). *Weaving complexity & business: Engaging the soul at work*. New York: Texere.

Lewis, H. A. (1990). *A question of values*. New York: Harper & Row.

Lipman-Blumen, J. (1984). *Gender roles and power*. Englewood Cliffs, NJ: Prentice Hall.

Lipman-Blumen, J. (2005). *The allure of toxic leaders*. Oxford University Press.

Lipnack, J., & Stamps, J. (1993). *The TeamNet Factor: Bringing the power of boundary crossing into the heart of your business*. Essex Junction, VT: Oliver Wight.

Lippitt, G. L. (1969). *Organizational renewal: Achieving viability in a changing world.* New York: Appleton-Century Crofts.

Lippitt, G. L. (1973). *Visualizing change: Model building and the change process.* Fairfax, VA: NTL-Learning Resources.

Loden, M., & Rosener, J. B. (1991). *Workforce America!* Homewood, IL: Business One Irwin.

Loeb, P. R. (1999). *Soul of a citizen: Living with conviction in a cynical time.* New York: St. Martin's Griffin.

Love, P. G., & Estanek, S. M. (2004). *Rethinking student affairs practice.* San Francisco: Jossey-Bass.

Lucas, N., & Anello, E. (1995). *Ethics and leadership.* Unpublished paper. Salzburg Leadership Seminar, Salzburg, Austria. November 11–18.

Lucas, N., & Koerwer, V. S. (2004). Featured interview: Sherron Watkins, former vice-president for corporate development of Enron. *Journal of Leadership and Organizational Studies, 11*(1), 38–47.

Lucas, N. J. (1999). *Lives of integrity: Factors that influence moral transforming leaders.* Unpublished doctoral dissertation, University of Maryland, College Park, MD.

Luke, J. S. (1998). *Catalytic leadership: Strategies for an interconnected world.* San Francisco: Jossey-Bass.

Lussier, R. N., & Achua, C. F. (2004). *Leadership: Theory, application, skill development* (2nd ed.). Eagan, MN: Thomson-West.

Luthans, F., & Avolio, B. (2003). Authentic leadership development. In K. S. Cameron, J. E. Dutton, & R. E. Quinn (Eds.), *Positive organizational scholarship: Foundations for a new discipline* (pp. 241–258). San Francisco: Berrett-Koehler.

Luthans, F., & Slocum, J. (2004). Special issue: New leadership for a new time. *Organizational Dynamics, 33*(3), 227.

Manz, C. C., & Sims, H. P., Jr. (1981). Vicarious learning: The influence of modeling on organizational behavior. *Academy of Management Review, 6*(1), 105–113.

Manz, C. C., & Sims, H. P., Jr. (1989). *SuperLeadership: Leading others to lead themselves.* New York: Berkley Books.

Mathews, D. (1994). *Politics for people.* Urbana, IL: University of Illinois Press.

Matusak, L. R. (1996). *Finding your voice: Learning to lead . . . anywhere you want to make a difference.* San Francisco: Jossey-Bass.

May, D. R., Hodges, T. D., Chan, A.Y.L., & Avolio, B. J. (2003). Developing the moral component of authentic leadership. *Organizational Dynamics, 32*(3), 247–260.

McCaulley, M. H. (1990). The Myers-Briggs Type Indicator and leadership. In K. E. Clark & M. B. Clark (Eds.), *Measures of leadership* (pp. 381–418). Greensboro, NC: Center for Creative Leadership.

McFarland, L. J., Senn, L. E., & Childress, J. R. (1993). *21st century leadership: Dialogues with 100 top leaders*. Los Angeles: The Leadership Press.

McGill, M. E., & Slocum, J. W. (1993). Unlearning the organization, *Organizational Dynamics*, Fall, 67–79.

McIntosh, P. M. (1988). *White privilege and male privilege: A personal account of coming to see correspondences through work in women's studies*. Wellesley, MA: Wellesley College Center for Research on Women.

McIntosh, P. M. (2000). White privilege and male privilege: A personal account of coming to see correspondences through work in women's studies. In M. L. Anderson & P. H. Collins (Eds.), *Race, class, and gender: An anthology* (4th ed., pp. 95–105). Belmont, CA: Wadsworth/Thomson Learning.

McIntosh, P. M. (1989, July/August). White privilege: Unpacking the invisible knapsack. *Peace and Freedom*, 10–12.

McMahon, T., Kochner, C., Clemetsen, B., & Bolger, A. (1995). *Moving beyond TQM to learning organizations: New perspectives to transform the academy*. Paper presented at the annual meeting of the American College Personnel Association, Boston, March 18–22.

Meadows, D. (1982) Whole earth models and systems. *Co-Evolution Quarterly*, Summer, 98–108.

Mizrahi, T., & Rosenthal, B. S. (1993). Managing dynamic tensions in social change coalitions. In T. Mizrahi & J. Morrison (Eds.), *Community organization and social administration: Advances, trends and emerging principles* (pp. 11–40). New York: Haworth Press.

Morrison, A. M. (1996). *The new leaders: Leadership diversity in America*. San Francisco: Jossey-Bass.

Morse, S. W. (1998). Five building blocks for successful communities. In F. Hesselbein, M. Goldsmith, R. Beckhard, & R. F. Schubert (Eds.), *The community of the future* (pp. 229–236). The Drucker Foundation. San Francisco: Jossey-Bass.

Morton, K. (1995). The irony of service: Charity, project and social change in service-learning. *Michigan Journal of Community Service Learning, 2*, 19–32.

Murrell, K. L. (1985). The development of a theory of empowerment: Rethinking power for organizational development. *Organizational Development Journal, 34*, 34–38.

Musil, C. M. (2003). Educating for citizenship. *Peer Review, 5*(3), 4–8.

Myers, I. B. (1980). *Gifts differing*. Palo Alto, CA: Consulting Psychologists Press.

Nanus, B. (1992). *Visionary leadership: Creating a compelling sense of direction for your organization*. San Francisco: Jossey-Bass.

Nash, L. L. (1990). *Good intentions aside*. Boston: Harvard Business School Press.

Nathan, R. (2005). *My freshman year: What a professor learned by becoming a student*. Ithaca, NY: Cornell University.

National Association of Student Personnel Administrators & American College Personnel Association. (2004). *Learning reconsidered*. Washington, DC: National Association of Student Personnel Administrators and American College Personnel Association.

National Business Ethics Survey 2005 (pp. 1–4). Retrieved February 8, 2006, from http://www.ethics.org/nbes/nbes2005/index.html

National Invitational Leadership Symposium. (1991). Proceedings from the 1991 National Invitational Leadership Symposium, College Park, MD.

Neilson, R. P. (1990). Dialogic leadership as ethics action method. *Journal of Business Ethics, 9*, 765–783.

Nicoll, D. (1984). Grace beyond the roles: A new paradigm for lives on a human scale. In J. D. Adams (Ed.), *Transforming work: A collection of organizational transformation readings* (pp. 4–16). Alexandria, VA: Miles River Press.

Northouse, P. G. (2004). *Leadership theory and practice* (3rd ed.). Thousand Oaks, CA: Sage

Oblinger, D. G., & Oblinger, J. L. (Eds.) (2005). *Educating the net generation*. Educause. http://www.educause.edu/content.asp?PAGE_ID=5989&bhcp=1#copyright

O'Toole, J. (1996). *Leading change: The argument for values-based leadership*. New York: Ballantine Books.

O'Toole, J. (2003). Why amoral leadership doesn't work. In *Business Leadership: A Jossey-Bass Reader* (pp. 279–306). San Francisco: Jossey-Bass.

Outcalt, C. L., Faris, S. K., & McMahon, K. N. (Eds.). (2001). *Developing non-hierarchical leadership on campus: Case studies and best practices in higher education*. Westport, CT: Greenwood Press.

Palmer, P. J. (1981). *The company of strangers: Christians and the renewal of America's public life*. New York: Crossroad.

Palmer, P. J. (1990). *The active life: A spirituality of work, creativity, and caring*. San Francisco: Harper & Row.

Palmer, P. J. (1998). *The courage to teach: Exploring the inner landscape of a teacher's life*. San Francisco: Jossey-Bass.

Palmer, P. J. (2000). *Let your life speak: Listening for the voice of vocation*. San Francisco: Jossey-Bass.

Palmer, P. J. (2004). *A hidden wholeness: The journey toward an undivided life.* San Francisco: Jossey-Bass.

Parker, G. M. (2003). *Cross-functional teams: Working with allies, enemies, and other strangers.* San Francisco: Jossey-Bass.

Parks, S. D. (2005). *Leadership can be taught: A bold approach for a complex world.* Boston: Harvard Business School Press.

Parr, J. (1994). Foreword. In D. D. Chrislip & C. E. Larson, *Collaborative leadership: How citizens and civic leaders can make a difference* (pp. xi–xiii). San Francisco: Jossey-Bass.

Pascale, R., Millemann, M., & Gioja, L. (2000). *Surfing the edge of chaos: The laws of nature and the new laws of business.* New York: Crown Business.

Pascarella, E., & Terenzina, P. (2005). *How college affects students: A third decade of research* (Vol. 2). San Francisco: Jossey-Bass.

Peck, M. S. (1987). *The different drum: Community-making and peace.* New York: Simon & Schuster.

Pedersen, P. (1988). *Handbook for developing multicultural awareness.* Alexandria, VA: American Association of Counseling and Development.

Peters, T. (1989). Foreword. In C. C. Manz & H. P. Sims Jr., *Superleadership: Leading others to lead themselves* (pp. xiii–xiv). New York: Prentice Hall.

Petersen, J. (1994). *The road to 2015: Profiles of the future.* Corte Madera, CA: Waite Group Press.

Phillips, J. M. (1995). Leadership since 1975: Advancement or inertia? *The Journal of Leadership Studies, 2*(1), 58–80.

Pickover, C. (1991). *Computers and the imagination: Visual adventures beyond the edge.* New York: St. Martin's Press.

Piper, T. R., Gentile, M. C., & Parks, S. D. (1993). *Can ethics be taught? Perspectives, challenges, and approaches at Harvard Business School.* Boston: Harvard Business School Press.

Pocock, P. (1989). Is business ethics a contradiction in terms? *Personnel Management, 21*(11), 60–63.

Pope, R. (1993). Multicultural-organization development in student affairs: An introduction. *Journal of College Student Development, 34,* 201–205.

Porter, E. H., Rosenbach, W. E., & Pittman, T. S. (2005). Leading the new professions. In R. L. Taylor & W. E. Rosenbach (Eds.), *Military leadership* (5th ed., p. 149). Boulder, CO: Westview Press.

Postman, N. (1992). *Technopoly: The surrender of culture to technology.* New York: Knopf.

Potter, E. H., III, & Fiedler, F. E. (1993). Selecting leaders: Making the most of previous experience. *Journal of Leadership Studies, 1*(1), 61–70.

Putnam, R. D. (1995). Bowling alone: America's declining social capital. *Journal of Democracy, 6*(1), 65–78.

Quinn, R. E. (1996). *Deep change: Discovering the leader within.* San Francisco: Jossey-Bass.

Quinn, R. E. (2004). *Building the bridge: A guide for leading change as you walk on it.* San Francisco: Jossey-Bass.

The quotable woman. (1991). Philadelphia: Running Press.

Raelin, J. R. (2003). *Creating leaderful organizations: How to bring out leadership in everyone.* San Francisco: Berrett-Koehler.

Rath, T., & Clifton, D. O. (2004). *How full is your bucket? Positive strategies for work and life.* New York: Gallup Press.

Rayner, S. R. (1996). *Team traps: Survival stories and lessons from team disasters, near-misses, mishaps, and other near-death experiences.* New York: Wiley.

Rheingold, H. (1993). *The virtual community: Homesteading on the electronic frontier.* New York: HarperCollins.

Rheingold, H. (2003). *Smart mobs: The next social revolution.* New York: Basic Books.

Rogers, J. L. (1996). Leadership. In S. R. Komives, D. B. Woodard Jr., & Associates, *Student services: A handbook for the profession* (3rd ed., pp. 299–319). San Francisco: Jossey-Bass.

Rosenthal, T. L., & Zimmerman, B. J. (1978). *Social learning and cognition.* New York: Academic Press.

Ross, R. (1994a). The five whys. In P. M. Senge, A. Kleiner, C. Roberts, R. Ross, & B. Smith (Eds.), *The fifth discipline fieldbook: Strategies and tools for building a learning organization* (pp. 108–112). New York: Currency/Doubleday.

Ross, R. (1994b). Skillful discussion: Protocols for reaching a decision—mindfully. In P. M. Senge, A. Kleiner, C. Roberts, R. Ross, & B. Smith (Eds.), *The fifth discipline fieldbook: Strategies and tools for building a learning organization* (pp. 385–391). New York: Currency/Doubleday.

Rost, J. C. (1991). *Leadership for the twenty-first century.* New York: Praeger.

Rost, J. C. (1993). Leadership development in the new millennium. *Journal of Leadership Studies, 1*(1), 91–110.

Ruderman, M. N., & Ernst, C. (2004). Finding yourself: How social identity affects leadership. *LIA, 24*(3), 3–7.

Schein, E. (2004). *Organizational culture and leadership* (3rd ed.). San Francisco: Jossey-Bass.

Schlossberg, N. K. (1989a). *Overwhelmed: Coping with life's ups and downs.* Lexington, MA: Lexington.

Schlossberg, N. K. (1989b). Marginality and mattering: Key issues in building community. In D. C. Roberts (Ed.), *Designing campus activities to foster a sense of community* (pp. 5–15). New Directions for Student Services, No. 48. San Francisco: Jossey-Bass.

Seligman, M.E.P. (2002). *Authentic happiness: Using the new positive psychology to realize your potential for lasting fulfillment.* New York: Free Press.

Senge, P. M. (1990). *The fifth discipline: The art and practice of the learning organization.* New York: Currency/Doubleday.

Senge, P. M. (1993). The art and practice of the learning organization. In M. Ray & A. Rinzler (Eds.), *The new paradigm in business: Emerging strategies for leadership and organizational change* (pp. 126–137). Los Angeles: Tarcher/Perigree.

Senge, P. M. (1994). Moving forward: Thinking strategically about learning organizations. In P. M. Senge, A. Kleiner, C. Roberts, R. Ross, & B. Smith, *The fifth discipline fieldbook: Strategies and tools for building a learning organization* (pp. 15–47). New York: Currency/Doubleday.

Senge, P. M., Kleiner, A., Roberts, C., Ross, R., & Smith, B. (1994). *The fifth discipline fieldbook: Strategies and tools for building a learning organization.* New York: Currency/Doubleday.

Shamir, B., and Eilam, G. (2005). "What's your story?" A life-stories approach to authentic leadership development. *Leadership Quarterly, 16,* 295–417.

Shaw, W., & Barry, V. (1989). *Moral issues in business* (4th ed.). Belmont, CA: Wadsworth.

Shea, G. F. (1988). *Practical ethics. AMA Management Briefing.* New York: AMA Membership Publications Division.

Sheehy, G. (1981). *Pathfinders.* New York: Bantam.

Simons, G. F., Vazquez, C., & Harris, P. R. (1993). *Transcultural leadership.* Houston: Gulf.

Sims, H. P., Jr., & Lorenzi, P. (1992). *The new leadership paradigm: Social learning and cognition in organizations.* Thousand Oaks, CA: Sage.

Sims, H. P., Jr., & Manz, C. C. (1981). Social learning theory: The role of modeling in the exercise of leadership. *Journal of Organizational Behavior Management, 3*(4), 55–63.

Smith, B. L., MacGregor, J., Matthews, R. S., & Gabelnick, F. (2004). *Learning communities: Reforming undergraduate education.* San Francisco: Jossey-Bass.

Smith, M. K. (2005). Bruce W. Tuckman – forming, storming, norming, and performing in groups. *The encyclopaedia of informal education.* Retrieved April 29, 2006, from www.infed.org/thinkers/tuckman.htm

Spears, L. C. (1995). *Reflections on leadership: How Robert K. Greenleaf's theory of servant-leadership influenced today's top management thinkers.* Hoboken, NJ: Wiley.

Spence, J. T. (Ed.). (1983). *Achievement and achievement motives: Psychological and sociological approaches*. San Francisco: Freeman.

Stacey, R. (1992). *Managing the unknowable*. San Francisco: Jossey-Bass.

Stogdill, R. M. (1974). *Handbook of leadership: A survey of theory and research*. New York: Free Press.

Strauss, A., & Corbin, J. (1998). *Basics of qualitative research: Techniques and procedures for developing grounded theory* (2nd ed.). Thousand Oaks, CA: Sage.

Sue, D. W. (2003). *Overcoming our racism: The journey to liberation*. San Francisco: Jossey-Bass.

Talbot, D. M. (1996). Multiculturalism. In S. R. Komives, D. B. Woodard Jr., & Associates (Eds.), *Student services: A handbook for the profession* (3rd ed., pp. 380–396). San Francisco: Jossey-Bass.

Tannen, D. (1990). *You don't understand me: Women and men in conversation*. New York: Morrow.

Taylor, H. L. (1989). *Delegate: The key to successful management*. New York: Warner Books.

Terry, R. (1993). *Authentic leadership*. San Francisco: Jossey-Bass.

Tichy, N. W., & Devanna, M. A. (1986). *The transformational leader*. Hoboken, NJ: Wiley.

Tjosvold, D., & Tjosvold, M. M. (1991). *Leading the team organization*. New York: Macmillan.

Toffler, A. (1970) *Future shock*. New York: Random House.

Toffler, B. L. (1986). *Tough choices: Managers talk ethics*. Hoboken, NJ: Wiley.

Transparency International 2004 Annual Report (pp. 1–24). Retrieved February 8, 2006, from http://www.transparency.org/publications/annual_report

Tubbs, S. (1984). *A systems approach to small group interaction* (2nd ed.). Reading, MA: Addison-Wesley.

Tuckman, B. W. (1965). Developmental sequence in small groups. *Psychological Bulletin, 63,* 384–399.

Tuckman, B. W., & Jensen, M. C. (1977). Stages of small group development revisited. *Group and Organizational Studies, 2,* 419–427.

Ulrich, D. (1998). Six practices for creating communities of value, not proximity. In F. Hesselbein, M. Goldsmith, R. Beckhard, & R. F. Schubert (Eds.), *The Drucker Foundation: The community of the future* (pp. 155–165). San Francisco: Jossey-Bass.

Vaill, P. B. (1989). *Managing as a performing art: New ideas for a world of chaotic change*. San Francisco: Jossey-Bass.

Vaill, P. B. (1991). *Permanent white water: The realities, myths, paradoxes, and dilemmas of managing organizations*. San Francisco: Jossey-Bass.

Vaill, P. B. (1996). *Learning as a way of being: Strategies for survival in a world of permanent white water*. San Francisco: Jossey-Bass.

Vaill, P. B. (1998). *Spirited leading and learning: Process wisdom for a new age*. San Francisco: Jossey-Bass.

Van Fleet, D. D., & Yukl, G. A. (1989). A century of leadership research. In W. E. Rosenbach & R. L. Taylor (Eds.), *Contemporary issues in leadership* (2nd ed., pp. 65–90). Boulder, CO: Westview Press.

Walton, C. C. (1988). *The moral manager*. New York: Harper & Row.

Watkins, J. M., & Mohr, B. J. (2001). *Appreciate inquiry: Change at the speed of imagination*. San Francisco: Pfeiffer.

Watkins, K. E., & Marsick, V. J. (1993). *Sculpting the learning organization*. San Francisco: Jossey-Bass.

Watts, D. J. (2003). *Six degrees: The science of a connected age*. New York: Norton.

Weber, M. (1947). *The theory of social and economic organization* (A. H. Henderson & T. Parsons, Trans.). Blencoe, IL: Free Press. (Original work published 1924)

Webster's Ninth New Collegiate Dictionary. (1986). Springfield, MA: Merriam-Webster.

Weick, K. E. (1979). *The social psychology of organizing* (2nd ed.). New York: Random House.

Wheatley, M. J. (1992). *Leadership and the new science: Learning about organization from an orderly universe*. San Francisco: Berrett-Koehler.

Wheatley, M. J. (1999). *Leadership and the new science: Learning about organization from an orderly universe* (2nd ed.). San Francisco: Berrett-Koehler.

Wheatley, M. J. (2002). *Turning to one another: Simple conversations to restore hope to the future*. San Francisco: Berrett-Koehler.

Wheatley, M. J. (2003). Change: The capacity of life. In *Business leadership: A Jossey-Bass reader* (pp. 496–517). San Francisco: Jossey-Bass.

Wheatley, M. J. (2005). *Finding our way: Leadership for an uncertain time*. San Francisco: Berrett-Koehler.

Wheatley, M. J., & Kellner-Rogers, M. (1996). *A simpler way*. San Francisco: Berrett-Koehler.

Wheatley, M. J., & Kellner-Rogers, M. (1998). The paradox and promise of community. In F. Hesselbein, M. Goldsmith, R. Beckhard, & R. F. Schubert (Eds.), *The Drucker Foundation: The community of the future* (pp. 9–18). San Francisco: Jossey-Bass.

Whitney, D., Trosten-Bloom, A., & Cooperrider, D. L. (2003). *The power of appreciative inquiry: A practical guide to positive change*. San Francisco: Berrett-Koehler.

Wijeyesinghe, C. L., Griffin, P., & Love, P. (1997). Racism curriculum design. In M. Adams, L. A. Bell, & P. Griffin (Eds.), *Teaching for diversity and social justice: A sourcebook* (pp. 87–109). New York: Routledge.

Willie, C. V. (1992). *Achieving community on the college campus*. Paper presented to the Annual Conference of the American College and University Housing Officers-International, Boston College, Boston.

Wood, D. J., & Gray, B. (1991). Toward a comprehensive theory of collaboration. *Journal of Applied Behavioral Science, 27*(2), 139–162.

Wood, J. T. (2004). *Interpersonal communication: Everyday encounters* (4th ed.). Belmont, CA: Wadsworth.

Wren, T. (1994). Interview: H. Norman Schwarzkopf, General, USA. *Journal of Leadership Studies, 1*(3), 1–6.

Yukl, G. A. (1989). *Leadership in organizations* (2nd ed.). Englewood Cliffs, NJ: Prentice Hall.

Yukl, G. A. (1994). *Leadership in organizations* (3rd ed.). Englewood Cliffs, NJ: Prentice Hall.

Zaccaro, S. J., & Bader, P. (2003). E-leadership and the challenges of leading e-teams: Minimizing the bad and maximizing the good. *Organizational Dynamics, 31*, 377–387.

Zaleznik, A. (1977). Managers and leaders: Are they different? *Harvard Business Review, 55*(5), 67–78.

Zigurs, I. (2003). Leadership in virtual teams: Oxymoron or opportunity? *Organizational Dynamics, 31*, 339–351.

Subject Index

renewal and, 301–324; strategies
for, 349–382; tipping points for,
338–340; transition *versus*,
303–306, 330; typology of,
336–337; understanding, 327–340;
web structure and, 255, 256
Change, rapid and constant: challenges of, 6–7; community and,
282; ethical leadership and, 210;
lifelong learning for, 26; marketplace competition and, 337; meaning making and, 108; new
leadership approaches for, 1–2, 5;
new leadership maps for, 59–66;
paradigm change and, 8–11, 59–60;
reflection and, 109–110; working
smarter and, 7–8, 325
Change agents: categories of,
352–353, 354; characteristics of,
354; college students as, 349–356;
in multicultural organizational
development, 269–270; see-feel-
change approach for, 344; of tipping points, 339–340
Chaos: connections in, 62–64; initial
conditions in, 63; learning organizations and, 270; nature of, 49, 59,
60–62, 63, 69; processes and,
103–104; self-organizing systems in,
64–66; stage of community building, 293
Character: "being" and, 77; elements
of good, 133–134, 135; and ethical
leadership, 133–136, 190; values
and, 132; working spiritually
smarter and, 8
Charismatic leaders and leadership,
38–39, 49, 52–53, 308
Charity, 372
Cheating, 99
Check-and-balance government, 219
Chemistry, green, 349–350, 361–362
Cherokee Nation, 414
Child development, gender roles and,
154–155
Child rearing, 154

Childhood and Society (Erikson), 303
Chinese pictogram, 170, 171
Chunking, 252
Circle-K, 248
Citizenship, 134, 135; faces or phases
of, 369, 370; Relational Leadership
Model applied to, 369; in Social
Change Model of Leadership
Development, 359, 361, 364
Civic engagement: concepts of,
369–370; defined, 20–21; social
responsibility and, 20
Civility: in community, 292; in dis-
course, 228, 230, 235, 240; in
Social Change Model of Leadership
Development, 359, 378
Clarifier role, 226
Climate: ethical, 115–116, 181–187,
211–212; group, 227–228, 228,
243; of learning and empowerment,
90–91
Closure, group, 221–223
Clowns, 224
Coadventurers, followers as, 58
Coalitions and coalition building:
advantages and disadvantages of,
367, 368; for campus issues, 365; for
change leadership, 345, 347; for
community action, 363–369; with
external stakeholders, 89; minority
and majority group issues in,
367–369; as models of cooperation,
366–367; participation in,
368–369; power dynamics of,
367–369; tensions in, 365–367;
typology of, 365, 366
Co-creators, followers as, 18
Codes of ethics. *See* Ethics codes and
standards
Coercion and coercive power, 92
Cognitive dissonance, 30–31, 401
Collaboration: cooperation *versus*,
106; emergent paradigm of, 11; in
hierarchical organizations, 406;
organizational structure for, 254; as
relational leadership process,

tion, 173; in extravert *versus* introvert orientation, 140; identity and, 130; international differences in, 160; social construction of, 22; in thinking *versus* feeling orientation, 138, 142, 155; understanding, 153–156

Gender roles and role development, 154–155

General Electric (GE), 80–81

General Mills, 199

Generative phase of citizenship, 369, 370

Generativity, 267, 303; stage of leadership identity development, 397, 398–399, 402–403

George Mason University, 340

Germany, 160

Global communities, 297–298

Global Corruption Barometer, 193–194

Global leadership, 159

Globalization, 150

Goals and goal setting: big hairy audacious, 308; SMART rubric for, 238–239, 246; for teams, 238–239, 243

Golden Rule, 205

Good leadership, 188, 189

Good-leader paradigm, 9–10

Google, 258

Government, distrust of, 99

Grassroots change, 353

Great man theories, 46, 48

Greek organizations. *See* Fraternities and sororities

Greeks, ancient, 197

Green chemistry, 349–350, 361–362

Greenpeace, 286

Grey's Anatomy, 236

Grieving process, 129, 332–333

Ground rules, 230, 240. *See also* Group norms

Grounded theory methodology, 393

Group development. *See also* Team development: Relational Leadership Model applied to, 221; stages of, 218–223

Group dynamics, 223–244. *See also* Group process; conflict and, 228–230; decision making and, 231–235; norms and, 225–228; roles and, 223–225, 226–227; teamwork and, 235–244

Group learning: in learning organizations, 272–273; personality preferences and, 143, 144–145; processes of, 240–241

Group maintenance roles, 224

Group norms: community, 290; concepts of, 225–228; for conflict resolution, 230; creating a "third culture" and, 174–175; development of, 220; for dialogue, 240; resistance to changing, 266; speech communities and, 168–169; for teams, 244

Group process. *See also* Group dynamics: barriers to inclusiveness in, 88; cultural influences on, 166–170; exclusion and, 104; importance of, 103–111; for resolving ethical dilemmas, 201–209; types of, 104, 105–111

Group values. *See* Values, group

Group-building roles, 224, 225

Groups. *See also* Renewal, group; Teams; Values, group: collaborative, 105–107; collective efficacy in, 389–390, 406; commonalities in, 151; defined, 216; dimensions of, 216–218; diversity in, 153, 166–176, 230; interacting in, 215–246; leadership development of, 406–407; leadership of, 241–244; leadership roles in, 217; moral talk in, 199–201; ongoing, 217, 220, 225–226; organizations *versus*, 248–251; perceptions of, in leadership identity development, 394, 396–401; pluralism in, 153; problems in, 302; renewal of,

406–407; importance of, 384; inter-dependence and, 401–406; personal identities and, 391–392; Relational Leadership Model and, 401–403; sample identity statements in, 396–397; social identity and, 392–393; stages of, 395–401; transitions in, 400

Leadership Identity Development (LID) study, 393–401

Leadership processes, for pluralistic contexts, 166–177. *See also* Group process; Process

Leadership Quarterly, 66

Leadership Reconsidered (Astin & Astin), 354, 382

Leadership study, 35–36, 40–42, 69. *See also* Leadership theories

Leadership styles: in authentic leadership, 67–68; context and, 39; in groups, 217; power and, 91

Leadership theories. *See also* Paradigms: behavioral, 47, 48, 50; categorization schema for, 45–46; complexity of, 44–45; evolution of, 44–59; great man, 46, 48; industrial *versus* postindustrial paradigm, 58–59, 70; influence, 49, 52–53; overview of, 69–70; reciprocal, 49, 53–59, 66–68; situational contingency, 48, 52–54; summary chart of, 48–49; trait, 46–47, 48

Leadership transitions, 304, 306, 330, 421–422, 423

Leading by example: authentic leadership and, 67; ethical leadership and, 101–103

Leading Change (O'Toole), 348

Leading the Way (Gandossy & Effron), 114

Leading with Soul (Bolman & Deal), 430

Learned Optimism (Seligman), 422–423

Learning: climate, 90–91; ethical, 189, 210–211; from experience, 28, 29, 33, 390–391; experiential model of, 28, 29, 33, 390–391; group and team, 143, 144–145, 240–241, 272–273; knowing-being-doing model and, 76–80; lifelong, 26, 164; model of, 26, 27, 32; from observation, 196–197, 389; openness to, 25–26; personal responsibility for, 26–28; trial-and-error, 252, 256

Learning as a Way of Being (Vaill), 430

Learning community: college community as, 296; reflection and, 110

Learning Model, 26, 27, 32

Learning organizations, 270–273

Learning style preferences, 143–146

Least Preferred Co-Worker (LPC) model, 51

Legitimate power, 92, 93

Let Your Life Speak (Palmer), 324, 430

Levi Strauss, 258–259

Liberation models, 270

Libraries, 11

Life and death, legal rights of, 204

Life change, 330–331. *See also* Change

Lifecycles, organizational, 267–269

Lifelong learning: in leadership development, 40; in multiculturalism, 164; for self-renewal, 411

Lifestyle, healthy and balanced, 412–416, 425

Linked (Barabási), 279

Listening: Chinese pictogram for, 170, 171; in community, 287–288, 293–294; in dialogue, 241; with empathy, 86, 109, 170–172

Live Aid concerts, 286

Living systems, 62–63, 64–66; interdependence in, 404–405

Long-term orientation, as dimension of culture, 265

Lose-lose outcomes, 229

Loss: helping people cope with, 342–343, 351; stages of coping with, 129, 332–333; in transitions, 305

Love, 427

Psychology: authentic leadership theory and, 66; behavioral leadership
theories and, 47; charismatic leadership theories and, 52; ethical
principles for, 207, 208; individuality construct in, 129–130; Jungian
typology, 136–141; positive, 66,
124–125; of transition, 303–306;
using theories of, 129–130; view of
leadership in, 24
Public good, as purpose of leadership,
19–20. *See also* Common good
Public humiliation, 184–185
Public perceptions: of global corruption, 193–194; of status of ethics
and morals, 11, 99, 185–186
Public sector, leader-follower dynamic
in, 16
Purpose. *See also* Common purpose: of
groups, 216, 237; of leadership,
19–20, 36–37; of organizations,
250–251, 255, 258–262
Purposefulness: awareness and, 116;
change and, 83–85; in community,
296; concepts of, 80–85; knowing-
being-doing model applied to, 78;
in leadership identity development,
402; organizational structure and,
255; renewal and, 308–311; shared
vision and, 80–83; in Social
Change Model of Leadership
Development, 362, 364; team performance and, 241

Q

Quaker saying, 419
Quantum world, 62–63
Question mark, 25
Quiet participants, 224, 227
Quotable Woman, The, 128

R

Race and racial identity, 130,
157–159
Race Is a Nice Thing to Have, A
(Helms), 177

Race—The Power of an Illusion,
157–158, 178
Racism, 22, 158–159, 161–162, 199
"Racism Curriculum Design" (Wijey-
sesinghe et al.), 382
Rapid change. *See* Change, rapid
Reactivity, 22
Real Change Leaders (Katzenbach et
al.), 353, 382
Reality *versus* competing expecta-
tions, 60, 61
Real-world considerations, 30–31,
405–406
Reciprocal leadership theories, 49,
53–59, 66–68, 230. *See also* Relational leadership; Relational Leadership Model
Reciprocal phase of citizenship, 369,
370
Reciprocal processes, in communities,
191–192
Recognition, for ethical behavior,
184–185
Recovery periods, 417
Recycling, in leadership identity
development, 400–401
Referent power, 92
Reflection: dialogue and, 240–241;
group, 111; on leadership identity,
387; as leadership process,
109–111; on one's existence,
418–419, 429; on organization as
system, 65–66; for self-renewal,
412, 415, 418–419, 420–422, 425;
working smarter and, 7–8
Reflective backtalk, 110–111
Reflective observation, 28, 29
Reframing: cognitive, 128; in meaning making, 109
Refreezing, 84
Rekindling Commitment (Jaffe et al.),
324
Relational leadership. *See also* Leadership; Relational Leadership Model:
community and, 282–284, 287,
295–296; development of,

Name Index